Mystic Utopian "Supermen"
A Private Training Course In The Use Of
Universal Magnetism And The Mental Control Of Others

With An Introduction By
Nick Redfern

Mystic Utopian "Supermen"
A Private Training Course In The Use Of
Universal Magnetism And The Mental Control Of Others

With An Introduction By Nick Redfern

Published in the United States of America By
Global Communications/Conspiracy Journal
11 East 30th Street 4R · New York, NY 10016

Staff Members
Timothy G. Beckley, Publisher
Carol Ann Rodriguez, Assistant to the Publisher
Sean Casteel, General Associate Editor
Tim R. Swartz, Graphics and Editorial Consultant
William Kern, Editorial, Format and Typesetting

Sign Up On The Web For Our Free Weekly Newsletter
and Mail Order Version of Conspiracy Journal
and Bizarre Bazaar
www.Conspiracy Journal.com

Order Hot Line: 1-646-331-6777
PayPal: MrUFO8@hotmail.com

UNIVERSAL MAGNETISM
EMBRACING ALL HUMAN POWERS

1. PERSONAL MAGNETISM In Seven Major Steps
2. ADVANCED MAGNETISM Control of Others Through the Feelings
3. MENTAL MAGNETISM Mastery in All the Conflicts of Life
4. SEX MAGNETISM Private Studies for Male and Female
5. OPERATIONS OF THE OTHER MIND Gigantic Powers of the Human Brain
6. SOLUTION OF LIFE Keys to the Deepest Mysteries of Existence
7. UNIVERSAL MAGNETISM Secret Lessons in Control of Self and Others
8. FUTURE SEEING AND DESTINY 1000 Profound Lessons in Philosophy

TAUGHT BY EDMUND SHAFTESBURY

1924

A publication of the
HUMAN BETTERMENT FOUNDATION
Pasadena, Calif.

HUMAN STERILIZATION TODAY

During the last twenty-eight years, California state institutions have sterilized nearly 12,000 insane and feebleminded patients.

JUNE

Physical Culture

THE PERSONAL PROBLEM MAGAZINE

15¢

A MACFADDEN PUBLICATION

NRA

Bernarr Macfadden
EDITOR

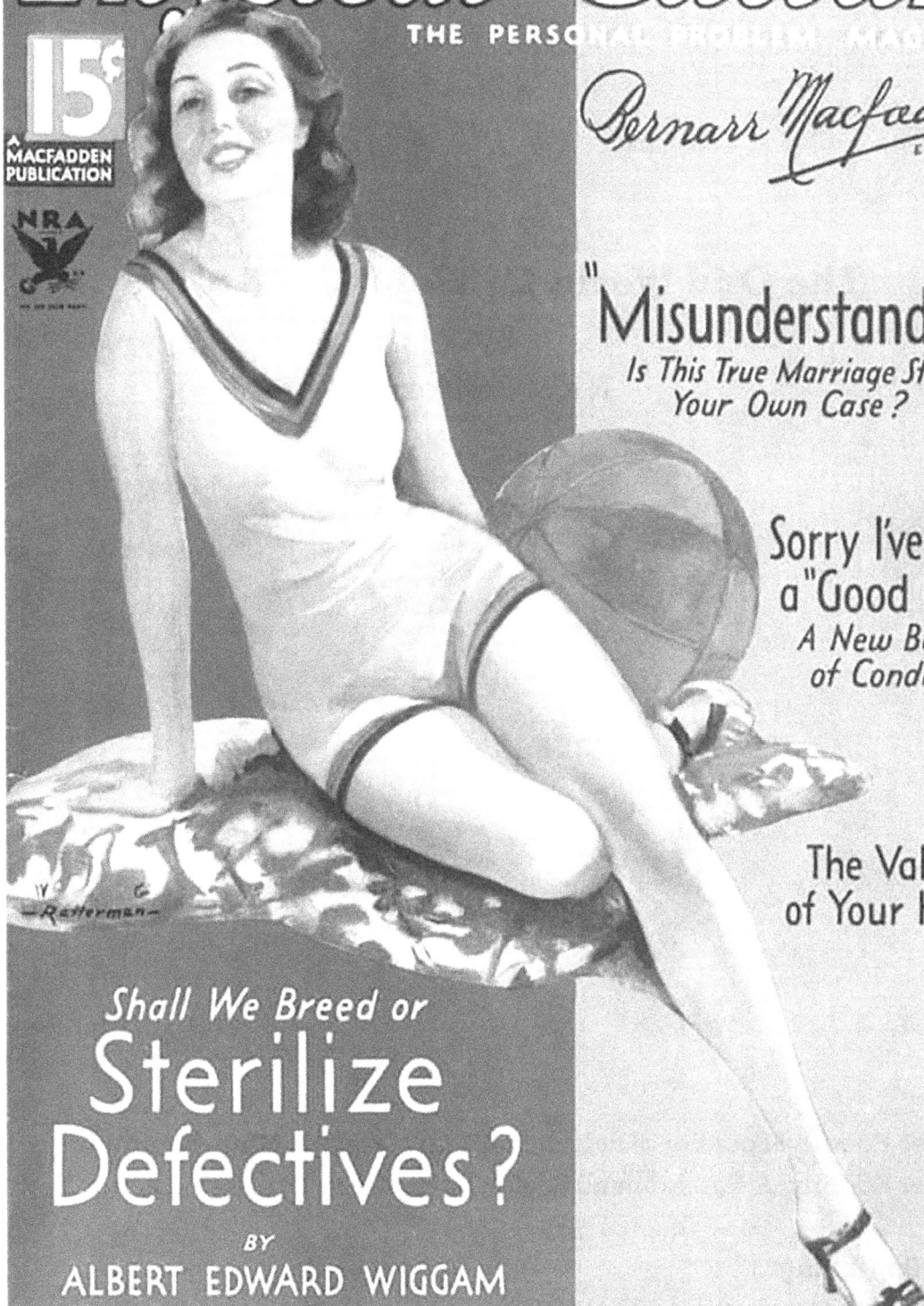

"Misunderstanding"
Is This True Marriage Story
Your Own Case?

Sorry I've Been
a "Good Boy"!
A New Basis
of Conduct

The Valves
of Your Heart

Shall We Breed or
Sterilize
Defectives?
BY
ALBERT EDWARD WIGGAM

The cover of Physical Culture magazine from June 1934. The abhorrent belief that societies can be improved by government mandated selective breeding initially got its start in Britain and the United States.

The Odd World Of Webster Edgerly
By
Nick Redfern

Webster Edgerly: Founder of Ralstonism, and Magnetic Mind-Controller!

Webster Edgerly, A.K.A. Edmund Shaftesbury, A.K.A. Everett Ralston

In the Beginning...

To say that the book you now hold in your hands is a strange, intriguing and highly controversial one, is putting things very mildly indeed. And much the same can be said about its author, too: Webster Edgerly; a name with which very few will today be familiar. Yet, Edgerly has a place in history, and certainly in infamy, that deserves to be told – if only to highlight the bizarre and, at times, dark and disturbing beliefs and motivations of the man.

MYSTIC UTOPIAN SUPERMEN

Born in Massachusetts in 1852, to Rhoda Lucinda Stone and John Foss Edgerly, Webster Edgerly was a social-reform activist and a staunch supporter of a healthy, and highly alternative, diet, and who ultimately became a man intent on perfecting the ultimate human being – in his eyes, at least.

Having graduated from the Boston University School of Law in 1876, Edgerly became fascinated – in fact, obsessed might be a far more accurate term with the idea that via certain highly controversial, and at times distinctly occult-based, techniques largely of his own design, the latent powers of both the human mind and body could be elevated to near superhuman levels. And as a result of this same fascination and obsession, Edgerly founded a now-obscure movement that became known as Ralstonism.

Edgerly loudly and eagerly proclaimed to anyone and everyone who was willing to listen that:

"We believe that Ralstonism, since it is becoming universal, is as necessary as food, light or water. This movement is the grandest, noblest, and already the most far-reaching power that has originated in the present age. Ralstonism is the grandest movement that man is capable of establishing."

And quite literally thousands of people did listen: astonishingly, at its height, Ralstonism attracted around 800,000 followers.

*****

Defining Ralstonism...

So what, precisely, was Ralstonism, and what was the true nature of Edgerly's belief system?

It all began in 1876, the very same year of Edgerly's graduation, when he founded what he called the Ralston Health Club – the same organization which also published Edgerly's writings, papers and numerous books. It was without any shadow of doubt a hierarchical organization, whose members were ranked according to the number of "degrees" they possessed – degrees that ranged from zero to one-hundred. Members advanced five degrees at a time, and each Ralston book purchased by a member counted as five degrees; which, of course, proved to be a very welcome financial bonus for Edgerly himself – and particularly so when one notes how many followers his organization attracted!

In the 1900 edition of The Book of General Membership of the Ralston Health Club, it was stated by Edgerly that the letters which comprised the word "Ralston" had their origins in the words Regime, Activity, Light, Strength, Temperation [sic], Oxygen and Nature. Curiously, however, earlier editions of the same book were credited to a pseudonym of Edgerly: one Everett Ralston. The implication (certainly in the early edition of the book, at least) was that Ralstonism was named after Edgerly's wholly fictitious alter-ego.

Regardless of the truth that lies at the heart of the origin of the name of Ralstonism, there can be no doubt whatsoever that it was a movement filled with deep, deep controversy.

Indeed, in Edgerly's mind at least, his disciples, devotees and followers were all the founding-members of what he firmly hoped would become a new order – possibly a new race and a new breed of human, even – that would be solely Caucasian-based, and completely free from what he disturbingly referred to as "impurities."

Specifically emphasizing this latter point, Edgerly loudly proclaimed to anyone and everyone that would listen that if Ralstonism was to work successfully and elevate its new Caucasian supermen to truly stratospheric levels, then all non-Caucasian males should be castrated at birth – and with absolutely no exceptions, whatsoever.

*****

Personal Magnetism and Mind-Control...

Edgerly's numerous "self-help" books that were all written under yet another pseudonym – namely, that of Edmund Shaftesbury – encompassed such seemingly unconnected issues as diet, exercise, punctuation, sexual magnetism, artistic deep breathing, facial expressions and even, rather oddly, ventriloquism.

And things got even stranger than that in the worlds of Edgerly and Ralstonism. Somewhat bizarrely, Edgerly recommended that all young Caucasian men should, whenever and wherever possible, engage in "probationary marriages" with old ladies; and he even decided that he was going to create his own alphabet: the 33-lettered "Adam-Man-Tongue."

Then there was Edgerly's Magnetism Club of America, which was established with the specific intent of giving its members mental-power over others via what he termed "Personal Magnetism."

In the book you are now reading, Edgerly outlines how the procedures that had to be followed to ensure such personal power could be successfully attained and maintained, too:

"The better way is to train the will at home and alone; always basing it upon some principle in the study of magnetism. With this in view, seclude yourself so as to be free from disturbing influences, and proceed as follows:

"Sit at one side of your room, so as to get as great a distance as possible between you and the object. Place any small object on the table as far away as the size of the room permits. Draw in your mind a straight line between the core of your brain and the object. It is well understood that intense thinking about any matter will produce an affirmative or negative effect. Try this, and see; let the matter be what it will, a wish, an object, or a fact. You will either master it or be mastered by it. Success in life is secured, often unconsciously, by concentration of attention."

Edgerly recorded for his followers the following, ominous passage:

"One person may be hypnotized by another without the latter's aid or knowledge. This is the Eleventh Principle. The brain of man is curiously divided into parts that think for reasoning purposes, into parts that think for mere muscular purposes, and parts that think for functional action. These are somewhat dependent upon each other beyond the conscious brain. When the conscious brain is put to sleep by a process that keeps the body awake, the subconscious faculty, which is the so-called inner brain, at once asserts itself and stands ready to obey any suggestions that may be given it."

As the above-passage makes abundantly clear, Edgerly was talking about, and exploring the feasibility of, what is commonly known today as mind-control.

MYSTIC UTOPIAN SUPERMEN

Further evidence of Edgerly's interest in the mind and its powers as a medium of both control and manipulation, can be found in his book, In Operations of the Other Mind.

Edgerly related that:

"Against the growing errors, vagaries, morbid theories, occult teachings, and wild beliefs that are darkening present-day life, depressing the mind, weakening the nerves, preying on the health and creating gloomy forebodings, this work comes as an inspiring guide and a practical instructor. It has been our wish and purpose to make this course of training one of the most important and valuable ever published. So, into the book we have put the great study, 'HOW TO EMPTY THE MIND.' Recall the countless times you have been mentally upset, worried, bothered with troubles. Think of what it would have meant-and will know mean to know how to cast all such mental torture out of your mind. The relief and peace of mind this one study alone can bring you can be worth thousands of dollars."

*****

The Odd World of Webster Edgerly...

All disciples of Ralstonism were ordered to follow strict dietary guidelines – many of which, like practically every facet of Ralstonism, were steeped in controversy and wacky beliefs. As a classic example, watermelons, Edgerly one day suddenly decided, were somehow poisonous to Caucasians, as, supposedly, were pickles, crabs, cranberries, cookies, tea, and "anything with crisp surfaces." It was only through a strict dietary regimen and regular physical exercise that a perfect body, and the ability to "read" and control the minds of others could be firmly achieved, he advised his followers.

In Edgerly's odd world, much of the physical regime that came with his unique exercise programs demanded that his followers and devotees moved in graceful curves and arcs, and walked exclusively on the balls of their feet. Edgerly's reason for this? Sudden starts and stops, and sharp angular movements, caused a "leakage of vital force," he confidently said – albeit with absolutely no justification for making such a statement, and without a clear picture of what, precisely, that "vital force" was.

Ralstonites, as those that adhered to Edgerly's ideas and visions rapidly became known, were even told that picking up marbles, from continuous circular patterns on the floor, was an integral part of the program – as was taking only dry baths, and ensuring that sitting, standing, sleeping, talking, eating and having sex were activities all undertaken in fashions specifically laid down by Edgerly.

As far as his personal life is concerned, Edgerly married one Edna Reed Boyts on July 5, 1892 in McConnellsville, Pennsylvania, and practiced law in Boston, Kansas, and Washington D.C.

In 1900, Edgerly's position in the world was elevated when he combined his activities with the founder of the Purina Food Company (which took the name of the Ralston Purina Company, and which today goes by the name of Nestlé Purina PetCare) and for a while produced the whole-wheat cereal that Ralstonites were expected (by Edgerly, of course) to consume.

Perhaps of equal significance (if indeed not more so), is the truly illuminating fact that a copy of his book Instantaneous Personal Magnetism was presented to none other than Britain's Queen Victoria by William Gladstone: a British Prime Minister during Victoria's reign. In other words, despite his strange beliefs and ideas, Edgerly culti-vated some decidedly notable interested parties.

*****

Ralston City: A Dream That Ended in Failure...

Between 1894 and 1895, Edgerly purchased huge areas of farmland along the north-ern slope of Hopewell Valley, New Jersey. It was there, in 1905, that Edgerly founded "Ralston Heights": a large and imposing house built to his own specific design and that was destined to contain a whole community of Ralstonites that Edgerly enthusiastically envisaged becoming the heart and soul of a futuristic metropolis that would be chris-tened the City of Ralston.

Interestingly, the rolling, curved contours of Edgerly's sprawling estate were spe-cifically designed in accordance with his firm belief that sudden stops, as well as walk-ing in straight lines, would result in dramatic and catastrophic leakage of vital force in his new race of supermen.

Edgerly's plans were highly ambitious: it was his ultimate goal to expand Ralston Heights to the point where it was comprised of literally hundreds of lots, at least sixteen small farms, no less than seven palaces, and the loftily named Temple of Ralston.

None of this came to pass, however; and perhaps that's a good thing, too. Edgerly died on November 5, 1926, in Trenton, New Jersey, before his dreams could be fulfilled. As a result, Edgerly's wife sold the property within twelve months of his death, and the eccentric, unusual and controversial world of Webster Edgerly came to a rapid close. Today, the Edgerly estate stands in ruins.

Needless to say, had Edgerly achieved all that he set out to achieve: namely, the creation of a race of elite super-humans with the ability to control minds via occult means, would have been a truly formidable and sinister force of undoubtedly fascist propor-tions – or perhaps a "Master-Race" would have been a far better description for what Edgerly had in mind.

And of course, on the subject of so-called "Master-Races," Edgerly was far from being alone in promoting the crackpot idea of creating a breed of superhuman beings – nor was he alone in incorporating matters pertaining to the occult in his teachings and beliefs concerning such so-called supermen. In the early part of 20th Century Germany, something evil was lurking – and about which, more very shortly.

*****

Six Ways to Control the Mind...

The power of the human mind – and specifically its ability to control the minds of others – was an integral facet of the work, research, theories and long-term plans of Webster Edgerly – and, of course, a central pillar of Ralstonism as he sought to create the ultimate superhuman.

Countless words have been written on the highly emotive topic of mind-control, some of it good, some of it bad, some of it over the top, and some of it right on target.

In his authoritative 1961 book on the subject, Thought Reform and the Psychology of Totalism: A Study of "Brainwashing" in China, psychiatrist Robert Lifton, M.D., detailed eight distinctly coercive means and methods by which it was possible to influence, and even completely and radically change, the minds of individuals without their knowledge. As Lifton capably demonstrated to his readers, such techniques had been used on prisoners-of-war in both Korea and China, and were highly successful, too.

Very notably, many of the scenarios that Lifton discussed had actually been identified, and even attempted, by Edgerly decades before. If nothing else, Edgery was certainly a visionary well ahead of his time – albeit without doubt a deranged and racist visionary.

First, there was what became known as Milieu Control: a form of mind-control that rendered the victim isolated from friends, colleagues, society and the environment – as well as controlling and carefully manipulating the limited information and communication provided to the person whose mind was being manipulated.

Certainly, in the planned Ralston City that Edgerly planned to build, isolating his followers from the outside world would have presented few, if any problems, at all.

Then there was Mystical Manipulation, a particularly ingenious form of mind-control. Essentially, the approach here was to secretly manipulate certain experiences to make them appear wholly spontaneous in nature; when in reality they were secretly pre-planned and executed. In almost all circumstances, such manipulation is undertaken by the "mind-controllers" as part of an en effort to convince the victims that their leaders, or hierarchy possess extraordinary skills and talents – perhaps even of a mystical, occult, and even divine nature, which is precisely what Edgerly attempted to do, albeit via claims that his mind-control techniques had "magnetic" origins.

Not surprisingly, mind manipulation of this specific type has proven to be particularly successful on those of a gullible and/or susceptible character – something that Webster Edgerly clearly understood, and realized was vital to his plans to make Ralstonism a movement of both significance and power.

Third, was what became known as the Demand for Purity. As Lifton explained – and as was one of the central aspects of Edgerly's Ralstonism – members of the relevant body are told that (a) conforming to the rules and regulations of the group is utterly vital; as is (b) always striving for perfection. And, as Lifton also revealed, when shame and guilt at not succeeding and not conforming enter the equation, a potent weapon of mind-control comes to the fore.

The role of sin in manipulating the individual and the collective group was also perceived as a useful tool. Invariably, those with a flair for mind-control encourage the discussion of sins, faults and flaws in those they wish to exert control over.

The concept of what became known as "Sacred Science" was a vital one, Lifton said, if successful control over the mind of the target-individual (or, indeed, collective group) was to be firmly achieved. In essence, Sacred Science states that the only things that define literal truth are (a) the beliefs, ideals and doctrine of the group; and (b) the person or persons speaking them. As a result, for those who fall under the spell of mind-control by these particular means, the leader becomes indistinguishable from a god, and for all intents and purposes becomes a deity – in the eyes of the followers.

Edgerly may not quite have seen himself in the role of a deity; however, he was astute enough to know that Ralstonism would only succeed if its members hung onto his every word, and his every belief – as if both were written law.

A particularly ingenious method of mind-control – that Lifton described as "Loading the Language" – was one that Edgerly planned to incorporate within Ralstonism from the very beginning.

In simplistic terms, Loading the Language is the means by which the controller utilizes words and phrases in new ways that those outside the group do not understand. Sometimes, the controller will go one step further and actually create new words, of which only the group itself has an understanding. This, of course, is precisely what Edgerly had in mind when he created his 33-lettered "Adam-Man-Tongue" alphabet.

Doctrine over a Person was Lifton's way of explaining how cult-leaders – and those specifically adept at mind-control – would subtly encourage cult-members to reinterpret their own personal memories and experiences to the point where they accorded only with the beliefs and ideals of the controller.

And, finally, as far as Lifton was concerned, there was Dispensing of Existence. The general description of this particular category stated that the group – along with its leader – has the right to decide who exists and who does not. Lifton stressed that this was not to be taken as a literal "life of death" situation; rather, it was meant to imply that those outside the group can only be "saved" and enlightened according to the group's beliefs if they join. If they decline to join, they must be completely rejected by those who are already under the spell of the mind-controller.

Yet again, this latter category of Lifton's demonstrates how surprisingly, and ingeniously, too, it is for the controller to isolate his or her victims from society at large. Doubtless, this scenario was firmly fixed within Edgerly's mind when he envisaged the creation of the sprawling City of Ralston.

Let us now turn our attention to some of the equally strange – and certainly controversial attempts to create super-humans, and the way in which both the occult and bizarre science have played key, integral roles.

*****

Nazis, Aryans and More...

The deranged Master-Race concept of Webster Edgerly was far from being alone: Adolf Hitler's Nazi Germany held that the collective Germanic and Nordic populations were the closest thing that existed to a pure race.

It was a much-disputed concept that caused wholly justified outrage in many quarters, and that had its origins in a 19th Century scenario that placed African Bushmen and Australian Aborigines at the foot of the ladder, and the Nordics (what a surprise...) firmly at the very top. Aside from in the minds of those racists that adhered to the theory (and who, in some cases, still adhere to it, to this very day), it was utterly lacking in any scientific merit at all.

And, interestingly, as was the case with Webster Edgerly, the Nazis were as fascinated with the occult as they were with the notion of creating the perfect superman.

As far as the Nazis themselves were concerned, they were firmly of the opinion that the people of both Southern and Eastern Europe were racially mixed with non-Europeans from across the Mediterranean Sea; while it was strictly the Northern Europeans who had successfully remained pure. Adherents of this belief additionally maintained that not only had the Nordics' remained pure: as a result of the cold, harsh climate in which they had mostly been raised, they also just happened to be the physically toughest and strongest of all peoples, too. And so, the ominous image of the blonde and blue-eyed Nordic superman of Nazi Germany began to develop – in leaps and bounds.

Somewhat ironically, however, the Nazis did not discriminate against Germans who were not blonde and/or blue-eyed, and who were considered Aryans (the term Aryan being derived from the ancient peoples who lived in Iran and the Indus Valley). The Nazi theorist Alfred Rosenberg argued that they were fierce, warrior people whose point origin was actually well into the northern hemisphere; but who migrated south in times past, and who were also the ancestors of early Germanic clans and tribes.

*****

The Thule Society...

In addition to this particular theory, a large number of Nazis were also influenced by Helena Petrovna Blavatsky's 1888 work, The Secret Doctrine, in which she postulated that the lineage of the Aryans could be traced directly back to the fabled island of Atlantis – a controversial theory also supported by the aforementioned Alfred Rosenberg, and the members of the Thule Society. Indeed, such theories were regularly, and very successfully, employed by the Nazis as they sought to justify depriving "non-Aryans" of citizenship and employment rights, and strictly prohibiting marriage between Aryans and non-Aryans.

The Thule Society was founded in 1911 and formally titled one year later. In 1918, it came under the sway of Rudolf von Sebottendorff, who was an occultist and the then-recently-appointed head of the Germanenorden Walvater. Sebottendorff later maintained that his original intention was for the Thule Society to be nothing more than a convenient vehicle to allow him to promote his own occultist theories; but that the Germanenorden pressed him to emphasize the society's political, nationalist and anti-Semitic themes – a claim which some historians accept as the truth.

The Thule Society attracted about 250 followers in Munich and about 1,500 in greater Bavaria. The followers of the Thule Society were, by Sebottendorff's own admission, little interested in his occultist theories. They were, however, very interested in racism, and finding more and more ways to combat both Jews and Communists.

On January 5, 1919 Anton Drexler, who had developed links between the Thule Society and various extreme-right-wing workers' organizations in Munich, together with the Thule Society's Karl Harrer, established the Deutsche Arbeiterpartei (DAP), or the German Workers' Party.

None other than Adolf Hitler himself joined the party later in the same year. By the end of February 1920, the DAP had been reconstituted as the Nationalsozialistische Deutsche Arbeiterpartei (NSDAP), or National Socialist German Workers' Party, generally known as the Nazi Party.

Other members of the Thule Society who were later prominent in Nazi Germany included Dietrich Eckart, Gottfried Feder, and Hans Frank. And Nazi interest in facets of the occult did not end there.

*****

The Nazis, the Occult, and the Spear of Destiny...

High-ranking Nazis, such as Richard Walther Darré, Rudolf Hess, Otto Rahn, and Heinrich Himmler are all credited with having an interest in the occult – albeit to varying degrees and at equally varying times.

For example, Rahn, who was employed in a wing of the "RuSHA Department" of Nazi-Germany's greatly feared SS, spent a period of time deeply engaged in a quest to find the so-called Holy Grail: according to Christian mythology, the dish, plate, or cup used by Jesus at the Last Supper and that was said to possess miraculous powers.

Then there is Trevor Ravenscroft's book The Spear of Destiny, which details a particular fascination Adolf Hitler had with the Spear of Destiny: the lance that supposedly pierced Jesus's body while he was nailed to the cross.

Ravenscroft's book (as well as a later book titled The Mark of the Beast) maintained that Hitler deliberately started the Second World War with the intention of capturing the spear, and with which he was said to be overwhelmingly obsessed. At the end of the war the spear came into the hands of U.S. General George Patton; and according to legend, losing the spear would result in nothing less than death – something that was said to have been definitively fulfilled when Hitler committed suicide.

Ravenscroft repeatedly attempted to define the strange "powers" that the legend says the spear serves. Notably, Ravenscroft found it to be both a hostile and malevolent force, which he sometimes referred to as the Antichrist, although that is somewhat open to interpretation. He never actually referred to the spear as spiritually controlled, but rather as intertwined with all of mankind's ambitions.

*****

The Buechner Story...

Interestingly, Dr. Howard A. Buechner, M.D., a professor of medicine at Tulane and later LSU, wrote two books on the Spear. Buechner was a retired Colonel with the U.S. Army who had served in the Second World War, and who had written a book about the Dachau massacre, to which he had personally been a witness.

Buechner claims he was contacted by a former U-boat submariner, the pseudonymous "Capt. Wilhelm Bernhart", who vigorously maintained to Buechner that the spear currently on display in the city of Vienna is nothing but an ingenious fake.

The real Spear, Buechner was told by Bernhart, was clandestinely sent by Hitler to Antarctica, along with a whole host of other Nazi treasures, under the specific command of a Colonel Maximilian Hartmann.

So the story went, the spear was said to have been recovered in 1979 by Hartmann himself. Bernhart presented Buechner with the log-book from this particularly secret expedition, along with photographs of the objects recovered. Bernhart also claimed that after the Spear of Destiny was recovered from the ice in 1979, it was hidden somewhere in Europe by a secret society that had deep Nazi roots. After contacting most of the members of the alleged expedition and others involved, including senior Nazi officials and close associates, Buechner came to accept the story as nothing less than fact.

MYSTIC UTOPIAN SUPERMEN

*****

Himmler, the SS, and More...

Acknowledged by many historians with being the driving force behind what became known as "Esoteric Hitlerism," and without doubt a character of prime significance for the officially-sanctioned research and practice of mysticism by the Nazis, was Heinrich Himmler who, perhaps more than any other high-ranking official in the Third Reich, was obsessed with the notion of pan-Aryan racialism and Germanic neo-paganism, the occult, and astrology.

In 1935 Himmler became a key player in the establishment of what became known as the Ahnenerbe: the ancestral heritage division of the SS. Overseen by one Dr. Hermann Wirth, its chief motivation was research in the field of archaeology; however, its work also spilled over into areas such as demonstrating the supposed superiority of the Aryans, and investigating the occult – the latter, primarily from the perspective of determining if it was a tool that could be useful to further strengthen the Nazi war-machine.

The SS also had its very own mystical religion, vaguely based upon imagery taken from Germanic tribal faiths that was then intertwined with certain aspects of Christianity – the prime purpose of which was to counter what the SS viewed as the Jewish-influenced religion of Christianity.

Similarly, the official newspaper of the SS, Das Schwarze Korps, or The Black Corps (to give it its English translation) which was published weekly from 1935 to 1945, ran articles that emphasized some of the occult-based beliefs of the organization, including the theory that the so-called Nordic supermen had their origins in the region of the North Pole that they believed was home to the original blood-line of the (equally so-called) Master Race.

Similarly, and specifically in 1935, Das Schwarze Korps commissioned Heinar Schilling, a Professor of Germanic History, to write for them a series of reports on the more significant aspects of early Germanic life. So popular did the reports become that they were ultimately bound together in a book titled Germanisches Leben, which was published in 1937, and covered such issues as nature worship; Sun-based religions; and various Germanic cults.

It's known, for example, that the Germanic peoples of the late Bronze Age had adopted a four-spoke wheel as being symbolic of the sun, and that this same symbol ultimately developed into the swastika of Nazi Germany; the notion being that the Nordics were the bringers of light – which is highly ironic in view of the fact that, in reality, they brought nothing other than darkness to the world, and killed millions of people in the process.

The utilization of runic symbology, as well as the existence of the aforementioned officially-sanctioned Nazi Government department devoted to the study of the Germanic ancestral heritage (including paganism), have given much credence to the idea that there was a pagan component to Nazism, too. Certainly, at least as early as 1940, the occult scholar and folklorist Lewis Spence succeeded in identifying a distinctly neo-pagan undercurrent in Nazism, for which he largely blamed Alfred Rosenberg, and which he literally equated with Satanism.

MYSTIC UTOPIAN SUPERMEN

*****

Stalin's Monster-Supermen...

Webster Edgerly and Nazi Germany were not the only ones fascinated by the idea of creating a race of super-humans: secret government files generated in Russia in 1926 (and declassified in 2006) under the regime of Premier Josef Stalin reveal that the Soviet premier had a crazed idea to try and create an army of supermen that would be a combination of half-ape and half-man, and that would be utterly unbeatable on the battlefield.

As a result Ilya Ivanov, the former Soviet Union's top animal-breeding expert at the time, was personally told by Stalin: "I want a new invincible human being, insensitive to pain, resistant and indifferent about the quality of food they eat." Somewhat shrewdly, Stalin added that the creatures should possess "immense strength but with an underdeveloped brain."

Certainly, in the eyes of Stalin if anyone could make the crackpot project succeed it was Ivanov. A highly regarded figure, he had established his reputation under the Tsar when, in 1901, he established the world's first center for the artificial insemination of racehorses. But more important to Stalin was the fact that Ivanov had already tried to create a "super-horse" by attempting to crossbreed such animals with zebras.

Despite the fact that the attempts to crossbreed a horse with a zebra failed completely, Moscow's Politburo forwarded Stalin's request to the Academy of Science with the order to build a "living war machine;" an order that came at a time when the Soviet Union was embarking upon a crusade to turn the world upside down, with social engineering seen as a partner to industrialization.

In addition, Soviet authorities were struggling at the time to rebuild the Red Army after the devastation of the First World War, and there was also intense pressure to find a new labor force, and particularly one that would not complain. As a result, in the warped mind of Josef Stalin, the secret creation of a super race of hybrid creatures that combined the intelligence of human beings with the physical strength of some of the larger primates, such as gorillas and chimpanzees, seemed to be the perfect antidote to every problem.

*****

The Program Begins...

The Russian scientific community swung into action and Ivanov was quickly dispatched, with $200,000 in his pocket no less, to West Africa where the first such experiment was planned: namely the impregnation of a number of chimpanzees with human sperm. Ivanov's now-archived reports reveal that the Pasteur Institute in Paris, France secretly granted him permission to use their research station in Guinea, West Africa, for ape-breeding research.

As Ivanov advised the Politburo, however: "The biggest problem is to catch living females." As a result, Ivanov's team learned that the answer to this tricky problem was to burn the trees and chase the apes into cages as they scampered down the trunks. Ivanov also reported, somewhat disturbingly, on the fact that his team had "seized" a number of local African women in the area who were "to be impregnated with ape sperm." No pregnancies resulted. More ambitious plans to impregnate female gorillas with human

11

sperm also ended in complete failure.

At the same time, a center for such experimentation in Russia was stealthily established in Stalin's birthplace of Georgia, where the super-apes were to be raised if impregnation was ever seen to be successful. Unsurprisingly, none of the West African experiments succeeded.

Undaunted, however, Stalin pressed on with an even more controversial plan: he arranged for a number of women "volunteers" in Russia to be impregnated with monkey sperm in an effort to determine whether or not following this particular route would prove to be more successful. Again, it was not.

That such experimentation did proceed, however, is not in doubt: only recently, workmen engaged in the building of a children's playground in the Georgian Black Sea town of Suchumi found a plethora of ape-skeletons, and an old abandoned laboratory.

In the eyes of the ruthless Stalin, and a result of the resounding failure to create an army of man-beasts, Ivanov was now in complete disgrace. As a result, Stalin sentenced Ivanov to five years in jail, which was later commuted to five years' exile in the Central Asian republic of Kazakhstan in 1931. He died a year later, after falling sick while standing on a freezing railway platform.

With that all now said, I will leave you in the hands of Webster Edgerly, a.k.a. Edmund Shaftesbury, a.k.a. Everett Ralston, and his largely-long-forgotten, strange, and almost out-of-this-world beliefs concerning mind-control and super-humans. Enjoy!

And if, after reading Edgerly's work, you are prompted to dig further into the life of this extraordinary man, you may want to check out the following books – all penned by Edgerly as he sought to fulfill his dream of bringing Ralstonism to the masses.

An A to Z of Further Books by Webster Edgerly...

A Study of the Unseen Powers That Control Human Life;

Advanced Magnetism;

Book of the Mind and Thought Society;

Book of the Psychic Society;

Brain Tests;

Child Life;

Complete Membership in the Ralston Health Club;

Cultivation of the Chest;

Edgerly Natural Reader;

Future Seeing and Destiny;

General Membership of the Ralston Health Club;

Higher Magnetism;

How to Make Personality Pay;

Immortality;

Lessons in Artistic Deep Breathing for Strengthening the Voice;

Lessons in Emphasis;

Lessons in Grace;

Lessons in the Art of Extemporaneous Speaking;

Lessons in the Art of Facial Expression;

Lessons in the Art of Ventriloquism;

Lessons in the Mechanics of Personal Magnetism;

Lessons in Voice Culture;

Lessons on Acting;

Life Building Method of the Ralston Health Club;

Life Electricity;

Life's Secrets Revealed;

Mental Magnetism;

One Hundred Lessons in Punctuation;

One Hundred Points of Character;

Personal Magnetism;

Ralston Gardens;

Ralston's Simplified Physiology;

Real Life, when Things are Right;

Right;

Sex Magnetism;

Shaftesbury's Secrets;

Solution of Life;

The Adam-Man Tongue;

The Authority Dictionary;

The Book of Books;

The Combination Book of the Ralston Health Club;

The Goal of Creation;

The Greatest Things in Human Life;

The Natural Reader;

The New Education;

The Origin of Man;

The Other Mind;

The Ralston Brain Regime;

The Ralston Health Club;

The Shaftesbury Recitations;

The Shaftesbury School of Philosophy;

The Two Hundred Year Club;

The Two Sexes;

Transference of Thought;

Universal Magnetism;

Yourself Behind Closed Doors.

*****

Nick Redfern is the author of many books, including A Covert Agenda; The FBI Files; Strange Secrets; Celebrity Secrets; There's Something in the Woods; Cosmic Crashes; Memoirs of a Monster Hunter; Three Men Seeking Monsters; On the Trail of the Saucer Spies; Man-Monkey; and Body Snatchers in the Desert. He has written for Fate; Fortean Times; UFO Magazine; Military Illustrated; the British Daily Express newspaper; the Anomalist; and many other publications. Originally from Britain, he lives in Dallas.

"Mystic Utopian Supermen"
A Private Training Course In The Use Of
Universal Magnetism And The Mental Control Of Others

UNIVERSAL MAGNETISM

EMBRACING ALL HUMAN POWERS

1. PERSONAL MAGNETISM In Seven Major Steps

2. ADVANCED MAGNETISM Control of Others Through the Feelings

3. MENTAL MAGNETISM Mastery in All the Conflicts of Life

4. SEX MAGNETISM Private Studies for Male and Female

5. OPERATIONS OF THE OTHER MIND Gigantic Powers of the Human Brain

6. SOLUTION OF LIFE Keys to the Deepest Mysteries of Existence

7. UNIVERSAL MAGNETISM Secret Lessons in Control of Self and Others

8. FUTURE SEEING AND DESTINY 1000 Profound Lessons in Philosophy

TAUGHT BY EDMUND SHAFTESBURY

1924

DEDICATION

To the thousands of men and women whose experiences have confirmed the teachings in private life of the principles and laws that are now fully presented for the first time in any published work, and whose appreciation has grown as the years have multiplied, this new form of magnetic control is respectfully dedicated by their fellow student and friend, the Author:

Edmund Shaftesbury.

1924

THE ODD WORLD OF WEBSTER EDGERLY

In this year, 1924, new knowledge of the wonderful secret forces of life is being given to the world in these many lessons, and new results in the use of the greatest power in the universe are being assured to our students. Those who have followed our past teachings will be pleased to note the vast advance which has been made recently in this system of training. This progress is solid, for it is built on countless experiments and tests that have never known failure. Magnetism is the most valuable of all studies. In itself it is the power to influence or control mind and matter. Such control exists everywhere; as between matter and matter we see it in the law of gravity, the law of cohesion, the holding of the mariner's needle to the north, and the drawing of one substance to another; as between mind and matter, it controls all the physical functions of the body, including health and action; as between mind and mind, we know there is a channel of communication through which influences are sent by powers not answerable to the ordinary senses. Every human being possesses some control over others, or some means of controlling others, although they may be unknown and unused. .

Magnetism and hypnotism are opposite ideas and opposite terms; yet most persons believe that the person who is magnetized is hypnotized. This is a serious mistake. To magnetize is to make more awake, to attract, charm, enliven and vitalize; to hypnotize is to make dull, sleepy, repugnant, weak, cataleptic and dead as far as the natural functions are concerned. One is always grand and noble; the other is always mean and contemptible. A person who is magnetized is made better for it; one who is mesmerized is made worse for it.

The young woman who recently hypnotized herself to get rid of certain misfortunes that haunted her, went crazy; the doctors said that, had she developed her magnetism, she would have expelled the first condition and avoided the last. All persons may hypnotize themselves; all persons may magnetize themselves. To hypnotize, it is necessary that all magnetism shall be driven out of the body; to magnetize, renders it impossible to hypnotize. This distinction must be well understood, and should be kept constantly in mind during the study of this volume. You cannot be thin and fat at the same time. You may pass from one condition to the other, but not readily.

A magnetic person may control the hypnotic only so long as the latter lacks magnetism. The former makes an effort to drive out what little vitality of this kind the latter may possess; but the sure way of thwarting all such efforts is by the study, culture and accumulation of magnetism. By such means, the hypnotic rescues himself from the contact of another. Fright, fear, superstition, mental weakness, hysteria and insanity are all over-come and forever expelled by the acquisition of magnetism.

On the other hand, let a person study and practice to become an hypnotic, and he will find his mind gradually giving way, illusions will come across it, fancies will disturb his sleeping and waking hours, figures of outlined forms will flit in his path, sounds will disturb him, and little surprises will startle him. As one woman said, who thought she would like to become a clairvoyant through the process of hypnotism, "Then began my wretchedness." The cure of such a condition is through magnetism. The cure of darkness is light.

Despite the dangers of hypnotism, we present the most complete analysis and discussion of it that has ever been published; and, if the personal assurances of those who have paid hundreds of dollars to other instructors can be believed, the lessons given in this volume are better, more scientific, more thorough, and more effective than any that can be obtained from teachers of the highest rank. We present herein fully ten times the scope and space of any department of previous editions that has been devoted to this one study.

The object is twofold. First, there should be nothing lacking in a work of this kind and purport. Second, the reason, theory and process of mesmerizing should be understood by all classes, especially by those who are liable to be easily influenced or led astray. There are grades of mesmeric control, from the well known "lapse" of thought to the cataleptic sleep. Magnetism benefits the user and the person influenced. Mesmerism degrades the latter, and is chiefly a plaything for the former. Whether you decide to acquire the art of hypnotizing or not, you should never be hypnotized.

REALM ONE
THE POWER THAT BINDS MATTER UNDER THE INFLUENCE OF MATTER
MATTER TO MIND, MIND TO MIND, AND SOUL TO SOUL.

UNDER THE CLOUDS a lad lies dreaming. Beneath the branches of a widespreading apple tree, on the browned and worn sod, he rests in open sleep, his mind locked in study, while overhead he views the idle vapors as they float dreamily by. The verdure above bends down to give shade and cooling protection to the verdure beneath, so that he catches glimpses of the sky only through spaces made by the yielding boughs.

He wonders at many things. The trees, the shrubs, the plants, the flowers all nod obeisance to the sun and its flooding light. They lift themselves up continually. The rock clings close to the ground. The volume of air outspreads itself around the globe, yet has so much weight that to lift one inch of it from the earth even so slightly, would require pounds of force. On the bosom of this air, the clouds glide like boats in the heart of the sea. They do not attain the top, nor reach the bottom, until they condense and become heavier than their buoyant master. At times they reach dizzy heights; then again they crawl along the crests of hills; or, in sheer weariness, they approach the ground. Yet in all their wanderings they are chained to this planet by a single law.

The apple tree is strong and mighty. Its roots are giants. They have gone down many feet in search of perpetual moisture. They have spread in all directions, seeking food from the rich stores in the soil. Their commerce is borne on the bosom of climbing streams, even tending to the top, outward and upward to the light of day as it is poured forth from the sun. This central fire and force seeks all life; and, to answer its call, matter itself is carried up out of the solid earth along with the living tendencies that subdue it. Thus inert material rises from its bed of clay and is kissed by the god that molds it into being.

Hanging aloft on the freely swinging branches of the apple-tree, the fruit is glowing in newly painted colors, bright from the freshest touch of nature. Drop by drop, particle by particle, the juices and the substance have been drawn out of the ground, from depths profound, up through the trunk and branches to the stem on which the golden apple hangs. The dreamer beneath watches it swaying in the breeze; sees it hesitate for a moment; and notes its quick flight to the earth. It came, not by some force that hurled it down, but by an attraction that drew it.

What that influence was, that could return matter to the material fund from which another power had taken it, seemed too subtle a problem for human intelligence to solve;

and, though centuries have elapsed since the dreamer first caught the spirit of its meaning, it still remains unsolved. To ascribe a misunderstood process to supernatural control is always the height of error. No thinking person who respects his own intellect will fall back upon the occult excuse for an explanation of what he cannot comprehend. If this is to be the goal of investigation, the child will never become a man. "Superstitions would soon die out if so many old women wouldn't act as nurses to keep them alive."

The masses that court superstition pass by the greatest mystery of the universe. Why does an object fall to the ground ? What holds the planets fast within the influence of the sun? If you answer one, you cannot answer both. It will not do to say it is the attraction of gravity; for the heavier a thing is the less it falls. If the object were as great as the earth, the earth would rise up to meet the object, and to that extent lessen its fall. The giant orbs that sail in majesty through the still skies of night, cannot get away if they would. A rope of influence binds each to its place, beyond which there is no wandering. To our humble minds it would seem as though some actual chain must be employed, else why could not the planet fly away at will.

Holding myriad tons of matter in easy sway, checking their advance by consummate skill, and never releasing its momentary interest over little things, some influence as powerful as the universe itself pervades all existence from the least to the greatest, and there is no analysis of science that can solve the mystery; so it goes unchallenged. Turn whichever way you will, this influence is always at hand. It is found in the microscopic sea, in the teeming ocean of visible life, and in the vast ether of the sky.

Magnetism is universal.

This is the First Principle. Much of the mystery of existence may be accounted for when we come to recognize the fact that the forces of nature obey the great law of magnetism; although man is powerless to explain the reason or the origin of this law. It is not necessary to shut ourselves up in a narrow world of belief, and grope outward in the dark, wondering what this mystery is. God works through recognized forces, fixed in their laws and natural in their results. Superstition is merely the inability to account for causes.

Life is more easily solved if we can come to understand that there is a force called magnetism which holds all existence together and impels all growth and all change. A body flying through space would go on in a straight line until it collided with another, and it would never cease going if no other were in its way, were it not for some magnetic influence that called it back. This earth is as free as any such object; it starts every year to go off into space and gets a few millions of miles farther away from the sun in June than in December; but if it were not drawn back, it would soon become an iceberg wandering in a void and bearing on its bosom nearly seven billions of entombed humanity who had frozen to death.

It is wise and merciful that this earth is held to her course, and is brought back when she begins to wander off. What holds her in place? A cable over ninety millions of miles in length might fasten her securely to the sun; and, swinging at its end, she might whirl through space in joyous security; but the sun has other children to control; the many cables might become tangled; the weight might be intolerable; the end in the planet might be difficult to fasten against man's attempt to cut it loose, and the heat of the sun would surely melt the other end; so a long distance magnetism is employed to hold the earth in place.

What this magnetism is that throws out a far-reaching control so many millions of miles in space, and keeps all the planets in their proper realms, cannot be known or explained. It is best to call it an influence. It is not a substance. It is not an ether. It has all the power of a cable, or a rope as many miles in diameter as you choose to imagine, but it is neither. All stars that shine in the sky are supposed to be the central orbs of systems like our own, each holding their subjects in sway by the same law of magnetism; and it is a wise provision that these systems are far apart from each other, for they would draw one another out of shape if they could.

The centrifugal force of the planet is said to keep it in motion and ever tending to fly from the sun, while magnetism holds it in check, or calls it back. This may account for the fact that the orbs in this solar system are kept regularly in their places, and move with the precision of clockwork. But it is either true that the magnetism of one solar system is limited to its own realm, or that it extends into space beyond its own realm. In the latter case, no matter how feeble it might be, some influence would travel to other systems; and, as time is nothing, such influence would eventually bring the whole heavens together. Such is possibly the destiny of the universe, or one of its changes; though the same laws that now prevent conflict in our system might protect the orbs in the more general melee.

From the larger influences of magnetism, you may come down to any lesser use and still find this force at work managing things. Rays of sunlight are undoubtedly atoms impelled forth by the sun; and they might travel on forever and be lost in space, but for the influence of their own magnetism which causes them to unite and join the nearest orb in making up its hulk; or else they might go back to the sun, and no planets be built. The earth and its sister orbs are all thus taken from the sun; and scientists have shown that the latter is losing some of its light and size, as you may ascertain by reading any extensive work upon the subject of the sun. From the greatest to the smallest, and through all matter from an atom to a world, magnetism is universal. It is the executive power of creation and of creative progress.

All matter is endowed with magnetism.

This is the Second Principle. We may judge of the whole universe by what we are able to ascertain in and on our little globe. As it is well proved that the earth is made out of the sun, the material of one must be the same as the material of the other. Even rays of light are infinite mineral atoms of sun-matter, out of which molecules are made. Time, which is nothing, is alone necessary to the construction of all objects, from particles of dust to great planets out of a single structure, the indivisible atom.

Let this atom hold in itself the power of attraction, and we see at once the solution of all questions relating to magnetism. By a certain class of affinities, molecules, which are the basis of the chemical elements, are built out of atoms, each and all alike. It is not what a thing is, but how it is put together, that determines its size, shape, weight and strength. Chemists tell us there are about seventy elements from which all matter is made, whether liquid, gaseous, or solid. These elements are changing in number, as discovery reveals their identity with, others, or separation from old affiliations. We will assume there are seventy. They account for all the material world, with its contents, animate and inanimate; and for all the orbs in the solar system, as well as for the sun itself.

These elements are arrangements of molecules, and what they are depends upon the construction of their molecules. The latter need be nothing more than fixed arrangements of atoms. Single atoms flying loose are light. This is elementary, and is the beginning of all matter. Let atoms come together as twos, or in pairs, and the result would be the lightest gas known. Magnetism is eternally tending to bring atoms together. The impulse of fire is tending to separate them, and thus in the dark night a fire produces light. The greater impulse of the sun drives them forth separated, but light soon changes to gas of some kind. One kind of atom, one shape, is all that is needed. Arrangement in pairs, and in fixed conditions, will produce gases, liquids and solids; first by forming molecules; next by the affinity of fixed classes of molecules for each other.

Magnetism expresses itself in every act of material construction. As soon as the atoms are sufficiently released from the impulse of the sun's force, they obey their own laws of affinity, and come together under some guiding intelligence in fixed conditions. The same thought that tells the seed of the flower to send down roots, and its root fibers to draw certain sustenances in particles from the soil is able to make classes into which atoms may arrange themselves. Thus there are but two necessary forces behind all creation, mind and magnetism; and of these the single, indivisible atom is the agent and instrument.

That force which calls the atoms out of their onward rush from the impelling energy of the sun and draws them together, is atomic magnetism. That which holds them in combinations for the construction of chemical elements, is molecular magnetism. Scientists call it molecular attraction, which is the same thing. That which causes a mass of matter to hold together is cohesion; and this is also magnetism. That which draws one mass toward another is gravity; and this likewise is magnetism. In fact, it may be safely asserted that the same original atomic magnetism attends the particles and follows them all through matter, causing the phenomena of cohesion and gravity. Without this primitive energy, it is not possible to explain either force.

Whether the precise statement of the theory is accurate or not, something akin to it is the fact, and that is the important part of it. Therefore, when atoms, mind and magnetism are at hand, creation may begin. Nothing else is needed. Atoms furnish the basis of all material construction; magnetism is the force that constructs; and mind determines how and what shall be made. Atoms could not create themselves; magnetism is an endowment, and endowments imply a giver; mind is thought whose limit is omniscience requiring a supreme intelligence behind it; and all these essentials are results, not original causes. They compel a recognition of the Creator; unless it is true that something can originate from nothing. As the study proceeds, we shall see the use of the endowment of magnetism in every act of life and in every operation of matter from the least to the greatest. Without it, all substance would fly apart, all growth cease, and all thought be barren.

There are no nonmaterial forces.

This is the Third Principle. We would not think of calling electricity a spiritual force. Its operations are becoming more and more known; but what its substance is, and much of its real nature, are yet undiscovered. Still we regard it as a material force. The same is true of other laws, such as gravity and cohesion. The object falls to the ground, but the power that brings it down or holds it there is not spiritual. The atmosphere is lighter than the earth, but none of it is lost in space, for the same law of gravity keeps it within the range of this orb's attraction.

No more serious puzzle is possible than to explain wherein gravity has its existence, or what it is; for we know merely what it does. Is it matter? No one thinks it is. It dwells in matter, so we are told, and yet there is no evidence that it dwells anywhere. The law of cohesion is fully as mysterious. We see masses held together by some silent power, each molecule clinging to each other without hook or lashing cord. Such a force is marvelous, yet it is not spiritual. No one pretends that a spirit keeps iron together. Perhaps the power itself has no material existence, but it lives in matter, and for that reason must be classed as a material force.

Electricity is called a fluid, chiefly because it emits a spark in small currents, or a ball of fire when larger masses or volumes are expended. This evidence of fluidity or of fire may be purely deceptive. A cold stone, a meteor flying through space is invisible; but let it strike the atmosphere that surrounds this earth, and the speed will create a friction that will make the object red-hot, sometimes consuming it by reducing its solid material to gas. Why may not lightning and electricity set the air itself on fire, or the gases in the air? When the current is perfectly conducted from place to place, it is invisible. Resting in a storage jar, it shows neither light, heat nor fire. It is in breaking that it shows itself, and its breaking is merely an attempt to leap some distance which impedes its course; or the ball that seems so clearly visible and so powerful may be a collection of matter caught up and carried along by the fearful rush of the current.

It is in interrupting the perfect course, in making a break in the line of travel by which it is conducted, that every known quality, attribute, characteristic and power of electricity, are known; and any instance that seems to contradict this statement can be analyzed down to its exact truth. On the other hand, there is no fire, no light, and no heat in either electricity or lightning when uninterrupted. The message that speeds from Boston to San Francisco gives no evidence, night or day, of its existence; nor would the operator be able to recognize it unless he were to check it and read the meaning of its interruptions. The principle of the telephone is in the disc-vibrations which interfere with the electrical currents by the action of the vibrations of the voice. Light is produced by imperfect conduction, which amounts to the same thing as partial interruption of the flow.

Our purpose in this line of thought is to suggest that perhaps electricity produces, but is not, fire, heat and light; because these appear only when the current is active. If so, then it may take its place with such forces as gravity and cohesion; the former causing large bodies to approach each other, the latter holding molecules together. These all affect matter, yet have no material existence; and are probably endowments of matter. They are not nonmaterial forces; for, if so, they would be endowments of spiritual life. Because a ball thrown in the air will drop to the ground, does not prove that its falling is due to some spiritual attribute. Gravity is not matter; it is an endowment of matter; and is therefore a material force.

The time is ripe when, in the history of mankind, the fear of the unknown should be abolished. No one hopes to grasp the reins of knowledge whose mind is unable to travel; for we are shut in on this little orb, without opportunity of stepping off to visit the sister spheres of the sky, and all beyond us must be viewed in wonderment. What we can learn is the nature and purpose of the laws at work in our own bodies, in our minds, in our souls, and in the operations of life about us, reserving the discovery of the great universe itself to some happier era, and in some nobler clime, to which we may be invited, or from which we may be excluded.

The two necessary forces behind all creation are mind and magnetism.

This is the Fourth Principle. It is not what matter can do, but what can be done with matter, that makes life powerful. Forces count for everything; matter for nothing. Archimedes could have moved the world had he been able to find a fulcrum on which to place a lever, and the energy would have controlled matter, even though it were not material. It so happens that chemistry can analyze nothing but matter, or that which is used, not that which uses it. This is a small field of analysis in the realm of creation; though complete in itself.

Creation involves the necessity of something to build with. The architect first ascertains what he is to do, the size, shape and uses of the structure that is needed.

He plans it; this is mind. He then turns it over to the energy that is to do the work of building. Magnetism is the builder of the universe. In order to erect a structure, mind and energy must spend themselves on something material. This is true when God builds, or when man builds. Matter is merely the substance to be used to give shape and reality to the forces that exist; and it cannot be possible that there is any existence without matter. This assertion does not intrude upon the idea of the life of the soul.

All energy comes from magnetism, whether individual or collective. Individual energy is that which each atom possesses to attract others to itself. Collective energy in chemistry is that which each molecule expresses in establishing its affinity for others of its class. Collective energy in life, whether animal or vegetable, is the nervous force behind the muscles, or the mental force behind both. These concern us most in this present study. As life comes up the scale, and as matter increases in the size and importance of its arrangement, the collective power of magnetism becomes greater and more useful. It reaches its climax in mankind.

Mind is associated with organic matter. By this kind of matter is meant not only that which is part of some organized body in the animal or vegetable kingdom, but also the general fund of disorganized life which is wanting to enter again into organized bodies. This fund may be associated with inorganic matter, yet be no part of it. Wherever protoplasm will form, there is mind. The cells from the tiniest bacteria up to amoebic structures, and every form of plasmic growth, are impelled in their natures by intelligences that lie in the nuclei in the parts called ids. Each perfect cell, or life, contains a nucleus, and each nucleus contains an id. Here we see matter, magnetism and mind. The mass of the cell is the material part; the nucleus the nervous or magnetic part; and the id the intelligence. These are collective energies, and dwell in matter as endowments of it.

It seems that these forces have been given to matter, and that it then has been left to work out the problems of growth under the direction of accident and circumstances. The cell development of plants is necessarily the result of an ever present intelligence in the cells and plants themselves; but such an intelligence blindly follows wherever it is bidden. One variety goes on renewing its kind until a chance mixture in the seed, or the directing hand of culture produces a deviation; then the same intelligence within the life goes on as blindly as before. No human mind can conceive the full process, nor human skill execute the work required in the making of the simplest plant; and, were the thoughtful care suspended but a minute, the structure would collapse; yet such intelligence is altogether blind, while keener than the brain of man.

The same skillful but impulsive energy is seen in the magnetism with which all matter is endowed. No work could be more perfect and more far reaching, yet at the same time more blindly done. But we have the satisfaction of knowing that, as organisms rise from their lower planes, the collective mental and magnetic energies concentrate themselves in brain and nerves, and then assume command, not only of themselves, but of the matter and life around. It seems to be the will of nature that combination and concentration of the very forces that produce themselves shall come to direct and partly control themselves.

Magnetism is a positive force.

This is the Fifth Principle. There are many kinds of magnetism, but they are all probably resolvable into the same force. We believe that force to be electricity, and to be the same whether it is manifested as mere electricity or as some form of magnetism. It is common to hear of mechanical magnetism, of vegetable magnetism, and of animal magnetism; but, when that which is termed mechanical was found to be an associate of ordinary electricity, investigators began to see if one was really not a condition of the other.

The force that leaps from the clouds in the thunderstorms was suspected by Franklin to be of the same nature as that which was generated by the electrical machine. He believed that he had proved this to be true; and, as the latter was known as mechanical or machine electricity, it was perfectly proper to speak of the same energy in nature as mechanical, although a difference in terms might be of some slight value. These constitute the two great divisions of this force. It is, however, debatable whether that electrical energy which is well recognized as the foundation of animal vitality is identical with mechanical electricity, is one of its uses, or is an entirely separate force; and this may be worth considering elsewhere.

That animal life possesses electricity has been an established fact for some thousands of years. The skin and hair is capable of generating by friction the common mechanical electricity, and this we have no right to regard as anything further. By animal electricity is meant that which dwells in the life of the inner organism. We stroke a cat's back, we run a comb through our own hair, we rub our hands together, we walk on the carpet; a spark that flies from the tip of the finger, or that portion of the body which is first brought in contact with a conducting agency, must be classed with those types of electricity that are generated by mechanical devices, for they are identical in character.

Persons who throw off sparks developed in any of these ways are fond of believing that they are charged with an abundance of magnetism. In this they are mistaken. Energy so acquired is never retained; even the slight moisture in the air absorbs it. This may be seen from the fact that there is no storage resulting from friction of the hair, as the cat neither gains nor loses by the operation. It is very easy to excite surface electricity by rubbing the feet upon a carpet, and this is no deeper than the cuticle; it spends itself if not used at once. It has not been generated within, is not carried within, and vanishes almost in the making. On the other hand, the person who is able to generate electricity by controlling the life forces within the body, is also able to retain it and use it at will. One such person, possessing determined energy, will throw off hundreds of sparks from the tips of the fingers, and yet check them instantly if so desired. He can take the hand of another and send a current of fire through the body, or yield nothing but a cold and clammy touch, letting out or holding back as he may decree.

Animal electricity answers to all the laws of mechanical electricity; the only seeming difference being in the fact that the former is controlled largely by the will of man, while the latter runs free. This difference, however, is not real. Man collects his energy from the general fund of nature, and holds it in storage by some kind of insulation. He bottles some part of the lightning, draws this force out of the still atmosphere, or generates it by chemical action; the animal organism does all these. From the remarks thus far made it is apparent that the body is associated with both mechanical and animal electricity. But there is another and more important kind which is connected with the growth of the body; and this may be called vital electricity. Then the brain is a special organ whose thinking process depends entirely upon still another kind known as mental electricity. Later on in this volume we will discuss these and more besides.

Electricity and magnetism mean nearly the same, but there is a distinction between them. No sooner was it discovered that electricity was a standing as well as a moving fluid or energy, than the other fact appeared that it existed for the purpose of attracting or repelling. It was as though matter had been endowed with affinities and dislikes, and then electricity was a force extracted from these two characteristics. Held in abeyance or under control by being insulated, it is always seeking the means of escape .either toward some condition whose influence it obeys or commands, or from an enmity which repels it. It has been said of it that it is positive and negative; that two positive currents repel each other; that two negative currents repel each other; and that a positive current and negative attract each other. It has been claimed that these are opposite uses of the same energy.

No magnetism exists that is not electrical in its nature; and no electricity exists that cannot be turned to magnetism. This is true of every kind, mechanical as well as others. Those who are most successful in harnessing the forces of nature are free to admit that while much is understood of the uses of this power, little or nothing is known of what it is, or in what condition it exists. The spark, the flash, the ball of fire, or the bolt of lightning, may be matter consumed by the speed of this energy, and not the force itself; therefore, until more is known of its true nature, it is not safe to regard it as fire, heat, or any form of these. Water thrown upon a burning building in a quantity less than sufficient to drown the flames, will add to them and burn like oil; so the lightning that travels through vaporous clouds at the speed of many miles a second may turn moisture to fire and leave a gleaming path of combustion even at the end of its course.

If electricity is an energy merely, it may be of the same kind, or identical with gravity and cohesion. We know that particles are held together by the attraction of their atoms or molecules, and that these are not fastened by interlacing or hooking; we also know that under other conditions particles of solid matter fly apart and become antagonizing gases; these are due to magnetism and repulsion. We believe that fire is one form of this repulsion, and solidity its absence. Cohesion then is an energy. Gravity is a similar force, and may be identical with it. It is powerful enough to hold all the elements and properties of this planet together under one system of government, to hold all planets and their intervening orbs together in the sun's great family, and probably the sun itself in its proper place in the universe. It is possible that electricity is merely the energy of gravity collected out of matter for temporary uses; and it seems almost probable that this is so for all matter is imbued with gravity, all gravity is an attracting force that is at home or in equilibrium when undisturbed, electricity pervades all matter, is restive when out of equilibrium, and is quiet when back again in matter.

If you will imagine two particles of matter so small that you can see them only under the most powerful microscope, clinging together without an apparent reason; and the myriad millions of other particles holding themselves together in the same mass, you will have an illustration of what is meant by the magnetic property of common electricity. Where this property exists, whether in or through the mass, or at the edges or surfaces of molecules, is not known. Whether it is a mind, or an intelligent force with which all things are blindly endowed, amounts to one and the same thing. It is electrical energy, magnetic because it attracts, because it controls other substance, because it holds together the parts that must be bound to each other to make the strength of the whole, and because it obeys other masterminds.

Vitality may be a separate fund, and intelligence still another fund, dwelling apart by themselves and coming to matter when conditions are ripe for action; or vitality and intelligence may dwell in a certain division of matter through which they control such other portions as they may be able to influence. In the first case these forces make use of matter; in the second case they dwell in it and are blindly attached to it, following fixed laws in their operations. Like the energies which are called gravity and cohesion, vitality and intelligence may be uses of electricity; and, the more we study them, the easier it is to believe that all power can be traced to this one mother-force. How much of this may be true may, for the present, be held as problematical. Those who regard the universe as divisible into two parts, the material and nonmaterial, subdivide the latter part into energies of material, and into spiritual forces; but, until a single energy whether attributable to matter or spirit can be described, it is too early to construct a system of explanation based upon laws of the spiritual. There is as much mystery attached to the forces which we know govern them, as to those which are supposed to govern the soul; and the mind at times gives evidence of supernatural powers which defy all explanation. It may be true that one and all are merely different uses of one great endowment, electricity or magnetism. These problems and questions will receive full attention in the pages of this volume.

Magnetism, on its positive side, works for life and growth. When it welds particle to particle it gives form to matter; it constructs, and out of it we get the strength of iron, the tenuity of wire, the elasticity of rubber, and all those qualities which make these forms useful and yet of different characteristics. On no other ground than magnetism can these things be accounted for. Release its positive and affirmative nature, and form is lost, molecules drop apart, decay sets in and life, growth and constructs strength no longer exists. It lifts the vapor from the ground, separating it from water by a change in specific gravity; then, when it has attained its height in the atmosphere it is again given over to the magnetism of gravity by condensation. Under a similar operation it prevents rivers from freezing to solidity and thereby becoming useless. It interchanges the strata of air producing temperatures and barometric changes whereby vegetation is protected. In this way we might go on almost indefinitely citing instances of the usefulness of magnetism as a positive force; the loss of any one of which would instantly destroy all life on this planet.

Mind and thought are magnetic phenomena. The physical brain is a battery of electricity peculiarly adapted to those vibrations which occur for the reception of ideas, and those other vibrations by which ideas are generated and sent forth into the system to be enacted into realities. It is not the reception of an idea, but its formulation and going forth out into the great sea of human thought, that exhibits the positive power of man's magnetism in this realm. The power behind the creation of ideas, whether from the reasoning faculties or from the will, is something that becomes a tremendous energy under the stimulus of the being in control. Not only in what is said, but in the way in which it is uttered, in the vital energy that propels its utterance, in the magnetic fires that burn in the tones of the voice, and in the vigor of mind which makes the same idea a different instrument of power when put in a stronger framework of construction, does positive electricity show itself in the life of one who is supreme master of the faculties with which nature has endowed him.

Hypnotism is a negative condition.

This is the Sixth Principle. The word negative may have more than one signification. Ordinarily it means a denial or refusal to believe a certain affirmative proposition. Again it means the mere lack of anything, and in this use it denotes absence. In speaking of electricity it is merely a term of convenience supposed to distinguish one kind of a current from another, although the idea of repellant action is associated with it. We are speaking of a condition that is the opposite of magnetism, and in so doing our use of the word comes close to the meaning of absence.

On a sunny day we sit beneath the shade of a large tree and our principle reflection is that we are out of the intense light; but there is brightness all around us in lesser degree. On a cloudy day we see the earth entirely enveloped in the protecting shade, but the sun is shining above it all. In the night we ride on the dark side of the planet, not thinking or stopping to think that the very darkness in which we are enveloped is the negative condition of the sunshine; but no night is so dark, not even when the clouds shut out the stars, that there is not some light somewhere out of doors. It is only when we shut ourselves within walls more opaque than sky-clouds that it can be said that all light is extinguished; and even then the phosphorescence of the brain shining in the eyes, and of germ-life, steps in with atomic rays.

There is no shadow without light; so there is no hypnotism without magnetism; light is a positive force, shadow is a negative condition; it cannot be called a force as it possesses no energy. Take all the light away and darkness would be complete; take all the magnetism out of a person, and the hypnotic condition is then complete, assuming that life remains. As it is difficult to find absolute darkness, so it is rare that magnetism is entirely lacking in a human life. Light comes from the sun directly, from the electric current, from coal, wood, the candle and the many forms of combustible material, as well as from phosphorescence, which is the glow of elementary atoms widely scattered. Light is, therefore, of every kind and of every degree of intensity; and the same may be said of magnetism, except that, while it is more limited in variety, it has the widest possible range of force and quality.

What seems less intense darkness at one time than another is merely a variation of light either in its quality or quantity. We often meet persons of whom we might say, carelessly speaking, that they are entirely devoid of magnetism; being straws in the wind of others ' influence; so we often enter rooms, or pass through groves at night, where darkness seems to he complete, yet some light is there. These remarks are made to illustrate the point that few persons exist without some magnetic vitality. Strictly speaking, it cannot be said of them that they are in the negative condition referred to under our principle; so, strictly speaking, we can rarely ever declare any place to be absolutely dark. Darkness, however, is generally referred to as a condition opposite to that of light; and we designate that state in which the magnetic energy is low as partly hypnotic; although not involving complete unconsciousness of the natural mind.

It is necessary to understand that hypnotism does not always or generally exhibit itself in the sleep state.

There is a certain average line in which the magnetism of an individual may be said to be normal; above which it may be called abundant and therefore, positive, as we use the term; and below this dividing line, as the vitality departs from the average or normal, it enters into the hypnotic or negative condition. With this understanding we can make clear to our students the various degrees of influence by which persons are more or less deprived of their magnetism below the normal plane, and are brought into the hypnotic state, without showing any semblance of sleep. Thus hypnotism, in a partial state, manifests itself in persons who are wide awake and have no knowledge that their magnetism is being taken from them. This corresponds to the partial absence of light, when gloom prevails without actual darkness.

The true cataleptic sleep involves a loss of consciousness in the natural mind; all the functions of the body are at a standstill; breathing has ceased, so that death might be announced were it not for some symptoms which indicate the trance condition; and the nerves are insensible to pain, in so far that they may be subjected to flame without recoiling. This is a complete negative state, in which all magnetism is absent. Such a condition comes on of itself through the process of disease that separates the storage batteries of vitality from the nervous system, rendering the mind useless. The body is dead in a magnetic sense, but lives for days, and even weeks, as an insensible piece of plant life, its only functions that are alive being those that are directly inherited from the vegetable kingdom, and these in a minimum degree.

So extreme a condition is rarely met with in any human being who is not actually diseased. As in the case of Bishop, the mind-reader, it is sometimes possible for a person to put himself in this depleted state; but the clairvoyants, of whom there are a few who are genuine, rarely ever enter the full cataleptic state, as it is not necessary in order to open up the subconscious mind. This shows that the faculties which awaken under the hypnotic influence are not necessarily developed by a prior exhaustion of magnetism, after the first experiences. In the attempt to subjugate the will of a person, it is generally considered necessary to completely expel all magnetic vitality; but this is used in the sense of expelling all light from a room that is only ordinarily dark. The word complete, as will be seen, does not mean totally complete, except in true cataleptic conditions.

It was formerly supposed that hypnotism resulted from a peculiar influence exerted only by a person gifted in that direction. This is now known to be untrue. There is no such thing as the gift of hypnotizing; but it does require skill and a special talent for suggestion. Hypnotism brings on a cataleptic sleep, but cataleptics are not able to show the uses of the subconscious faculty until they have been led on by his art of suggesting to them the things to be done and said. Ordinarily the victim of the disease known by this name is worthless as a subject for experiment in this line; so would a person be who had been put into the usual hypnotic sleep without the aid of suggestions to open out this faculty. We, therefore, see that an operator is required, who must handle his subject with skill and turn the hypnotism to account.

Instead of the gift of hypnotism, we must speak of the gift of suggestion; and this is an art that is rare indeed. Perhaps we may be wrong in inferring that it does not require skill to bring on the cataleptic sleep; it does require skill to exhaust the magnetism of another person, but this belongs to one who is able, through superior magnetic vitality, to absorb what energy there may be in the subject, which of itself leaves him in mesmeric sleep. The first essential is to find the individual who may thus be overcome; the second, is to find one who has sufficient magnetism to conquer the other; the third, is to combine with the latter the skill of suggestion, so that to take advantage of the mesmeric sleep. All this would look as if there must be some person gifted in hypnotizing; and, taken in a popular sense, all persons are so gifted to a greater or less degree, except that they have not the skill to follow up the advantage by the art of suggestion.

Self-hypnotism is more common than that of personal influence. This being true, it may be understood how a man who had never practiced either branch of the art in his life, on catching a friend of his in the act of mesmerizing himself by looking at a silver ball, put to test what he had read in books by making suggestions just as his friend was falling into the hypnotic sleep. To his surprise the latter talked and acted like an experienced subject; he obeyed the amateur operator to a degree of perfection that finally alarmed him; and he had some difficulty in bringing him out of this condition. The most surprising result of all was the fact that he secured control over his friend so that he could put him into the mesmeric sleep at will. This shows that there is no such thing as the gift of hypnotism, that the state of subjection may be produced by other causes than those emanating from the influence of individuals, and that any person who is reasonably magnetic may step in with the art of suggesting and turn the sleeper into a subconscious subject.

A COMPLETE COURSE OF LESSONS IN THE DEFENSE AGAINST HYPNOTISM ON everything that can be acquired is worth acquiring. The privilege of putting a defenseless person to sleep, and then waking him up into a different state of consciousness wherein he is made the victim of your own whims and the stray influences of other minds, is sought because it is considered an evidence of power. The graver question is, whether it compensates for the trouble and efforts that are entailed upon the operator, and the injury it does to the nervous system of the subject.

As long as the matter remains so obscure as at the present time, so long will men and women seek the knowledge that will enable them to acquire the power of hypnotizing their fellow beings. You may not know it, but the numbers that are eagerly inquiring for this knowledge are surprisingly large. Most applicants disclaim the intention of taking advantage of* those they may control, even deeming it praiseworthy if good is done them through this means. In personal letters, almost without limit, we have for years advised all correspondents to drop the idea and cling only to the nobler art of magnetism; but, amidst it all, there comes the persistent demand for a clear understanding of hypnotism. Men and women will have the knowledge, cost what it may. Our duty was then made plain.

Deception and fraud are more rampant in this line of publications than in most any other. Those who know how the art of hypnotizing is acquired seem unwilling to part with their knowledge; for what good reason it is hard to say. Those who know something of this art, but not all, are most free to impart this and much more added. The result is that the public are never sure of what they are getting. Only recently we saw a private pamphlet for which a man of intelligence paid fifty dollars; and it contained sixty pages of impossible instruction, mixed with good and bad advice. We showed the uselessness of the work by comparing the pretended lessons with the genuine; the former wasting energy for nothing, the latter giving results in a satisfactory manner.

A wife asked for instructions of such a nature that would enable her to control her husband so as to prevent his ruin through drink. The request was a worthy one, the object in view most commendable; but hypnotism could not check his appetite for liquor except when he was in a subconscious frame of mind, or partly so; and we advised magnetizing the man instead of hypnotizing him. After repeated letters and arguments we succeeded in explaining the difference, with the result that the woman adopted magnetism and made a man of her husband. A similar request came from a woman who loved a young man and desired to secure his consent to marrying her; so she asked for lessons in hypnotism, thinking that a cataleptic would propose to her. He might do so while in that condition, but not intelligently. We showed to her the difference, and she used magnetism with perfect success. We cite these two cases, which really are typical ones, because certain advertising teachers strongly advised the use of hypnotism, and failure could not be avoided.

All persons may acquire magnetism, and most persons may learn to mesmerize. No one need fail to magnetize; many fail to mesmerize. Of those in the latter class who do fail, the majority do so, not from lack of knowledge or correct training, but from lack of courage and tact at the crucial moment; as, for instance, when the subject is poised in that doubtful mood when a quick release will seem like a gift from the operator, and he is left too long before being released; thus realizing his own power instead of the manipulators. For this reason and because of tact at the right moment, or second, many subjects are lost; and it may, therefore, be said that all persons who might become hypnotizers, will not. Yet the advertising teachers go on guaranteeing that all will acquire the art. If it were true that all may, it is not true that all will. A commercial college promised that every pupil in its charge would become a good penman, and learn to write a neat and beautiful hand; for the reason that the art was one that all could acquire. This may have been an honest fallacy. It is true that nearly every person, if not all, may learn to write a neat and beautiful hand; but it is not true that half of those who may do so, will do so. The same is true of hypnotizing. Very few of those who are unable to acquire the power, have the tact to win at the crucial moment. Some who fail at one time, succeed later on.

Patrons of reliable teachers are sure to blame their instructors because of this failure. In some cases the teachers are to blame; for they should make their work so clear and so plain that even stupid pupils may understand; but this does not give tact and skill. It may help. The fault may be with the method. It is wrong to take tuition fees from those who are not likely to succeed, unless there is a clear understanding that the primary purpose of the instruction is to show the way to avoid the hypnotic influence of another; or to save oneself from the horrors of self-mesmerism. This is always a worthy object, and should be encouraged.

There are several ways of taking lessons in this negative art. Many if not all traveling mesmerists advertise to give instructions in their work, and go so far as to guarantee success in a few lessons. The fee they charge is a very flexible one; if the applicant is poor, it is never less than twenty-five dollars; and a promise of secrecy is properly asked for and given. If the would-be-pupil is able to pay, the amount demanded is large; and there are instances of five thousand dollars being paid at the beginning, before a single lesson was taken; while more was stipulated for under a conditional contract in which no payment was to be made unless the mesmeric power was in fact acquired. The instructor saw that it was acquired.

It is the rule of mesmeric teachers, if they are traveling operators, not to give results even where they can. Some take a fee of twenty-five or fifty dollars, and impart correct knowledge, then ask for another fee on the ground that it is a difficult case. To do this they avoid making a promise to complete the instruction for the first fee. Some assure their applicants of success by word of mouth; then supersede this by printed or written contracts containing clause to the contrary, which have legal force. It seems to be understood that a successful operator does not wish competition. He tells as little as he can, and leaves his pupil to hunt for more, but in vain. Sometimes he checks the progress of the lessons by falling back upon a stipulation and demanding a further fee that cannot be met.

A young man acquaintance of the author, who was wealthy, but who seemed to lack magnetism, and who gave not the slightest promise of ever acquiring the mesmeric art, spent four hundred dollars in lessons with a very prominent public operator, and learned absolutely nothing. He then paid fifty dollars to a younger and less prominent operator, with a further agreement to pay more if he succeeded; and, as a result, he became as effective and as powerful a hypnotist as either of his teachers. In a conversation, he assured us that the greater of these told him half, and no more, and that the other was willing to finish the course; yet he did not tell either teacher the method of the other.

The number or proportion of those who may be hypnotized is growing less, and we are doing all we can to assist in the diminution. There are many reasons why the condition of catalepsy should be avoided. It indicates ill health of the nervous system, and causes an increase of this malady, while standing in the way of its cure; and this is true whether the mind is fully overcome by such control, or is merely in a state of lapsed memory, which is the least of the mesmeric or cataleptic degrees. There can be no gratification in this yielding to the will of another. Even the clairvoyant power, which has been turned to good account in a few instances, is useful to the operator but not to the subject, as the latter knows nothing of what occurs in its exercise.

Persons who are fully mastered by this influence, as well as those who come partly under its control, suffer from nervous weakness; although a few rare exceptions may be found among the fully equipped clairvoyants. There are hours of unrest in every day of life. Morning, following a refreshing natural sleep, is the only period of the day when the mind is free from hallucinations. As evening approaches and the darkness deepens the shadows along the road, vague fears startle the nerves, and a longing to be in the rooms within the house drives away all sense of pleasure in the scenes without.

This condition of unrest and fear is experienced by those who have come under the influence of the operator, whether fully or partly; but is more annoying in cases where self-hypnotism has occurred. This peculiar affliction should be first considered. It has been known for centuries that the optic nerve might be made the agent of mesmerizing the mind in a mechanical way; and investigation has shown that the condition within the body, as to life-functions in their influence on the thoughts, as well as outer.

Self-hypnotism is mechanically produced through the optic nerve.

This is the Seventh Principle. Few persons are aware of the fact that if they gaze at a small shining ball placed in front of the eyes slightly raised, the optic nerve will soon become tired and the mind will pass into a rapt or ecstatic condition; and those whose nerves are abnormal or morbid will become mesmerized, while the others will pass through a troubled slumber into natural waking.

The mental and nervous conditions are morbid when they are diseased or disordered. This comes from physical causes through illness that leaves the body weak and the nerves unsteady; or else through some interruption of the vital currents, as by misfortune, gloom, disappointment, and insufficient nutrition. The brain and the nerves are associated; being alike in their ordinary activities, and subject to the same laws of health and disease. Nervous excitement involves the brain before it does the body; and anything that startles or agitates the senses will derange the nervous system. Thus the scream of a child has caused a woman to drop a glass; the sight of a strange person, or of something that surprises or horrifies, may take away all power of motion, or so weaken the nerves that the limbs tremble and the strength gives way. It is on this principle that the hearing of bad news will cause a collapse of the stomach and stop digestion.

There are so many intricate problems involved in this connection that it is impossible to consider them all. Not a generation ago it was hard to find persons who believed in the power of mesmerism; and still harder to find those who could be induced to accept the theory that the body was the slave of the mind; although the few investigators of these subjects in every age had been acquainted with them from the beginning of history. The heartbeats, the pulsing blood, the flow of life along the nerves, the accumulation of power in the central batteries of the body, are urged to excess or drooped in weakness as the mind is buoyant or depressed. But what a shock of fear may accomplish in a mental way, the wearying of the eye may do in a mechanical. Yet something must exist beyond this. Lives are generally morbid. Habits make or mar the clearness of the mind and vital existence. Such a disease as superstition grows on a person and soon produces the morbid or abnormal state.

A test of one's condition is found in the use of self hypnotism, for, if the mind and system are normal, nothing but natural sleep will ultimately result from them; but, if there is morbidity, the mesmeric state will follow. Despite the advantages of clairvoyance as attained through hypnotism, it must always be borne in mind that this condition is the result of a combination of hypnotic influence and morbid nerves. Even the better things hoped for in future discoveries must pass through the mud of this low channel. One excellent hypnotist said very frankly that the nearer a person came to insanity the better subject and clairvoyant was produced; and this highly morbid state was favorable to clear seeing in the subconscious realm; an almost contradictory statement. It ought to be true that, if there is an inner mind possessing supernatural powers, it should be the offspring of health and not disease. Yet it is said that no great genius has ever existed who was not mentally erratic. In some cases, the more eccentricity, the more genius.

It is not advisable to practice self-hypnotism. If your condition is normal, nothing will come out of it; if morbid, you will suffer from hallucinations. If you desire to become a clairvoyant, you must pass through the lowest stratum of the sane mind in order to accomplish this end. Here are some reasons offered by intelligent persons, for resorting to the practice of self-hypnotism. A man writes to us as follows: "I wish your opinion. I think I am right in my way of reasoning; but you can tell me whether I am or not. I have read the biographies of many men and women of genius; and the world regarded them as eccentric. Take the idiotic careers of Goldsmith and Byron; were they sane! Study Napoleon and Alexander; were they sane! One author declares that all great men are out of their minds; that they show it in their way of living, and in their works. Another says no one is perfectly sane. My argument is this: If geniuses are insane to a degree, if geniuses possess the subconscious power of quick and clear seeing, if those, who out of ordinary life possess the same power, are also of morbid mental condition, why is it not true that self-hypnotism will awaken the spirit of genius?" Here is an association of similar tendencies without proof to connect one with the other, or to resolve them back to a common cause.

It is true that geniuses are endowed with something of the clear-seeing of clairvoyance; otherwise it is not possible to account for the great memory of famous men and women. Edward Everett and others declare that Daniel Webster committed to memory the Bible, Shakespeare, Paradise Lost, and other works; but common minds doubt the statement as it seems impossible of belief. Actors quickly commit to memory the leading roles of long plays, and some have done this in a single day, although few persons off the stage will credit the assertion. We once knew a statesman and lawyer of national fame, of whom it was said that he had committed to memory most of Shakespeare and all of the Bible; and, as far as we could test the accuracy of the report, it seemed true, for he was willing to recite from these works ad libitum. If the subconscious faculty was not at work, we do not know how to account for the phenomenon.

MYSTIC UTOPIAN SUPERMEN

Another reason given for the development of self-hypnotism is contained in the following letter: "I was bowed down with trouble. Night and day I prayed to get release; but, not being sincerely repentant, I only suffered the more. I thought of mesmerizing myself, for I knew a friend who did so and forgot all her troubles. Do you advise it?" In our reply we cited the case of a woman who had read a highly sensational book and was unable to divert her mind from the realism associated with the doings of certain characters in the story, so mesmerized herself and was last known in an asylum. This seems not to have deterred the inquirer; for she followed in the same course and likewise entered an asylum. It is possible that, in both instances, the mind was tottering; making both of them fit subjects of this influence. They did not become clairvoyants, although both might have done so had their reason not been dethroned.

The principle involved in self-hypnotism is elsewhere stated. To develop the true condition the nervous system and mind must be morbid. We will first treat of the mechanical kind, wherein the optic nerve does the work. Some subsequent explanations will show why such sleep is caused in this method of procedure. We will say here that a sharp, fine point of light such as may be caught from the tiny reflection on a small, shiny ball, say about a half inch to an inch in diameter, will exhaust the magnetism along the optic nerve from the eyeball to the juncture within the brain. Its influence goes no further than this. If the magnetism of the nerve cannot be sustained there is no vitality with which to keep it alive to use. A sensation of fear attends the loss of sight; the brain becomes tired in its sleep-acting functions; and, after a number of trials lasting from ten minutes to an hour each, for 5 or 10 days, a cataleptic sleep is produced.

This sleep is mild and unnoticeable in any peculiarities, if the mind is normal; otherwise it is fully mesmeric, and needs some other person to act as operator or suggestor of action. To turn it to effect, the suggestions must be made under the methods stated in the pages following, which are devoted to that part of the matter. The terms used in this connection are here stated.

Operator.—This is the man or woman who has charge of the hypnotic. The operator may induce sleep by manipulation, or by magnetism alone.

Manipulation.—This consists of handling the person to be mesmerized. It depends primarily on magnetism, but aids it by rubbing the parts of the body as described in subsequent pages of this department.

Free Hypnotism.—This is the putting to sleep without touching the body or any part of it.

To Hypnotize.—This is the same as to mesmerize. Hypnotize is derived from the Greek word meaning sleep. It is not strictly correct, for all sleep is not accurately described by a single word.

To Mesmerize.—This is the same as to hypnotize. Mesmer, in the last century, called attention to the art by lectures and experiments; and his name was associated with it up to recent years when a new word was coined from the Greek; so that "mesmerism" is less frequently employed today than "hypnotism."

Subject.—This is the term applied to one who is sought to be controlled by a hypnotist.

Hypnotic.—Any person who is, or may be hypnotized, whether by an operator or by self-processes.

Catalepsy.—This is a sleep in which the senses and ordinary faculties are suspended, and the conscious mind is completely clouded. It is the same as hypnotic sleep.

Subconsciousness.—Erroneously spoken of the soul; but properly applied to that mental state which is revealed by the operator after a subject has been mesmerized to such an extent that there is no consciousness remaining in the ordinary mind.

Part-hypnotism.—This means that condition which is not involved in sleep, but where the person is overcome to a slight extent, or suffers a lapse of consciousness. Nearly all persons are thus influenced at times.

Trance.—A supposed state of subconsciousness; usually the pretense of advertising charlatans claiming to be mediums and clairvoyants; but, when genuine, it is the term applied to cataleptic sleep, otherwise called mesmerism.

Clairvoyance.—The name of the subconscious faculty when it reads the thoughts of other persons, and sees objects and events, as though matter did not separate them from the senses.

Spiritualism.—The erroneous claim that what cannot be understood or explained by the reasoning faculties must, therefore, be the work of spirits. It is the weakest emanation of the human mind, and is on a par with the lowest order of mediaeval superstition.

To Magnetize.—This means to add and arouse vitality in another person. It is the opposite of mesmerize, which depresses vitality and puts to sleep.

Positive Personal Magnetism.—This is(used to increase the vitality of others, to arouse magnetism in them and to win them by enthusiasm or belief of an active nature.

Negative Magnetism.—This is used to depress or drive out the little magnetism possessed by a mesmeric subject so that all attempts at resistance may fail.

Hallucinations, due to hypnotic conditions, are destroyed by magnetism.

This is the Eighth Principle. It is of importance because there are not five persons in a hundred that are not prey at times to these abnormal conditions of the mind or nervous system. It might be said that all men and women and most children have had hallucinations at some period or other in the past; though perhaps but for a moment.

In natural consciousness we possess five senses. Of these, sight is most readily disturbed by temporary hypnotism, which does not put to sleep, but takes us away from full self-control for a minute or two at a time. What is called 4 'part hypnotism'' differs from the temporary influence in that it holds the mind in partial sway but docs not cause sleep. It is preceded or accompanied by depression. Hallucinations come in such moods. No magnetic person has them, unless there has been a temporary suspension of the vitality. As a rule all highly magnetic individuals are free from influences that tend to depress.

As hypnotic conditions are always associated with morbid states of the mind and nerves, and these are due to physical illness or mental affection of some kind or other, it would not be possible to consider them apart. A man is less likely to be harassed by hallucinations than a woman; she is more likely in her depressed part of the month than at other times. Some women declare that they are never free from morbid tendencies at such times. Of course the mesmerist has more success in throwing them into the cataleptic sleep in these periods, and the fact is known to them. But our duty in this connection is to consider the mental afflictions first.

From this line of testimony we find that some women have periodic hallucinations, varying in kind; while others have the same sort of troubles at regular times; and still others are affected without regularity. One woman describes her trouble in this language: "Nothing can be so annoying as the coming on of these sights at such times; I look down when I walk, for there is always sure to be a face ahead looking at me, and I avoid it if I do not raise my eyes." She then says that the faces "are never two alike; nor are there more than one each month." She never sees a pleasant face; once it is a child suffering pain; again it is a man with bandaged head; or a woman with chin contorted; and the strangest face of all was that of an old lady which seemed to be "lying on a pillow gazing at me; if I looked down I could not see it, if I looked up there it was as plain as day." The cure of this morbid trouble was completed solely by the studies of magnetism in the highest exercises obtainable.

The mere reading of the causes and operations of hypnotism has saved many a mind. It is said to be impossible to hypnotize a person who has once read or been told how it is done, for the means whereby belief may be captured are forever destroyed. In a number of instances we have known of the cure of hallucinations by merely reading of the story and laws which are involved in their origin; for, the foundation fear being gone, it is no longer possible to depress the mind and nerves. To read and to know is generally a great help in regulating the mental functions. A comet once caused the world to fall on its knees and tremble; now that the people know something of the nature of the comet, they cease to be awed by fear. The same law holds true in hypnotism; it is generally the fear that the operator has the power to obtain control, that yields it. So in hallucinations; when the real cause of them is known the terror is gone.

To illustrate the effect of reading alone of the way such morbid troubles originate and are overcome, we cite the following instance: A woman writes, and sustains her claim by other evidence: "At this period every time I started to go from the house I saw a form, half man and half dragon, crouching just around the corner, leaning its head and part of its body forward, looking at me. Its eyes were torn open and horrible in their gaze. You can imagine my feelings when I first witnessed it. I screamed and went back into the house, telling the folks that there was a man demon around the corner. They went our cautiously, saw nothing, came back and looked pityingly at me. I realized it all. A month passed, and I had the same experience. I felt that my reason was being dethroned. This continued till I received your explanation of the cause; and I instantly got relief. It is a fact that the knowledge of the cause was sufficient to release me from this bondage. I then knew it was not trouble of the mind, but depression and fear that increased the influence over me." Two important facts are educed from this case. In the first, we see that she suffered from a recurrence of the same hallucination; in the second, she cured herself by knowledge which drove away fear.

A man who had failed in business became so depressed that he suffered from hallucinations of the most horrible kind. They came upon him at all hours of the day or night, waking or sleeping; but they were not constant visitors. He went for days without seeing any; and rarely saw more than one in twenty-four hours. This made him believe that it was worry and not mental disease that was the cause of it; but still had enough doubt about it to be depressed and fearful. He says: "I fought this horror as bravely as I could. I did not succeed in drowning it, and I write to say that if I do not get some relief I shall put a revolver to my temple and blow my brains out. That may relieve me and kill the devils." No doctor living would have refused to certify that the man was mentally deranged. Yet he was not. Many a person has gone to the asylum, or to the suicide's grave, who might easily have been rescued. Remove fear from half the candidates for insane wards, and full reason would be restored.

The foregoing case is typical and should be considered more fully. The man's first hallucination was that of a widow with her child, lying bleeding at his feet. He was about to step aside, when a mass of clothing rolled over, pale arms came out of a bundle of white, and bony fingers almost clutched his hands,—all causing him to shrink suddenly. His wife, who was walking with him, saw his actions and tried to pacify him. In a few seconds all had disappeared. He rubbed his wife's hands and asked if she was at his side, although he was looking straight down into her eyes. She said that his pupils seemed to be dilated and his gaze wild and weird.

Later on in the week he opened a closet door and thought he saw a skeleton, which toppled toward him, raised its arms to clutch his neck, and disappeared as he shrank back to avoid it. He shut the door, said nothing to his wife, and had never opened it again up to the time our attention was called to the case. His purpose was expressed as follows: "I will not tell any member of my family what I suffer unless they are with me; but some morning I will be found free from it all." He then goes on to relate the worst of all his hallucinations: "I was sitting in the front room reading. I would not spend another evening in the sitting-room where that closet-door is. My wife crept in, always speaking before she entered, so as not to startle me. She sat at the table opposite me, her face partly toward mine. I heard a rustling at the window, then a scratching sound. I was afraid to look up. It was a warm evening, and the top of the window was down. The shade would every now and then blow out as though the wind lifted it. Soon a pair of hands appeared, one on each side of the shade, extending into the room and shaking about, while the fingers wriggled and snapped. I laughed to myself, and looked down. Then I heard distinctly the throaty sounds of a man trying to attract my attention by exclaiming 'ahem!' very loudly. I looked to my wife. She heard nothing. The sound came louder than before. I looked up. The long arms had lifted the shade clear to the ceiling, and under it, leaning over the top of the sash, was the unshaved face of a hideous tramp, with eyes running streams of blood. He raised one knee as if to climb over the window and spring into the room. I threw my book at him and ran away. My wife found me on the bed upstairs, my face buried in the pillows." We could not refuse to act in his behalf. He thought himself insane, and his wife thought so; but he had yet time. This art saved him.

The probable cause of these hallucinations was the oppression of his creditors. It is a fact that some minds are sensitive to evil influences, or malign dispositions. This is seen in the case of a young man who, on a certain evening, felt that somebody was plotting to do him injury. The feeling was so keen and clear that he stated the matter to his elder brother, saying, "I am to have trouble. Who can be at work against me!" They made a note in writing of the time to a minute. Subsequent events verified the belief. A secret meeting was held at the hour and malice predominated. In the case of the man who had failed in business, it seems that on or about the time when he experienced his most horrible vision, his creditors were in conclave seeking to get evidence, or plan proceedings to arrest him for fraud.

The first step in such a case was to explain fully the cause and the operation of self-hypnotism produced by fear. We wrote frankly: "You have probably done wrong in some part of your failure, and are looking at every turn for the sheriff to enter and take you into custody. This fear has hypnotized you." We explained fully the process whereby apprehension would drive a person into a part mesmeric condition. In the instance cited, the mere knowledge did not effect a complete cure; it expelled the rougher hallucinations, which seemed to satisfy him. He then took up the study of magnetism, and, a few months later, when the crisis came, he met it manfully, settled with his creditors, was allowed a liberal reduction, and gained their confidence to such an extent that he resumed business, and is today prosperous. He now writes: "I am not afraid of closet-doors or windows. Your work of magnetism is worth a hundred thousand dollars to me. You know that I am sincere, because I have brought you many converts. It is true that no doctor, no asylum, no treatment of any kind, except magnetism of the higher estates could have rescued him from insanity and suicide. A fact of so much value as this cannot be escaped or passed lightly by. The man in question believes in this method sincerely, for he sees that other persons who need just such help as magnetism are induced to get it in time to save disaster.

A certain business man had became overwhelmed by success. He made money so fast that he could not attend to the thousand cares that were multiplied thereby. From morning, at the earliest hour, to the dragging period of midnight, he fought away at the intricate problems; until at last the nutrition that fed his brain and nerves gave out. These little ministers of life cried night and day for sustenance which he could not give, for his thoughts and plans were too intensely strong to admit of cessation. He could not sleep. The newspapers, which serve to suggest every horrifying idea that will hypnotize weakened minds, published the picture of a business man who, under similar circumstances, went to the bathroom at two o'clock in the morning, and blew out his brains. This was the final straw. In a state of hypnotism, he arose from the side of his wife and proceeded to do the same thing. She heard him as he stole out of the room, followed him, and caught his arm, just as the revolver discharged, and swerved it from its aim. The shock of the sound aroused him from his hypnotic mood, just as any quick, sharp noise may awaken one who is in a light cataleptic slumber. Could suicides miss the first shot, it is likely that they would not fire the second.

A person may be self-hypnotized and greatly injured by the operation of fear.

This is the Ninth Principle. There are various kinds of fear. The most common is that of misfortune and poverty. It has sent millions to an untimely grave. The usual fear of the mediaeval ages is no longer universal; it was the continual apprehension of murder. Then no human life was safe; and those who retired at night were in doubt of rising in the morning.

Later on this feeling of insecurity changed to that of assault or attack. But this kind of fear is rare, except in Kentucky among the mountaineers, and on the borderlines of civilization where the far West blends into the population of the Pacific slope. Fear of bodily harm is not common at this date where laws are respected and enforced. When one kind of apprehension gives way another takes its place, and the mind is kept busy extricating itself from its moods. In this age the fear that the means of living will be taken away, is probably paramount to all other mental depressions. This was not so when people got their full sustenance and support from the land,—nor would it be so if the acres that are prostituted to waste were made the basis of human supply as they did in the wealthy colonial days.

Conscience is the cause of fear to a much larger extent than is believed. Not only as a moral influence, but in its alarms that portend danger to reputation or liberty, it drives the good man and the bad man on to the reefs of wreck and misery. The desperate criminal is an animal, not a human being; and animals sutler neither remorse nor regret. To rise to the plane of humanity, a felon must either fear or command by the possession of a supreme magnetism which knows no fear; and in the latter case he would be too honest a man to commit crime. The acquisition of magnetism is directly opposite the tendency which makes wrongdoing easy.

Most crimes are committed under hypnotic conditions, and the prevention is to be had more frequently in the prior training than at the moment of the offense. Absolute certainty of apprehension and punishment will deter all persons who are sane, and nearly all who are insane, as we shall see in later pages. But there is doubt of being punished and thus the man is lost. In a subsequent realm of this volume, the conditions of hypnotic influence will be considered fully, and perhaps some new light may be gathered on the question of criminal responsibility. The dazed condition and the animal nature that seems to invite it, are entitled to examination. We now have the direct laws of this art before us.

Hypnotism puts to sleep the conscious will and awakens a morbid condition of the subconscious faculty.

This is the Tenth Principle. The science and art of mesmerizing, which word is being displaced by the older term hypnotizing, have been known in one form or another, generally crudely, for several thousand years. Briefly stated, the effect of the practice is to shut off or put to sleep the conscious or regular faculty of the brain, and open up the subconscious or intuitive faculty.

The absence of any really scientific laws on the subject, the belief that the practice was quackery, the limitation of it to certain undesirable uses, the confining of the power of hypnotizing to persons of generally low standing, and the fact that the brightest minds failed to acquire the art while the dullest succeeded, all conspired to make it an undignified if not a disreputable profession; and it drifted away from its true base to such an extent that few works of authority are obtainable on the subject, while the world of sensational literature is crowded with its extravagances. Even at this day the public are considered gullible, if we may judge from the advertisements that appear in magazines and periodicals, seeking purchasers of books and courses of study on mesmerism, hypnotism, personal magnetism and other similar matters.

That the art was practiced thousands of years ago, is known to any close student of history or of the Bible. No nation was exempt from the practice. The credulity of the masses was such that, aided by a prevailing superstitious fear, they quickly accorded to any man who could wield the power, the rank of healer, doctor, priest or almost anything he sought. Humanity does not change in forty centuries so that one age would differ materially from another in this regard; and it is not only reasonable, but certain, that the hypnotist had his favorite subject always attending him to give evidence of thought-reading, clairvoyance, warnings, predictions, and the like.

The lowest types of minds have been successful as hypnotists more often than those above the average. It seems to have cropped out by accident, and to have as much surprised the operator as anyone else. Indolent men and lazy hags in the days of witchcraft fell into the practice as though by natural endowment; and the popular fear of the black art helped to make victims in great numbers. As most persons, to some extent at least, may be hypnotized; and, as those who produce the influence are not always able to undo its effects; the result is demoralizing, and must have been seriously so in the dark ages.

When persons are saturated with fear, even the half qualified witches, as they were then called, could produce sensations akin to the possession of devils and all the hallucinations that fell upon the lives of those who were bewitched. As there was a firm belief in the existence and power of the witches, and as the evidence produced at trials was conclusive of their work though not always of their identity, we must regard the practice as an established fact. To laugh at the errors of belief is not in our province. Only ignorance doubts the history of the facts. We know it was wrong to put sorcerers to death; just as it would be wrong today to execute hypnotists. They are one and the same.

To put a person into mesmeric sleep, it is necessary to catch his belief, and this is obtained in one of two ways, either by willing consent or by inspiring fear. As the reasoning faculties are eliminating superstition, that greatest of all hypnotizing influences, the opportunity for bewitching large numbers is much less now than in former ages. In 1793, when the last witch of the world was officially put to death at Posen, the better judgment of mankind had come to see that the so-called witchcraft was the fault of those influenced rather than of those who wielded the strange power; for, twenty years earlier, in 1773, Dr. Mesmer gave to Europe the results of certain experiments that coincided with the work of sorcery.

A person may be a witch and not know it until some other person makes the fact apparent. The word witch is applied to both man and woman; but generally to woman, from the fact that the German tribes for nearly two thousand years gave over to their women the profession of healing by laying on of hands, by mysterious herbs and peculiar ceremonies, that may or may not have been akin to hypnotism. The male-witch was sometimes called a wizard, though not generally. It was a belief in England and Germany that out of every one hundred witches one was a wizard and ninety-nine were hags. From evidence of the nature of their work as compared with that now at hand, it is clear that witchcraft was hypnotism, that the subjects were easily bewitched because of the credulous condition of their minds in those ages that were darkened by superstition, and that the witches were blameless in most cases, for the reason that the power is generally possessed before the owner knows it.

Both sides of this matter may receive light from the following experiences which have been verified, as stated and corroborated by other similar cases. We cite the simplest of them, as they show the principle clearly enough. A woman makes the following statement: "I am not a clairvoyant, nor do I know anything of it, one way or the other. I am ignorant of hypnotism. A year or more ago I was visiting a friend for a few weeks. She was neither a clairvoyant nor hypnotist, and had no interest in anything of the kind. I found her one day looking so steadily at my eyes that I was frightened, but she seemed more afraid than I was. I did not dare look at her; but at times did so briefly as one looks or glances at others. In each instance she seemed to lose control of herself. I cut my visit short and came home. A few days later I received a letter stating that she was under my influence, and describing her condition." As advice was asked for in both cases, we directed the unfortunate subject to take up the study of personal magnetism which invariably cuts off all hypnotic power. In the case of the woman, who so suddenly found herself thus qualified to influence others, we advised a study of this higher course, whereby she became enabled to withdraw her control at will.

A subject of the same woman two years later sent a very vivid description of the first influence exerted over; for it seems that the hypnotist, finding herself with the power, chose to use it occasionally, and we have since learned of eight instances in which she controlled others, two of them men. The case referred to was that of one who, like the first, was influenced without the intention of the operator. She writes: "I thought Mrs. -'S eyes seemed brilliant, one more than the other. This caused me to look at the brighter one at every chance I got, even when she was not looking at me. When she did look, I felt myself getting restless, and my eyes rolled. I was conscious of becoming drowsy, and then fell asleep." After this description she goes on to relate some hallucinations that frightened her; one of which was the fear that she was losing her mind. In another case the subject, after being freed from sleep, saw dark birds in every corner of the room.

So common have been such experiences that it is waste time to enumerate more. The study of witchcraft shows exactly the same conditions; but it must be remembered that the subjects in those days were all, or nearly all, affected by some phase of religion. The belief in a personal God, a personal devil, and angels good and bad, led to the further idea that there was a malignant spirit abroad empowered with the right to cause misery and disease. Men, women and children often hypnotized themselves with the infatuation that they contained devils, as did the people of old Palestine; and, being under the control of this belief, they did then just what would be done now under the same conditions; they acted as if devils were in them.

Although too horrible for the ordinary experiments of modern practice, some hypnotists, desiring to show the resemblance of witchcraft to hypnotism, have made the suggestion of "having devils" to their subjects, with the results as expected; and everything that was associated with the old days of witchery may be brought out. It must be remembered that self-hypnotism has always existed; that a person may come under influence without the effort or even the knowledge of the one who owns the power, and that readiness of belief is the strongest known stimulant to this end. Doubting minds are rarely ever affected. In the study of ignorance it is found that belief is more absolute, and more easily captured, in proportion as the intelligence is low.

The hypnotic experience, formerly known as witchcraft, can be followed or traced through the centuries from the dawn of history; but it burst forth in the fifteenth century as a mania, no doubt receiving its impetus from he edict of Pope Innocent VIII, in 1484, charging the Inquisition to hunt up and put to death all witches and sorcerers. As Germany had been the birthplace of the medicine women, or "healers ,' 9 the papal bull was intended primarily for them; and two zealots of that country, in 1489, drew up the famous " Witch-Hammer, " in which you may find the whole doctrine of witchcraft set forth in systematic form, and rules set down for the detection and trial of the crime. These rules afterward became a sort of authority, and were believed in for a long time after their authors, Kraemer and Sprenger, were dead; although they are ridiculous at the present period.

Other edicts followed and produced untold misery. It seems strange that the heads of the Christian church, the representatives of the best prevailing education should originate this suffering. In 1494, Pope Alexander VI; in 1521, Pope Leo X, and in 1522, Pope Adrian VI issued bulls to the same effect. In Bamberg, 600 persons were burned or hanged for sorcery in four years; in Wurzburg, 900 were executed; in Geneva, in the year 1516, 500 persons were burned in four months; and over 1,000 in Como district in 1524; all for this one cause. In England, in 1562, the statute of Elizabeth made witchcraft a capital crime, whether it was practiced to the injury of another or not. These laws implied that those who possessed the power were able to control it. In the reign of James VI, of England, following the dawn of that splendid renaissance, the frenzy burst out in its full fury. The king wrote a treatise on the subject, and his "witch-finders" went forth to scour the land for the offenders.

In enlightened England during the Long Parliament, fully 3,000 persons were put to death because of witchcraft. The mania appeared in America, the Salem tragedies of 1691, '92 being the culmination here. As the people believed in the reality of the sorcery, and attributed their misfortunes to these maligned persons, it became an easy matter to hasten their arrest and execution by the concoction of lies without limit. No more picturesque and highly illuminated falsehoods have ever been invented, than those which surrounded the witches of the seventeenth century; and few persons were guiltless of this malice.

Times have changed. When the renaissance arose with its promise of better light, the dark clouds of superstition would not dissolve till they had shadowed a majority of the homes of England with the gaunt figure of death, either for creed, sorcery or politics; and, were it not for the fact that all persons must die sooner or later, the wide swath cut by fanaticism must have materially reduced the population of that country. But times have changed. What was then witchcraft is now hypnotism. The art that held religious devotees, including potentates, under the sway of self-appointed leaders in other ages and climes, and that wrought such havoc in the shifting centuries of a later era, is now recognized as a reality in modern science, possessing some qualities that entitle it to careful investigation. It has long enough been handled by charlatans in lectures and treatises of a highly sensational character; and it is now time for the facts.

Animals other than man may be hypnotized, although they are not reasoning beings capable of holding a fixed belief. Yet their minds do, in fact, adhere to ideas; and all animal training proceeds on this basis. It seems that some fear, or some fancy, is aroused by a small shining spot, especially if it is set in surroundings different from itself. That which will excite attention in a human being is known to do the same in animals; with the exception that it is harder to hold the brain of the latter. A bird sees the glitter in the eye of the snake, or of the cat; at first watches it out of curiosity; then becomes dazed, and is caught. A small shining ball will rivet the attention, but it lacks the depth and peculiar scintillation of the live eye, and, consequently, it requires more time to produce stupor.

Many persons have gone into mesmeric sleep, induced wholly by a small, bright object. Birds can sometimes be made stupid in the same way, though the fascination is lacking. When you enter a dark room in which a cat is seen only by the two shining orbs, a peculiar phosphorescence dances before you. In the light this changes to green and gold. You watch the dancing streams of the aurora in the cold northern skies, and they hold your attention. What you may find in the glitter of a tiny ball is intensified by the coloring and swinging of little masses of light that are strange enough to cause you to wonder at them. No wonder the bird looks till the will is paralyzed.

Some writers go so far as to claim that the mesmeric power is a kind provision of nature, intended to lessen pain and fear when the animal of prey seizes its victim. Some testimony has come from persons who have been rescued from the jaws of beasts after losing consciousness. Of course it is understood that humanity is not intended by nature as food for animals; but the general law covers all life, and suits each individual case. From private and published accounts, some facts come to us that seem to corroborate this theory. In the attempt to find a reason for the existence of everything good and bad in this world, it has been suggested that hypnotism is a condition of painlessness established to release the prey from all suffering; and, being a general provision, all animal life is affected by it. This cannot be the only use of the condition. Most gifts of nature have two or more uses.

In getting testimony from the prey themselves, we may look to dumb creation first. A mouse taken from a cat was uninjured and free from bruise as nearly as could be ascertained. Although it ran about when in the power of the cat, it gave no evidence of suffering. The bird flies about the head of the snake, making its circles smaller, and goes peacefully to its doom as though to die were pleasanter than living. The lamb shows no sign of suffering when the hot breath of its slayer is upon it. A large wolf carried a ewe nearly a mile as tenderly as the mother cat carries her kitten; and was shot just in the act of plunging its teeth into the lamb's throat. The latter had no bruise whatever, nor did it give evidence of pain. It seemed dazed for quite a while, as though some influence still over-awed it; as does a human subject whom the hypnotist fails to release from the spell.

A child was carried by the clothing in the teeth of a bear to the place where the savage beast intended to make a feast on its life. A hunter lay in wait at the spot and by a good aim slew the bear without harming the child. The latter who was six years old gave an accurate account of its feelings when it saw the animal coming toward it; showing great horror at first, then a light from two big balls of fire, and finally a sleepy condition. It seemed to regard the journey in the clutches of the bear as a dream; and said it was not a bit frightened till the gun was fired, then the sleep changed to wakefulness and fear.

In another case a child eight years old was caught up by the shoulder and held in the jaws of a bear for some minutes before it was rescued; and, although the flesh was badly torn, there was no pain at the time the teeth went in, nor until the wounds were being dressed. Hunters in the jungle have told many experiences that corroborate this law of

44

relief from pain. One incident is as good as a hundred where the same thing is repeated. A man missed in his aim at the vital region of a lion and was seized and carried to the lair, where the young cubs were given a lesson in dining on human flesh; much in the same way as the mother dog yields some of her food to her young. He felt them devouring his legs from the hips down to the knees, and the old lion had commenced to bite out a chunk from his shoulder when a party of hunters came up in time to kill the animals. The unfortunate man lived four days, and stated that he felt no pain whatever from the time he was seized to the time he was brought away from the scene.

This arid numerous other incidents confirm what has been well said by writers, that when the beast of prey seizes its victim the latter is thrown into a state of hypnotism and suffers no pain. On the other hand it experiences a dreamy, happy feeling that causes the tragedy of nature to lose all its sting. This should be so. It is ordained that one life shall eat another, and the torture and cruelty should be considered sufficient in the fact and constant fear of such disaster, without adding the excruciating suffering of tearing flesh and nerves asunder, while the act is in progress. Why life should devour life is not within the province of this book to consider. It seems that no species escapes this fate at times. Even the toughest have been slaughtered for food.

One person may be hypnotized by another without the latter's aid or knowledge.

This is the Eleventh Principle. The brain of man is curiously divided into parts that think for reasoning purposes, parts that think for mere muscular uses, and parts that think for functional action. These are somewhat dependent upon each other. They constitute the regular Work of life; deal with plans, with action, with organic operations; and cooperate with the senses. Where such brain divisions are located is known to a slight extent only, except in a general way.

Beyond the conscious brain above described, somewhere within it, or concealed in the body, is another faculty that cannot be so easily discussed; and, although the regular brain involves great problems in itself, this embraces others far more stupendous. Many things are known about it, but there is yet much to learn. It is agreed by those scientists who have been able to reach a satisfactory conclusion on some points, that the subconscious brain attends regularly to its duties night and day without need of rest, that it does so without the knowledge of the regular brain, and in a realm exclusively its own. One other point, and the most important to which they agree, is that the subconscious brain comes to the front as soon as the regular brain is hypnotized.

From a close observation of experiments it seems that the inner brain is always at work and always conscious of itself; but that the only time it has any connection or cooperation with the outer brain is when intuition is strong, as in catching some scent of danger, some thought from another, or some idea out of the vast realm of knowledge as by inspiration. It seems willing to allow the outer brain to have full sway in its associations with the details of this life, and is apparently making provisions for something beyond. These are surmises, drawn from the fact that the inner brain works so quietly and untiringly.

When the conscious brain is put to sleep by a process that keeps the body awake, the subconscious faculty, which is the so-called inner brain, at once asserts itself and stands ready to obey any suggestions that may be given it. This kind of sleep is induced in a number of ways, as we shall show; and one of the most common is that which proceeds from the unintended influence of another individual. An instance has been known of a boy fourteen years of age being hypnotized by a cat; another of a girl of fifteen falling asleep whenever she watched the eyes of a parrot; and most cases of the cataleptic order have their origin in some kind of unintentional hypnotism.

Self-mesmerism is different from this just described. It is caused from within by fear or some other agency which absorbs the belief, annihilates the will and opens up the subconscious faculty. In cases under the present principle, the sleep may be partly aided by some inward influence, but it is really induced by the unintended power of an individual, who may be unaware of it. Many persons have exerted some such control as much to their surprise as to others. A young lady entered the room where a dozen or fifteen persons were present, and was instantly seized with a peculiar sensation which she avoided by going to the next room. She stated the circumstance to a friend, and they resolved to ascertain the cause.

After passing in and out several times she located the person who held this control over her; a young man who really was innocent of any intention in the matter. They had never met before, nor was there any recognition when she first entered the room. It seems that he was gazing fixedly at a picture that hung by the side of the entrance, and the light of the room was reflected in a peculiar manner from his eyeballs. This caught her gaze and she was compelled to retire from it. It was a mere stimulus, however, to the effect; for the young man was in reality an embryo hypnotist and did not know it; nor did he understand the art in any way. Other cases of unintended and unwilling control are known; and it is probable that partial influence is exerted in thousands of cases every day where neither party is conscious of the fact. They experience the condition and account for it as due to a headache or some bit of indigestion.

Magnetism must be absent in the person hypnotized.

This is the Twelfth Principle. It has been claimed that the hypnotic state is induced by animal magnetism. This is not true, except in so far as magnetism is the determining force which gives one person the power at that juncture when thought-waves have neutralized each other. This point should be clearly understood, as it is the key to the whole matter; and what is said here should be considered in connection with the next of our principles.

Under nearly all circumstances most persons possess magnetism; and what is said throughout this work explains the meaning of this statement. There are times when magnetism runs low or ebbs away, and life seems weak. The muscles may have some strength, and the vegetable functions, as of respiration, circulation and digestion, may continue their work; but nervous life and thought seem suspended. When these conditions are mild they are called lapses, and are brief in point of time. When they are severe they resemble, or pass into, catalepsy; which is a complete absence of magnetism or nervous vitality.

In the cataleptic condition there is a suspension of mind, memory and will. The face retains whatever expression may be on it at the time; if a smile, that lasts through the whole period; if a look of pain, the same remains to the end. The muscles are likewise fixed; if an arm be raised it will stay where put; a limb will assume and hold any attitude given it; and the whole body responds to any change willingly and makes no motion of its own. Pain is not felt. The arm may he cut off without suffering. This is the true cataleptic condition. It is akin to hypnotic sleep, except that in the latter state the subconscious mind awakens and governs the body not of its volition but by suggestion from another.

Physicians see no real difference between catalepsy and mesmeric sleep, except in the fact that the subconscious faculty may be awakened in the latter. It is true that some hypnotists fail to arouse their subjects and thus leave them in catalepsy, from which they are released with some difficulty, and always with more or less injury. The genuine trance mediums, of which there are but few in the world, pass into this condition; and occasionally seem dead to all appearances as far as the uses of the body and mind are concerned; the only physical life being in the vegetable functions of respiration, circulation and digestion, and the only mental existence being in the subconscious faculty. It is not true that catalepsy develops the trance-medium, or the hypnotic subject; but it is true that a trance-state and hypnotism result in catalepsy.

This supposed disease is associated with every kind of revelation or supernatural sight into things, realms, and worlds that cannot he penetrated by the perception of the ordinary mind. When the evidence is entirely lacking no one is able to say what was the condition of a person at the time of some special exercise of this extraordinary power; so the result is accepted without comment. But where all the attendant facts are known there is never an exception to the statement that catalepsy always accompanies the revelation. One explanation accounts for it by the assertion that the conscious mind is the agent of the senses and their memory; acting for them in the relation of the body to the earth; while the subconscious mind is directly employed in the service of the soul. How much of this is true need not be considered at this time.

There is one personage in history of whom enough is known to show the nature of the results that may come from the cataleptic condition. We refer to Mohammed, the founder of the religion bearing his name. There are two classes of critics among Christian scholars. While both classes believe him to be wrong, and his millions of devotees to be misguided, one great division of the best students of the man and his work assert that he himself was honest; and the other division assert that he was a mere pretender. There is sufficient reliable authority to prove that he was constantly subject to fits and spasms of epilepsy. Any history, however large or small, admits this fact, and it is considered to be as completely established as is the fact that he conquered his own residence city.

In a cave in Mount Hara near Mecca he constantly retired for meditation, commencing at about the age of thirty-five. Here he spent hours and days in religious contemplation. At the age of forty, while in epileptic fits, he received the first of his revelations which were ultimately printed as the Koran. His own honesty could hardly be doubted, when his wife was the first of his converts. Pretenders begin elsewhere than at home. In his own city of Mecca he counted 40,000 fervent believers prior to his death; so that if he deceived men, it must have been those who were closest to him and knew him best. In our opinion he was not a pretender; but this does not admit that he was not the honest dupe of his own fancies.

MYSTIC UTOPIAN SUPERMEN

The genuine products of a cataleptic condition may be as wrong as the genuine products of honest but erroneous reasoning. One thing is true; the subconscious faculty performs wonders, and there is yet no evidence that it may not perform tricks. The case of Mohammed was undoubtedly that of a genuine trance-medium; and it may have been much more. In an age when fraud and pretense are prevalent, and the public has been deceived numberless times by so-called trance-mediums, it is well to calmly contemplate the history of one who is above the charge of charlatanism; for, as Prof. James, of Harvard University, said of Mrs. Piper, of Arlington Heights, Boston, if there were but one white sheep in a hundred it would prove that all sheep are not black. This woman was studied and investigated by the English and American scientists of the highest rank; and was universally admitted to be genuine in her work. All possibility for fraud has been eliminated.

Compare these two cataleptics, Mohammed and Mrs. Piper, and you have two similar examples of the same wonderful power, with an immense intellectual gulf separating them. Give to the modern personage the same breadth of brain and skill of execution that Mohammed possessed, together with his ability of leadership, and the age in which we live, with its millions of undecided minds ready to grasp anything within reach, would witness the foundation of a new religion. Yet the sum of the whole story is merely that catalepsy is an open gateway revealing to us some things that the ordinary mind cannot understand because they are not in its line.

The conscious mind is a magnetic use of animal intelligence. It does not know how to interpret experiences not within its province. When something happens through the action of the subconscious faculty, the regular mind seeks to explain it, and thus it flies away into the spiritual realm in the search after reasons. What man does not understand he ascribes to superhuman causes, to spirits. This was so when comets and earthquakes overawed the people; it is so when the subconscious mind manifests itself. The intelligence of the masses may be something better in this century than it was in the dark ages, but the case with which enormous numbers of people accord their belief to such doctrines as spiritualism, faith-cure and the like, shows that the brain is far from perfect. They are not able to see that certain facts, which are clear enough as facts, may be accounted for in more than one way. Their limited intelligence compels them to say that because "such is so and so," it therefore is proof of something else.

The lack of magnetism is the cause of catalepsy. A person who has died in this condition, as was the fate of Irving Bishop and others, shows a low state of the ganglionic electrical cells throughout the body; and this is the surest indication of a depleted vitality or magnetism. It is equally true that the lack of the very same vitality, not the vitality of the functions that keep the body alive, but that of the nervous system, is always apparent when a person is hypnotized. Magnetism is more or less fleeting in weak characters. It is an essence, a quality, an endowment that comes and goes, and is held within one's grasp only by life's energy, in which mind and will play important parts.

Let this magnetism be withdrawn by the will itself, as when a person hypnotizes himself; or let it be expelled by a stronger personality; and the condition is ripe for the influence of another who understands how to take advantage of it. The operator may not know what opposes him, but he feels that something stands in the way, and he proceeds

48

to remove the obstacle. Thus many break down the barrier of magnetism in the subject with no knowledge of its nature. When disease destroys the magnetic vitality, catalepsy follows; when a superior will removes it, hypnotism follows.

Hypnotic depressions are contagious.

This is the Thirteenth Principle. The rise and fall of the tides of magnetism in any human being are as frequent as the movements of the ocean, although they occur without regularity of interval, and are dependent upon moods rather than habits. Thought and will are more evanescent than is supposed. They yield to influences of the day, to the power of circumstances, and especially to the will of others. Most persons are partly hypnotized without knowledge of it, and would indignantly deny the charge if made to them. Of course this kind of influence is depressing. Magnetism arouses one because it gives him some of the energy of another. Hypnotic waves have the opposite effect.

In some degree, however slight, the contagion of this depression spreads and may reach a room full of persons. Gaping or yawning often does this. The act is, in itself, evidence of weak vitality, and this is depressing. One person starts to yawn; another follows, and the movement goes around the room several times. Experiments have been made in the same line, by imitating the act of gaping with the hands, opening and shutting them from contact at the wrist; and other persons, seeing them, have been set to gaping. This has been done without suggestion of any kind. Even the reading of the description of this imitation has created a desire to gape.

Depressions in mass, involving many persons, have frequently occurred; and few are free from their influence at some time or other in life. Many are very susceptible. They do not call it hypnotism, as that explanation is an unpopular one; but there is no doubt that the same law reaches all cases of this kind, varying merely in degree.

Bad news affecting one person, is felt by others in sympathy, and even by those who are not. It often happens that one in a party, or one member of a household, will receive a so-called presentiment of misfortune, and others present will feel the same depression. Reports from numberless sources confirm this kind of experience. There is no doubt that it is due, in its spreading at least, to the action of hypnotism in a slight degree.

While it is not so easy to completely hypnotize a person as it is to magnetize one, it is much easier to partly hypnotize than to magnetize. This law is almost paramount to a principle. It is important enough to remember at all times. Following out the idea, without knowing the law, many speakers and persons in conversation seek to take advantage of it, and gain a temporary influence by relating sad stories, cases of distress, and the like. We know a clergyman who ended every sermon with some such narration, and dismissed his congregation while in a depressed condition. It required some hours for some of them to wake up.

Hypnotism appears in all degrees of force as a controlling power.

This is the Fourteenth Principle. We do not hesitate to declare that in proportion as vitality or magnetism is strong all tendency to being hypnotized is weakened. While complete control is not possible until the magnetism of the individual is entirely overcome, it is true that the stock in store by the latter may be so weak as to be easily driven out.

MYSTIC UTOPIAN SUPERMEN

Few persons, however, are made to give up their magnetism, for the attempt to overcome them usually causes a reaction; whereupon the will sets to work and new energy is at once created. It is not always the open operator who is thus resisted. Lecturers, evangelists and other depressers, who, instead of winning by magnetism, seek to obtain control through the opposite course, are not hypnotizers, but are merely agents of depression that lead to a condition which in itself is hypnotism. One who gapes cannot lay claim to power; it is the gape that does it. The picture of a person yawning was hung up in a schoolroom as an experiment; as a result every student there began to yawn, all unconsciously. These things show that there is such a condition as self-hypnotism.

We are nearly all of us subject to it; and this could not be true if it did not appear in degrees. The scale of control is a long one, extending from the slightest influence to that of complete sleep. The few persons who never came under the spell are those who are highly magnetic, and they are altogether unimpressionable. They seem cold in their nature, and lacking in sympathy for the misfortunes of others; while possessing an attractive personal power. They are recognized as strong in all their faculties and as leaders of mankind. All others, however, come under some degree of hypnotic influence sooner or later; and few are aware that they are thus partly controlled.

Clairvoyance is induced by hypnotism.

This is the Fifteenth Principle. The word clairvoyance means clear seeing, and is supposed to have its origin in the idea that all material objects are transparent. If the fact exists at all, it is true that the perception annihilates space and time, and penetrates solid walls as easily as the physical eye leaps through the matter of the atmosphere.

No case of genuine clairvoyance ever existed that was not induced by hypnotism of one kind or another; that is, by the influence of an operator, or by the action of self hypnotizing. The latter is well proved. Most trance mediums, or clairvoyants, are so in name only; in reality they are either out and out frauds or are weak in the powers they profess. While many of them may have been the subjects of mesmerists and have thus ascertained their ability to act as clairvoyants, it is claimed that the majority have never been operated upon but have discovered that they were endowed with the faculty of putting themselves into the sleep. We shall show how this is done, a few pages later.

From information at hand it is probable that thousands of men and women are living in this country who have been hypnotized, and that many more are added to the numbers yearly. Of these, nearly all might become trance-mediums if they were followed up and trained in that line of development. There are such mediums who lack all power except when hypnotists are in attendance to put them to sleep; some pretend to carry on the business alone, and, no matter what might be the genuineness of their work when under control, they are impotent as self-mesmerizers. On the other hand it is rare that a trance-medium is also a self-mesmerizer; a few such exist, yet they are valueless most of the time. One who is genuine suffers much loss of vitality by continually closing out the conscious faculties; and the cataleptic sleep is dangerous if persisted in too frequently.

We therefore conclude that the genuine clairvoyants are not always able or willing to exert themselves except upon important occasions; that those who are trustworthy at times are not generally so, but depend upon a few remarkable strokes of success for the maintenance of reputation and patronage; and that the general crowd of advertisers of this kind are pure shams, some admittedly possessing a faint degree of telepathic energy, while others have none. We have met those who are genuine, and find that they are discredited because they advertise to foretell events. Knowing that they are endowed with clairvoyant powers, but hardly coming in contact with the details of their own work, they assume the impossible, and are charged with dishonesty while not actually guilty.

Clairvoyance is the operation of the subconscious mind; a faculty that is alert night and day in every human being, but of which we have little or no knowledge except by intuition, for the reason that by some kind of doom which seems unaccountable, the connection between this inner mind and the regular mind has been severed. The subconscious faculty lives, acts and attends to its duties with untiring zeal. Its chief power is the clear perception that travels any distance in a second, and sees without the aid of the senses. This is universally admitted to he the fact. If we could only know what is known by the inner brain, we would be omniscient. Fate or nature has ordained that we cannot secure such knowledge while the regular mind is conscious; so this must be put to sleep, the body must become dead through the suspension of its action in catalepsy, and then the inner mind partly reveals itself to others but not to the individual.

Such is the fall of man. Let any person succeed in uniting these two minds, so that the conscious faculty may take advantage of the knowledge that comes within the grasp of the subconscious, and all things would lie open, revealed in every detail. A few persons have been rarely endowed in this respect, and but partly so; yet they have been the world's geniuses. It must be that man has fallen from the loftiest of pedestals, or has yet to attain his noblest of estates. The proposition is as plain and as accurate as the most exact of mathematical statements. It cannot be refuted. The goal is too great to contemplate. Whether any of this race will ever reach it or not, is beyond knowledge. It would require a revolution of all faculties, and of all methods of living, to enable mankind to step into a realm so close at hand and so far away.

Under present conditions the penalty of clairvoyance is a severe one. It comes only from catalepsy; and this is merely a dying of the normal life of the body; or such a suspension as resembles death, and for the time being is its equal. When the life is removed, for it seems to be an obstacle, then the subconscious faculty may become alert. It probably does, although there is no way of finding out unless others are present. Sleep is not catalepsy, and the dreams that come may have no relation to the subconscious life. The latter is presumably awake, but we cannot connect with it. Death, as near as we can produce it, removes the barrier, which is life; then the inner faculty may be partly connected with. This would argue that death is the opening of the life within; but the fact known may have no relation whatever to the assumption. Things are not proved in that way. A great gulf of other possibilities separates the fact from the assumption.

Some day we may come nearer to the proof. Investigation is rapidly tending that way. It is your duty to go no further than facts, and to avoid conclusions that only seemed warranted. For years it was considered proof positive of a spirit communication when a medium talked with the memories of those who lived or died; the fact being that the various personages who speak through the medium are characters that live in her inner brain, just as all kinds of characters dwell in the regular mind; and that inner brain, having clairvoyant powers, can see far beyond all ordinary expectation. It can perceive thoughts, call out of the great fund of lost memories many exact things, reproduce persons and talks that have existed and now are nearly forgotten, and startle us with speeches, descriptions and details that no ordinary faculties could acquire; yet because we, with our ordinary faculties, fail to comprehend them, we certainly have no right to set up the claim that these are spirits from the spirit world talking through the muddy vesture of this medium.

Such a claim is not only without foundation, but it is ridiculous. The power is that of clear-seeing, and it is a remarkable one; we freely admit that; but its clear-seeing merely results in its partial interpretation of what it sees, and it plays many fantastic roles in these translations. When a dead woman speaks, as it seems, she does not speak at all; it is the subconscious faculty talking. The dead are far away and know nothing of it. The idea that Alexander, Caesar, Napoleon, Shakespeare and earth's most prominent personages must be turned over in their graves at the request of some greasy woman, and made to indulge in jargon at her sweet will, is too absurd to be discussed; and the fact that great masses of hollow-eyed people believe in it is proof of the hypnotized condition of the modern mind.

The subconscious brain talks for any and everybody, in and out of all subjects. Being clear-seeing, it can go where our reasoning cannot. Still it is the talker. Its men and women, dead and alive, with their descriptions, loves, languages, styles, methods, are caught out of the minds of others, present or absent; and its assertions are generally echoes of the wishes or expectations of those at hand. When a man says, "I died eight years ago last May, on Monday, at 2.16 P. M.," it is nothing but the brain of the medium talking. But some one says, "How can the medium tell what she never knew?" In the first place, she is not telling it; her subconscious mind is telling it; and, being clear-seeing, it can know that, and a million other things, which the medium could not learn in ten thousand years of normal existence.

Then comes the further claim that the clear-seeing faculty ought to be believed, or taken at its word. Thus, when the supposed spirit says, "I am dwelling in heaven, and your sister and brother, who died since I did, are here with me," we are called upon to believe that the spirit must be, in fact, speaking, because otherwise it would be untruthful. Even this statement, in effect, is often made by the inner faculty of a medium, "I am the spirit of Henry Brown; I am living in the spirit-world." In such cases, the genuineness of the medium is open to question. But, assuming that she be honest, such statements are wrung from her by great efforts, if at all; and they can be easily ascribed to the echoes or expectations of persons at hand, no matter how clear-cut and startling the assertions may seem.

It is always the subconscious mind that talks; never anyone or anything beyond it. The connection with normal minds at best is very imperfect, like a badly constructed telephone-line. The clear-seeing faculty has unlimited range among all minds, present and absent, and among all places. It must contend with this crowd of visions, this debris of memories, this hoping, wondering and expecting that linger in other minds; and it would be strange if it did not furnish all kinds of information. Still, it is the subconscious brain that speaks. There is nothing beyond it, except its perceptive abilities. In the case of Mrs. Piper, herself acknowledged by all to have been a perfectly genuine clairvoyant, the scientists, who employed her for years, admit that, while she was honest, the characters who spoke in her were rarely truthful when talking of themselves, and generally truthful when detailing events and descriptions. So it is largely a muddle, with some startling accuracies at times that overwhelm the mind.

The future cannot be told by clairvoyants. Those who claim to do it, are either deliberate frauds or else are the dupes of their own powers. We have already stated that the medium, when honest, is not conscious of what is done or said when in the trance; therefore she cannot know, as a matter of fact, whether or not the future is foretold. Believing in her powers, she is led to advertise more than she can execute. As clairvoyance is clear-seeing, and as the future has not yet been unrolled, it would follow, naturally, that it could not be seen. Coinciding with this view, is the universal experience of investigation. The past has been brought up, and the present penetrated, often to the wonderment of others; but there is no case of prediction or foretelling that has any color of genuine clairvoyancy about it. Here and there, a few things have been stated that can readily be accounted for as guess work; and some instances of sight into the future have been traced to telepathy, by which hopes or plans are read in the minds of others prior to fulfillment.

Spiritualism is founded upon defective clairvoyance.

This is the Sixteenth Principle. We might well say that all clairvoyance is imperfect. There is a limited amount of accurate knowledge concerning it; and what there is cannot be taken as a basis for any system of religion, or belief relating to the soul. All persons at times have had some evidence of the presence of the subconscious faculty; though most have been slight and unimportant. The passing of a face, the touch of a finger, the noise of some faint sound, some call, or music, the reading of a thought, as when we speak an idea that another had intended to utter at the moment; these are common glimpses of this faculty.

In response to a large number of requests for reports, we received the general statement from nearly all whom we asked to state if they had ever seen ghosts, or believed in them, to the effect that none had been seen, and were not believed in. But a few persons asserted most positively that they had seen ghosts; and one clergyman declared that nothing could shake his belief in spirits, as he had seen one and believed what he saw. This seems logical on its face. If to believe what is seen, is to be taken as a guide, the dreamer, the delirious patient and the victim of tremens are able to prove all sorts of spirit worlds.

Investigators have never considered it worth while to account for the objects seen in such visions. Some say they are the creation of the fever in the patient, the conjuring up of the disturbed brain of the dreamer, the contortion of ideas in the drunkard; but, as something cannot be created out of nothing, this does not account for them. A keen and sensitive mind may build creations, so it is said; and this is used as proof that the visions of a disordered brain so originate. If a clear mind may build creations, it does not follow that they are built out of nothing. In delirium there is inflammation of the brain, the nerves of vision are involved; they are never free from the association of bacteria, and microbes in general; and we are satisfied that the smallest particles, even the atom itself, may be perceived, in rare instances, under great stress of excitement, not of the mind, but of the finest strands of the brain where impressions are made in the sense of sight. As microbes compete successfully with shapes of demonology and the reptile world, this would account for most anything seen by a delirious brain.

It does not account for the evidences of telepathy and clairvoyance. These are akin, with the exception that the former is merely the power of interpreting, in an exceedingly slight degree, the facts known to the subconscious mind. One who can look into the thoughts of another brain, or who can see events not present to the eye, is a telepathist. All persons are such at times; some to a much greater extent than they imagine. All persons possess an inner mind; it knows all, probably; few persons ever catch the knowledge of that inner mind, because the connecting links of consciousness have been taken away; still the inner mind is always at work; it leaks occasionally, and the regular brain grasps the knowledge, but in such little bits that no real service is rendered, except in rare instances. This is telepathy.

Clairvoyance differs from telepathy in that the latter occurs under all conditions, asleep, awake, sane, insane, or in or out of the mesmeric state; while clairvoyance is possible only when the normal life is made as dead, and the subconscious life is called forth for interpretation. As most persons are able to put themselves into some degree of catalepsy, or become depressed in some degree of hypnotism, which is the same thing differently stated, it is true that they may experience some of the conditions of clairvoyance; and, under this consideration, it may be claimed that telepathy is its mildest degree; or that one may merge into the other.

In either case the phenomena of ghosts may be accounted for on the theory of self-hypnotism, or that imposed by circumstances. Fear and expectancy are common causes of this condition, either mildly or strongly. A person had been told that a woman in white appeared nightly behind a certain tree on a certain estate, that she never had been seen elsewhere. He became so impressed with the thought that he looked for the apparition, but in vain. One evening, laboring under a special spell of depression, he thought he saw the woman, and his mind soon confirmed the fact, as he believed. The experience was repeated night after night for a week, when his mind cleared and the woman disappeared. It originated in a hoax, yet the ghost was a fact to him.

A girl ran screaming from her house to that of a neighbor, telling the story of a ghost that walked across the road near the house. A month later she repeated the same transaction, telling the same story. This occurred for three months; the apparition passing from one side of the road to the other, east of the house, and always choosing the same place for its rendezvous. A brave young man, who boasted that he was anxious for just such an opportunity of disproving the existence of ghosts, undertook to hold watch in the neighborhood. In the meantime the family had moved away, the girl was in a distracted, nervous condition, and the house was deserted.

The young man secured a description of the apparition through a third person, and set about his task. He wasted valuable time for some months; but, at length, was rewarded by seeing the ghost. It appeared on the west side of the house, and was clad as the description stated. Before seeing it, he had become depressed by an affair that drove him to the verge of suicide. He was alarmed at the sight, and ran from it, almost in hysterics. The strange part of the story is that the intermediate party purposely located the ghost in the wrong place, and clothed it in garments that differed considerably from those seen by the girl; thus proving that expectancy had provided the sight. It was a clear case of self-hypnotism in a degree, occurring in depression; while the ghost was the clairvoyant perception of the description taken out of the mind of the intermediate person.

What one sees may be doubted, but we are told that the evidence of two or more proves a thing beyond question. This supposes all persons to be honest. The individual who sees alone may be charged with telepathic or nervous disorder, so that he is not able to credit his own senses; while two or more may not be open to this charge. A case is in point. A hand was seen protruding from the hole in the ceiling of a schoolhouse. It was a very thin, white hand, as of death. A female schoolteacher saw it; fainted; revived; went about her duties; saw it again, and had to be taken home. She was nearly dead with fear. Although she declared that she could not be induced to go into the building again, she minutely described the occurrence, and anxiously sought a solution.

Crowds were attracted to the place through sensational and grossly false statements published in the papers; but the hand did not appear. The teacher was finally induced to return in company with some friends. She saw nothing. One afternoon, late in autumn, she was at the building with seven young women who had made request to go with her. One of these was a sad-faced girl who seemed to labor under great fear. She saw the hand first; next the teacher saw it; and, finally, the others. An investigation of the testimony of the eight persons showed that all were greatly depressed by one thing or another, chiefly by the situation, and the shrinking of the teacher, and especially the disconcerting appearance of her sad-faced friend.

The expectation of something superhuman about to occur, and the fear of seeing it, placed all the visitors under the law previously stated, that hypnotic depression is contagious. A familiar illustration was that of gaping, as given in connection with the principle. The teacher says she looked once or twice at the hole where the hand had formerly appeared, but refrained from gazing steadily at it, as she seemed conscious of a growing condition that would naturally invite the vision. The sickly woman looked for it and afterward said that she was sure she would see it. "Something told me I was going to see that hand," she exclaimed at the time. The fact that the others witnessed the same vision may be explained either by the law of telepathy, or the principle that hypnotic depression is contagions.

If either of these laws is in operation, the only concurring condition needed is that the persons present should be weak in magnetism, so that they could not, or would not, resist the hypnotic influences. Then it would be strange if all did not see the same apparition. The testimony of the two or more, instead of proving that the ghost was a reality, would confirm that rule that what one hypnotic subject witnesses, all witness. Were it not for the contagious element involved in these matters, no magnetic person would be able to thrill hundreds with his power, or depress a whole audience at will. It is true that there are experiences which come to one alone, and which cannot be transmitted to others, even if present; but it will be found that such others are free from depression and out of sympathy with the occurrence.

Spiritualism has no standing. A quarter of a century hence the world will laugh at the idea of spirits talking back, and especially in the supremely silly way in which they are made to do under the regime of their tormentors. The laws of depression and its contagion have undoubtedly helped to establish experiences where partly hypnotized persons, or the usual attendants at seances, are made to see, hear, feel, taste and smell according as the subconscious faculty wills; but all the claims taken as made cannot for a moment warrant the assumption that they prove any connection between the spirit world and our own. To adhere to such belief is evidence of a partly hypnotized mind in the believer.

The loss of all personal magnetism must precede complete clairvoyance.

This is the Seventeenth Principle. Vitality, the spark of life and personal magnetism are all one and the same, except in the uses to which they are put. All these must be suspended in the person who wishes to become a clairvoyant; and the supervision may be directed by the person himself, by fear, by expectancy of a morbid character, or by a mesmerist. Sometimes it originates in catalepsy as a disease, but this does not generally develop the condition desired.

One of the rules usually given to a candidate for this kind of work, is to subdue the will and to try to come into subjection to the operator. Efforts of the sort do not succeed as a rule. A person may be very anxious to become a clairvoyant, but personal magnetism is in the way. It does not depart by order of the will; for the more power the will has the more magnetism is generated. Teachers say: "Now exert your will all you can, and give yourself up." This is a contradiction. It is like saying: "Eat all you can and try hard to get hungry by eating." The exercise of the will generates magnetism.

The art of losing one's vitality is not easily acquired. It becomes the basis of hypnotism, and the latter must always precede clairvoyance. So these steps must be understood. How to take the first is the primary consideration. After that the process is much easier. While we do not recommend such practice, it is our duty to prevent the full course of procedure; for, if we do not do so, some one will, and the result will be the same. The fact remains, however, that the losing of one's magnetism is injurious to the health, while the cataleptic condition of body and mind is harmful to both. Some operators give back all the magnetism they take away, and occasionally more, so that the loss is compensated in such instances.

The union of magnetism and telepathy produces extraordinary genius.

This is the Eighteenth Principle. There are always exceptions somewhere. A telepathic condition is one in which the conscious mind has connection with the subconscious. The latter is clear-seeing, has access to all other minds, and to all events everywhere. It knows everything. If the conscious mind were to connect with it, there would be no need of studying and memorizing in order to acquire knowledge.

Whether these two minds have ever been united we cannot say. It is possible that the ideal man, the Adam who fell because he tasted of the tree of knowledge, was deprived of this wonderful power because so much knowledge meant infinitude. This is mere speculation. It may be true that the union of the two faculties awaits man in another world or a future life. If it ever occurred, or ever should occur, the results must be beyond all measurement. One thing is amazing; the subconscious mind is a fact, and a concealed one. It can be proved, but the steps to be taken are arduous and unsatisfactory. From this we conclude that the concealment is intended; or it is possible that the glimpses of light are guiding lines to direct man to discover more.

To possess a faculty so powerful and to be unable to use it, is somewhat puzzling to the aggressive spirit of our species. To be compelled to assume the attributes of death, in order to awaken the inner, all-knowing mind, and then to remain ignorant of its disclosures, is even vexing. Once in a while an extraordinary genius appears on earth, and an analysis of his nature shows that he is endowed with magnetism in the highest degree, and breaks the rule of depression by possessing a consciousness of the knowledge held by his inner mind. Let this become a perfected union and the man is a god.

Hypnotic depressions may become epidemic.

This is the Nineteenth Principle. So weak is the human mind on matters not personal or selfish, that error spreads like ink upon the wave. One idea hypnotizes the country, and a wrong notion becomes idealized and goes into history as a virtue. When the public are thus swayed, the contagion is irresistible. It divides itself only as the interests involved may warrant. Among the political parties, the epidemic is confined to one or the other of them, thus showing the weakness of the mind; for an apparent fact cannot be a fact at will, and a fiction at will, as the beliefs of partisans insist they are.

When the whole population of the civilized world in the last decade of the tenth century, then confined to Europe, saw and felt the approach of the year 1000, a fear of great magnitude seized them. Almost without exception, men, women and children were depressed and hypnotized into the belief that the world was coming to an end. Wars ceased; peace reigned; and a spirit of love swept over the savage breasts of the times, opening the way to the Crusades, religious fervor and finally the Renaissance. Out of fear comes repentance. No better illustration of an epidemic of hypnotic depression has ever been furnished by history.

Beliefs are likewise spread through masses of people, depending on their condition of mind as to the readiness of acceptance. No matter how absurd an idea may be there is always something to believe in it. The claims of the origin of Mormonism are accepted as honest facts today by thousands; and if you assert this to one of them you will get the reply: "Of course we believe the story to be true; and if you wish to understand the sincerity of our belief come to Utah." This is the type of all other cases. You may begin with a fiction, a hoax played as a practical joke, set it up in pretended seriousness for the attention of others; and, years after, you will find a people swearing allegiance to it, and their children reverencing it as sacred.

The sects of faith curists, known as mental scientists and several other kinds, have a following that is not large but is earnest, including men and women who are openly above the suspicion of being weak-minded; but the enormous proportion of them that go insane proves the rule that mental depressions or defects attend most cases of hypnotism where superstition is the stimulating cause. Every upstart finds some followers. Religious fanatics are not without devotees. Schemes to make money are sure to allure investors of a class that ought to have sense enough to know that nothing but total loss can come out of them.

Politicians are shrewd enough to know this defect in the popular mind, and they proceed to serve bait on the hook. Falsehoods fly like wildfire along party ranks. The people believe and are fooled; believe again and are fooled; and go on taking bait blindly. A million voters accept the skillful invention and stake their whole course of suffrage on its being true; always flocking like sheep to its standard; while as many more yield their faith to something exactly opposite. This following in herds cannot be accounted for, except upon the theory that masses of people are afflicted with hypnotic contagion.

The manipulators of political beliefs during campaigns know wherein their party followers are depressed mentally, and they study to supply the needed excitant.

When a mesmerist secures control of his subject, he suits his suggestions to the nature of the person and the probability of their being adopted. This principle is seen everywhere in political and newspaper sensations. What is most likely to fit into the hollows of human nature is most paraded, and it is a profession in itself to concoct such matters. In the dearth of news in 1893, the papers started the rumor of hard times, exaggerated every common occurrence and gave it color of disaster; so that the panic was a natural consequence. The depression was epidemic.

History furnishes many examples of men who have done their country great service through years of sacrifice and toil, yet who are suddenly overwhelmed by unpopularity, and almost in a day. Ingratitude is not explained on any other ground than that the people, being deficient mentally, have no power to resist the influence of meanness that runs rampant through the land. Hypnotic epidemics are always on the dark side. The public will eagerly devour ill reports, and scoff at good ones. A newspaper libel will take a page of type in leading columns; its denial will occupy a few lines in an obscure corner; or a page to a lie and an inch to the truth. This the people believe in and prefer.

Hypnotism is induced by one person whose thought waves coincide with the thought-waves of another.

This is the Twentieth Principle. Waves of water, waves of sound, waves of light, waves of thought exist and flow in rhythmic action, each in its domain. In a water-wave the body of water itself need not move onward for a wave to pass over its surface. Sound will travel through still air. Light shines in absolute quietude. Thought is impulse of the ether that pervades all matter. It moves in waves of action as peacefully or as turbulently as the force behind it shall determine.

A thinking mind is necessarily a magnetic one. You cannot separate one force from the other. When the magnetism is weak, the mind is also depressed. It does not follow that wisdom, judgment or depth of intellect are sure to come from the acquisition of magnetism. You can give the mind health without making it fit for a philosophy, as you can give the body health without producing the skilled artisan. The foundation makes the other qualities possible, but does not provide them. Where there is depth and breadth of thought, there is some degree of magnetism, and the two are associates.

It was formerly claimed that no minds except those that were weak could be mesmerized. It is generally true, but not always so. If a strong mind can be deprived of its magnetism, the mesmerist may succeed in getting control over it. Persons who have become exhausted through overuse of the brain, or who are depressed, or otherwise out of normal balance, may be caught at such times, but would soon react, if their ordinary faculties were strong. In this way the ablest of men and women have been partly controlled, and these periods are called lapses. They are rare, and should hardly be taken into consideration in the pursuit of this study.

Will and thought and magnetism run together, as the same or parts of the same things. No mesmerist can make any progress against either the one or the other. If the subject shows any force of will, the first thing to do is to ascertain if this can be broken; and a moment or two will generally suffice to tell if there is a likelihood of weakening. So one who is engaged in strong thought is not apt to come under the influence; yet the waves of thought may be driven out with some skilled efforts. Likewise, magnetism will repel the operator. Whether these three good qualities are considered as separate forces, or as one and the same, varying in uses, they, or any one of them, will stand in the way of the success of a mesmerist.

Thought-waves are alike when they take the same view of the same subject. If one person is thinking of one thing, and another person of another, they do not coincide; and, until there is a supreme command of attention given to one or the other, there is no hope of hypnotizing either. If one person thinks of the same subject, but has a different view of it from another, the same law holds true. The very first step in securing hypnotic control of an individual is in compelling him to think of the same thing that is in your mind, and in the same way.

PROTECTION AGAINST HYPNOTISM
IS ABSOLUTELY NECESSARY IN THE CONTROL OF OTHERS

All humanity is divided into two classes: The hypnotic and the magnetic.

This is the Twenty-first Principle. It may be a matter of inquiry why we devote so much attention to this subject. But when it is understood that the hypnotic condition must be swept away and the road cleared for action, before it is possible for one person to actually secure a valuable control over others, the necessity for becoming familiar with this, the greatest of all obstacles to success, will at once become apparent.

There are in fact only two classes of human beings on earth; and from the beginning of time there have never been more than these two. If you are in the hypnotic class, you cannot be magnetic; and the chances are ninety out of a hundred that you are in the hypnotic class. If you are in the magnetic class by virtue of birth or the gift of Nature, or the result of acquired power through habits that beget it, then you are in a position to go on with these studies.

This does not mean that if you are in the ninety per cent class, your case is hopeless. It is to make it hopeful that this book has been written. But let us look at a sort of summary of the facts that confront us, and prepare for the encouraging methods that are to follow.

There are still grades of hypnotic influence at work; some in the home; some in the marriage relationship; some in ordinary association; a vast number in business; a still greater number in politics; and we find them in court proceedings, especially in jury trials, and markedly in most churches; while no profession is free from them.

As a familiar illustration let us take a typical case. There is a church in a great city in America where the charge has been openly made and repeated in the newspapers that the preacher holds his congregation under a hypnotic spell during his sermons. The control he exerts appears in two prominent results. One is in the fact that the collections he demands are all oversubscribed. The other is in the fact that the church is always crowded, while the minister is not famed for great eloquence. We made it our business to visit this church many times during a three months stay in the city; and in this connection let us say that the hypnotic class of people are influenced by one or more of the following conditions:

1. Eye strain.

2. Monotony of gaze.

3. Monotony of voice that is alive.

4. A bright light, if of very small size.

5. Monotony of physical activity.

6. Monotony of mental activity.

7. Lapse of Mental Activity.

8. Entering the DARK SECTION OF THE MIND. —The latter is so important a condition that it is made a prominent part of the Estate of Hell which follows in this book; and will not be discussed here. It includes the most recent discoveries in this line of study.

Let us review briefly in new language the main points we have presented in this Estate of Protection Against Hypnotism:

It does not require an hypnotic operator to manipulate a person; when in fact not one in a million of the hypnotic class has ever been under the manipulation of an operator, or professional hypnotist. This influence is constantly exerted in every phase of daily life; by others who have no knowledge of what they are doing; and by the persons themselves, who likewise would be surprised if told they are making themselves easy subjects to such a power.

In the world of Nature the use of the bright light combined with the monotony of a voice that is alive is quite common; as is seen when a cat, sitting some distance away, fixes its bright gaze on a bird, and chatters in a monotonous voice, quite low, and not easily heard by people, until the bird is thoroughly hypnotized, and even flies to the cat. This method is employed by Nature probably to maintain the life on earth, having in view the fact that the bird assists in sustaining the cat, and dies with less suffering than if allowed to starve to death by the slow process of the decrepitude of old age when it is neglected and helpless. Of course we do not see why the cat should be sustained in the wild state of Nature; but it seems to be on earth to stay for a while at least; and if the bird takes other life for its food, the cat may not be denied the same right. Fish in the sea feed on fish; and this feeding goes from the smallest to the largest kinds.

Eye strain comes from the interest the bird takes in the glowing light in the eyeballs of the cat. A large mass of light would not do this work.

Eye strain comes always from looking higher than the level of the eyes themselves. Great lawyers who, in the olden times, had permission to talk to juries until they won their verdicts from them by sheer hypnotism, as was the case always with Rufus Choate, "the ruler of the twelve," as he was called, and with others of the profession, have realized that when the jurors are seated on the level floor in front and slightly beneath the advocate, they fall more readily to the power of the superior speaker; but when the jurors are located in raised boxes, or when the six in the back row are higher than the front row, those that are higher are the last to be influenced except by the actual evidence. Choate used to say that he talked until the last man yielded; and that he was able to tell when he had won them all. In one case he talked for two days to one man; as the other eleven were with him; and he did not desire a hung jury. We know that a great advocate understands the leanings of the juror he is addressing and that he understands when they are with him.

This brings us to the church in question, where it was claimed that the preacher hypnotized his people. The first thing we noticed was that the seats of the main floor were on a level line; not raised as they were placed in theaters; so that every person present was compelled to look up; and those in the nearer seats were quite a distance, relatively, below the pastor.

The next thing we noticed was the fact that the pulpit was unusually high; being elevated so that the minister could be seen by everybody, as the officials explained to us. They said, "We either had to raise the floor to an inclined plane as in theaters, or raise the pulpit; and the latter course involved less expensed." The result of this condition in the structure of the church was that a large portion of the congregation were compelled to lift their eyes to see the minister; and as his gestures were forceful and illustrative of his meaning, they did this willingly and constantly.

But a poor preacher, judged by an oratorical standard, would not have produced an hypnotic effect. It required a man with vital ideas, a vital mind, a vital will power, and a pleasing delivery, to secure this kind of control; but we are sure that these qualities were aided by the height of the pulpit which produced an eye strain on the part of his listeners.

Then his voice helped to some extent. It was very much alive, but inclined to a monotony of pitch. You can take this combination into any church in the land and you will have a congregation swayed in a hypnotic sense. It has been shown in a great number of other churches where the pulpits are placed high and the speakers are attractive, the contributions are of notable size. In other words, you cannot force a listener to hold the eyes uplifted without producing eye strain, and some form of weariness of which the hearer is generally unconscious, as the bird is when it flies to the cat.

Looking long at any one thing has a similar power over the mind, even if there is no uplifting of the gaze; but the influence is weak, and requires much more time. It appears in the habits of people who work and drudge day after day at home and in factories, shops and other places. Farmers are almost to a man, in a large part of their lives, members of the hypnotic class, and it is for them that the blue sky laws have been enacted. Monotony of physical activity, no matter where carried on, leads to hypnotic conditions. It has been often said that the world is full of suckers, meaning people who yield their money and support to schemes that wise men would avoid; and this has led to the most vital axiom of all time that "one is born every minute ."

If you wish to learn to what extent the world is populated by hypnotized men and women, answer all the advertisements in the periodicals for a week or month; remembering that these advertisers would not spend their millions a year for such claims unless they got their money back with a profit from the dear people. More than one thousand million dollars have been sent to fake companies since the recent war, in the belief that a big income and profit would be secured as promised; when in fact the whole amount has been a total loss. It is not always that the hypnotized person is a "sucker," for there are grooves in the mind that run under control, while other grooves are in the opposite condition. The most pronounced of all "suckers" is the great financier whose astuteness has made him many times a millionaire, and who is swept off his base by the rustle of a feminine skirt. His mind has two sets of grooves; one place him in the hypnotic class when the influences are right; and the other makes him the monarch of finance and business. Look to your history in the last two generations where men are known to you by their publicity, and note the number of really great men who have fallen under one set of grooves. A collection of these histories would furnish the colossal surprise of the century.

There is no doubt that many other causes enter into the work of making a person a member of the hypnotic class. These we will consider in the briefer but more important Realm, the Estate of Hell.

But let it be known that all forms of monotony are hurtful to the mind and weaken the power of the individual. One line of work too long pursued, the sameness of home life, the weariness of country existence, the humdrum repetition of things day after day, all tend in this wrong direction. Did you ever know that there are ten digits on the two hands; that each digit leads to a separate brain activity; that the use of one or two, singly, or the whole in a bunch, deprives the brain of its developing nourishment, and that here we have one possible form of monotony. We know from many tests that the person who uses all ten digits daily, separately, but not in a bunch, has a much more vital brain power in all things; for you cannot help one part of this organ without helping all.

The habit of putting a child to sleep nights by a monotony of interest is not a bad one; for the child's mind is more likely to be normal than otherwise; and there is little to fear of hypnotic results at that age. This monotony can be employed in a singsong style of melody, quiet and having much sameness, as the crooning songs of the mother; or in telling a story in which the same things are closely allied, with no vivid plot, like the marching of sheep through a gate, each sheep being about like his associate, and with no purpose in view except to march through the gate; these and other methods have been successful in bringing sleep to the child; while a spirited and alarming anecdote with danger and narrow escapes, will work injury and lead to bad dreams and fears. It was once a familiar rule with elders to put themselves to sleep by counting' sheep mentally; this has its value when the nerves are not tortured by indigestion, late meals, or indiscretions.

Jurors are almost always members of the hypnotic class; or else they would get excused from jury service by some method or other. Like the noble bankers and great merchants who have fallen victims of the rustling feminine skirt, they are controlled by the emotions set going by great but dishonest lawyers; for no matter how great a man may be in his profession, if he pleads for the release of a murderer, or murderess, he is not honest when he knows that he is exerting undue influence over the jurors by trickery. It may be thought that there will not again be heard the rustle of the feminine skirt referred to, owing to the change of style in dress, but ere these pages have been long before the world, the skirt will be back; and in its place we have the lack of skirt, which produces another but extremely powerful form of hypnotism.

Owing to the lack of willingness on the part of men to engage in the venturous voyage of matrimony, which condition is largely due to the expense of supporting two or more persons on an income that does not provide properly for one, the women of the world since the great war was inaugurated, conceived the idea that men could and should be hypnotized by the exposure of parts of the female form; and it is a matter capable of proof that the recent styles in feminine dress were established solely for this purpose, while ostensibly made necessary by the cost of the material. But women on the average spend relatively more money on dress today than before the war, even taking into consideration the increase in price. The beautifully shod feet, the shapely ankles, the fine forms of the lower legs, the contour of the calves, all combine to make a form of hypnotic influence that does its matrimonial work successfully.

The question arises whether this form of attraction brings about the right kind of mating that makes marriage a desirable bond; but with that we have nothing to do. The lowering of the upper portions of the dress fore and aft was also a bit of hypnotic scheme to help on the man's desire for giving up his freedom, as some philosophers facetiously state; exposing the chest down to the limits of legal permission; and eventually bringing the back into the struggle.

This kind of attraction like thousands of others, takes advantage of the mind in its mental lapses. It ceases to do coherent thinking. The professional hypnotist seeks to throw the mind of his subject into a mental lapse; during which interval of thought, his own ideas are substituted for those of his subject. A remark often does this very thing; as when a person is trying to induce another to sell something for a price less than that asked, the owner throws the prospective buyer off the track by the remark, "The thing costs me more than you offer." The party addressed does not stop to think that the assertion is an oft repeated one in business, and he believes it to be true. Traveling agents who invent many excuses for securing the attention of those to whom they desire to sell their goods, make use of this lapse in others' mental operations, and thereby obtain a hearing. But it must not be assumed that this condition exists solely with the country bumpkin.

With fully ninety per cent of all humanity in some kind of hypnotic state, it is no wonder that there is so much cheating going on in the world. People would not be dishonest in their dealings if there were no such condition as that of hypnosis to cloud the minds of their victims. The lawyer who deceives the jury or preys upon their emotions would not be able to succeed, and we doubt if he would try, if juries were not, as a rule, members of the hypnotic class. The same lawyer addressing the United States Supreme Court would hardly dare to appeal to their maudlin nature, as does the advocate who asks the jury to return the murderer to the bosom of his family and sixteen children in time to have them all reunited in a happy Christmas celebration. With tears in their eyes the jurors yield to this appeal, and do as they are requested with the suffering felon.

It is necessary to separate humanity into two hemispheres of influence.

This is the Twenty-second Principle. If you will look back to the first book in the cultivation of personal magnetism you will learn that there are enemies of this power all on the negative side;' and there you will find that, when such enemies are removed, Nature quickly builds the power in any person. The quickest way to acquire natural personal magnetism is to remove the enemies. Millions of people do not like to practice tests or exercises who would enjoy driving out these foes; and, to their surprise and gratification, they would find themselves gifted in the art, and all naturally, without having practiced any of the tests. Of course it is better to include the whole system. But it is the fundamental law of life that when the barriers are removed, the result always is power. All this relates to the work of acquiring the power.

Universal Magnetism relates to the work of using it.

The same fundamental law follows us now. There is but one class of persons who are capable of exerting control over others; and this class is found in the division that we call The Positive Hemisphere of Influence. The one gigantic enemy of these persons is the fact that they are dwelling in The Negative Hemisphere of Influence; and here we see what is meant by the hypnotic class. It is they who live in the Negative Hemisphere.

If you dwell there, you must move.

This one act of getting out, instantly gives you the control that is most important, most powerful, most supreme; and if you add to this act of moving your dwelling place, the victory over the enemies of personal magnetism that are set forth in the first book, you are already master of the greatest of all arts, Universal Magnetism.

In our private classes, and among the thousands of our private pupils for nearly half a century, we have found many men and women of great prominence in the world, which means that they have no time for exercises and tests; and they have invariably desired to achieve the most potent results in the shortest possible time; and our methods with them have been summed up in the following training:

1. Fight down the enemies of personal magnetism, as stated in the first book, and thereby come naturally into that power.

2. Move your dwelling place from the Hemisphere of Hypnosis to that of the opposite Hemisphere; and you are at once master of Universal Magnetism.

This does not mean that the remaining parts of the system are not of advantage; they are, because they quicken and increase both powers, and should be adopted by all men and women who have the time to devote to them. But the results of the above dual method, being natural gifts only, are so marked that there is at once the inclination to follow through.

You will not at first believe that hypnotism played so great a part in life; but that is because it embraces all people in all walks, and under all forms of association, dealings, communication and contact with each other. It is a vastly larger and broader term than when applied to the practice of putting a subject into a cataleptic sleep; that form of it is less than one per cent of its whole scope.

We are coming now to the lowest form of hypnosis, which is known in study as The Estate of Hell. You will find there, perhaps, yourself living on the wrong side of the world of Influence.

Our duty to you is to take you away; but before we can do that we must show you where you are, and how you can get away. Then if you do not go on any further in this great study, you will have at once come into possession of the power of Universal Magnetism. We hope that you are not dwelling in the wrong Hemisphere. We shall see. The next Realm will tell the facts.

Having moved into the Hemisphere of Control, you will then find your subjects in both these Hemispheres. Those that you will enjoy best as subjects will dwell in the same Hemisphere with you, that known as the magnetic. But they will not be numerous. In dealing with them, you will find that it will be necessary to employ what is called The Crystal Mind, which is being now made public for the first time. Without it, you will find that all dwellers in the Hemisphere of Control have more or less power to protect themselves from all kinds of influence; hence the Crystal Mind must determine the question of supremacy.

But ninety per cent of your subjects will be found living in the other Hemisphere; those that are too far in the DARK OF THE MIND will be most pitiable, and you may feel inclined to help them into a better condition. The others are the usual dupes; some are always dupes; others only in certain lines of activity and thinking. We will make you acquainted with them, and will show you how to deal with them.

Now we enter a briefer Estate, but one of the utmost importance.

REALM THREE

The Estate of Hell

IN THE BLACK SHADOWS OF EXISTENCE

THE magnetism we teach is of the kind that conquers; and we propose to show, before this book is ended, that there is but one kind that never fails to conquer; but one kind that wins at all times, in all places, under all circumstances, and achieves a total victory, complete in every particular. Other methods may extol the advantages which a stronger personality is able to wrest from a weaker, but such victories are cowardly. The grandest man is he who is master of his peers.

The word hell means anything you choose to make it. In the lowest planes of barbarism it indicates a country somewhere beneath the surface of the earth, where occupations and penalties are suited, not to the demerits of the wrongdoers, but to the fancies of the inventors of the place itself; always reflecting the mental characteristics of the age and people from which they emanate. Thus the idea of hell changes continually; it broadens its fancy, and losses its sting as civilization makes progress. If there were no penal codes there would be no realm of punishment.

The human heart is so constituted that the more refined and sensitive it becomes, the more it suffers. Life is full of rough places; thorns abound on every side; and that person is most in harmony with nature who is rough and thorny, for he has less to pain him. It is the tender hand that is pricked. A gang of laborers are hounded and abused by the man in charge of them, but they pay no heed to the oaths; yet a sensitive fellow pines and pales at the mere intimation that he is not active enough for his age. The actresses whose character creations on the stage are ideals of life are scolded at rehearsals, until they have a right to believe themselves the trashiest of human beings; yet woman shrinks from the least of insinuations in a more sensitive sphere. Miss W. says of herself: "I was told by a gentleman acquaintance that I ought to improve my mind by reading the best and loftiest works of literature. I asked him if he thought my brain deficient, and he said he supposed most women were a little below the average of their sex's ability; and I became very angry with him. I went on the stage, and lost my ultra-sensitiveness in a short time. When the manager told me that I was the lowest specimen of female ignorance he ever saw, that I would never know enough to go in out of the rain, I agreed with him" These are facts, illustrating the two phases of life; one, the hothouse nature, that quails before the least chilling breeze; the other, the sturdy oak, that enjoys rough weather.

Conscience is supposed to regulate the amount of suffering to which a person will be subjected by reason of errors or sin; but training and habits control conscience.

The more sensitive you are, the more you will feel the pangs of this attribute of the heart. The first breaking away from right-doing is fraught with severe anguish; the second amazes you; the third lets in some light on the ease with which you can sin and forget. The worst of crimes may be committed, if there is no fear of punishment. It is human to go as far as the evil bent of the heart can go without running the risk of detection. Take away the continual check on wrongdoers, and they will not stop at any limit.

The blackest ages of history are not many centuries away. Then all power was robbed from the State and given to the Church, whose imperialism concentrated the armies and machinery of civil governments under the leadership of one great head; and blood ran in rivers through the realms of the most advanced civilization. There was no conscience. Men felt willing and able to say aught they pleased if in power, to the best of their race if out of power; and sensitiveness to rebuke of the tongue was absurd in an age when the sting of the torch executed the malice of the heart. What must have been the feelings of those who could put their fellow beings to death, watching them writhe in flames, is understood only as we study the possibilities of evil action in the present age.

Pulling away more and more every decade from the grosser cruelties of a rougher humanity, we find the torturing fear of physical harm to be superseded by a much keener suffering of the mind and nerves in each new era. They once said it was not hard to die, and a body could be killed but once; we now say it is worse than a dozen deaths to pass through the anguish of mental fears, such as a finer age has brought upon us. So little is death dreaded in the barbarous and semi-barbarous countries, that the most horrible of punishments must be invented as deterrents of crime; and the agonies are long drawn out, so that the unconsciousness of death may not bring sweet peace to the individual. A step lower brings us to the savages, who not only laughed at such things, but actually courted the opportunity of enduring physical pain in excess. The American Indians never flinched a muscle when the red-hot irons were held gently against their flesh, and slowly burned holes into their bodies.

Against the defiance of death and torture in the more physical races, we find the excruciating horror of a broken mind in this era of intelligence. The probability of a life in the asylum is haunting a million men and women in our own America today; for the rush, the hurry, the excitement, the hysteria of living are sapping the peace of the brain and tearing open the ever-healing wounds of the heart. There is no contentment. The rich are driven to distraction by their cares; the poor are planning to become rich; the middle classes are the fulcrum on which both extremes ply their leverage; the learned hate ignorance, and the ignorant have contempt for learning. In each class the war of discontent, envy, jealousy and competition turns the hope of peace into a red flame of conflict. Fraud is rampant everywhere. The desire to cheat some one is responded to by deception from every source. There is no peace. The human heart is not an instrument of peace. Therefore the man or woman who can call all these warring forces into one compact organization wherein conflict is turned to a united energy, will be clothed in supreme power.

The magnetic hell is confusion.

This is the Twenty-third Principle. The confusion referred to is that of the nervous system that may or may not associate itself with the mind. We all recognize the mind that is clear at one time and confused at another. It may he mixed or muddled by propositions too deep for it to grasp, and these scatter its magnetism if it attempts to deal with them. It is a fact that some of the most magnetic of individuals are not of a high order of intelligence; but they know when not to enter upon a line of thought that is too difficult for their understanding.

The acquisition of knowledge, the riper state called wisdom, and the possession of intelligence are three distinct matters, each apart from the other. As a rule, the crowding of the mind with facts weakens its real usefulness. A college professor may know one hundred thousand things, culled from history, science or philosophy, more than the president of a bank or the manager of a railroad system; yet, with all his knowledge, he is a useless well, valuable to others, but of no avail to himself. A man from the city, who knew city ways and methods, looked with pity on the blooming face of the country girl who was ignorant of all ideas that belonged to metropolitan life; and she, in turn, felt a deep sympathy for his ignorance of country ways; yet, while both lacked knowledge, they might have been highly magnetic.

Confusion appears in the mind as a reflex action of the nervous condition. No matter how much a person knows, he cannot express it, or even think it, if his ideas are scattered by his own nervous confusion. Hawthorne was accorded a high rank among the brainy men of literature, yet he suffered continually from this trouble. Actors have what they call stage fright on first coming before an audience in the beginning of the evening's performance, and no matter how often they have appeared before, it takes some minutes to overcome this condition on each new occasion. History is full of instances of such uncontrol in the private and public careers of her favored individuals; they succeed in part, and fail in part.

But the most distressful confusion is that which fills the lives of men and women who have no knowledge whatever of the method by which they may marshal their vital forces. They are one restless torment within the body. They arise in the morning in a state of discontent, struggling to adjust themselves to the duties of the day. If they belong to the more stupid ranks, those that are always on the negative side of life, they may feel no responsibility, and by this lack of touch with a progressive existence they may be happy in a measure. This they can never be if they are on the positive side, for their very activity means unrest. A captain without an army has no reason to worry over his martial responsibilities; give him soldiers in force; and he is a commander only so long as he is able to marshal them in rank and file and control their aggressive movements. Let them move along as a motley mob, and he suffers the pangs of confusion in his management. So it is with every person on the positive side of life who is unable to take charge of his forces.

Such persons are unhappy. To be ignorant and dull, stupid, careless, and a negative part in the social relations of humanity, perhaps invites more happiness than to realize that life is worth living, and to try to live it successfully. "Only the simple minds are happy," says a writer. This is not true. The fact is that all who are on the negative side of existence are contented with less of the fruitage of living, because their wants are limited and their opportunities for enjoyment are less. They are often miserable in the little mind they have. Their periods of content and hilarity are due to alcohol or other stimulants, and in times of leisure, such as Sundays and holidays. Out of their classes come the socialists, the mobs and the tossing masses of criminal humanity.

To be actually happy there must be positive life, and this means magnetism; but herein the most acute suffering and confusion are found, when the vital energies are not marshaled. Existence is like a battlefield; self is the general in command; there must be an army or the commander can never realize the pleasure of victory; yet, in taking charge of an army, his responsibilities begin, and he may live to see his forces torn asunder, scattered, demoralized, and all rending his mind into shreds. He is unhappy without his army; he may be unhappier with it; yet he can never be happy without the possibilities it may afford him of achieving the grandest victories.

This condition of confusion is one that should be studied and recognized in every life, for it comes to all, and some are never free from it. We look for its cure in vain if we seek it outside of ourselves. There is no cure except in marshaling the forces within us and leading them on in battle; but it is true that there is less of suffering if we abandon the captaincy and drift into the ranks of the negative souls that are blown about by the winds of misfortune and finally tossed on the rocks of disaster. There are no compensations for such existence; even the moments of rest are bubbles of deception. We must be going up stream if we would find happiness.

Confusion of the magnetic forces shows itself in many ways. Every bad passion and emotion is touched. You do not feel right toward your fellow beings. You are angered at anything, no matter how trifling. The success of others weighs down upon you. Malice and a desire for revenge live at your elbows, spurring you on in your conduct toward enemies. Erratic fires burn in your soul, and their flames sear every honorable motive that ever had dwelling place in your heart. Policy sometimes holds sway over your tongue and over your deeds; but it is hollow, and the gain it brings is the progeny of greed. You are not happy, but are restlessly hunting for some means of acquiring happiness; always finding yourself thwarted by circumstances which you charge to an unjust fate.

Some experiences may prove valuable as examples of the workings of this confusion of the magnetic forces. We predicted years ago the suicides that would occur among certain prominent men of this and other nations, particularly of the French. When confusion has produced anarchy of the magnetism, suicide is almost a certainty. The French hate to outlive their excitement. The self-destruction of Boulanger was as much to be expected as the natural death of Gladstone and Bismarck. A stormy and erratic career is a sea of disorder, involving mind and soul. Most persons, who are too strong for suicide, wear out suddenly, like a machine running wild, or jump the track and are ditched.

The feelings are never at peace. An hour or a day of quietude within is a symptom of alarm, engendering the fear that it is too good to last, and that something is sure to happen to bring greater misery. Then, when a trifle occurs to mar the even tenor of one's way, the dark cloud of malice arises and overspreads all the horizon. A woman, in conversation with a friend who had been loyal to her for fifteen years, happened to make a remark that was a little extravagant, whereupon the friend said, "I hardly think you mean that; do you?" "Well, I like your impertinence. You accuse me of deliberate falsehood." "I did not intend to do so, but what you say is not true, and you know it." "If you will find the door, you may do so," exclaimed the woman in her own house, and her guest departed. In the evening this quick-tempered woman told her husband the circumstances, and added, "I do not know why I spoke so hastily; but I have done it, and we are both too proud to ever speak again." And it is true that, although a mutual friend tried to heal the breach, they have always remained enemies. When the thought of the old friendship comes up, the spell of malice fights with it until it is downed, and there is less hope than ever of peace.

Magnetism is greatest and most powerful in the colder climes. The heat of the warmer zones tends to make a spirited person altogether too unreasonable to be classed as a higher example of civilization. This is seen in the South, where the feuds indicate that the magnetic vitalities run wild. Most of these difficulties have originated between the wives of the contestants, and over the slightest of causes. In one case the families were neighbors, and a pet dog would emanate from the home of Mrs. A. to the flower-beds of Mrs. B., until the latter sent a polite request by her boy, asking that the trips of the canine cease altogether. This was regarded as an insult, though any reasonable mind would have thought it perfectly proper and neighborly.

In the mind and soul of Mrs. A., the stormy unrest of hell began. She brooded over the note, over the dog, over the flower-beds, and over everything, until confusion reigned supreme in her nervous system. Herself counted a magnetic woman, she gave an exhibition of an army disorganized, running pell-mell upon an enemy with eyes shut. Her only thought was revenge for the writing of that note. Its language was polite, even affectionate, and the grievance was not imaginary; but she could not forgive the sending of it, as they had always been the best of friends. She could not see that it was her duty to obey the request. She could not appreciate the fact that a gentle endurance of a real offense, in this world of cross interests, is far better than enmity and bloodshed. "I do not know what actuated me to do this," she afterward said, in the usual groping about for an excuse, "but I believe it was the devil himself. " If this is so, there must be many devils about; for her conduct was in line with that of millions of others who are unable to control their impulses.

The husbands took up the matter; then they became enemies; then the grown-up sons entered into it, and thus the war of the families began. One night the son of A. met B., and crossed the street apparently to avoid him. B. had an errand at the store on the other side, but lingered behind, so as to keep out of the young man's way. The latter reasoned as most persons do, and was quite sure that he was being followed; indeed, he felt so certain of it, that he went home and told his father. Mr. A. then came out, and demanded of B. why he was hounding his son. B. declared that he had not intended to do so; that he took his usual course home, and proposed to attend to his business if other persons would attend to theirs. To this A. declared his disbelief, and the lie was passed. Then came threats.

After the foregoing preamble to the feud, it was necessary that each should arm himself. The mere vision of the other was the signal for putting the hand to the pocket; and, as they came upon each other quite unexpectedly one evening, they drew and fired. One died instantly, the other in a few hours. In a year more one of the sons killed the other; a cousin killed the survivor, and the relatives and friends of each side joined forces, until twenty-six were slain. In some of the Southern feuds the causes are slighter, and the fatalities greater.

There is no prevention for this slaughter; for, once the restless heart is aroused, it has no peace till death ends its owner's life. The reasoning faculties never act in such dramas.

Women are no more subject to the confusion of their magnetic forces than are men. They may be more relentless and revengeful, for they act by intuition or instinct ; yet men are as frequently given to these disorders as women. Two merchants, whose lines of trade were conflicting, met and entered upon an altercation that had no sensible cause; yet they became lifelong enemies, and were made miserable by their experiences. One man takes affront at some simple grievance, and he is no longer of use to himself, for he cannot harbor malice without losing his true value. We recall the case of a young lawyer, who met his death under the following circumstances: He held a claim for collection against a man more than a thousand miles away, and wrote him a letter demanding immediate payment. The man replied that he would pay it when he was able, and said that he could not be forced to pay by any "young snipe." Here was the beginning.

The lawyer wrote back a letter in the same vein, adding the words, "I do not propose to be insulted by a cur." The man was deeply offended, although he had begun the malicious part of the correspondence. He wrote an intemperate letter, containing a score of opprobrious adjectives, some of them too low to repeat. The lawyer then replied in like vein. On receiving the letter, the man demanded a retraction at once, or he would come on and thrash the lawyer. The latter, who had not begun the attack, showed that he was not frightened, for he followed up the mud-throwing by another abusive letter. The recipient came on and killed him on sight. He was hung for it. Both men were built of intelligent stuff, and would have been accounted magnetic were it not for the fact that their vital forces were scattered and wild, lacking leadership.

A large majority of men, on receiving the slightest provocation, will answer in kind, paying interest in so doing. Nothing but policy, the desire of gain, or the fear of punishment, holds most persons back. You may do a friend a favor, and receive from him a scathing rebuke in case he fails to get another favor from you. The foulest of letters have been written to benefactors who limit their kindness. We are referring to the intelligent classes, who are supposed to possess magnetism in some positive degree at least. They are at enmity with the world and with themselves. Not one of them is free from this incoherence of energy.

Women carry revengeful feelings to the grave. It is their nature. They refuse to yield.

MYSTIC UTOPIAN SUPERMEN

When two women quarrel, both are free from blame, and it has never been discovered that either is in duty bound to make overtures to the other for a healing of the breech. Sisters and brothers, in a majority of all families, have fallings out that are generally of lifelong duration. It seems easier for those who are of the same flesh and blood to enter upon feuds than for others, and this may be due to the fact that more privileges and liberties of remark and action are permitted among relatives.

Lovers quarrels are bitter and generally groundless. Magnetic young men and young women lose all control of these forces when disturbed by the counter influence of love. They expect all from each other, and, like the perfectly polished marble, show to disadvantage with the slightest defect. When they part it seems like the opening of a great gulf between two vast hemispheres. If obstinate, these misguided heads turn away, and point their noses of scorn in opposite directions for the rest of their natural lives. It can easily be ascertained that nearly all engagements are broken, very few of the original mating couples hanging together through thick and thin.

Married life is a hell in many cases. This is due to a loss of magnetism, or a confusion of the forces that might be united and produce the noblest and the sweetest of peace if both parties would have it so. It takes but a word, a hit of neglect, a criticism, a rejoinder, or something "light as air," to explode the magazine and set off the ignitable energy. Men and women will not strive to control themselves. There is satisfaction in showing fight, in the pangs of resentment, in the silent tongue and "cutting" of life's partner; so they let loose, and the sting sinks in, never to be removed. The pictured fancy of honeyed bliss is a dream that has its awakening in the realism of vinegar and gall. Some marriages are filled with happiness, and God blesses them.

Irritability destroys magnetism.

This is the Twenty-fourth Principle. You get up in the morning; something goes wrong; your garments do not fall into place easily; your hosiery clings to the heel; your elbow will not go through the armhole; the shoe is too tight; a button is off something, and you are irritable. Perhaps the vicissitudes of the dressing period are passed over successfully, but other matters go against the grain. It is a common saying that the day is begun wrong, and everything will go wrong till night.

Few indeed are the persons who are free from this disease of the nervous system. It is more fearful in its results, both in physical and moral effects, than any other malady. It grows rapidly by letting it have its way; it is diminished by trying to check it; but once it has been allowed free scope, the disposition to suppress it is lacking. In its physical injury it involves the brain first, and then the mind becomes irresponsible, and the morals give way sooner or later. Solitude develops it very rapidly. A man made the statement that he could not be alone a half hour without uttering oath after oath, which he never dared to do when others were within hearing. Another man declared that he had the reputation of never using a profane word, yet that, in fact, he swore fearfully a hundred times a day. He knew that he could restrain himself, for he never gave way in the presence of others.

A wife in court testified that her husband was a man of mild temper, never having uttered an oath in all his married life; and she was much surprised when the attorney for the defense drew from him the admission that he "swore to himself when alone." Asked how often, he said it was "pretty often if things bothered him." A young man, who stood among the leaders of his class in the university, and of whom a great future was predicted, soon after graduation began to show a deep indentation between his brows. This became noticeable to his friends. He was occasionally overheard in a rage, and was taken to task for it by those who were interested in him. He made this statement: "I was once able to control my irritability, but I formed the habit of yielding to small influences that tended to distract me at times, when I was busy and had much to accomplish. This habit grew on me insidiously. It soon asserted itself my master." He was induced to see that it might be controlled, for he did in fact control it when others were about. His books told him that irritability was the first step toward insanity, and he saw in his own example that he was slowly and surely tending that way. He has been a student of advanced magnetism for several years, and is today a perfect master of himself and now of others also.

Irritability is of two kinds : the one is the forerunner of insanity, being impelled by that malady, and not easily held in check; the other is the outcome of habit, and leads to insanity if not suppressed. That which is the symptom is due to mental and nervous confusion, and is the natural accompaniment of depleted vitality wherein magnetism is lacking or is chaotic. The gentlest cares of derangement are those which are on the negative or hypnotistic side of life; and the severer cases, as of madness, are found among magnetic persons whose energies are not controlled. They are like engines running wild, without master hands to direct them.

The kind of irritability that brings on insanity is always the creature of a careless habit. It begins with a sound mind, and possibly a magnetic nature. No person likes to be thwarted. Life of all kinds resents interference. The ant, the bee, the fly, the cat, the dog, and all species, when not frightened, are quick to snap at intrusions, as though to fight them away. On this principle of resentment it is natural to fly up" at anything that goes wrong and thus interferes with whatever you are doing. A little thing is in the way; with a snatch at it, a curl of the lips, and a knitting of the brow, you ejaculate some ill-natured remark that cannot help reacting on the heart.

One of the brightest young men we have ever met lost all his magnetism, all his good nature, all his self-control and, finally, all his mind by allowing this habit or irritability to grow on him little by little. Another professional gentleman gave way, year after year, to this same habit, until he was unfit to remain in his office. He said this of himself: "I often meditated on the condition in which I found myself, and I often remarked that I could stop the habit at any time if I chose; but it got the better of me. Now I am going at it in earnest, and I will conquer, for I wish to get back the prestige I have lost."

He failed again and again, until his physician recommended the study of these advanced lessons in magnetism, and they alone saved him.

It may be easily proved that a lack of magnetism is the cause of, and is also caused by, irritability. Vitality of body, of nerves and of mind will show itself in some degree of positive magnetism, and when the latter has been accumulated it will give rise to the former or some one of them. These causes and effects work both ways. Let some act of the individual lessen the vitality, and the magnetism suffers; then irritability sets in, and the condition becomes worse. Many men and women say that they are never irritable until they are all tired out. "1 have full patience until I am weak from weariness; then I have no patience at all; I am cross, even ugly, until I get rested. What is the remedy? The body and mind may become exhausted without depleting the system of its magnetism, but this is difficult of attainment; it is a condition the average reader will never encounter.

If you are irritable you should ascertain the cause of it, or what it indicates. First, learn if it is due to an approaching loss of your mental powers; and, if so, go to work in earnest to supply the needed magnetic vitality which alone can avert the failure of this great organ. Then you will save what is more than life; you will avoid the wreck of your own existence and the peril of others. There is not the slightest doubt that this is the only means of cure. It not only furnishes the life that is slowly fading out in the mental faculties, but its vitality causes a healing, as far as anything can, of the nervous structure that is breaking down. The thorough study of this volume, and the adoption of its regime, as well as the following of this system of training, may be fully relied upon as a cure if one's time and full attention are given to the work. Improvement is noted almost from the beginning, after the first reading of the book, for its influence tends to shape the plan of thought and action at once.

On the other hand, the probability is that your irritability is due to carelessly giving up to feelings that are aroused by each little annoyance. It is not because your mind is failing that you are fretful, but because you lack the willpower and purpose to check such feelings. Here, again, there is but one effectual cure, and that is found in the realm of peace, in the following pages of this volume. We feel sure that you will adopt the plan therein furnished, for it is designed to accomplish such a result. Every step of the way is stated and explained with the most ample description, so that nothing can be lost or misunderstood. A change of habit is not easy. Great goals are reached only by strong efforts. If you neglect this golden opportunity, your career will be down hill. If you believe in yourself and in your magnetism, remember that some of the sublime wrecks of manhood have come from the most magnetic of men and women, who permitted their energies to run away with them, like unmanaged horses dashing to the cliff.

Worry kills.

This is the Twenty-fifth Principle. A minute of worrying drives out a mine of magnetism. It collapses the brain, the mental force, the vital functions, and all the operations of life. It destroys appetite. Many a person has commenced a meal, and stopped eating when some bad news arrived. The saliva stagnates, the gastric juices of the stomach stop their flow, digestion ceases, and there is no taste in the mouth. Don't worry.

A person may be good-natured and yet worry; it does not follow that the latter habit will either invite or accompany irritability. Some of the ill-tempered persons never worry, and others, who are as gentle as may be desired, are so weak in character that they are always softly worrying. The philosopher knows the uselessness of wasting his energies over what cannot be helped, and says, mentally, that it will not make any difference a century hence, so he will not worry; yet, what his mind so easily solves, his nervous system will not always obey. Temperament, health, habit, all are involved in the cause. Indeed, it has been claimed that ill-health is the only producer of worry, on the theory that perfect health is buoyant and sees nothing but the bright side of life. This might be true if perfect health could be found; but as most persons are in deficient health, and are given to worrying, it is not possible to say that one is the promoter of the other.

The first and most fruitful cause of this habit is the anxiety which is felt about the means of living. There have been such unpleasant stories circulated about the discomfort of the poorhouse that all persons instinctively shrink from the prospect of ending their days at that resort. There is a horror attached to it; and rightfully. The very poorest of humanity cherish the romantic idea of dying at home in the bosom of their family, lamented as the curtain falls, and tenderly put to rest amid the shedding of hallowed tears. These humble creatures look forward to work that shall bring them fifty cents or more each day, but as no employer is bound to keep them steadily engaged, they are always thinking of the hour when they will be idle. The only soul who is sure of unlimited work is the miserable wretch who is underpaid, who gives a day of toil for an hour of compensation.

He who knows that employment may be had for a year will worry about the time to follow; if he is sure of four years, he frets about the blank fifth; if his contract runs for ten years, he is uneasy about the eleventh; and we know a Baltimore lady, who leased her land at a large annual rental for ninety-nine years, who said she was always uneasy at the thought of the lease being broken. John B. Gough told the story of a spinster, a thin, dried-up woman of forty and over, whom he found weeping bitterly at the side of a curbstone. He sought the cause of her anguish, and she said she was thinking that if she should get married and have a child, and the child should fall into the drain and be drowned, she should go distracted the rest of her natural life. While the story is probably not true, it well illustrates the tendency of humanity to borrow trouble.

Worrying may be done in silence and yet be as destructive of the vital forces as though it were done openly. Some women withdraw to have a cry where no one will know what is going on. Men often go apart to think out the problems alone. It is sometimes thought that if the means of living could be provided in ample abundance clear down to the end of the longest life probable, there would be nothing to worry about. This is far from true. The rich are always anxious. At a gathering of more than a score of ladies the question was asked, what was the most troublesome thing in life, and all but two answered, the servant question. Those who are too poor to hire a servant escape a large field of worriment, while those who are endowed with the good fortune to be able to hire help are to be more pitied than their humbler fellow mortals.

We met a young man of unusual capabilities; one who was bright, smart, magnetic and of the highest intelligence. He delivered a course of lectures when less than a quarter of a century old, the most powerful of which was a strong assault upon the evil habit of borrowing trouble. Ten years later we met him under changed conditions, and our first remark was that he looked worried. "Ah!" he said, with a sigh, "You have not forgotten my lecture. I was a guidepost, was I not, pointing the way but not going thereon. Let me tell you how it is. My income never exceeds two hundred dollars a month. I pay forty dollars a month for house rent, and it is the cheapest that will do me. Lighting averages seven dollars a month; heating, seven dollars; my grocery bill, forty dollars; my butcher's bill, thirty dollars; my wife has three children and is ill, which requires two nurses and a cook, the wages of whom aggregate forty dollars. You see, forty is my lucky number. How much is that? One hundred and sixty-four dollars, so far, per month. The doctor runs up a bill of ten to twenty dollars every blessed month I live; last year he made it fully that, and he comes right along now. My wife's mother is homeless, lost her fortune, and lives with us. My wife's sister was abused by her drunken husband, and had no place to go, so she came to live at our house. She is getting a divorce. Being penniless, she must be taken care of at my expense, and being an invalid, I must hire and feed her nurse. Then the cost of medicines, clothing, and a hundred little things, must be met. I run behind more than a hundred dollars a month. When I was courting my betrothed—and she is the best of wives —I pictured to myself and to her a future in which parties, dances, theaters, drives and pleasures galore would make us weary with their abundance. How is it now? When I come away from the house each day I hang my head; when I approach it, I never look up. In it or out, I am unhappy. What can I do? If I go to a less expensive place my chances of earning as much as I now do would be destroyed, and while I might make more by starting out for myself, there would be a long period of time in which I could not earn anything, during which my wife and three children, her mother, her sister and two children, and the four servants would have no means of sustaining life." And lie dropped his chin to his chest as he plodded on.

The foregoing case is an actual one, every detail of which is true. We ask our students to tell us for him what he should do. Solve the problem, if you can; send us the solution, and we will forward it to the man. His case is but one of hundreds of thousands in which the same principle is involved. What can he do? Shall he go on incurring debts that can never be paid? He tries to be honest. He does not spend a cent for pleasure while he is in debt. He allows himself nothing, not even a cigar. It is true that the two hundred dollars per month is a large income, but it is possible only in a city where the rents and other expenses are proportionately great; if he were to curtail the latter, he would lose the former. You may tell him not to worry, and of course it would be heroic for a refined and sensitive soul not to feel any anxiety for the future, whose opportunities he had mortgaged, and whose only hope lay in the operation of the statute of limitations. To advise him not to worry is not to solve the problem. If you are in a bottomless pit, and climb up one foot, then fall back two, and continue to move at this rate, how long will you keep at it without some worrying?

Between the case just cited and that told by Mr. Gough, we see the two extremes; one with something to worry for, the other with really nothing. History shows us one kind of solution in the lives of men who have been recklessly careless, whose lack of worrying has been a total lack of interest. They have attended to the battle of the world while giving no thought to the struggle at home; and wife and children have died, leaving these husbands to carry on the conflict with less burdens, like the swimmer who sank with three children clinging to his neck, and rose to the surface without them. The statement was recently made in public that men were not attracted to married life because of this condition; that they preferred the certainty of their freedom and its independence to the other certainty of being unable to support a sickly wife and children. It is a fact that the most suitable men, otherwise, for matrimony will not allow themselves to be carried into the vortex; fewer of the desirable men marry; they admit this to be the reason, and the condition is getting worse every year. Only yesterday a gentleman remarked, "I am a bachelor, or soon will be so-called. I owe nobody. Single life means to me freedom from worry." And he gave his reasons in full.

Let us see what they are. He went on to say, "I have an income of two or three thousand dollars a year from my business. I spend one thousand a year on myself. The woman who would be my wife would desire a thousand for herself. She would be right. The rent and plain expenses would eat up all the rest of my income; and to half live, I must run in debt. Now I save up a thousand a year against the future rainy days; if I were to get married I would exhaust the rainy day fund, incur debts I could never pay, and worry myself sick." Another man said: "I earn a thousand dollars a year, and have an extra income of two hundred dollars, making a total of one hundred dollars a month. This is good. I proposed to a girl, and we got ready to be married. I told her what my income was before the proposal. Her mother kindly figured out that we could not possibly live in a house, as the daughter could not cook, and a servant would be out of the question; therefore we must board. We cast about to find a suitable place for boarding; the least desirable was twenty dollars a month, each, for meals and twenty-five for a room if we had but one room; a sum of sixty-five dollars. Then there must be at least twenty-five per month allowed as pin-money to the wife, five dollars for laundering, ten for theaters, as she had always been so brought up; and here we exceeded my salary. So I stopped. Not a cent remained to pay for my own clothing, and there was no chance of laying by a little every month as a nucleus for a home. When the suggestion was made by the good lady, to the effect that a baby might appear once in every year or two, and that nurses, doctors and help must then be had, we turned pale as death." This man has never married. The girl is a spinster with no prospects. His recent words on the subject were: "We both did right. Marriage under those conditions would have been a hell, and I am glad I am out of it." When deliberate thought and judgment are paramount to love, few marriages occur. The woman cannot be blamed; the man cannot be blamed.

Fussing and faultfinding are detrimental to magnetism, and these things arise in marriage more than in single life. It is not that we would discourage wedlock, but that we wish to state the facts when we say that, in that state, the man and woman both have more difficulties to surmount than otherwise. The wife is harassed by little cares, each trifling in itself, but wearying in the accumulation; and the husband, who has always been selfishly wrapped up in himself, now finds demands made on his time and patience that he never would have dreamed possible. Then he begins to fret, to fuss, and find fault, as though the f's were following him like an avenging spirit. His magnetism flies away; it is in chaotic confusion.

When we look into the lives of the most magnetic men of history we find them selfish in their devotion to their public work, and neglectful of family. These great men do not take their wives and children with them in their careers; they may provide well for their maintenance, give them fine estates, and spend their vacations at home, or bring them to some place of residence that may suit their prominent stations in life, leaving them there as they go forth to their greater work. Daniel Webster rarely ever took his family from Marshfield, Massachusetts, in those years when he was a rising star. Rufus Choate tore himself away from all home cares in the professions of law and politics, and rarely ever knew what was going on, except when within the walls of the dwelling, and then only so far as himself and his books were concerned. Edward Everett had won international fame before he was married, and his brilliant public career was free from home cares even to the last days of his usefulness. He traveled without his family in that remarkable tour of lectures in which he raised sixty thousand dollars for the fund to rescue Mt. Vernon from the hands of speculators. Charles Sumner had but a few days of married life, walking out of his home never to enter it again. And we might go on without limit, citing the lives of the world's magnetic men who have been compelled to live in freedom from home cares in order to secure control of themselves in careers of grandeur.

Exceptions to this rule are so few as to not bear examination; their very scarcity being proof of the main fact. The successful men of genius, whose magnetism has paved the way to fame, are either unmarried, or are free from home cares and worry. Gladstone is cited as an example to the contrary; but what are the facts in his case? His wife, either by an acute knowledge of life, or by some kind spirit of intuition, did in fact accompany him on all his tours of oratory in which his magnetism was most displayed; yet she did this not to place the burden of her care upon him, but to relieve him of that and of all thought of himself. She watched his health momentarily, listened to his speeches, arranged through her own efforts and those of others all the details of travel, and left him free from all worry. Indeed this case, that is quoted as an exception to the claim that magnetism cannot endure or survive the wear and tear of trifles, such as surround the married man, is proof of the efficiency of such freedom, for Mrs. Gladstone had the rare faculty of protecting her husband from such annoying influences. She even knew what was best in diet, day by day; she went so far as to select the clothing needed by the changing temperature, and it was her pleasure to watch every effect made by him for success or weakening, so that she might guide him by her advice. Such a wife would save any man a vast amount of magnetism. Such a wife was Mrs. Blaine, who watched her husband as devotedly, although she did not always accompany him.

Opposed to these queenly influences are the fretting and fussing wives that lean altogether upon their husbands, exacting not only all the large and small attentions due, but requiring them to manage the household affairs from the least to the greatest details. The man who plays nurse at home, who is housemaid and kitchen adviser, whose little moments are consumed in petty chores that yield no return for the time expended, can never hope to rise above such conditions. He is anchored in a small rivulet, and will never hear the waters of the mighty river of life sweeping past him, much less catch the sound of the magnetic ocean beyond. We advise all who can control their fate to develop the greatest magnetism in those years which precede marriage, as did Everett and others; then success is within reach before the cares come, and the fretting things may be ignored or thrust upon attaches.

The habit of borrowing trouble starts with very little provocation, and sooner or later grows to be a mountain. Those who suffer from it are useless to themselves and almost so to others. It is the looking ahead, and taking to heart the possibilities, however remote, of something befalling. Due care is necessary at all times to avert much of the sickness and misfortune that would otherwise come; but there is a vast difference between stepping aside to let the carriage pass, and sitting down on a rock to bemoan the chances of your distant relative being run over by the same vehicle. One act is caution born of judgment, the other is a vision of distress created out of a weak brain or deficient character.

MYSTIC UTOPIAN SUPERMEN

Trouble-borrowers are always in debt to unknown happiness, and are always making their payments to the account of misery.

Owing to an imperfect adjustment of things, there are real troubles that come to all persons; some seem to arrive in droves, like cattle on the stampede; others hold aloof till later life, and are gentle in their approach. It is natural for parents and elderly relatives to be taken away before you are called to go, and you may be compelled to see these dear ones laid to rest, one after the other, although it is possibly your wish that they outlive you. "I hope to die first," said the wife to her husband. "But what of my loneliness V 9 he asked. Funerals have a most depressing influence over many persons, as they realize the fact that they must pass through the agony of dissolution. Not one can escape its dread toils. The older we live, the less we fear death. We get tired of life by having too much of it. So the reasoning goes. The better way is to realize the great responsibilities of living, and let death stand out of your thoughts.

Most persons make some mistake in life and are weighted down by the thoughts of it. They seem to see the finger of scorn always pointed at them, as though there were no erasing of misdeeds. Conscience did not prevent them committing the error, but remorse follows the act like a dark bird whose wings overshadow every good purpose. There is no past. Actions proceed in chains, and the links of sin may forge their consequences in divine goodness. The after effects of wrong are vision's that live in fewer minds than the sufferer supposes. Good men and women fall, some suddenly, and some from great heights; but there is no crime, however black, that cannot be lived down and wiped out on earth and in the records of the hereafter by resolute goodness. There is no< past. You of yesterday, who broke the commandments, are not the same person who today honestly keeps them.

If you worry because of the errors of the past, take courage in the thought that the past dies in its going. There is no past today, nor will there be tomorrow. He who resolves, and actually begins, to do right, overthrows the soul, that was steeped in crime. The same body changes continually; the soul is driven off, and a new being enters in its place. Only the minds of mortals, only the memories of defective humanity, are able to recall the iniquities of the past in the lives of those who are honestly resolved to act right. Neither God Himself, nor any angel in heaven remembers the evil committed by one who is saved. It is an impossibility, because there is no past. If it were not so, what pleasure would there be for you to go to heaven, and there meet the girl you have wronged, the father who slew your mother, the sister who brought shame upon her home, the wife who was unfaithful, or the brother who robbed the bank?

Life is in the present, though always searching out the path for the future. Hugo could not remember much of the first years of his existence, and nothing of the epochs in which he had previously been on earth, as he chose to believe, for to him there could be no past. He had no positive proof of such prior living in the flesh, but merely entertained it as a belief. Knowing the calmness of mind that is produced by such a glance backward and a look forward, he worried about nothing. It is sufficient for us to secure our calmness from the fact that a hundred years hence not even our grandchildren's posterity will know anything of our having dwelt upon the planet. As our ancestors of a hundred years ago are not known today, except perhaps by name, so we must be brushed off the globe as indistinct characters, whose only force will be in the spelling of the words that may be attached to our place in the lineage.

Under such circumstances is it worth while to worry? Care should be taken to avoid all the mistakes, miseries and misfortunes of this life; no duty should be neglected ; the best of earth that is honestly attainable should be secured to our use; love and pleasure, enjoyment and happiness should be courted and won; but no man or woman should worry. "Is it worth while?" Look at the opening illustration of this principle; think where your ancestors of a hundred years ago are today, and where you will be a century hence; then become philosophical. Napoleon was immovable when he chose. Not a line on his countenance revealed the impression that the most exciting circumstances made within. Some of the most successful men and women have trained themselves against display of feeling in the presence of others, and this must come out of a perfect control of self when alone. Worry is full of life-destroying influences. It sends its millions to the grave every year. It kills life, heart, magnetism and brain. It is the enemy of ambition, the executioner of happiness.

Pain weakens magnetism.

This is the Twenty-sixth Principle. The nervous system yields out its vitality during pain, and it goes from the body in large quantities. It is not possible for a person who is thus afflicted to remain calm, except under so great a strain in the effort that weakness must follow, and this is almost as wearying as the suffering itself. It is true that some may cultivate the power of forgetting or not feeling the agony that is racking the system; but this requires will of the strongest kind, and while the mind is thus closed against the sensation, the loss of energy is going on just the same.

Pain is always accompanied by a rapid waste of magnetism. It is claimed by some that pain is caused by this waste. If not, where does pain originate ? It is in the nerves, felt by the nerves, and conveyed to the brain by the nerves. A pulling, stretching, pressing or severing of the nerves may awaken their action to the sensation called pain. But why not the bones or cords likewise? Why should the nerves alone contain the power of suffering ? The answer may be: To warn us of danger. But why not any other part as well? And how is this alarm produced? Do the nerves vibrate in pain? Are they contorted? Does not the electric fire flash in minute subdivision along the fine fibers? These are certainly the facts, and we may resolve them into a simple law, somewhat as follows:

Pain is an excitement of the nerve fibers caused by a violent movement of the electricity of the body along the fibers , thereby heating them intensely.

In support of this theory are the following facts:

1. Electricity is heating.

2. Pain is always attended by heat.

3. The electricity of the body is part of its vitality.

4. The vitality is quickly exhausted by pain.

5. Great pain is liable to deplete the body of all its vitality, producing death.

6. When we burn our flesh the nerves alone suffer, and their destruction ends the pain.

7. The cure of pain is not in conflict with this theory.

MYSTIC UTOPIAN SUPERMEN

It is known that if a nerve be pressed by the finger so as to shut off its flow of electricity, or if it be severed, or drugged to accomplish the same end, all pain above the cutoff still remains, but all feeling below or beyond the cutoff is instantly lost and cannot be restored until the current is allowed to flow there again. Devices of every kind have been thought of to hold in check this fluid of life, so as to cause less suffering. The gum at the teeth is frozen by cocaine to make extraction painless; but the half-destroyed flesh will not heal rapidly, and the idea is not favored by all dentists on that account. Hypnotism is considered an excellent anaesthetic, for the most difficult amputations may be performed by its aid; but the loss of vitality is just as great, and the deadening of all the other functions, as in catalepsy, makes it harder to revive the patient. "Now wake up" exclaims the operator, after the leg has been removed; but the patient does not wake up.

Troublesome teeth should be removed if the pain cannot be overcome in any other way. There are very decided reasons why decayed teeth should not be allowed to remain, the foremost of which is the loss of magnetism and the lowering of all vitality throughout the body, including that of mind, of heart, of stomach and of respiration. These losses mean less pleasure as well as less health in life. Decay of the teeth always contains bacteria of disease, and some of these are of the diphtheria species. There are numerous instances of continued sore throats, bronchial catarrh, sores, abscesses, and other maladies, that have been cured only by the removal of decayed teeth. We recall over a hundred cases where persons have been unable to develop any magnetism on account of this condition, who, under advice, have had the upper teeth taken out and plates substituted, thus putting in clean, strong teeth that cannot ache or decay; and the result has been almost marvelous in health and vitality as well as in the acquisition of magnetism.

Pain should not be endured, and especially not in these intensely aching little agents. Even the lower teeth are now substituted by the bridge system, so that much misery is averted. A dull, throbbing, unending pain in so sensitive a thing as a tooth is always a drain upon the vitality of the body. A neuralgic headache is equally deplorable, and ninety per cent of humanity suffer from this one malady alone, not knowing that the cure is within the reach of all, as set forth in the fifth degree book of the Ralston Club. Yet few persons take the required interest in themselves to keep off this kind of pain. To endure it is to make a magnetic life impossible. Neuralgia is simple in its cause and as simple in its remedy.

Other forms of pain, as of dyspepsia, rheumatism and sore lungs, are detrimental to a magnetic existence. They can be conquered, and should be expelled from the system as soon as possible; not only because they drain it of its vitality and health, but because they are unnecessary. They are due to varied causes, one of the most prolific of which is the reversing of the order of eating, or taking the heavy meal at the close of the day, and then having little or no appetite for breakfast. This is the height of stupidity, and, like most other kinds of nonsense, is popular with the sickly classes. The absence of the morning meal, or of a strongly nutritious breakfast, is the cause of some forms of headache and stomach trouble, which most persons prefer to endure rather than try the cure.

Insomnia is caused by erratic nerves.

This is the Twenty-seventh Principle. In the present age of reckless disregard to the health of body and mind this malady is on the increase, and that most rapidly. We do not propose to discuss the remedy, as it is very simple as well as completely effective, as stated in the fifth degree book of the Ralston Club. We wish to state, in this connection, that when the tendency to insomnia is apparent, it is useless to spend any time in the present course of study, except so much as may be necessary to accumulate willpower enough to follow the cure stated in the book we have mentioned.

It is however quite true that where sleeplessness is due to conditions that do not arise from a wrong diet, or from wrong physical habits, its cure is within the province of this volume of advanced magnetism, and then largely through regime and the use of willpower. Sleep is not likely to come to one whose magnetism is kept too active late in the evening, unless the ability to open and shut the brain at will has been acquired. This is discussed under another principle herein. The eating of foods that produce excessive vitality, as of the phosphatic kind, will tend to keep the nerves awake if eaten within four hours before retiring. So the use of muscle-making diet will keep the muscles twitching, and thus prevent sleep. All these matters are discussed in the Ralston Health books.

In the present age, which is the least magnetic of any, the custom of going without breakfast, or eating one that is too light, because of a lack of appetite, and which originates from the still more dangerous custom of eating a heavy meal in the evening, is fast destroying the vitality of the people. It is never safe to commence the duties of the day without a good breakfast to lean upon. The usual idea of working or exercising early in the morning, in order to create an appetite that cannot possibly come with an overloaded system from the night before, is as ill in its results as it is wrong in principle, for it calls into circulation and into the organs that need the best blood, the very worst; giving the stomach and heart the matter that is becoming effete. The yellow and bilious skin is evidence of such a reversal of the proper plan of eating.

Add to the weakened organs a lessened vitality that comes from the lack of sound sleep at night, and the explanation of the fact that this era is the least magnetic known is easily understood.

A condition that prevents sleep is always a dangerous one, and no time should be lost in correcting it, not by the senseless proceeding of taking drugs, but by going at once to the source and starting there. Of all the modern schemes, for shortening life, and destroying happiness while life lasts, the most inane is that which fails to recognize that an inverted method of living is the cause of disturbed slumber, dreams that tire, and insomnia itself; while drugs that deaden the heart and nerves are used to force sleep against the continued abuse of life. It is exactly as sensible for a person to place a flame under the extended hand^ and then seek to rely upon anesthetics to deaden all sensibility to pain while refusing to withdraw the fire.

Nearly all kinds of weakness in this age are traceable to such a lack of judgment. As far as health is concerned, the matter rests in the care of those who wish freedom from disease. As far as magnetism is concerned, it is necessary to have the best of health as a basis, and there must be release from continuous pain; there must be natural vitality and sound sleep. It is true that, after a fund of magnetism has been secured, a person may take greater chances with health than before, as the extra vitality will permit abuse. The greater the life, the more reckless its owner may be, but while vitality is being sought it is dangerous to abuse it.

MYSTIC UTOPIAN SUPERMEN

A lapse of thought is a brief hypnotic condition.

This is the Twenty-eight Principle. When the engineer of an express, under pressure of excitement, opened the throttle of his engine and crossed in front of a flying train, he did so because he could not think. His mind was a blank. Another engineer, who had struck a carriage, killing two human beings, stopped at the place of the accident, then went ahead and took a siding to await the passing of a "flyer." As the swiftly-going locomotive approached, he advanced his train and was killed in front of the 6 'flyer .' 9 His lapse cost his life and two engines.

These absences of mind are very common, and show that incidents may temporarily hypnotize. They are too serious to be passed over lightly at this time. It is a common experience with nearly every person to pass through moments or parts of moments in which consciousness is a blank; and this is excused on the ground that the mind, being busy with more important things, could not attend to lesser details. Such an excuse should never bo tolerated by one who wishes to be useful to himself or to the world. An animal can think of but one thing at a time, and it is generally known that if we can engross the attention in one direction, advantage may be taken in another; but this is not true of human beings who are mentally able to guard their interests. It is through the maintenance of a single idea at a time that educators of animals succeed in mastering them.

The lapse of thought gives opportunity to tricksters as well as to those who seek legitimate control of their fellow beings. Nothing is more interesting than to watch the sleight-of-hand performer as he openly introduces or removes details of his entertainment while engrossing the attention of his audience in some matter that is strong enough to keep them engaged for a minute or two in following its action. Thus, standing at one comer of the platform or stage, he will hold up something under circumstances that give rise to suspicion, and will ask his audience to watch him closely, so as to detect any attempt on his part to deceive them. The matter is well worth watching, for it would react upon him if he should expose this part of his work as a mere trick to keep their eyes away from some more important change going on in the center .of the stage. Every eye is focused upon what he is doing; and, no matter how important any other action on another part of the stage might be, the audience would not notice it, unless something occurred to transfer their attention. It is very hard to watch two or more proceedings going on at the same time some distance apart.

So well known is this fact that dramatic companies do not hesitate to take advantage of it. When an actor is delivering his lines, or two or more are engaged in a portrayal of absorbing interest, others of the company, who happen to be on the stage at the same time, are content to merely balance the scene and form an entertaining tableau to which a little byplay is added. It is only when the general action is evenly distributed in several parts of the arena that audiences attempt to catch what is going on in more than one place at a time. Even those who have attended the performances of skillful prestidigitators for the purpose of detecting what is done in those moments when the attention of the audience is being held to one corner of the stage are generally unable to withdraw their gaze and scan other portions of the platform. We recall a party of investigators who could not possibly follow the details which were enacted by an assistant in the center while the performer stood lower down, close to the footlights, although both could have been clearly seen; but a more practiced observer noted the bringing in of properties, the presence of which could not afterward be accounted for by the audience.

Lapses of mind occur in everyday life; and it is sometimes claimed that the busier a person may be, the more frequently these vacuities happen; but this assertion can be challenged. A person may be on the positive side of magnetism and yet allow the mind to suffer a lapse. The subconscious faculty, even when it gives rise to the brilliant evidences of the highest genius, is in a lapsed state; its gifts of fancy, its dreams of coming realism, its charming leaps into the realm of intuition, and the glimpses it often catches of the inmost secrets of life, are all born in subconsciousness. During the moments, hours, and sometimes days, in which genius revels in this realm, the mind is not a negative magnetic force, although its condition is lapsed; yet, in such moods, the poet, the author, the orator, the artist or other dreamer may he taken advantage of.

Evidences of this character are found in the lives of most geniuses. Daniel Webster was always without funds, although he received as high as one hundred thousand dollars for his services in a single case. His money disappeared as fast as he received it; he was preyed upon by all kinds of beggars, by his impecunious friends, and by claimants in every station of life, even being so forgetful as to pay the same bill six times. The Biggs Bank, of Washington, D. C., still holds an unpaid note of his for the amount of one thousand dollars, which he endorsed for the accommodation of a friend, he receiving five hundred dollars for his own use. Any biography will show greater aberrations of mind in lesser geniuses; but we cite the case of Webster for the reason that a man whose brain outweighed those of his contemporaries, and who carried upon his shoulders the weight of the American Constitution, would be able to attend to the lesser details of his own affairs.

Under another principle it will be seen that the ablest men and women possess the gift of subconsciousness in slight degree at least, while wielding a majestic power on the magnetic side; and this doubling of two opposites separates the few individuals from the great masses of mankind. In analyzing such characters we find that the magnetism on the positive side does not save the individual from the lapse on the negative side, and this is why persons who are gifted in some department of life are so easily taken advantage of and become the marks of schemers. It is recorded of one person, whose exceptional ability gained for him more than two hundred thousand dollars in a single year, that he lost it all to sharpers within the space of one week.

Passing out of the realm of genius we come to the everyday ranks of life, and find included herein many capable men and women, and those of high as well as low intelligence. Lapses, with them, are perhaps not so common as in the limited class to which we have just referred, and they show a negative condition generally unattended by any periods of positive magnetism. As we have previously stated, these are often charged to crowded duties or the many cares of the day. We know that the genius would be more successful in life if he suffered less from the consequences of his own vacuities, and the same is true of all men and women. In fact, the penalties to be paid by the ordinary individual are always greater in proportion, for there is not usually the gift of recuperation. Edwin Booth was led into an enterprise that cost him his entire fortune of nearly a million and an indebtedness of almost as much more; but his genius was of such a high order that he recuperated completely, paid his notes in full, and left a vast fortune at the time of his death. General Grant was taken advantage of at a time of his life, when, owing to sickness, he was unable to recover from his losses, and became the object of a princely charity.

Nearly all errors of judgment, nearly all accidents, nearly all missteps in life are chargeable to lapses of mind, when, if the magnetism were only a positive force, an unbroken line of victory might be maintained. Experience is a splendid school, but does not come to the aid of him who needs it most until severe losses have been endured. The farmer who, by hearing of misfortunes of his neighbors, has schooled himself against similar experiences, and who is taken advantage of by the cheap magnetism of some traveling agent, wonders why he could permit himself to be fooled in this way. Were it not for such negative conditions among those who enjoy the training of city experience, the three-card-monte man, the green goods dealer and the bunco-steerer would not count as their prey so many men of supposed business sagacity.

Forgetfulness is one form of lapse, but it is strictly an absence of memory, which need not indicate a lack of magnetism, although most persons who are magnetic have remarkably retentive memories. The true lapse appears in the vacuity of mind, where there is no tax placed upon the memory. Common illustrations of these are seen daily; and it is well known that the lapse is most frequent where the mind has the fewest cares. You may talk to a person in a voice loud enough to be heard rods away, and with enunciation that does not miss the full execution of a single syllable, yet the person addressed may know nothing of what you say, although there may be a pretense of having heard it all. Shame sometimes prevents the admission of such a lapse, so that the thought, with whatever of value it contains, is lost upon the air. Against this lapse the ordinary speaker is continually contending, and so common is it that he ejaculates, at the end of every idea, the interrogation, "See?" and waits for the response, "Yes," before proceeding further.

We recall the case of a lady who, in her desire to avoid the usual interrogatory ejaculations of "See?" "Don't you know?" "Don't you see?" "Do you understand?" uses a rising inflection, and asks the question merely by her intonations, and waits, before proceeding, until the person to whom she is speaking replies, "Yes." This peculiar mannerism is an exact substitute for the ordinary expressions which we have just cited; and it is safe to say that, as her attention has never been called to it, she is entirely oblivious of it. The following will serve as an example: "We went down as far as the bridge, and saw the train coming (?), so we stopped for a few minutes until the train had passed (?). It was going very fast and made a great deal of smoke (?). We hurried on, and waited at the side of the bridge for a freight train to pass (?) on the other track." At each place where the interrogation mark (?) appears in the foregoing quoted sentences the speaker raises her voice, uses a rising inflection, looks at the person addressed, waits until she receives some sign of acquiescence from the latter, and then goes on. If you ever have occasion to listen to a conversation carried on by two or more ladies during a social visit, you will notice that one of them continually reverses this mannerism by ejaculating "Yes," by which she indicates that she is paying full attention to what is being said, and thus prevents the use of the inquiry, "See ?" which would otherwise be used.

MYSTIC UTOPIAN SUPERMEN

Persons who are busy mentally while engaged in the performance of duties often suffer vexing lapses. This is so common with some persons as to be almost a nervous disease. We recall the case of a carpenter who would lay down a tool in one part of a building on which he was working, and who would spend considerable time in hunting it up. It is true that skilled laborers can easily recall where each tool is placed, unless they are afflicted with this vacuity of mind. The lapse occurs more frequently with those who are not pursuing their usual vocations at the time. In the use of garden tools it is very common for the amateur tiller of the soil to lay down a hoe, a rake, or spade in some place, and one minute after not have the slightest idea where it was put. This fault is so common as to prove annoying in the life of almost every individual. But it is a habit that can be cured by means of the methods we teach.

Exposure to colds and conditions that tend to lessen the vitality and bring on disease may occur during a lapse of the mind or a weakness of the will. A person who is clad for indoors will escort a friend out of the room, and stand talking at the open door, where a chilling atmosphere is quickly stealing away the vitality, yet has no mental knowledge of the great risk which is being run. Carelessness of this kind has filled many a grave where the health seemed perfect, and the person has passed through the days and weeks of suffering, making a brave fight for life, and dying without for a moment having realized that the fatality was due to this almost unaccountable lapse. So children are continually being exposed to the dangers of dampness, draughts and colds, and parents wonder why so many children are lost.

Lapses of mind are dangerous in many cases and have led to misfortunes that might easily have been averted. There is no doubt that they are due and chargeable to negative magnetism, and could be prevented by the study and acquisition of positive magnetism. It seems to us that this is a duty. Not many years ago the practice began of examining all applicants for railway positions, to ascertain if they were colorblind; and there is no doubt that the rejection of such as were so afflicted has led to greater security in the service. It is fully as easy to test the magnetic condition of men and women and their susceptibility to lapses. Nearly all the marine horrors and railroad holocausts would then be averted.

Strangest among disasters are those that come to reliable men, whose many years of experience should guard them against accident. This disposition to lapses comes with oft repeated monotony. An examination should be made once every year after a long period of service. Suppose the test in the time of first applying for a position should prove that the individual is not subject to lapses; then, after many years of faithful employment, another test is made, and the same person is found deficient in this regard; the only conclusion is that the constant attention to one line of duties has served to develop a state of negative magnetism, as any monotony will do. Hence comes the unaccountable accident to the old and reliable engineer or sea-captain; and most of the terrible calamities are attributable to them.

What caused the engineer to continue his train at reckless speed, contrary to custom and to signals, knowing that another train was due to pass in front of him on a cross-track? He was not a drinking man, nor had he shown evidence of mental weakening. He rode openly to his death, and carried over eighty souls with him. He ranked among the most experienced, the coolest and clearest-headed of the engineers of the line. What caused another, equally careful and skillful, engineer to neglect to take the siding as usual, to allow a regular train to pass, instead of which he went blindly on, and collided at fearful speed on a sharp curve? What causes so many signaling men to give the wrong order, or to forget a plain duty? These must be lapses.

The majority of the fearful wrecks at sea are due to these temporary vacuities of mind. It is otherwise unaccountable that the best masters of these ocean palaces should deliberately take their boats into positive danger. They do not commit the blunders thoughtfully, in an effort to get greater speed, or shorter distance out of the course; for then the results might be attributed to mistaken judgment. They do it thoughtlessly, stupidly, amazingly. When the question is put to one of them, if he has survived, the answer is: "I found myself out of the true course, but how I got there I do not know." And this is true.

The bridegroom-elect who slipped one cog in his memory and went to his wedding one day late, was not as cordially welcomed as one who went on Tuesday, instead of Wednesday; in the latter case the bride forgave him, and made him comfortable for twenty-four hours, while in the former instance she married the best man, and left a cold meal for the latecomer. It seems that there are certain persons in whose minds a complete vacuum is formed for everything except the routine details of life, and these may go amiss. The actor who is unable to remember his lines in the early days of a play is quite different from the one who, after knowing them perfectly for a year or more, suddenly loses them; in the first instance it is a failure of the memory, in the other it is a lapse of mind. For this reason, when companies in such profession perform the same play for a year or more, the custom is to have prompters for the first few weeks, and, about a year later, to return the prompters. "Saying the same lines so frequently makes me lose them," says a well-known actor.

On the witness stand many an honest man and woman has been made out a liar, and so ignorant are judges of this phase of the mind that they often turn to the witnesses and severely rebuke them for contradicting themselves. Reputable citizens are compelled to submit to insult, browbeating and chicanery from lawyers who are unfit to be received in the plain homes of our land; they are tricked into wrong answers by misleading and foxy questions; they are denied the right of continuous reply under cross-examination, being required to answer parts of things to suit the whims of attorneys, whose low animal cunning is palmed off as the current coin of ability; and thus hemmed in between a desire to tell the truth, a wish to obey the court, and a contempt for the lawyer who is nagging them, the most honest witnesses are led to say things in one breath and to deny them in another. When cases are tried and adjudged in a businesslike manner and under the rules that would govern the settling of mercantile affairs, then the courts will be held in respect by the public. It is to the shame of the supposed system of American justice that nine cases out of every ten, ninety out of a hundred, nine hundred out of a thousand, are disposed of on technical grounds called law, wherein honesty is dwarfed or ignored. A board of directors of any institution, even one that involves millions of dollars, will satisfactorily transact an enormous amount of business in three hours, whereas courts of supposed justice, ignoring business principles, and sneering at common sense, will drag a fifty-dollar suit for three years. The uncertainty of trials, the petty brains of trickery, the flood of technicalities which men called judges childishly administer as evidence of wisdom, and the reverse of all rules of honest procedure, have made witnesses the target of doubt, stupidity and cheap cunning; hence the fact that trials smut and besmirch the reputations of honorable men and women through the conditions involved in mental lapses, need not excite wonder. The only prevention of this deplorable result is in the study of magnetism, as was seen in the perfect mastery that Henry Ward Beecher, during weeks of cross-examination, maintained over Judge Fullerton, who took rank as one of the most skillful and adroit examiners of his era. Never for a moment did that splendid genius of magnetism relax control over his would-be tormenter. It was the battle of giants, with but one victor.

So much distress and suffering are the consequences of lapses that life cannot be considered secure with one who is subject to them. Compromising bits of conduct, answers not intended, consents, agreements, contracts and transactions that involve irreparable loss, are due to lapses. Many an old man skilled in business matters by years of experience, has lost all the savings, all the wealth of a lifetime of accumulation, because, in some lapse of mind, he has sanctioned some foolhardy undertaking, or entered in a losing arrangement. In such ways old men are ruined. When asked why they made the errors, they reply that they do not know.

Superstition destroys magnetism.

This is the Twenty-ninth Principle. This is a fertile and abundantly fruitful subject for discussion; but, being so well understood by the public, very little need be said at this place. When life was not worth living, persons looked for death from almost any source; and, in some of the centuries, when better things should have been expected, very few died natural deaths. Mystery, uncertainty, violence and ignorance made a quartet that caused humanity to dance attendance on every kind of fear and apprehension.

Natural phenomena puzzled the minds of all until science came in with her rational explanations; noises of rumbling thunderclouds far away, or of unusual heavings of the ocean, were taken as sounds of approaching earthquakes, causing the utmost fright; the howling of the dog within a year after somebody had died was the forewarner of another death within the same community during the coming year, especially if the locality was thickly settled; the blood-red sky told of war in any degree of horror that the rich coloring depicted by its depth of hue, and the same was fulfilled in such periods as those when England entertained the conflicting hordes who called themselves the champions of the roses; the presence of the black cat causes cold shivers to trace themselves up and down the spinal column, because this visitor brought evil, and his going away was the harbinger of luck; and so on, through a hundred thousand volumes of description, we might proceed to unfold the vagaries of those dark centuries.

That superstition is the master of most men and women in this day of enlightenment is too apparent to be denied. Few are exempt from its hypnotic influences, despite the soft denial of the fact. Look at any person whose mind passes into a lapse, and you will find one who is highly superstitious. Brooding over the latter will cause the former; and by this means a person may become self hypnotized; for fear, monotony of thought, and brooding tend to develop negative magnetism. Superstitious business men sooner or later go under. In their affairs the keenest judgment is often called for, and transactions that require action one way or the other, involving mental decisions based on a careful weighing of the prospects of success, are guided by the cheap claptrap of superstition.

When placed in the balance the element of chance or luck takes precedence of judgment. A splendid opportunity for securing property, or of trading in some way, is allowed to go by because the day is Friday, or may be the thirteenth of the month. Actors religiously avoid managerial officers on Friday and Saturday, and crowd them on the first days of the week; it is no longer fear that deters them from signing contracts on unlucky days; it is a settled business habit, just as fixed in its nature as the path of a lamb around a certain stump. Young men in business often "toss up" in deciding what to do when in doubt, although they would soon learn that judgment is a good guide if they would train it to act for them, and they oftener allow some bit of superstition to control their action.

The belief in a thousand and one details of daily conduct hampers the life of many a well endowed man and woman. The fear that to do a certain act, or at a certain time, or in a certain way will invite maladies or disasters, is like a weight of lead about the neck, strangling the breath, and hindering all attempts at progress. A woman sums up well when she says: "A fool told me that to walk under a ladder meant death sure within the year. I discovered, alas! too late, that I walked under a ladder one morning, and for twelve months I was useless in my family, in my duties and in my studies. I was in a state of weakness all the time. When the year was ended I was relieved, and you may be sure that I gave that fool a piece of my mind for the suffering she had caused me." This brief letter is a concise presentation of the case.

The ablest business men and the most successful persons of either sex have openly and fully defied the claims of superstition. A New York merchant opened his store for the first time on a Friday, another on the thirteenth of a month, and Daniel Frohman postponed the opening day of one of his most successful plays from the eleventh to the thirteenth day, in order to challenge superstition; and all these enterprises were eminently prosperous. The true man need not go out of his way, either to challenge or to avoid the claims of superstition, unless he wishes to test their stupidity.

There can be no magnetism of durable quality where there is a belief in any superstition, even one. Such belief forces the acts of the persons out of the direct line of good judgment, and destroys some part of the freedom of the will. If a single one of the many notions now prevalent can be accepted as having weight, others will follow; for any hypnotic habit grows rapidly. " Proof positive/ ' so-called, that these notions have proved true, is nonsense sheer and simple. The weight of fear, based upon some apprehension of calamity, may break down the vitality and lead to dire consequences; but such result is due to self-hypnotism, inspired by the fear. This point is well illustrated in the invented superstition, which was originated some years ago by three men whose purpose was to ascertain if negative magnetism could not be induced by mere fear. They asserted that six was a more fatal number than thirteen; that if six persons sat down together, one would die within a year and all within three years; and each cited cases without limit to prove the truth of their claim. This they delivered to a selected party of six women, whom they overtook as by accident. All were impressed; their belief was captured; they separated; one died within the year, the other five went into a decline, two more died in a few months, and it was only by the intervention of third parties that the others could be rescued from their fear. Superstitious belief is hypnotic. It destroys magnetism.

THE dark-section, OF THE mind THE MOST ABJECT FORM OF MENTAL SLAVERY

Everybody has heard of the Dark of the Moon.—The Mind is susceptible of being illuminated by the vitality of the life about it; it also has its shadows, its twilight, and its dark phases. The only phase that is magnetic is that which we call bright. When in the shadows it is uncertain of itself, and lacks the aggressiveness that goes with power. Gradually drifting into the gloom of the twilight it sooner or later enters its dark phase; and it is then unable to see any horizon; its purposes are broken and erratic; there is no course in view; it drifts about under the driving force of false beliefs and is useless to itself and to the world; and may in time either reach the asylum of the insane, or become a source of danger to itself and to others.

In this section of the present Realm we shall endeavor to assist all victims of this condition into safety from its perils.

Certain tests are given here to serve as guides to your own knowledge of yourself; and when you are satisfied that your mind is in its dark phase, the methods of release from this abject bondage will be found in the newer division of this book known as the Realm of the Crystal Mind. You can all see the DARK OF THE MIND must of necessity be the opposite condition from the Crystal Mind. The two terms are self-explanatory. It is hardly necessary for us to say that the professional hypnotist takes advantage of this DARK PHASE in order to find his most ready subjects.

FEAR is first aroused as a test if this condition prevails. There is fear that comes from physical collapse, or what has the appearance of physical collapse; and this is secured through trickery. If the operator places the subject in a standing position facing him, and asks him to stand with the weight of the body on the back part of the heels with the feet together, and gently presses his hand against his chest, there is instantly a feeling of falling; this produces fear in a mind that is in its dark phase, and leads to hypnotic control if the subject is susceptible. If in conjunction with this trick, the operator seeks to weary the eyes of the subject by having him look up either at dancing fingers, or at some bright small object, there is a sense of sleepiness. Let these two sources of fear be combined, and it will be quickly seen if physical fear is present.

The foregoing test applies only to the muscular control of the body and of the eyes; but has served the purpose of professional operators for generations.

As opposed to these examples of physical fear, we have what is known as mental fear, and this may or not express itself through the mood of worry, or a kindred feeling. This we have discussed fully.

As the mind grows darker, there comes a more dangerous mood which is recognized by the coming on of a feeling that something is PORTENDING, that something is about to happen that will bring trouble or reverses. This sense of something impending follows the person and tinctures every act and thought. It is this class that visit the fortune tellers, that have their palms read, and their futures mapped out for so much a sitting. From this class are obtained the recruits to every new cult, and to every abnormal belief.

MYSTIC UTOPIAN SUPERMEN

They are as often people of wealth and social standing as they are poor and unfortunate in this worlds possessions. Great men have been known to fall under the spell of the DARK OF THE MIND. History tells of this mood in some of its most notable characters.

The cure is in finding the Crystal Mind.

The most serious phase of this realm is found in the climax of mental darkness, in the form of obsessions. An obsession is an absorbing belief that cannot be shaken by facts or circumstances. Men who are leaders in the world, who sway masses by their influence which generally asserts itself by statements either in print or byword of mouth, know their subjects; and while not one of them perhaps has ever practiced the art of hypnotism, as an art, they have controlled hundreds and thousands, and in some cases millions of people, by taking advantage of the obsessions that enslave them. It is true that an obsession is a slave master, and its subjects are the most abject of slaves.

The mildest form of domestic obsession is the belief of the mother in the child; leaving the latter to bring itself up; and accomplishing what is known as "spoiling" it. No greater harm could be done the child than to allow it to bring itself up; to shape its own desires and their gratification; and to allow it to learn after bitter disappointments that other human beings have rights. This obsession of the mother who thinks the child could do or think nothing wrong, is that of mental blindness. The result is that the parent is under the unending influence of the offspring; will do anything for it, make any sacrifice, waste energy and money, and eventually give up health and life in order that every whim and notion, wish and demand may be gratified. There are two general classes of criminals in the world: the inherited class and the "spoiled child" class. The latter become headstrong, vicious, quarrelsome and ungovernable; simply because they have always had their own way when young, and insist on overriding all those who stand in their way when they grow up.

Diseased love is a common obsession;, and often leads to murder. It is generally confined to the male sex. The man or young man selects some one of the opposite sex for whom he displays his slimy affection; and becomes persistent and annoying, until the climax comes. This male person believes that his love is worth having, and cannot endure being repulsed.

Bigotry has existed for countless generations. It is always offensive and always steeped in its own convictions. The bigot can be swayed by those who fall in lines with his views; but his belief cannot be shaken. There are some religions that begin in the tenderest years of a child's life to teach it false doctrines, and these beliefs are so deeply wrought into the blood that they are carried to the grave. Many of these victims grow to be successful men and women in other lines, but are always intolerable in religious matters. They are narrow and one-sided. Their minds are like diseased fruit that is healthy on one side only; with the taint of the decay permeating the whole of the flesh.

Inherited obsessions are the most marked when they appear in the form of partisanship. This mental disease came out of the constant conspiracies of groups and sections of people against the established government, leading often to civil strife; and the thirty years' war of the roses in England is the forerunner of the political parties now at strife in America, as well as in England. On analysis it is easy to trace this love of national conspiracies to the desire to overthrow the prevailing government; for one political party has for its goal the destruction of the other party; the party out of power seeking by every means, fair and foul, and foul in ninety per cent of the cases, to drive out of power the party that is ruling the country. A mind that is free from obsession would clearly see that the elected officials of the government were commissioned to perform the business of the nation in the same businesslike manner that prevails among the employees of a great corporation. Look at the management of the business of the greatest railroad in the country; supposing the employees were to divide themselves into two conflicting groups, each seeking the destruction of the other employees, and spending most of their time in abuse and detraction of their fellow employees, would it be safe to travel on that railroad? Yet that is the spectacle we behold of our American Congress, the elected employees of the people; and they retain their hold on office by hypnotizing the public. This condition cries out for correction.

Step into any political meeting anywhere, if you wish the opportunity of studying whole crowds that are hypnotized to the number of thousands; first by their own obsessions, and by the thrilling addresses of their orators who are trading on those obsessions. One form of this mental malady is akin to insanity; such as may be witnessed in the national nominating conventions where thousands cheer the mention of a favorite candidate for fifty-five minutes; while the next mentioned candidate is cheered for fifty-six minutes; and the opposing convention cheers its chief hero for fifty-seven minutes, all of one variety. Men jump high into the air, throw their hats higher, tear the coats from each other, and present a picture that would make bedlam look like a Sunday School session. The hypnotic operator makes his subjects do all these antics, but one or two at a time. The controlling influence of the great convention does the same things by the power of excitement that displaces mental intelligence.

Given an effective speaker, an audience of partisans obsessed by their belief in the necessity of political parties, another party to attack, and a lot of falsehoods as the munitions of the assault, and you have the most pronounced evidence of mass hypnotism in existence.

Party votes in Congress are always examples of hypnotism swaying men of supposed intelligence in the name of party necessity. All members of all parties are hired employees of the nation; they have no other business than to perform the work of the government, yet when a measure comes to a vote these hired employees line themselves on sides, fight each other like cats and dogs but in a mental sense, and quarrel, bicker, make venomous attacks on the honesty of each other, and hold up the business they were sworn to perform, all in the hope that one party may destroy another party. What kind of service would these employees render the great railroad if they divided themselves into two warlike groups and fought for advantage, giving ninety-five per cent of their time and effort to their own greed for office, and their struggle for reelection, while the railroad received only the remaining five per cent of their time and effort?

If you cannot see that partisanship is all wrong; that the reelection of office holders is all wrong; that parties are nothing more than conspiracies; and that the business of the government should be conducted in a businesslike manner; then you are laboring under this same obsession that keeps you in the hypnotic class, and out of the magnetic class. Nor will you ever pass from one to the other until your brain is clear enough to recognize these vital facts.

The mind grows darker as obsessions become free to take full possession of it. The really dangerous stage is reached when crime and violence to others follow this disease. Thousands of murderers have testified that they have been compelled to commit crime by the evil influence of others over them; and the subject has been much discussed by criminologists. Whether the claim is fully true or not, it is a fact that a person may readily become self-hypnotized by an obsession. Religious fanatics are numerous who offer up human sacrifices to their gods, not only in savage lands but in intelligent America. Many children have paid this penalty at the hands of obsessed parents. In like manner, the refusal of a certain cult to call in the services of doctors when members of their families are critically ill has compelled legislatures to enact laws making this homicide or manslaughter; in some States punishable as misdemeanors; but the fact is recognized that it is a crime.

Other religious cults devote themselves to self injury, even in our own America, while still others perform idiotic rites; showing the massed hypnotic influence that is able to sway thousands.

BRAIN STORM is the final climax, this side of actual permanent insanity, that an obsession reaches.

It appears in individuals who are driven by hatred, envy, suspicion, or jealousy, to engage in crime, generally murder, and who are in an hypnotic mood while under its influence. Juries excuse this crime unless it is excessively brutal. The law says that a man who permits himself to get drunk knowing that he may do some act of violence, is not entitled to acquittal, for it was his duty to guard himself against the irresponsibility of intoxication; so the same principle applies to a man or woman who permits an obsessing idea to dethrone the reason even long enough to kill another.

If some woman runs out into the streets screaming that a man has attacked her, whether she does this for revenge as has been the case numerous times, or is justified in making the charge, if the incident occurs in certain States, a mob is quickly formed and the culprit, whether innocent or not, is summarily lynched. The mob is controlled by the hypnotic power of the obsession; it does not dethrone reason, for the rioters are as sane then as before and after the event; but it takes the place of intelligent thinking, and drives the mind to its nonthinking state. The match that fires the magazine of powder is no more dangerous than the suggestion that fires the mob. One county in the middle West has been able to defy the law of the State and of the nation; and could if put to the test defy the law of all creation up to the point of absolute extermination of every man and woman living in it, simply because it is under the hypnotic sway of passion, and lives in a perpetual brain storm.

Wherever riots occur, no matter for what purpose, there we find this mental slavery. There can be no civilization under such conditions.

It is not always the low classes that are swept into massed criminals by an obsession. The fanatic crowds at ball games lose all control over themselves; and it is only the thinnest veneer of self-control that holds them in check from throwing thousands of bottles and other missiles at the umpires and opposing clubs. They are temporarily obsessed and rendered mentally deranged by the desire for victory; just as the fighting Arabs contort their bodies in battle to harmonize with their contorted minds, when they become flying windmills in their plunge against the enemy. The snake dance and other barbaric displays of students through the public streets of a city, ending in riot and destruction of property and danger to the public, are massed forms of hypnosis setting aside all intelligent control of minds that are supposed to be a grade above the savage intellects.

It is necessary to come out of the obsessed class in order to come out of the hypnotic hemisphere and enter that of the magnetic control of others.

SUCCESS in life, whether in the fields of mind, of business, or of body; whether in the acquisition of knowledge, of happiness, or property, or of power, is directly -dependent upon a sustained elasticity of temperament and the buoyancy of hope. Fear depresses and handicaps. Courage is needed to meet the contingencies of battle; and it must be the full, round courage of a broad nature, an unfaltering determination to win all honest victories that can possibly be achieved in the range of one's powers.

We are now entering the estate of peace. By this we do not mean that we are about to retire from the great battlefield of life. On the contrary, we seek to put an end to the warring factions that rage within our own selves, to gather the millions of scattered forces, enlist them all under one grand marshaling, assert control over them, and, wielding a united power, lead them on to success. The greatest victories are achieved by those armies whose purpose is a unit. Man ordinarily is a collection of untamed and widely dispersed energies, over which he has never sought, except in rare instances, to" wield the master's wand. He does not know what is meant by the advice to conquer himself, nor is he aware of the tremendous forces that are possessed by him, awaiting organization and use.

As may be seen by referring to the preceding realm, the chaotic condition of most magnetic persons prevents their use of the powers with which they are endowed. They are not at peace with themselves. They possess energy enough to wield a great influence over the lives of others, and this could very readily be turned to magnetism of a positive character; but they feel too much the impulsive force of this energy, as though it were leading them always astray. They must have excitement. A day of rest, an hour of recuperation is to them a dull period; the tour is slow; life is not worth living, unless they can be always on the go; and thus their vitality runs wild and wastes itself.

There are two classes of persons who enjoy peace within themselves; one is that large division of mankind who are almost devoid of magnetism; the other is a rather small portion, who possess positive powers of magnetism, which they control. The former do not always get peace, for it seems that when they are in a struggle to shake off the weight of influence from outside, that crushes them always to earth, they are in the agonies of suffering. The lower strata of men and women, those who are utterly devoid of magnetism, are the dullest and most stupid of humanity. They are always poor, and are not wide enough awake to wonder at it. They labor and toil on, willing to be led or driven, and are molded by the influences of others. You see them in the lowest classes of contented workmen and women.

Give to the under folks any magnetism, even if it is far below the line where the positive force begins, and then the torment is inaugurated. Then commences the struggle to arise out of the humble estate into one toward which the finger of ambition points the way. Discontent with present conditions, coupled with the handicap that checks progress, indicates such magnetic qualities as, when free, will revolutionize the life that seeks to better itself. Out of their rank have come all, or nearly all, of the supreme minds and courageous leaders of the world. The roll of fame is crowded full of names taken from humble conditions and forced to the front by inherent energy. It is not true that all who are discontented rise to higher planes of life; most of them might, if they knew how to marshal the powers they possess; but about one in ten thousand makes up the mind to go ahead, and then goes ahead. Resolute will never fails; it carries its owner to the loftiest plane of success, no matter how low may be the estate out of which he is taken.

Conflicting emotions, restlessness and discontent, if they are aimed at the lowly condition of unsuccess, if they complain of the meaner stratum in which they are compelled to exist, if they scorn the past and look always to the future, seeking an upward course to better opportunities, these are sure indications of a developing and growing magnetism. Yet they force their possessors to live in confusion; there is no peace; the energies are not mastered, and it is to them that this course of training will come with tremendous force, leading them up out of their vale of conflict. Of such persons about one in ten thousand rises by sheer power of resolution, shaping their destiny by the genius of an undaunted will. Let us see if more than one in that number can be helped.

We will leave the hopelessly stupid class to themselves. As has been said, they include the humblest of toilers, those who seem contented with food, clothing and shelter. A very small proportion of the richer or higher social classes may be said to belong to this rank; they are the sons or daughters of wealth, who are not full-witted, who are unable to think for themselves, and for whom the courts appoint guardians. It is always true that any such person may be wonderfully assisted in overcoming such negative conditions if once they may be made to take an interest in the study and training of magnetism. They rarely care for self-improvement, however.

The most numerous class of persons who are subject to conflict within themselves are not those who are discontented with their present rank and are always looking up, but those who are discontented with everything, and are looking down. Let us fully understand the distinction between the two. Both possess magnetism that might be made positive if the energies within were brought into peace. The first class is on the rising path, with magnetism increasing and the positive vitality coming to them, if they are able to control themselves; and from their ranks come the greatest men and women. They are in conflict with their conditions, but they are looking up to some higher hope. The other class consists of those who are already endowed with positive magnetism, or who have had it; but, being unable to marshal these forces, and to control their use, they have allowed themselves to come under their sway. They are nervous, excitable, irritable, restless, and always at war within themselves.

They are beings run away with by splendid forces which they do not choose, or cannot acquire the energy, to control.

Out of such class come the greatest sufferers. They constitute those of whom we wrote in the preceding realm of this study. It is not easy to know that you are equipped for the best heritage of earth; that in mental endowments, or in the possibility of acquiring them, you take rank with the first classes of mankind; that you were intended by nature for a position far above that which you occupy; that you realize that there are within you the magnificent forces on which you should ride to the grandest success; yet that all is conflict, confusion and waste. Your magnetism, once positive, is now chaos. You see no longer the outlines of that highway over which you had hoped to travel many years ago. All within is at war; you are restless.

From this class you must take the speediest departure possible. It is the realm of distraction. You are already irritable. Many a man and woman has acquired in this incipient malady the seeds of mental breakdown, of the direst disaster. You are given to worrying; this engenders unhappiness. Misery is about you, colored by the hue of your own orbs. Restless in quietude; reading anything and everything to keep down the stormy conflict; seeking something new to satisfy your unquenchable thirst; arising in the morning without taste for the day's duties; going to bed at night, unhappy because the day has been wasted; this routine of half misery and hectic pleasures is taking you down grade very rapidly. It is hoped that you do not belong to the class we have described. If you do, turn about; marshal your distracted and warring forces, and transform defeat into victory. We will help you. More than that, we will guarantee to you the highest rewards of absolute success, from no other source than in the very pages of the present volume.

You should first ascertain if you belong to this class. Remember they are the restless persons who have had, or may have, some positive magnetism, which is running to waste. It is a dangerous class, for the reason that its end is generally disastrous. The excitement that brings no satisfaction; the unrest that knows no peace; these are fast sapping the vitality of heart and brain and nerves. It is a hard class to get out of. You cannot leave it as easily as you think. But it is necessary that you shake all such entanglements out of your life if you ever wish to find solid happiness on earth. Therefore you should talk honestly with yourself, and decide whether or no you belong to this class.

Your chances are better if you are in the discontented underling rank, for that has been the training school of greatness from time immemorial. By underling is not necessarily meant that you are poor, but that your positive magnetic forces are yet in process of formation. In the other class you may have now, or have had at some previous time, such vitality; but it has gone to waste; or, being without mastery, it is on the wane; and to retrace your course is like backing up hill with a team of unruly horses. In the discontented underling class you feel the impulse of unborn energies, which need an intelligent head to lead them on. From the standpoint of a conceited imagination this class is the least desirable of all to be found in, but from the better viewpoint of the chances of progress, and the attainment of success, it is by far the best class. If you are in it, all you need is the guiding help of such a course of training as this book furnishes in order to help you to rise in the world.

We now see four classes spread out before us in the field of our study and examination. Highest above all is that which contains the few but the great men and women, not always famous, but powerful in their influences over the rest of mankind; and this is the magnetic class. Next in rank are the discontented underlings, whose fate it seems to have been these many centuries to send about one in every ten thousand of their number into the higher class through the operation of magnetism acquired by energy of will and an unfaltering determination of purpose. Third in order are the restless, chaotic individuals, who are partly successful in life, who take rank, socially, perhaps above some of the others, but whose magnetism, being uncontrolled, is running to waste. Finally, at the bottom of the scale, are the stupid, contented classes, who have no magnetism of a positive character, who never had and never will; they serve the other strata of humanity.

To which one of these four classes do you belong? It is perhaps of some importance to settle in your own mind this problem; for your method of procedure may be somewhat varied by the answer. More will be said of this later on. It is our duty, at the present juncture, to go directly to work upon the course of training, which is now at hand. Avoid superficial reading and skimming practice. Get down deep into the theme, and make it the most important duty of life for the time being. It masters everything else; it leads to all the success you may ever achieve; and why should it not receive the highest recognition in this world? As Charles Spurgeon said: "If there can be such a thing as having but one great accomplishment, let it be that which will accomplish the most; its name is personal magnetism."

Normal consciousness is normal magnetism.

This is the Thirtieth Principle. It is perhaps a somewhat technical proposition, but may be made clear by a little explanation. The word, consciousness, means the power of the faculties to recognize conditions, impressions, ideas, thoughts and transactions. Here we see the clearness of that force in life which is known as intelligence. Some persons retain more than others, but it may be merely the bulk of accumulation in the memory, most of which would do as much good as the shelf in books. Worms of that class are stupified by the weight of facts they never absorbed, and are not magnetic.

The wisest man is not he who has stored away the greatest number of facts in his memory, but he who recognizes the most of what is going on about him., and is able to turn the largest proportion of it to his account. The bookworm wriggles among people day in and day out, or walks amid the sumptuous wealth of nature, seeing nothing, hearing nothing, feeling nothing, appreciating nothing, because he is groping in his brain among the numberless facts that are jammed into it like shoestrings in a valise; the brooks run on in merry laughter; the birds sing their melodies of glee and plaint; the trees rock to and fro on the cradle of the breeze, swaying in lullabies to the tunes that mother earth first sang when she hushed her children to their primeval rest; the clouds float by like argosies in seas of blue; the sublime painter of earth and sky outspreads before the gaze the richest colorings that ever sprang from the soul of genius; yet this wise mortal is blind and deaf to it all.

In every day's experience there are thousands of details transpiring, out of which a little at least may be drawn into one's life and absorbed into one's being. The individual who does not recognize this is poor indeed. Counted wise, he is ignorant. His consciousness is not active. He may be a member of the lowest stratum of humanity, contented and void of all positive magnetism. The meaning of consciousness, then, is the power of recognizing life in and out of self. It cannot be disassociated from magnetism, for it is dependent upon this force. Normal consciousness is normal magnetism. It is the dividing line between negative and positive magnetism. Below this line there comes the possibility of lapses and hypnotic control; above it, the possibility of self-mastery, the marshaling of the forces of life, success and peace. When you are below the normal plane of consciousness, or clear recognition of life in and about you, then you are on the negative side of magnetism; when you are above such normal plane, you are on the positive side.

Life is a mass of energies.

This is the Thirty-first Principle. These energies are so numerous and so powerful, each in itself, that it is difficult to keep an account of them or their operations. They seem to permeate the body from head to foot. The physical forces are of all kinds, capable of executing great deeds of prowess or small details of the most delicate fineness. They cannot be studied without exciting admiration and wonder. Nothing more amazing is known in this line of miracle, when subjected to analysis, than the varied ability of the muscles to throw a missile of any weight to any distance within a given range. For an engine to do this, or a cannon to hurl its projectile, there must be the summary of brain-power in directing the details, the adjustment of the quantity and force of the power, the resistance of the machine, the angle of elevation, the observation of distance, and a long prior investigation of the laws by which each may be instantly controlled. Man, if new upon the earth today, would require centuries to accomplish so much; yet, in his own muscular energy, he soon reaches such end. This is but one of a million uses of the power that is lodged within the body.

Then the energies of the nervous system are still more amazing. They run the longest gamuts, from the daintiest and most exquisite impressions to those wild bursts of power that the actors of the heroic stage have so often loved to imitate. The varieties of nervous force are multitudinous. It is true that they sway the muscles, but they are always lost in muscular exuberance when the nerves are not in full command. They have a power that is not seen at all times, a reserve energy that compels the body to do work the extent of which defies all the computed rules of expenditure. That they are too often weak is a fact that should not be tolerated while man is able to give them training. Behind the emotions and passions, back of the voice, the heart and all expression of the faculties, the nervous system stands ready to enhance or belittle their uses, as its own condition may be weak or strong.

There are multiplied and complex energies of the mind, so many, indeed, that they are beyond computation. It would be needless to attempt their classification in this place. The mind has five channels of communication with the world, through which it receives and sends those impressions that constitute intelligent existence. Each of these channels represents a world of power to and from which it continually runs. Sight excels all others, and its value is so great that the greater share of life goes out with it. By its operation there may be communicated to the life of man much that affects it in numberless directions; that which appeals, pleases, uplifts or destroys; that which educates, conceals, deceives or reveals, that which stimulates to love or hate, transforms the soul or dethrones the reason; in fact, there is no limit to the scope of the mind's energies as affected by this one channel alone. Then the other senses play their parts. Beyond them are realms of invention, fancy, contemplation, and hundreds else. All these are living, powerful energies belonging to the conscious mind. In addition to that sphere of thought, the hidden or subconscious faculty deals in its own magic, to solve which the philosopher would sacrifice all his other glories. Yet our present day research is fast penetrating amazing depths of this mysterious power-giant.

The fourth world of energies is that of the soul, that moral force that is kept in the background in the majority of lives. It concerns itself with the life that follows death. The many varieties of energies of which it is composed are less understood because they are not usually brought to the front, are not dissected in the analysis of life, and do not obtain the culture in this existence that is best calculated to develop them. If the soul lives at all, it is a complex and fully endowed being; not a mass of spirit essence, but an embodiment of character, energy, intelligence and executive ability. All this seems foreign to you, perhaps, as you never have thought of the soul apart from the mind. To you the two seem inseparable; for when sleep or unconsciousness overwhelm the faculties, you have no sensation of the soul that might indicate its presence or existence.

Left to nature, all energies are at war and in confusion.

This is the Thirty-second Principle. It may be asked, why nature produces war and confusion. She has always done that. When she supplies the forces that work out the ends of existence, all is not done. We trimmed a grape vine today. It was in a fearful tangle. The fruit was well set, but the tendrils were choking its growth. The branches that should have been pinched back to a few leaves, had fallen down toward the ground, and were winding themselves around the trunk, three in a snare, or else were becoming inextricably confused with other parts. A man who had a vineyard that was neglected year after year, received no fruit whatever; his neighbor, who gave constant and skillful care to his vines, plucked large and luscious bunches year in and year out.

Nature furnishes impulses, God gives them a few laws to avoid destruction or extermination, and man's duty is to train these impulses under such laws. Left entirely to nature, man himself would become a hapless savage. Deprived entirely of nature, he would be a sickly model, devoid of life. The wild grape, like the wild cherry, is too sour and crude for use; fed on the impulses of nature, it becomes a beautiful product of culture under the guiding hand of man; made apart from these impulses, it must be a thing of artifice, constructed of wood, and painted in imitation of that which is genuine.

All these things are true of those energies which constitute human life. The fixed routine of functional existence follows the same laws, whether in vegetation or in the animal species, as of blood circulation, breathing and digestion; and around these three chief operations all the common faculties of plant and body find their divergence, in which they reproduce the sum total of ancestral traits. Without a direct intelligence to guide them they grow wildly; they run to waste, and suffer much in so doing. It would seem that nature is exceedingly cruel in all directions, were she responsible for the anguish that is endured on her account. Her children are born in pain, and die in pain. The short lives of birds, animals and fish that become the prey of others are too brief to serve any use; yet there is less suffering in being devoured than in being left to die from age. Follow any animal you will, in your mind at least, and note the long days and weeks of pain in the forest during that struggle which precedes death from starvation.

We see the birds about us and envy them their happy freedom, but we never inquire what becomes of them. Youth is full of play and cheerful glee in the merry efforts to use their wings from tree to tree; but age is one long waiting for death through the processes of slow starvation. There is no palatial couch on which the king of the jungle lays himself down to final rest amid the soothing attentions of love or the anesthetics of science; when he can no longer roam at will for food, when the bones are stiff with age, the blood thin with lack of nutrition, and all the impulses of that once noble frame are smothered in decrepitude, he is a thing of dependence on the meagre charity of his consorts, a tottering temple of despair; and, against the driveling out of life in the months that must follow, the speeding bullet of the hunter is an act of mercy.

We may praise nature all we will, for she is grand; but she is helpless. Long eras passed while she waited for the coming of man to take charge of her runaway forces. So, in the body of man himself, there are these millions of energies running to waste; engines that have no equal in power for their size; wires that carry enormous loads of vitality; a heart whose expenditure of force is far in excess of all calculations in the world of mechanics; a brain that originates and propels volumes of power, and countless others, large and small. Behind every faculty there are millions of infinitesimal forces, whose collective vitality has enormous power. Except in the performance of the vegetable functions of breathing, circulation and respiration, all this energy runs to waste in the ordinary life; yes, in the extraordinary life, a large share of the time. Few and rare are the men and women who are able to assume mastery over them. So we claim to possess the genius of generalship at once, offhand, without knowledge of the armies placed under their command, and without cognizance of the goal toward which they are tending. As well might a raw recruit be given charge of the great armies of the nation.

Peace dispels confusion.

This is the Thirty-third Principle. By peace is meant the cessation of internal war, as has been previously stated. This quietude is the earliest step in the story of self-command. We do not fall back upon the old homily, that he who is able to conquer himself is greater than he who taketh a city. That is good enough. But our simile is closer to the facts in the case. To conquer one's self implies that one's own life is at war with its head, or its brain. This is the equal of saying to Wellington: "You are at the head of the flower of the English army. This army is at variance with you; it is your enemy, and should be your friend; go ahead, conquer your own army, and then strike for the enemies of your country." This sounds well.

On the other hand it would have been closer to the true facts to have said to a general, whose soldiers were in the same relative condition as those of man as a human being: "You are at the head of millions of the best fighters a commander ever saw. These fighters are not waging war against your outside enemy, nor against you, for your existence is the sum total of theirs; but they are in confusion. Some of them are fighting among themselves; some are at a standstill, not knowing which way to go, what to do, or why they have being at all; others are on the run, racing at hazard, without guide, and expending all their energies for naught." Now, it is not true that man must first conquer himself in the sense that the general must either whip or subdue his own individuality, or in the sense that he must march in victory against his supporting army; but it may be said to be true that he must assert his authority, and hold his fighters in subjection to his will.

So much is certain. Peace in the ranks, the end of dissensions; the checking of retreat or runaways; the abolition of all the influences that breed confusion; these are the first essentials of conquest. But it is not to be a conquest of self. We teach mastery as a quality of grandeur; we do not teach humility. Man must rise and tower above his own forces, as did Caesar and Alexander; and, with obedient followers, he should make his conquests felt abroad. Peace comes from a desire to have peace. It does not require much more than knowledge, in a case of this kind, to bring about the results which are really sought. Life is motion. Along the complicated highways, if we knew the road that we ought to take, it requires no greater effort to march that way than any other. We cite this illustration as evidence of the ease with which a person may change plans and purposes, and thereby reach goals quite opposite from those at first sought; so wonderful a power is knowledge. Training the vine is less trouble than unsnarling its tangled growth; it is more quickly done, and the fruitage is better beyond all comparison.

The mere reading of magnetic thoughts may change the whole current of life.

This is the Thirty-fourth Principle. Here is the pivotal point of culture. A man has attended a lecture; he does nothing but listen; he catches bits of information which are new to him; the manner of delivery may have been inspiring, and the language elevating; but the facts are the things that he takes away. That night he falls asleep amid his ponderings over the new idea; in the morning he awakes, and is still delving into the possibilities that open up to him in new avenues of progress; during the day they linger about his work, his duties, his other thoughts; and so on, for weeks and months, they continue to impress him. He is a changed man.

We walk one road or another; or, to take the water for our means of illustration, we sail in one current or another, in one path through the ocean to a certain port, or otherwise if we seek another harbor. The captain who steers his prow toward the north coast of Ireland, might have gone as easily to the English Channel or to the Canaries; it was merely the combination of knowledge and purpose. The energies of the boat, its machinery, furnace, engine and steering apparatus obey his command as well when making one port as another. The sailing vessel is the creature of other influences than its own; it must yield to the whims of wind and storm; man of negative magnetism is buffeted about, but when his power is positive, the engines that propel his course are all within him, and are subject to his will. Then knowledge of the true way, and a purpose to pursue, are his chief agents of success.

So much for our illustration. The same law holds true as to the effect of reading as of hearing. Fine efforts do in fact dress things well; but after all the mariner of life needs facts. We must be dreadfully in earnest. The captain astray on the high seas, whose compass is broken, and who has no means of making his calculations; or who, being cast a long distance out of his course, finds himself in waters that are unknown, needs information; he asks the coming voyager for knowledge; facts, and nothing but facts, will serve him. There is coal enough to make port; the machinery is intact; the engines work splendidly; the ship steers aright, but the pathway of the ocean has been lost, and a friendly craft is sighted. Now the captain is in a position to obtain the needed guidance. He is after knowledge. Do you think he cares for a flowery display of rhetoric, for fine language, for the dress and garniture of words'? Does he need exalted, lofty, inspiring description? No. He wishes plain facts—the one thing that alone can bring him safely into port.

There is often a vast amount of magnetism in a fact that comes at the right moment in the juncture between victory and defeat. Napoleon lost Waterloo because the Prussian army was allowed to join Wellington. He had the latter well under defeat, and saw the star of destiny rising over the horizon, when Blucher broke through the forests and came to the rescue of the English. Grouchy took the wrong road. With French forces enough at his command, he went out to meet the Prussians. At the juncture of two roads he was in doubt whether to take that to the right or that to the left. Had the knowledge been vouchsafed him, a single word, teeming with magnetism, would have changed the destinies of Europe. Display, style, ornaments of speech, elaboration of delivery, all pale before the power of the word that carries the precious freight of a fact.

You ask how mere information will change the current of your life. It may or may not. Much of the knowledge of the world is incidental to the main progress of existence. Advice is so little followed that its giving is a luxurious waste. The minister who hammers away week after week in volumes of advice and censure, does not see any change in the faces or lives of his congregation; they come Sunday after Sunday, with that same patient, half-stupid, all enduring meekness that bears the stamp of duty. They have read the deluge of mind in the Sunday paper; they have broken off rather suddenly in the midst of some foul sensation, and they come to church for grace with an ill grace. Advice never did much good. " Your sermon was so inspiring," said the grocer at noon; and on Monday morning he put the same proportion of sand in his sugar.

There is an immense distinction between the promulgation of a fact that gives direction to the main course of life and the offering of advice that affects only the incidentals. A preacher who had told his congregation how to live so as to have clean hearts, found that they one and all regarded the advice as first-class, but as belonging to their neighbors; thus A thought B needed it; B thought A needed it, and so on. One Sunday he told them all that they might make a thousand dollars apiece, for a certain wealthy philanthropist offered that reward to each man, woman and child in that church who would read the Bible through in a year, and who told no untruth, nor spoke an unkind word in a twelvemonth. That afternoon the dusty volumes were unshelved; next morning orders by telephone were flashing over the wires for Bibles at once, and on the following Sabbath inflamed eyes and sweet smiles greeted him from a packed auditorium. The acquisition of a thousand dollars affected the progress along the main course of life, as every person knows; the getting of a clean heart was a matter that had no reference to the struggle for an existence, and could wait awhile.

The same thing is true of advice that affects health. Persons must have confidence in its efficacy, and must also feel sure that their carelessness in living has not yet reached the limit of their vitality; it is only to save themselves from death, from a costly sickness or from severe pain, that they will accept any advice even if it is fully credited and known to be efficacious. Such is human nature. The reason of this is in the fact that ordinary ill-health and its cure are incidentals in the journey of life. The course of travel is not an incidental. There are four such courses; all main highways. One is the hypnotic, which is pursued by the contented underlings ; they are the masses over whom the capable classes rise; and were it not for such masses, there would be no means of ascent. The traveler who sat on the peak of a lofty mountain thanked the ground for supporting the mountain; he thanked the base for supporting the upper part; he thanked the breast for supporting the top; he thanked the top for supporting him.

The second class comprises those who are struggling along the highway of discontented subjection. They will release one in ten thousand from their number, and he will ascend to the top of the grandest eminence. The others will follow agitators self-chosen from their own ranks; they will furnish the great faultfinding hordes that vote one day at one election, and another way at the next, always tearing down without hope of building. From this subjected but discontented class there come out master minds year after year as intelligence is acquired to help them; and they are the best candidates for the study of magnetism. The third highway is lined with those who have started well, but whose armies are in confusion.

The fourth is the finer and more sparsely occupied road over which travel men and women who control their energies and are magnetic. We may add recruits from the other three ranks, and uplift all four.

Thus is it seen that magnetism affects the main course of life. To those who are determined to rise the offer of knowledge is a training influence in itself. More than one ambitious person has said, "I have awaited some guiding principles to help me. I know now what I am and what I may become." We have seen lives completely changed by nothing but a course of reading, or a course of instruction, consisting, not of advice as to what to do, but of information where to go. The signboard tells where a certain journey will end, but offers no advice or suggestion as to the propriety of going there or elsewhere. When a man enters upon a certain highway, having at its termination the goal he seeks, he proceeds along that course, and adapts himself to its conditions and circumstances.

While there are other and perhaps more decisive methods of training in magnetism than the furnishing of knowledge as to what road to travel, there is none more important or effective than that which presents the facts that lead to such information. Few books, indeed, are helpful; they contain too much verbiage for the slight amount of solid knowledge. Principles are always an advantage, for they present laws, and laws are fixed rules founded in the impulses of nature and the modes of giving them guidance. No man can read them without finding himself already leaving the wrong road and seeking the right one. A few principles in a lecture, in a lesson, in a book, have swung individuals around, changing forever the currents of their existence. This we have known over and over again among students of this science. The glory of living is that a man can alter his course for the better if he so chooses.

The union of the wasting energies of the body creates great magnetism.

This is the Thirty-fifth Principle. The laws that precede this should be reread until they are understood. From their reading and absorption, there will come the desire, then the determination, to enter upon the right road. These are important influences, and they cannot be lightly regarded. We have seen that the confusion that arises from the discordant and warring forces within the body should be brought into a state of peace. That this will be done, we believe there is no doubt.

Peace alone is not enough. The general who unifies his untrained troops has done something toward preparing for conquest, but not all. Their confusion ceases; they are no longer in conflict among themselves, but they may yet be a disintegrated mass, whose parts are not trained to work together. The estates and dominions that are contiguous in a country may cease to war with each other; but, like the German Empire, they may do more; they may form a union for offense and defense, a cemented nation composed of smaller peoples, each potent in its own forces, but mighty in its joining.

The way in which this union should be brought about is a matter of the highest interest. There are always various suggestions that may be offered in most any subject of importance; and here we find it easier to treat this line of study in such offhand manner than to deal more seriously with it; yet the full responsibility must be met. We know that a man who can achieve so much as to quell the confusion within him is already a monarch in his own realm; and we are sure that few there are who are strong enough in willpower, in purpose, in iron resolve and solid determination to command their own being, for it is the most wonderfully constructed and the most magnificently equipped temple in the whole realm of creation. He who maintains harmony in such an array, who is its acknowledged head, and who is able to lead it to victory, is a king indeed.

These remarks lead us naturally to the method which we propose to adopt, after having given it thorough trial in a wide range of cases during more than a quarter of a century. While at first it may seem as if the plan is not directly concerned in the cultivation of magnetism, a few weeks of trial will convince you to the contrary. It must be remembered that those persons who are said to be naturally gifted in the possession and use of these powers have come by them through methods of living that have tended toward such development. They know no exercises. The part of the process of culture is fully as important as any that may be associated with practice.

A self-pledge has far more value than any specific action, for it involves the use of all the powers of the body, even the common drift of nutrition, and turns them into any desired channel if the intent of the obligation is fully observed. Three men start out to acquire the arts of magnetism. One thinks about it, sees the needs of the body, the mind and nerves, notes their wasting of energies, and his good sense tells him that no life can run itself without intelligent guide. He finds that he is a machine, a furnace, an engine, a boiler, a storage battery, an electrical dynamo, a full strung system of live wires, and that all this wonderful display of mechanical invention has an engineer, the brain, that knows not one thing about running it. He thinks this over, and all the while his good judgment, his fund of sense, is unconsciously throwing an influence over his daily career, and he may truly boast that he never took a lesson in magnetism, although he is giving himself the best of lessons.

The question is often asked why some men and women are so cultured in this attainment, while others are deficient; and it is said of them that they are endowed by nature. There is no such thing as endowment by nature. A quality, a talent, a gift, or any advantage may come down from former generations, but they do not arise out of the ground where nature had its birth. If you are more refined than other persons, it is because you have lived where there is less roughness, or you have decided not to live as roughly as others, or your parents or ancestors have so lived, and their tendency has not been thwarted in your life. This is true of anything that is called an acquisition or a gift.

MYSTIC UTOPIAN SUPERMEN

Magnetic persons who never practiced or studied the subjects are sometimes those who have inherited the manner from their predecessors, but the latter have come by it through proper living of their own or of those whose blood flows in their veins. In no case is it a clear gift out of the bosom of nature. The three men, of whom we have made mention, start out to acquire this art. The first, as we have said, finds what a wonderful piece of work he is; is surprised that it is without engineer or manager, and is soon under the influence of this thought. He lives with it night and day; it goes with him in his work, in his pleasure, in his moments of idleness, just a thought; yet he cannot escape its influence. Soon he finds himself advancing along a highway that is new to him, and he wonders what has brought about the change. To his surprise, he believes a thought has turned the key of a greater life, and he begins to examine that matter, to see if his belief is well founded.

A magnetic thought is an operation of the mind that influences matter.

This is the Thirty-sixth Principle. It is hardly necessary to repeat what all persons may easily ascertain to be a well-established fact. Out of a million thoughts, perhaps one may be magnetic; if it is, and you are affected by it, your life, your body itself, will be influenced by its power. This is not in any way connected with telepathy; nor with any phase of mental science; nor has it any occult value. It is a plain, simple, easy proposition; and—, for fear some readers will misunderstand it, we will explain its meaning at once.

If you tell a man that he is not as nearly well as he ought to be, he will agree with you; the thought has fallen on barren ground. If you tell him his health is failing rapidly, and that he will not live many years, he may or may not agree with you; and, in either event, he will pay but little attention to the statement. If you tell him there is a pocketbook full of ten-dollar bills waiting for him as soon as he gets well, he will go to work at once to secure the reward. The thought has struck home. It influences him by reason of the fact that he acts upon it. His acting upon it required neither exercise, practice, nor training of any kind, but merely a better method of living; the rising at a more suitable time in the morning, the eating of more wholesome foods, the seeking of sufficient sleep, pure air, and normal conditions everywhere. These things done, the natural impulses set to work and give him perfect health.

The occultist or visionary mental idealist will assert that mind influences matter. So it does, and in a variety of ways. The method now under consideration is free from all occult associations. The thought that bore the burden of power was of sufficient interest to arouse the man to action; that is the sum total of it all. You may call it motive, selfishness, or what you will; the fact remains that something that entered the mind operated to change the whole current of the man's life. So, in another case, the mere statement that if you give certain persons rope enough, they will hang themselves, was of sufficient power to touch a man who had been unfortunate through talking too freely; he did nothing in particular, except allow those with whom he dealt to have their say, and the result was that his life became one of success, instead of failure. It is a very well understood fact that a course of living, like a mighty stream of water, may be deflected by surprisingly small things, although a thought is often great.

The simple illustrations we have taken are not within the range of a magnetic thought.

MYSTIC UTOPIAN SUPERMEN

Our object was to show that any idea, however conceived, might sway the body of an individual upon whom it seemed to have effect. Even if it appealed to nothing but motive or greed, it was sufficient in its purpose. Thoughts may live as powers either in or out of magnetism, although it is claimed that all thoughts are necessarily charged with mental vitality, which is one kind of magnetism. Thinking, if conscious, is of such a class; but much of the ordinary thinking is automatic, and nothing automatic is magnetic. It is when a thought is having birth, when the desire, the effort or the seeking after it, brings it into being, that it is conscious and powerful, even though its value is small. The originating of anything is evidence of some vitality, and conscious attention is necessary to such a process.

Magnetic thought is an aggregate unity of the separate thought cells of the body.

This is the Thirty-seventh Principle. What is meant in this place as a magnetic thought is one that not only is attended by the conscious effort of the person producing it, but has behind it the whole nature of the individual. It is not enough that it is capable of changing the current of a life; it must take a direct hold on that life. The difference should be understood.

When the information is received that water has been discovered in the central district of an arid country, its force sends families thither, breaking up homes, and affecting the future conduct of hundreds of persons. There is nothing magnetic in this thought, in the sense in which we are now presenting the matter, for the information did not of itself take direct hold of the people. In order to become an influencing power, it was necessary that there should be an arid country, and that there should be suffering because of a lack of water. The news of a better locality was welcome in the highest degree. In this and the other cases cited the life within the body was not affected; the influence went no further than to change the place of residence and the circumstances incidental to that.

On the other hand there are thoughts that are born in the very being of a person, backed by all his faculties and energies, which are sent forth to other persons, or which sway the individual himself. Such thoughts come from life, out of the realm of human feelings, and are destined to affect not merely the conduct, but the personality they touch. Instead of making a man move to a new country, they make him a new man, and it is the purpose of every magnetic thought to thus affect some life. It influences matter far more powerfully than ordinary appeals to motives or selfish interests. In a flash it marshals one's entire attention.

Such a thought takes hold of a person and involves his whole nature, even being felt in his muscles and flesh, from the sole of his foot to the crown of his head. "I experienced a thrill that made my skin grow cold," said an auditor to a famous orator in referring to a certain passage in his speech that took the house by storm. "I felt just the same," replied the speaker. We listen to some powerful thought uttered in a force of magnetism that pervades the whole body, and the feeling that we experience is also found in that of the person who produces the idea; and the same is true, whether it is written or spoken. "When the line flowed off my pen, I realized its power even to my feet,'" said a writer. "When I read the line, I was conscious of its power, and it took possession of me," said a reader; and it is true in one case as in the other.

MYSTIC UTOPIAN SUPERMEN

It seems that the whole being must live in the thought, must be behind it, and unite in giving it a living strength. It does not come from the mind alone, not from the brain, the nerves, the soul, the flesh, but from all together. Mind is the larger collection of gray matter in which vitality dwells; the ganglia, and all other minor collections, are likewise endowed with intelligence, which is one of the expressions of vitality; but every atom of the body is charged with some mentality, which appears in comparatively larger form in cell structure, where gray matter seems to first congregate. It cannot exist unless intelligence exists with it; therefore it must represent some degree of thought; and, in the countless millions of these cells that are present in every cubic inch of flesh, there must be a greater proportion of magnetism than we have ever imagined, and this will account for the tremendous concentration of power that is felt in a thought whose life is charged with the magnetism of the whole body.

Any person who has ever given birth to such products of the mind, is aware of what is meant. The way to distinguish them is in the fact that a magnetic thought makes the body feel it from head to foot; while a mere mental idea has no influence over the flesh, over the material substance, or matter of the body, neither in the person who originates it, nor in the one who receives it. A line sometimes contains a book. A word or two may move a multitude. We have all read the famous remarks of generals in battle, whose single flashes of genius have burst forth in almost unpremeditated sayings, pregnant with force and stirring to the soul. They have without doubt turned defeat into victory at critical moments. In vain have historians attempted to analyze their mysterious power; admitting always that a half dozen words, springing from human energy, have changed the face of a continent.

We have seemingly diverged since we left our three friends in search of the way by which to acquire the art of magnetism. The first saw the natural processes, and quickly found himself confronted by some living principles, and these we have stated. He next proceeded to see why certain men and women possess great energy of purpose, and he thought these might be ascribed to temperament; yet the more he examined the propositions, the more was he convinced that temperament did not make magnetism, but was made by it. Then the problem became deeper.

Why is it that some persons are magnetic while others are not? The brutal saloonkeeper, the savage that forces his gains by bullying, the foxy gambler, the coward that adulterates his goods and shrinks from the observation of mankind, the manipulator of stocks, the cheat and fraud, these are often money-makers without the aid of magnetism; so it is not true that success is the gauge whereby such vital power may be measured. With magnetism all persons should succeed; without it, the dishonest may. All these facts were disclosed by our searching and inquiring friend. He himself wished to acquire the art, and so betook himself to ascertain the science that directed its operation.

This first man depends entirely on his powers of observation for the information. He simply becomes satisfied that the body is a machine of great complication, which can no more he left to run itself than can any other machine; that the faculties are diverse and marvelous, and they, too, need an engineer at the throttle to guide and control them. These facts, coupled with the lessons derived from other lives, lead him to conclude that the power of magnetism is a resultant energy that is generated by life itself, and that its degree of power is dependent upon the amount of intelligent direction the mind may give to the body and its faculties. He goes to work on this principle, and soon finds to his satisfaction that his conclusion is correct. He then progresses further, and is delighted at the power he has obtained. He is right. Man's body is a far more delicate, and yet more effective, machine than ever has been seen elsewhere, and it is the only machine that man permits to run itself. Without an engineer it goes at will, and is ineffective; it merely struggles along, and to mend the errors that naturally arise from allowing it to run itself, there are thousands of drug stores and thousands of doctors waiting at every hand. Let a little intelligence of the right kind come into play, and these errors will not happen; force will he conserved; vitality will grow on itself, and soon the man or woman who is bright enough to find out these things will be credited with the possession of the gift of magnetism. This is the first way.

The second man who starts out to acquire this art, takes a course slightly different from that of the man whose methods we have recently described. He does not wholly believe that magnetism is the natural accumulation of power coming from energies that have been made to serve the control of an intelligent mind. The first man concludes that these forces are running away or to waste, all the time they are left without an engineer to guide them; he studies other lives, and watches the same law at work within himself, and finds that his claims are true. The second man does not see how magnetism, which he supposes to be a gift, can be acquired without doing something. He goes to work to ascertain what a gift is, and, from all light that he can get from those who are so blessed, he is of the opinion that it is the result of a certain way of living, the constant tendency of which is to stimulate and excite into development the powers within the body.

Even being true, as he thinks, he cannot understand why this development takes place in one who only thinks about living in the way that favors such influences. What has the engineer to do with the engine that is running itself? He takes control, and permits it to run only as he chooses. Then the machine is quite another piece of construction, for it is valued because of what it does. Knowledge and skill are required, to be sure; and here a volume of instruction of the right kind may be indispensable. Yet he believes in regime. He cannot satisfy himself that the engineer without training, practice and skill in the art of managing himself, would be able to manage his powerful and complicated engine.

So this second man studies the lives of men and women who are acknowledged to be magnetic; he watches them in movement, in conversation, in idea, in action, until he is almost able to follow out their plan of living; and this he proceeds to reproduce. His one great lack, as he afterward states, is a book or system of law to guide him.

This he procures, and he finds his magnetism developing rapidly, and making him a power among men. He has really entered upon a life of regime, of exact and careful conduct, in which he is but a stronger degree of the first man, who did less. The real difference is that one saw what was necessary to remove opposing influences and take a general supervision over natural faculties, so that these energies might not be left without an intelligent guide, while the other did all this, and more too, adopting a life of general regime to aid the development of the power.

MYSTIC UTOPIAN SUPERMEN

On comparing results the second man found himself the better of the two, and the reason was because he held the reins always in his hands, or had the running of the machinery always minutely under his control. He saw that magnetic persons who left their powers to go as they pleased, except when they chose to direct them, were always breaking up in periods of life when they most needed them, as Napoleon, Blaine, Disraeli, and thousands of others, who might have avoided wrecks had they marshaled their faculties under a system of regime that held them in momentary sway. Hence the less brilliant man in the earlier years may go down into old age suffused with the glory of a longer victory and crowned with the laurel of unbroken success.

The third man is perhaps more interesting. He knows all about the first and second, and still more wonders how any power can be acquired without something besides regime. He would like to enter into a system of practice, gather electricity as does the machine constructed for that purpose, and become a fully charged battery. He reads that this can be done by any person of ordinary intelligence. Herein he is right; but he will find by experiment that it is possible to generate more of such power than he can use, and that, unless he actually assumes control of his forces, he will be adding one more to the energies that are already running away with him. Here the distinction is one of importance. The prime demand is for a controlling engineer, and this he can secure by allowing his own good judgment, his common sense, to govern his powerful army of energies, to bring them into a state of peace, and to unite them for action.

Having considered the three methods that are possible of adoption, and found them all valuable; having looked into the minds of the classes of ambitious persons, who are most likely to succeed in the acquisition of this power, we will now proceed to offer the very best means of making the start. It is not so much the specific thing you do, as the road on which you travel, that determines what the results will be. This should be remembered. The difficulty in getting on the right road is not a great one; it requires decision, or a making up the mind, to do it, and then the step is taken. If you wish to go to one city, and are on the road to another, the first thing to do is to ascertain where the other road is, then how to get on it; after which, if you fail to go, the fault is your own.

Self-pledges, honestly made, are sources of magnetism.

This is the Thirty-eighth Principle. A self-pledge is made to yourself, not to us or any other person. If you break it, you alone know it; the responsibility is with you, and you alone can mend it. A pledge is, and always has been, a great means of help to a strong character, and a fair means of help to a weak character. The argument that a man or woman of energy needs no such tether is not sustainable under examination. The strongest boats need the strongest moorings; the greatest ships require the most certain as well as the most secure of anchors.

Any definiteness of purpose is magnetic because it unifies energies of the body; and the more complete that purpose becomes, the more it will concentrate the millions of powers that make up the faculties behind the resolve. This ability to unite the divergent forces of one's life is seen in the affairs of state in the policy of a great nation. England's civil wars gave way to meet the dangers of a foreign enemy. Rome united her discordant factions under the skillful manipulation of Caesar, who sought to conquer all the world without her gates. Greece reached the climax of her power while her States fought side by side against her Asiatic enemies, and it was because of her political agitators at home that she fell a prey to nearer foes. Napoleon could not hold France together in time of peace; he broke his oaths in order to excite foreign war and thus retain control of his stormy people. The American Revolution was serious enough to weld the thirteen Colonies into one amalgamated nation; and when the country was divided into North and South by bloody war, the scars of dissension were obliterated by the conflict with Spain, in which the blue and the gray fought side by side.

A pledge is made for the purpose of entering boldly into the battle of life, and its first effect is to unify the army with which victory is to be won. It is a purpose crystallized. Any resolve has some value, and on the same principle. Magnetism awaits use; not getting it, the power wastes away. With a lack of regime, there are millions of energies running wild, which would prove tremendous batteries of magnetism if more regime were to be employed to hold them in check. What is meant by resolve, purpose and such higher conditions of the mind, must be understood in the sense referred to in the realm of The Will, as set forth in this volume. Names are somewhat technical when used in a specific study.

This realm is now coming to a close. It is one of collecting forces and harmonizing them, preparatory to the greater battles that are to follow. It is the realm of peace, the estate of quietude such as precedes the movement of a vast array of battalions toward the enemy of success. Too many students of these problems make the unpardonable error of supposing that willpower and magnetism are evidenced by the mad plunge into the ranks of the foe, before an attempt is made to collect and count the forces at command. As sensible would it be for any general to hurl his columns against the enemy while yet his soldiers were carousing and fighting among themselves.

THE ESTATE OF THE WILL—THE REALM OF POWER

THE human will is in no wise like the will of lower animals. It may set itself to a fixed purpose and conquer, all the while urging on the progress of its action; while the will of the animal is more like the stubbornness of man. One takes a track, and does not deviate from the course to be pursued; the other fastens itself to a certain idea, and cleaves to that with tenacity. There are points of resemblance, but in the main the distinction lies in this separation of the mind's activities; by which is meant that in the exercise of the will there is a continued activity carrying it along, while in stubbornness, as in animals' purposes, the idea is fixed beyond recall or variation, and any interference with it is regarded as an intrusion.

For fear that this is not yet clear we will explain further what is meant. The seat of all willpower is in the brain. That which decides what to do or not to do is called the mental action; and although animals are said to lack minds as organs of reasoning, they possess mental faculties not very far below some of those accredited to certain members of the human family. They decide to do or not to do a hundred or more conscious acts daily. It is an operation of the will that causes each decision, but after the point of action has been reached in their thinking processes, the muscles, or else the physical division of the brain, the cerebellum, takes possession of the whole being and knows no change.

This limitation of activity of the brain to merely the deciding of what to do or not to do, is peculiar to animals and to stubborn human beings. The cat in earnest sees its prey, it measures the distance, and decides that it can or cannot make the leap successfully, for it is familiar with its own powers through prior experiment. For this the cat plays in kittenhood; it jumps about in every possible use of the body, until it knows the length of its range in making the spring; and not until old age withers its vigor does it cease altogether to play. The same is truth of all animals, even the most savage. The lion in the jungle lies in ambush, and prepares to make the leap only when the prey is within reach; it may wait, and wait in vain.

The peculiar characteristic of the animal brain is to see its way clear to doing a certain thing, and then proceeding to its execution on the theory that it is surely to be done. It cannot understand nor brook disappointment.

The little ant shows every indication of a hot temper if its purpose is interfered with; so does the familiar bee that busies itself about the flowers at the porch. Most wild animals are terrible only when they are checked in their attempts to do what they undertake, and the ugly dispositions of domestic pets are due to being thwarted from time to time. Like obstinate men and women, they rage or grow sullen when something occurs to make a change of purpose necessary. You know how almost unbearable it is for a mulish individual who says he will not do a certain thing, to be compelled to do that very thing; yet how pleasant it is for any sensible person to change the mind when the exigency requires. The one is animal by proclivity, the other is human in the best sense of the word. To close the mind is to stop the will's action after it has merely decided to do or not to do a certain thing.

Stubbornness is a physical, fixed and nonmagnetic force.

This is the Thirty-ninth Principle. What is the real character of stubbornness should be well understood, for it is common to mistake this unprogressive condition for will-power. Such a man is reputed to be of strong will. Why? Because he never changes his mind when once he makes it up. Then he is a fool. There are some men and some women who take special pride in having it known that they never change their minds. " Mother is slow to make up her mind, but when she does, nothing can alter it," says a proud daughter, as she glances at the mother who rocks sternly in her chair.

You can examine and analyze every such case of obstinacy, and you will never find one of magnetism among them. This mother, who is so slow to make up her mind, justifies herself on the ground that she would be very fickle to decide one way, and then another. A father, who adopted a rule of uniformity with his children, would adhere to it through thick and thin, because he knew he would look weak if his word could not be relied upon. When he told a son to do a certain thing, it must be done, even if the circumstances requiring its performance had changed, or if a mistake had been made in the order. One day he told him to lock up the house at eight o'clock, and not open it for any living person, as he himself had a key and would open the door when he came home about eleven o'clock. It was a cold night. The boy's mother and sister, who had gone out of town on a visit, arrived back a day sooner than intended, and found all doors and windows locked. They called to the boy, who declared, in the exact words of his father, that the door was not to be opened for any living being, and that he did not dare to disobey. He clung to the idea, and the father praised the boy, while deploring the sad annoyance and subsequent fatal pneumonia that ended the foolishness. To this day that man, like millions of his stripe, believe that it is a matter of valor to make up the mind and not change it.

Fathers who have young sons, or daughters in their teens, are more likely to become obstinate old fools than other men, who are unencumbered with such offspring. Here is a case: One father of this kind told his boy to carry a letter to the post-office, and be sure to get it there before the mail closed at six o'clock in the afternoon. His clock was wrong, and the boy found it out when half way to the post-office. He was told he could put the letter on the train, which he did; it was handed to the postal clerk of the mail car, where it was as safe as in any post-office. The boy had done right; it would have been foolish to have done otherwise, yet his father whipped him, saying that when he was told to do a thing he must do it as told, no matter whether he knew it was right or not.

Such obstinacy was the worst training the boy could have received. In this world the art of living well and successfully is the art of adjusting one's self to the ever varying tide of circumstances. It is an ocean crowded with craft; not a barren sea in which the obstinate helmsman is the only man afloat. The swells are always at work drifting one out of his course, and throwing other craft in one's line of progress. The father whom we have described would have told his boy to steer the ship for a certain port, no matter what came in the way. The wise man would have explained contingencies to his son, would have instructed him in the art of adjusting himself to changes of conditions, and have praised his sagacity. In no other way can life be made a harmony and its progress a success.

No policy, no plan, no operation can be so clearly outlined ahead as to require no change. The greatest battles of history have been fought out on lines that varied materially from those intended. Even where the farseeing sagacity of the keenest general has caught in advance the inevitable moves that must lead to the battle's end, he has had to meet contingencies by departures, one way or the other, in order to force the moves as he saw them. Change is the law of life. A man may aim to reach a certain goal, and may keep steadfastly to his purpose, but his road must be suited to the direction in which he is traveling. "I will go to that end," says the determined man. "I will go to that end by this route," says the obstinate man. The one gets there by adjusting his journey to the conditions with which he must contend; but he gets there. The other starts out on the road he himself has ordained to be the one that must be traveled, and when he finds that it is not the right one, he stands still, and will not budge.

Such conduct is too often supposed to be evidence of a magnetic character; but it is quite the opposite. If you have an electrical dynamo that is capable of supplying your house with light, you must know how to set it in motion and keep it going. The fact that the power is there is not sufficient; you cannot afford to cut off the current by deciding in your mind that the power will do the work. Turn on the current. The will is supplied by a steady energy that comes from the strength of your purpose. Now, suppose that the energy is there, and is strong enough, of what use is it if you shut off the mind ? The current must be turned on, must remain on, and the energy of purpose must not be slackened.

Look at the case of the man who bitterly complained that he had met only failure in life; nothing but reverses from the moment he began to take care of himself. "Why is it?" he asked. "I have been industrious, but that has not brought wealth. I have worked into the night for years to keep out of the poorhouse; and I have never got far out of its shadow. Why is it? Then, why do others hesitate to deal with me? I pride myself on my honesty. I am worthy of their confidence. In business I can get a reasonable amount of credit, all I ask; but I cannot buy as low as others; I have to sell for less, and very few seem anxious to have anything to do with me. " His wife also spoke of him in the highest terms. "Why has not Hiram succeeded better? He is a man of iron will." This added light to the mystery. It seems that some misguided guardian had instilled into Hiram's mind that art of making it up and sticking to it. When he got an idea well lodged in his cranium, he hung to it. He locked his mind up, and threw the key away. It was that or nothing.

This man who so bitterly complained of his fate, can be better understood by referring to an incident that illustrates his whole career. He owned some land, and managed to mortgage it for nearly its full value, so that his equity in it was very small. Still he owned it, and took an interest in its surroundings. A natural brook ran across the corner of the rear end, at a place where he missed none of the land by reason of its rocky condition; and through this brook the rains washed from the adjoining ground. This he considered an encroachment on his rights, so he dammed the brook, and forced the overflow elsewhere to the annoyance of his neighbors. They requested him to take down the barrier. He declined. They threatened, and he laughed at them. He had closed his mind. Once shut, it was an engine of power that had stopped running. He did not, for he could not, think beyond the one idea that the land was his; what was his he could do with as he pleased, and he pleased to dam the brook. That was the beginning and the end, the all in all. When he made up his mind, it was made up. Hiram was a man of iron will. So was the jackass that planked his feet in the roadway of the forest and would not budge, not even when they built a fire under him. Hiram made it known that he would not remove the dam. They summoned him to court, and he stayed at home. The judge ordered a removal of the dam, and he tore up the paper. He was cited to court for contempt, and would not go. They took him there by force. He was fined, but would not pay. He was ordered to jail until he had purged himself of the contempt, and this he would not do. His good wife finally paid the money, kicked out the dam, apologized to the judge, and secured her husband's release. He even did not seem anxious for that, but as he had found it impossible to get some of his favorite dishes in the jail diet, he concluded to get back home once more.

The Iron Chancellor, Bismarck, was a man of determined will, as set and steadfast as he could be, but he never permitted his mind to close itself against change.

While adhering to a purpose with bulldog pugnacity, he used all means to win, even at times pretending to abandon it. He obeyed his friends; he respected all authority above and below him; he shifted his course a dozen times when it was policy, but he clung to the idea of ultimate victory. This is magnetism. It is not obstinacy. Had he dammed a brook that served to carry away the water from the neighbor's land, he would have removed the dam on request if he had ascertained that the law so decreed. Able men take soundings. Small men are sometimes great in this regard, and they have magnetism in relative degrees, rising above the strata beneath them. Good judgment is discretion; discretion is valor, and both are the opposites of obstinacy. To not get the mind fixed, for it will close and shut off the power of the will.

MYSTIC UTOPIAN SUPERMEN

The will is an active progressive force.

This is the Fortieth Principle. The difference between making up one's mind and executing its purpose is a vast one. What is called the will is a force; it is not a condition or situation. It is a train in motion, not a mule standing in the path of progress, and refusing to move one way or the other. Under the special circumstances of life, the habit of making up one's mind and holding it unalterable, is both dangerous and disastrous. The future is always before us, and it is not possible to see its vicissitudes. What you have passed through in the last ten years is quite different from what you contemplated. You could hardly have foreseen half of its incidents.

All these propositions appear to conflict with one another. But they do not. Obstinacy is the closing of the mind, shutting it up, and turning off its currents of action as the engineer may close the throttle by making up his mind to do so. Willpower is the turning on of the current, the starting of the engine. Here is the first distinction, and it should be borne in mind. It seems also to be a contradiction, for it deprecates the idea of making up the mind. A resolve to do a thing that is really undertaken is quite different from a setting of the mind blindly. If you seek a certain goal, if you are taking your ship toward a port, the willpower is in full operation; but there is no need in setting the mind. It should be open and active, ready to consider any matters that are likely to arise. Obstinacy is not always a negative position. What we maintain is that it is a position, and not an activity. Thus if a captain decided to go to a certain port by a certain route, he is carrying out his purpose so long as everything favors his progress by that direction; but if he refuses to change the route when good judgment requires, either for safety, for lessening the time, or other reason, he is obstinate; his mind has become set and is no longer a machine of the will. It would be as unwise to lash the helm and see nothing, know nothing, determine nothing, after the one making up of the mind in the start.

It is necessary to make up the mind. This cannot be denied. But it is necessary to keep it active and under control as a power. A resolve may open or close the mind; if it opens it, it may become a magnetic force; if it closes it, the result is obstinacy. It is necessary for the general to determine what he will do in battle, and if he gives orders for the advance upon the enemy's breastworks, he must be ready at all times to change his method of proceeding without abandoning the purpose to carry the position. It may be necessary for him to call his troops back a number of times, or to change the route of the advance, or to retire when the firing is too heavy, or otherwise maneuver as the vicissitudes of battle may demand. Here it will be seen that the purpose remains unaltered, and the willpower is alive in the fullest energy; discretion and valor clasp hands; the skillful resting, the withdrawal, the constant change of tactics, are all evidences of an open mind, willing to do whatever is best for securing the end which is in view. Had the general blindly ordered the troops to advance in a certain way, or by methods of action which were at variance with good judgment, he might have been ignorant or unable to make himself master of the art of war; but if he persisted in a course of conduct that could not be justified even under the theory of a mistaken judgment, he would have been obstinate, for the mind would have been closed to all suggestions or thought of variation necessary to save his soldiers from unwarrantable bloodshed.

From these illustrations it will be seen that a person may be obstinate affirmatively by closing the mind upon some determination to act or take a particular course, and allow no variance from that. It would be the same as if there were no mind at all after the initiative had been taken. As well might a locomotive be started blindly upon a journey without any one to guide it on the way, as was done when a discharged employe of a railroad company opened the throttle of an engine, and jumped from the cab when it got under way, watching it as it sped out of sight. Most persons fail in life whose willpower is of the wrong kind. They have the ability to make up the mind to win success; they see ahead of them the goal which should be reached, and they start for it, thinking that all that is necessary is the aim and the getting under way.

There are two considerations relating to the importance of making up the mind, which should be understood in this connection. Shall a person keep the mind open and give it free opportunity to change at will, or shall the mind, when once made up, remain steadfast to its purpose and allow no change? If the former proposition is true, then there is nothing but vacillation in any project of life, and the world is too full of these uncertain persons, who do not know what they want more than a day at a time. If the latter proposition is true, then a mistaken idea must be pursued to the end, even if nothing but disaster awaits it. What has previously been said may now be crystallized into the following summing up: There must be known in advance the goal toward which one directs his journey; this goal must be determined upon in a proper way, without hazard of judgment or the prospect of certain success; and then the purpose must go on until the end is reached. The only thing important, and the only thing that should be unchangeable, is the goal; all else must yield and shape itself to this bit of human history. The best way of proceeding may or may not be understood at the start, and it is along the journey's course that an open mind is required, for the energy of an active will must not be relaxed until the victory has been attained.

Development of the will requires the cultivation of straightforward thought.

This is the Forty-first Principle. The answer to the questions raised may be found under the law we have just stated. If it is true that so sad an error has been inaugurated as that a person has started toward a goal that is not worth the effort to reach, and has sacrificed perhaps some of the best years of his life in toil that must now be regarded as wasteful, the graver problem arises, whether the steps should be retraced and a new goal sought. Of course the root of the whole trouble is due to the mistake of choosing the wrong road in the beginning, and this can only be lamented, not remedied.

The remark is often made that it would be a great blessing if the right goal could be chosen at the start. It is undoubtedly true that some failures in life are ascribable to the selection of a wrong purpose; but the chief causes of disaster are not due to the choice so much as the way the journey is made. We shall briefly discuss both phases of this matter. In the first place, no person should make an error in the choice of the goal, whether it be that of his life work, or some one of the lesser ends that are necessary in the great struggle. If his judgment be poor, he should seek the aid of one whose advice he respects, and even then he need not run much risk of making a mistake. When MacMahon, a poor boy of France, saw the dazzling glory which surrounded the office of marshal of that great country, he resolved to devote his life to the one purpose of reaching that position. After events justified the statement that it was not a wild flight of his mind, but a fixed design, which had been thought out with some knowledge of the difficulties that would stand in the way. Some persons might regard him as demented, others as foolhardy, still others as ignorant of what he was undertaking; but MacMahon was evidently thinking in what we call a straightforward direction. He knew that the office might be attained through merit, that the first requisite was the ability to perform its duties, that he must be a soldier in the ranks before he could hope to become an officer, that he must win his way from one grade to another, as thousands before him had done, and that he must seek such elevation as would place him within easy distance of the goal; and while this might be in sight, the most difficult step of all was the shortest. There is nothing impossible, nor improbable in so much of the journey. From the condition of poverty and obscurity to that of high official rank in the army of France was a long but reasonably certain advance; he saw that it was within the range of the right kind of a youth, and he knew that the right kind of a man could bridge the final gulf. He succeeded; he became Marshal of France; he became more.

We have selected an extreme case as an example of what is meant by straightforward thought in the development of the will. Had this young man decided to become emperor of that nation, he would at no time have been reasonably sure of the fulfillment of his purpose, and he might have been open to the charge of weak-mindedness. When Napoleon stood on the bank of the Seine, about to plunge into its waters to obtain that relief which his fevered and disordered brain demanded, he saw no hope of anything in life; nor is it true that, when he led the army of Italy through its series of brilliant victories, he was then contemplating the mastery of France. His fate unrolled to him page by page, and he himself said that he was a man of destiny, being led on whithersoever its powers decreed. We can hardly imagine a young man seeing his way clear to the overthrow of any power, even a provisional government, until he had a reasonable assurance that such an end was possible. MacMahon had such assurance. Napoleon's career was a series of goals, each carrying him higher and higher, until he became dictator of Europe.

It is probable that destiny opens up in a series of prospects these goals to every earnest life. Starting with a fixed determination to make the most of the conditions at hand, and bending every energy to do the very best that circumstances will permit, a mind of iron will does not have to proceed far before a new plane of action appears beyond the horizon. Destiny is at work. Again the true heart toils well and aims high; the footing is becoming more secure each day, and soon there is no doubt that something awaits further on. Whether the compass of living be small or great, the noblest successes are achieved in this way, and the end of one's career need not be sought or even known in the beginning. What is true of a whole life is true of any part of it. To make the very most of what is within reach is sure of rapidly extending the lines of the horizon and increasing the compass of our possibilities. Lord Beaconsfield determined to become a member of Parliament; he was a young man of about twenty-two, possibly, at the time, and it was probable that the premiership was not in his mind, although it was not out of his reach. Had he thought to make himself king of England, the whole purpose would have been chaotic. Nothing daunted him. When he finally obtained a seat in Parliament, and obtained a hearing, he made the most dismal of failures; yet his purpose was unshaken.

MYSTIC UTOPIAN SUPERMEN

An analysis of his character may throw some light upon our principle. He was not seeking his election for the purpose of filling his purse or gratifying a temporary whim; he wished to come before the nation as a man of power, and, having come into possession of the opportunity, he immediately proceeded to use it to that end. At first he was a Liberal, but the party was unpopular, and he deviated his course to one that would place him on the winning side. His first speech was laughed at and jeered; he felt the weakness of his abilities, but he told his hearers that the time would come when they would listen to him, and this indicated that his will was supreme. Having become a Conservative, and having made himself a power in Parliament, he quickly succeeded in showing Peel that he was a lieutenant of no small value. Able leaders of great political parties must have assistants about them capable of executing their wishes. Greatness lives in the men who serve it. Disraeli never swerved from the purpose of his ambition, but he altered his path and changed his methods as often as he could gain some end by so doing. He saw the vulnerable points in the character of his leader, and forthwith proceeded to take advantage of them. In a speech in Parliament, ostensively intended for another purpose, he placed, Peel on trial, succeeded in overthrowing his government, and was chosen to heal the breaches he had made.

The story of Beaconsfield's life shows him to have been a man who was thwarted often in his progress toward the goal which he sought, but who never swerved from its ultimate attainment. He was willing to step aside when the obstacles were too great to be surmounted, to thrust them aside when he felt that he had the power, to compromise when neither was possible, and to make them his tools if something was to be gained thereby. His career is an illustration of what is meant by straightforward thought, for he kept the end in view. Had he made his plans in any other way, as most men do who are weak, he would have altered his purpose for some immediate success. As long as the thought in mind is straightforward, it will not deviate from the purpose, but will change only its method of pursuit.

The will sets the goal of purpose.

This is the Forty-second Principle. It is very easy for weaklings to depart from a plan which they have entered upon with some display of energy, and the lives of most men and women show that they are incapable of maintaining the straightforward thought which alone sustains the will and brings success. The case is so common, and may be so easily recognized, that a single instance will be sufficient to explain what is meant. A young man enters the university, and knows nothing of what course he will pursue after graduation. He says he will be older then and in a better position to determine. In this he is right, for a general education may be made the foundation of most any kind of a worthy career. He becomes a lawyer, and resolves to reach the head of his profession, clear way up in the top ranks, where there is so much room, as Daniel Webster once said. In the first year of his practice his receipts are in the neighborhood of two hundred dollars, and as this is in excess of what Webster and Choate earned in the same period of time, he plods on very well satisfied. At the end of five years he is able to squeeze out less than one thousand dollars per annum, and some of this by questionable methods. On again comparing his career with that of Webster and Choate, he finds that he is far in the background. He places the snuffer over the candle of his ambition, extinguishes the flame, and runs for office. He is elected to some county position, and receives a salary of fifteen hundred dollars or more a year. He becomes a political wirepuller, assists his Congressman in the campaign, and is rewarded with a temporary position of private secretary. When the fortunes of his leader begin to wane, he is helped into one of the departments of the general government at Washington, where he seems reasonably certain of a salary sufficient to live upon; and here he enters upon a career of slow decay for the rest of his active days.

The case we have cited is, as we have said, a common one. The particular details may be varied to suit the difference in any other instance which involves the same principle. Thus many young men, who start out in business with the determination to become merchant princes, turn to the law; a surprising large number of practicing attorneys seek the ministry, and the change of purpose thus goes on to suit the probabilities of success in these weak characters. These departures from one drift to another are not steps in the line of a fixed purpose. Beaconsfield would never have played such a part, nor would any other person whose willpower was sustained by straightforward thought. This means that shifting deviations for temporary policy that start life toward an entirely different goal make the mind an instrument of crooked purpose, and they show the lack of willpower as well as the lack of magnetism.

We are sure that the goal may be determined upon without mistake. Let it be what it may, the will that fixes it should be sustained and developed into greater and greater proportions of power by a straightforward direction of the mind, willing to deviate in the steps that are taken, but not in the end to be secured. No person can afford to make a mistake in the selection of any great goal, nor can he afford to depart from the attainment of that goal. These two things are certain. The will is rapidly developed by seeing that those mistakes do not happen. It is developed by the constant adherence to the purpose already formed. Without such a purpose it has no port to make, no pathway to pursue across the ocean of life. There is really no such thing as a fixed life work; the best journeys are those that keep in a well chosen course and make the most of what is at hand.

The will must never be relaxed in its active urging onward of the individual career. It should not refuse to adopt the best means and the best methods. It should go ahead. But, on the other hand, it must not set itself upon some particular detail that can be circumvented with greater ease than it can be adopted. There should be no useless resolving to do something of minor value, no wasting of energy on trifles. The young man who had no aptitude for the stage, but who studied therefor because some phrenologist, who was paid to say something, told him that the shape of his head was exactly like that of Edwin Booth's, could not be persuaded from his purpose, and he went on to the direst failure without one opportunity for winning laurels in histrionics. What was his method? He studied and waited. He did not do anything aggressive; he made no effort to test himself alone; he merely studied in a desultory manner and waited. He shut his mind off, refused obstinately to be swerved from his purpose, and waited for the prediction to come true. Had he used his willpower as an aggressive force, he could have accomplished his end. He could have climbed to the top round of that ladder had he been in earnest. No obstinate man is in earnest. Aggression, backed by will, makes magnetism, and failure is impossible.

MYSTIC UTOPIAN SUPERMEN

Be in earnest.

This is the Forty-third Principle. To be sincere at all times is to be faithful to those trusts which have been placed in your keeping by Nature and God. Faculties that might be cultivated in the highest degree should not be regarded as things for trifling. Mind in itself is an organ of vast powers; it may be made more commanding year after year if it is nurtured and used aright; but it leads its owner down many steep declivities of disappointment in life when it is slightingly treated.

Many a beautiful mind, of promise far exceeding the ordinary cast, has been warped by the trifling methods of living. The trashiest kind of reading presented it as a regular diet, and were a remonstrance to be made, the reply would come back to the effect that there is but one life to live, and it would be monstrous to commit that to seriousness. Such a reply is trifling. Such a life is trifled with. Such a mind is useless, as the after story may show if it is learned at all. Few care to know it. Here is a young man who sleeps late, rushes through his meals, crams his brain with the sensations of the papers while his feet are above his head, and spends night till long past midnight hour in reading cheaply written novels, and being told that he is destroying his faculties, he sneers forth the word "crank," and goes along his course, rotting on the way to the grave. Too many men and women are mere triflers.

We believe in sunshine, in cheerfulness, in the happiness that leaves no sting. We do not believe in the sickly flush of diseased joys that spring out of laziness, lounging, morbid thoughts or lecherous habits. Nature gives beauty to the flower that grows by the impulses she furnishes, and it is her loathing to behold the painted daub on the walls of the brothel. The man or woman who shouts "crank" at one who is in earnest is as much out of the joys of life as though the worms had already begun their borings through the coffin. No such person is sincere. To mock others is to chaff at God. Few are those who respect the powers with which they are endowed; great is the reward of such respect.

Many of the great men have left their testimony to the importance of being in earnest. "What must I do to succeed in life?" asks an ambitious young man of one who has tasted the pleasures of fame through merit. "Always be in earnest," was the reply. Another asked a similar question of Burke, who said: "Be in deadly earnest." From an acquaintance with the biographies of many of earth's favored sons and daughters, the same counsel seems to have been the golden thread that controlled them in the growing years, when the struggle required the utmost zeal in order to win. "Be in earnest" has been the motto of all who have conquered.

It is necessary to be in earnest in little things as well as great. The purpose of the mind should be sincere, honest, clear, definite and thorough. Talk to the least of your fellow beings as if you believed them worthy of your attention, and be in earnest. Do not trifle with body, with health, with mind, or with any of the faculties that are entrusted to your care. In every deed, in every remark, in play, in sport, in love, in labor, in all things, be in earnest. This virtue will stamp itself upon your thought, it will affect your daily habits, it will be seen by others, and ere long you will be believed in, and your power over others will rapidly become recognized. It pays.

Courage is the magnetism of aggressive action.

MYSTIC UTOPIAN SUPERMEN

This is the Forty-fourth Principle. When you know that a certain course is right, that harm to justice cannot come from it, that you will achieve a grander standard by adhering to it, then you must not be swerved from it by any considerations of danger or fear, and certainly not because it may be inconvenient to do what needs to be done. It is not always in moral questions that courage claims action, and the mind requires courage to spur it on. Sometimes there are crises in business, in society or in friendship that can be met only by the energy of this virtue; and in self-conflicts as well the power of courage is capable of turning defeat into victory.

Look at some difficult case and see what courage will do. A young man from the country applied at various places in the city for something to do. He was uneducated, unmannered and uncouth. They laughed at him in his home and in the fields about when he said he was going to the large metropolis to get a chance to rise in the world, for he was too ignorant to know what to do. "You don't know enough of the world to go to the city," they told him. "Well, I can't learn to swim till I go where there is water," he replied. Once in the city, he was laughed at there for his fixed country ways. In a few days he was thoroughly discouraged, yet he had courage. The only way of keeping alive was by working for a dollar a day, and this he did while he struggled to find out what was necessary in order to succeed.

His goal was a fixed one; he intended to throw off the crude habits of country life, a self-inflicted misfortune among most farmers, and get up in the world in some honorable way. He knew his goal; he did not know the road to it, nor even the direction in which it lay. He knew what was honest. It was not setting his mind to say that he would do no dishonest act, for obstinacy comes from a specific and not a general determination. In two weeks, by faithful toil, he proved his value to be more than he received. Any person can do as much. He did not labor to be watched; when he knew no one could see him, he still kept on, and results justified an increase of wages to slightly more, which, in a month, became nine dollars a week.

Now he began to feel independent. He asked questions, took notice of men in better positions than himself, and found out something new each day. The goal before him was to rise in the world, although he still had no knowledge of how it would be done in his case. He wished to go back to his country home, and prove to his old friends that they had laughed without cause. This he determined to do. In the class of laborers with whom he was associated there was not one who had any ambition; most of them saw nothing better than what they then had; they lived from day to day, from hand to month, and a few hoped for good fortune in some way, either by change of political parties in power, or some other notion of demagogues. This young man saw that they were all destined to be merely low laborers, for they did not determine to rise. He made up his mind that will-power must set the goal.

A friend of his at the place where he lodged told him that he needed more education. When asked what kind, he was informed that grammar, spelling and pronunciation were the essentials, to which a knowledge of common arithmetic should be added. For a few cents each, copies of the required books were obtained, and he set to work, unaided, to learn what he could. There is not a laborer in New York City who would buy books on grammar, arithmetic, pronunciation and spelling, or any one of them; and there are not ten laborers in America who would do it; yet all of them howl at the misfortune that keeps them poor. When once the will sets the goal of ambition, it takes a heart full of courage to execute its behests.

Any person now bowed down by the misery of poverty may find out what to do to get out of the slough, if there is a will to get out; and it does not require that the way be seen, known or understood. Let but the mind be made up, and the body will act. Any human being who is grieved at the unfortunate turn of fate that bars the way to success, who wishes to turn this defeat into success, who wishes it hard enough to will it, may accomplish it in the fullest measure; but there must be a making up of the mind that is all earnestness. Few care to do this; they prefer to have the golden apples drop in their laps from the clouds overhead. The young man from the country had decided to rise; he looked with pity on the laborers around him; he knew that they could better themselves, for lie felt sure that he could do so in his own case, which was a hard one; yet how he could not tell.

He toiled away at the books night after night. The spelling book first interested him; he could understand it better. Three hours a night are eighteen a week. All outside attractions were nothing to him. He had a talk with a nice gentleman, who saw his ambition, and who advised him to attend church on Sundays. He followed the advice unostentatiously. He talked with men, but did not force himself upon them. 4 'Can a laborer rise in the world V 9 asked a correspondent. "If so, what is the best advice in starting to do so!" "Get a few books of common studies; insist on learning how to spell, pronounce, talk grammatically, and do ordinary arithmetic; go to church every Sunday; talk to your superiors, and find out all you can." Any man, young or old, who does this much will soon find himself above the ranks of mere physical labor.

Our young man found that it was not so easy to understand what was required in pronunciation as in spelling. His plan was to read the book through aloud, so that he might hear the sound of his own voice in uttering the words. He heard educated men talk in various places, and caught the sounds of words. His memory thus began to grow. Out of a sermon he would collect fully one hundred words, and compare them with the book on spelling. Once in a while, though not often, he had the privilege of talking on the subject with some person who could give him information. After once the ice was ~ broken and he began to understand the rules of pronunciation, he made rapid progress. Then came grammar, which he dreaded. It was all Greek to him. He read the book through twice very* slowly and aloud. A dictionary was necessary, and this he bought. Some introductory words in the grammar seemed to be abandoned as the study proceeded, so he merely marked the meanings and went ahead into the parts of speech, and it was all very dark to him.

While plodding along in this vale of discouragement, he got acquainted with a laborer who could not read. He was so ignorant that he could not tell one letter of the alphabet. He was about twenty years old, and had come from a mountain home far away, where they never saw a hook or paper in use. "What are you in the city for?" "To get a living." "What will you do after you find out that you are able to get a living?" "Don't know. " "There is but one other thing to do, and that is to die. See these men about you? They know nothing. They work with their arms and legs. Every one of them could get up higher, but they are not willing to use their heads." These remarks came burning out of the country boy's heart; they impressed the mountaineer, who wanted to learn the alphabet, and he became a sort of pupil of the ambitious boy; he called once a week, and the latter found how much easier it is to learn a thing himself if he tried to teach it to another. This is very true. The little episode turned out to be the starting point in a new career, for it sent the mountaineer up into the realm of ambition also, and he succeeded in many aftersteps.

It was a severe test of the willpower, when the grammar proved too much for the country boy. He did not like to ask the necessary questions of his elders, for he feared to intrude too much on their good nature, beyond getting general advice. So he read the book through a third time, and in so doing found it possible to discern the simple parts of speech, as the article, the noun, the pronoun, and sometimes the verb. In this he aided himself by the practice of copying a sentence and then marking the words that he knew. It was in so doing that he realized his inability to write plainly. An old man, who kept a secondhand hook store, told him what to buy, and showed him how to hold the pen. It was not long before he improved in this art.

He gained some knowledge of the rudimentary construction of grammar very soon after this, and was pleased to know that he understood every one of the parts of speech. It was with unusual pride that he meditated on the fact that no living being had given him one bit of light. He had discovered it all himself. The use of cases in pronouns had a fascination for him, and he learned to say I and he, me and him correctly. This change came to the attention of his employer one day. It was also noticed among his church friends, who were not altogether cool to him. Such a man is bound to attract attention. Willpower never strives alone in the haunts of one person's life. Grammar, now that he saw it, really changed his use of language to such an extent as to command the attention of others, was to him a magnet of attraction. It is surprising how rapidly a little bit of learning will accumulate force in its progress. Once he was able to catch hidden meanings, he plunged ahead, and found the higher books of rhetoric and literature awaiting him, while arithmetic now became easy to understand.

He was too valuable a man to be lost sight of. A vacancy above him soon occurred; and no life is kept crowded down when its wings are spread to rise. He was soon earning one thousand dollars a year. At this time pride did not trip him. He kept to his books all the harder; for, as he once said to his employer, he saw clearly that it was his books alone that took him out of a position of nine dollars a week to one worth more than double. He found that the little volumes that were everywhere for sale at the stores were so written as to enable any person, however stupid, to understand them if there was a disposition to do so. "What I did not understand, I would read, then lay aside and sometimes read again, repeating the process till I did understand it. I also started the worst case of ignorance I ever saw along the same road, and he has conquered." Here he referred to the mountaineer. Both careers proved successful in the highest degree. Where was the cause? What was the source of that cause?

Strength of purpose develops magnetism.

This is the Forty-fifth Principle. The case we have given at some length lends its answer to the questions we have asked. What could have caused an ignorant country boy to rise out of his condition, to acquire an education, to succeed in making a fortune, to go back to his old home, pack up his timeworn parents, and take them to a sumptuous home in the city? What could have done this? Every ignoramus in that country region exclaimed, "Luck." This is a false answer. Luck played no part whatever in his rise. It had no more to do with it than did the moon or the north pole. Luck is sometimes a factor in the turn of events, if we call the law of chance by this term; but it came not into the life we have mentioned.

When the pleasures of carousal night after night were neglected for the study of books, not for mere information, but to really fit the young man for a better plane of labor, there was no luck at work. When repeated readings of that abominable grammar did not shed light on the science, he did not throw the book down, and go out for a pitcher of beer. What luck was at work when he read the volume again? What luck was shaping his career when a fellow laborer, blear-eyed through continuous soakings of beer, laughed at him because he preferred the companionship of books that he could hardly understand to that of men whom he understood too well? Not for a moment in all his career did the element of luck play any part whatever. But, says some one, his rise to a better position was due to good luck. Not by any means. There are all grades of employment, from the humblest to the highest, and some one must fill each position therein. No person holds a position forever. The place hunts the man. He who is ready is the one wanted every time. This toiler made himself ready. There was no luck in his dropping into the place that awaited him.

What was the cause of his success ? Willpower. But what was the origin of that willpower? It was not magnetism. It was nothing but a blind energy. This we must examine. Such an energy is possessed by many laborers; probably by millions now in this country, who can never get any further along for the reason that the spark is lacking. Let us imagine any one man to be the type of these millions who are destined to remain always at their present low level. We look into his character, his habits, his good qualities and his imperfections, and we find him to be possessed of unlimited energy, all running wild. He works hard and faithfully, thinking it will always insure him employment if he does a full day's work. He wishes and even hopes to rise in the world, but to him the idea of rising is in no way connected with progress, the taking of steps, or the movement up into a higher stratum.

Right here the secret is found, for his life is a drift around a whirlpool without direction ahead. When asked if he is satisfied with his condition, he almost convulsively shouts, No. When the further inquiry is made as to what he hopes for, and how he hopes to get it, he invariably says something in this vein: "I want better wages and cheaper foods. The pay I get is too small; the price I pay for living is too high. Something is wrong in the government. They ought to tax the rich more and make them pay us more. There will be a political party come to the front some day that will do this for us, and every laboring man will vote for it." No wonder the fellow is poor and wretched. No wonder the millions of toilers are hopeless and tied hand and foot by the cords of misery.

To every one of them there is just the same opportunity of succeeding as came to the ignorant country boy, whose story is absolutely true. They and he possessed the same common energy; but theirs was blind, spending itself in the whirlpool of wasted forces;

his needed the one instigation to give it magnetism. So all energies may be turned into a direction, set going on a road, and be made magnetic. What was the spark? It came to him in the one idea of rising out of his low condition. It furnished a goal. He looked ahead. Other laborers hoped for higher wages, lower prices of living, and cheaper beer; things that never occur together. This toiler did not look for higher wages in his rank, but resolved to get up out of and away from that rank. Thus he fixed a goal.

Toward this goal he looked at all times. His thoughts bent to it. He allowed no deviation from that straightforward energy of his mind, which saw no other goal to be desired; not temporary ease, not pleasure of the heart, not carousals, not the rainbow-chasing of demagogues who allure toilers away from themselves toward the dangerous shoals of anarchy, which is the real purpose of political harangues; he threw all his life into that one struggle, which had for its helmsman the straightforward thought of rising in the world. Such thinking is sure to develop magnetism, and if you do not believe it, try it. Such thinking collects together the discordant energies of the mind and body, unites them as one puissant army of purpose, and hurls them in solid column against the ranks of the enemy of success, breaking the illegitimate array into fragments. Try it.

Nothing is more certain than that most persons possess energies which are allowed to run to waste. Nothing is more certain than that such energies, if their confusion is allayed, may be marshalled into an aggregation of fearful aggression. Here the will is needed, and the will is in itself an active progressive force, not a standstill energy of the mind; it is an open mind, always looking for means to affect an end. Development of the will requires the cultivation of straightforward thought; the road ahead may lead about and deviate a hundred times or more, but its end is never abandoned. The will sets the goal of purpose. This is the spark that ignites the fire beneath the boiler. This is the one distinguishing feature that separates the millions of laborers who cannot hope to rise, because they do not decide to rise, from the one ignorant fellow who is sure to forge ahead simply because the will sets the goal of purpose. He wants, wishes, proposes, decides to rise in life; and that is all that is needed to start the magnetism of his whole soul, mind and body into the way of succeeding. He is in earnest.

It is not the frothy impulse of a quick nature, but the steadfast earnestness of courage. Aggression requires courage. Success in anything, large or small, must brush little natures aside, for they block the road; and malice barks in proportion as the earnest man rises in the world. It takes courage to pass them by. One man, a pitiable weakling, says: "It hurts me to find that I acquire enemies as I climb higher. I almost wish I had never climbed at all." He must know that hatred has existed since the beginning of time, and will continue for some centuries yet; and no man or woman has lived well who has not felt the sting of savage humans among civilization. Courage is not so hard to hold under circumstances of success of any kind. It is when the failures come, when the tide hears you away for a while down toward the opposite goal, when little things prick up their ears and bite viciously at your feet, when a cloud of impenetrable thickness shuts out all view of the world about and you are wrapped in the gloom of despair; at such times courage is the highest virtue.

In a way, as a type of needed courage, take the case of the country lad, who could not get one ray of light out of his grammar. Imagine, if you will, any ignoramus of a laborer taking a grammar to look at, much less to study. You and his acquaintances would laugh at him. Even if not laughed at, if he could go away to some room where he would be alone, you can very well imagine him squinting at the covers, turning the book upside down a few times, hunting for some tobacco and beer advertisements in the opening pages, placing leaf after leaf carefully over each other, until he gets to a few long words that are hieroglyphics to him, then hurling the volume across the room, and settling back in his chair, clasping one knee in his two hands, and go to dreaming of the time when some political party will bring prosperity to the laborer. Yet the fellow has energy. He lacks the willpower to set a goal that will cause him to move on. Any goal that is not ahead, or that does not require progress, is like a stake in a whirlpool around which one is ever dashing, and which, when reached, means nothing.

Better than leaving a farm and going to the city to add to the crowd of non-producers, is the reverse determination of staying at home and rising there; for the great centers of population must be fed by farmers; their clothing comes from wool cut from sheep raised by farmers, or from cotton cultivated by farmers, or from linen spun from flax planted and grown by farmers, or from silk made by worms tended by farmers; their shoes come from cattle, sheep or goats reared by farmers; their houses are built of wood that is produced outside the cities, and all that is used or consumed must come from these sources. The real man brings something from the soil; and, great as others may be, there is no vocation that can place a human being above the directing genius that compels nature to serve him. Yet the reverse seems true.

Why the noblest of all callings, that which harnesses the mighty power of the sun and whips along the elemental steeds, should be forced down to the lowest strata of humanity, and there degraded, we cannot understand. Many years ago we succeeded in convincing a young man, who sought the glories of the legal profession as the highest end of living, that God held other professions in higher esteem, none being more honorable than that of honest farming. The laughter of his friends, the ridicule of his enemies, did not deter him from following the advice. He made the art of farming a noble one. From the soil he won all the comforts, all the luxuries of life. The same brain energy that can wrest a large income from the practice of law can secure a larger one from the soil, and the wear and tear are lessened.

When ignorance directs the plow the house gets a mortgage. It requires thought to make an acre yield a hundred dollars a year, yet he did it; a business skill is necessary to turn a hundred acres into ten thousand dollars, or five hundred into fifty thousand dollars; not one farmer in a dozen can get much more than twenty dollars from an acre; yet brains can take a fortune every year from a farm; and the best of it all is the fact that the man whose head holds the brains need not lift a finger. He may be in the city much of the time, or in the country amid the scenery he has helped to beautify, enjoying the products of nature and the healthful air of the fields.

One more case may be cited as showing the way in which a seemingly impossible feat may be accomplished by the magnetism of the will. A young man desired above all things else to become an orator; not a mere talker, shouter, haranguer or demagogue, but a real orator, earnest, eloquent, convincing; not that species of speaker that drives the public away or is tiresome to listen to, but a man such as those who have attracted great crowds, and the more they talk, the more they are desired. This young man at first did not select his goal, therefore he had no magnetism in the line of this effort; for it is one of the laws of magnetism that the goal must be decided upon.

The concentration of the energies of the body, including the mind, the nervous system and all the faculties, acts very much like the lens that collects scattered rays and directs them into a certain fixed channel of force. The sun is hot enough to make the blood suffer from its intensity, but it has not sufficient heat to set any substance on fire. The steel and flint throw a faint stream of delicate sparks that cause the fine tinder to ignite, owing to its supersensitivities. The sun cannot ignite the tinder, even when its rays are the hottest. A lens collects scattered lines of light, and throws them to a single line, the power of which is due to the fact that this single line is the concentrated force of many; yet it can set fire to nothing that is not readily ignited. Add to this lens another, and still another, till countless thousands of rays are focused upon one point, and you can set a ship on fire miles away.

By this it is seen that energies that are scattered are of less use by far, and in most respects are quite worthless, compared with the united force that is derived from their combined efforts. A thousand little powers, helpless in their separation, are resistless in their union. The mighty river that bears upon its brow the giant craft of nations could hardly float a log on any one of its upland streams. It is in exactly this wise that the will-power makes man a conqueror when he fixes a goal and concentrates all his nature upon the purpose of reaching it. He may become what he will.

Without losing sight of the young man who desired to attain the highest success in oratory, and who had to contend with difficulties that seemed insurmountable, as we shall soon see, we must examine the conditions that give a man the power he requires. It must not be supposed that any one thing will accomplish this end, nor that so multiform a use as magnetism may be summoned by one bend of the rod. There is no single line of training that develops this power, except for that single line. All that is said in other parts of this volume should be understood and acted upon, and a general all-round cultivation of magnetism should be adopted.

We may become what we will.

This is the Forty-sixth Principle. Any man, any woman, may determine the fate that awaits the unfolding of life's history. If you could but know this, and know the method by which you can shape your own career, it would be worth half the years of living, would it not? We stand ready to prove the fact even to the uttermost; to prove it in your case, or in the life of any person. If you wish the matter put to the test, we will do that. Here is the full explanation, the process of development, the line of action. Nor is it so hard as it might seem.

In the first place it is necessary to assure those of our students who are careless in their mental conclusions, that the action of the will is easily accounted for by everyday rules, and is not dependent upon the occult powers so-called. To use the will is not to exercise faith. What that is may be worthy of discussion, but at this place we are considering the simple processes of our open, unhidden natures. We need not say more. This book has none of that overflow around its statements of mysterious sayings and problematical phrases that charlatanry must fall back upon in order to impress. The purpose here is to show how much vitality there is in the plainest processes of life. Truly it would seem as if there were no limit to what a man can evolve out of himself if he will take Thought thereto.

You may become what you will, and it makes no difference how foreign to your nature the goal may be; if you are really in earnest, it is yours. That you must be thoroughly and completely in earnest requires no iteration. That much is taken for granted. In order to be in earnest it is necessary that you believe in yourself and in the possibility of success. Able men have always believed in themselves and in their power to accomplish what they undertake. This is not faith, at least not in either a religious or an occult sense. It is plain, everyday common sense. How absurd it would be to start out for an end that you had no expectation of reaching!

Suppose the great Englishman who when a lad decided that he would be the foremost power in that nation—suppose that he really never thought he would succeed; how could he be justified in retaining the ambition! It is not a blind faith, a trusting faith, to reason out that a certain goal is ahead and within reach of the man who is fully in earnest, and who proceeds to reach it by every available means. He is not absurd enough to select a purpose that he himself discredits; nor is he crazy enough to shut his eyes in choosing, so that he sets out upon an impossible journey by a road that leads the other way. He has many reasons for believing in himself.

The average daily life is surrounded by thousands of details.

This is the Forty-seventh Principle. The man who selects the goal of his ambition wins because all the operations of his own existence begin to throw their influence his way. This means a great deal. There is no silent, mysterious force playing occult pranks. We assume that he is active; if he is not, he cannot hope to succeed in anything. A magnetic man or woman loves to be doing something, to arise in the morning ready and eager to live a full day through, to see as many books, persons, friends or not, as many transactions and activities as can be well crowded into a single day.

Sometimes these thousands of details appear in what is read and in the long procession of thoughts that pass in line through the mind; they are pictures of action, and make their impressions vividly upon the personality. How many things have occurred today? Oh, a few only; none of importance, you may reply. This is not true, unless you are living aimlessly. Take a pencil and paper, and note down the myriad activities that have been going on all around you; and if none of them touched you, your day has been a void. It is not necessary that many of them should affect you, but some should interest you.

It has been estimated that an active man is surrounded in his daily life by fully ten thousand details out of which he could draw at will such as he chose; and sometimes it seems as if an excessively active life must be centered within a hundred thousand details. We write to explain what is meant by this claim, for it means much to an earnest individual. Suppose a woman is a lover of flowers; she has her books on botany, containing thousands of ideas from which she can draw one or more as she pleases; then there are references to the science in her ordinary reading; the paper, the magazine, the history, the novel, all may in some brief way present information within the line.

Now she sees pictures in books, on the wall, and elsewhere, which are bettered by the broad fields that stretch away to make the landscape; and here and there are garden plots bearing more items of interest, all in the one particular line of her fancy; yet these are but a small proportion of the thousands of details that lie within her reach. No person makes use of a tenth of these; few ever see one-fiftieth of what is taking place; but a magnetic person does. He has reason to see and to appreciate the value of what transpires; and this leads us to a most important law in the present study.

Magnetism attracts its own kind from surrounding details.

This is the Forty-eight Principle. Given ten thousand details of occurrence in the ordinarily active world of one man's life, and a hundred thousand in the day of a very energetic person, the question arises, how many of them will touch him? If he is a man of magnetism, he will exclude the most, and draw the few that are in the line of his interests. This we all know in a general way. The banker sees banking events chiefly; the grocer lives in an atmosphere of flour, spice, beans and goods of his trade; the lawyer watches the courts and human discords; the clergyman has an horizon of his own, and its fruitage is church membership, missions, donation parties and slippers; the doctor feels the pulse of the day's events in new serums, chemicals, powder, internal explosives and nitro-glycerine pills; and so each sees and seizes details that escape all the others.

Take any example and follow out this law of magnetic attraction, and you will see it ever at work shaping the career of each individual that comes under its operation. Here is a young man who determines to become the judge of a court of high grade, not a justice of the peace, nor a criminal magistrate. He aims toward the Supreme Bench. If he is fully in earnest, he will get to that position; and it is not by any means easy, for such an exalted rank requires many, many years of preparation. Yet he will get to the goal. He must be in earnest in selecting it. It would be the height of foolishness for a man in mature life, without training or experience, to select such a goal; he could not be in earnest if he did so. But the younger man will succeed in this most difficult of undertakings; and it is safe to assert that no person ever set out to win this particular end that has failed.

The justice of one of the Supreme Courts of this country told in private the story of his ambition, and the way it worked out. The principle is exactly in accord with ours, and the case is fully a representative one. He made up his mind fully to reach that goal, and in his own State. He was a student in a law office, where books were at hand for study. He desired to become a Supreme Court judge. Naturally he began to look up the duties of the judge, and found that they involved a general knowledge of the law, a full knowledge of law libraries and digests that told where cases could be readily found, and experience in the rules, customs and precedents of practice and procedure. In addition to this, the judge must be perfectly familiar with the rules of evidence, those that were imperative and those that were discretionary, and he must be able to maintain the dignity of the office.

A young man who would like to be a judge is quite different from one who is determined to be. The former still has all his energies; the latter focuses them upon the one goal, and his magnetism becomes powerful and irresistible. It draws out of the thousands of daily details those that appertain to his one resolve; and it is interesting to see how this is done. Little things that are of no value to the general drift of mankind appear to him important. In conversation he hears a thousand remarks during a single day; and he is where he can hear such as are in his line of study, of which number perhaps three or four only are worth retaining. They relate to some judge or some judgment, to some unusual decision, or some ruling that has been passed upon in the courts above the trial sessions. These are attracted to his mind, and held there as the magnet draws little particles of iron from a mass of dirt.

Not only in the thousand remarks of an active day, but in the numberless items of his reading will he catch such ideas as add to his general knowledge and grow into his being. No other individual on earth collects as much under one idea, unless the same determination has been formed; there may be fifty thousand men with a similar ambition, but not with a full mind made up to achieve it. With him it is different. He is in deadly earnest; and, day by day, there is an absorption of ideas out of the great fund of details that surround his life. It is necessary to practice law. He does this in all the integrity of his soul. In every trial he is armed with a flood of decisions. When the settled law of his own State is undisputed he does not drag in the far away decisions of other States and thus win dishonestly, although the opportunity to do so is everywhere offered him. Thus a case was won in a trial court by a firm of lawyers who cited over sixty decisions of the far Western States, all agreeing to their proposition, while the other side did not know enough to look into the decisions of the State where the trial occurred, for they were the other way and took precedent.

This young man was always armed with the law, and amazed those about him. The judges came to respect his own sincerity, for never had he tricked them by trying to force down their legal throats a wrong conclusion, if there was such to be had. He had, in the first ten years of his practice, won the admiration of every lawyer and every judge within the wide range of his acquaintance, and many a judge remarked that when he started in to state the law, he was sure to succeed. His positions were tenable, subject to human error, of course, and always as liable to be wrong on problematic points as other learned minds; but he had a judicial clearness that enabled him to get the right logic out of mooted questions, and this was the result of his years of absorption. A remarkable thing above all was the fact that he cared more to assist the courts in arriving at the true conclusion than he did for winning his clients ' causes.

To view this method in the abstract, one who is not altogether honest might say that it is the lawyer's first duty to win his case, as his fees and living come from his clients, and his obligation to them is reciprocal. Therefore he should let the law's correction come as a secondary consideration. There are two reasons why this suggestion is not a worthy one. In the first place, a lawyer ought to be an honest man; and if such are hard to find in the profession, it does not follow that honesty will not succeed better than first successes. In our opinion there is no real magnetism unless it is honest; for a dishonest man cannot make himself in earnest and thoroughly sincere, no matter how hard he may try to crowd the belief into his mind. If every person doubts the wonderful power of an honest, actively aggressive life, let him try it. In the hands of able men integrity is a magnet capable of controlling all opposing interests. Not to pretenders, not to those who pose as modest and sincere, nor to that class of clever feigners of every noble virtue, does mankind pay homage long; but to him who is proved honest will tribute come. In a world where white souls are almost unknown, in an age of rarest truth, the honest man, who couples ability with his deeds, must draw mankind to him. He may control them at will; and experience shows that even the hypocrite, finding integrity such a magnet, has educated himself to become honest. So many a pretender, who has joined the church for fraudulent ends, has finally been truly converted and has repented.

For another reason the lawyer who wishes rather to see justice done than to win his clients 9 cause, will increase his practice. Few such lawyers exist. Most of the bar are human, and love the limited glory of having won the case in question. Says a rich man: "You secured the verdict for me. You are a clever lawyer. But your methods were not sound. I shall hesitate to employ you again, unless I have a very bad case." It may be known that capable business men are even keener in mind than the best lawyers; they know how much real integrity an attorney has, and they are shy of him in the future. Trickery may be concealed from the jury, but never from the court and rarely from the client. There are some lawyers in existence, though very few, who will not advance a wrong legal proposition to the consideration of the courts, and they are safe counsellors. They will not go into court on a side that must depend upon such a wrong, and the public soon finds it out. Litigants who wish to win when wrong, may employ the other class of attorneys; but every sensible human being who is in the full possession of his faculties desires to know the law in advance, and to act accordingly.

Too often, altogether too often, the lawyer advises his client that the law is on his side, or is sufficiently in doubt or unsettled to warrant making the fight, when he well knows that he will be defeated unless he can change the facts a trifle, and then he commits subornation or perjury in order to save himself from his client; and most clients are willing to vary the truth just a little bit, a harmlessly little bit, rather than be forced to yield to a hated rival. All this is wrong. It never touches the honest lawyer, for he will not permit it to. Being capable, learned and truthful, he becomes a power in his profession; and, wherever there have lived such men as these, they have reaped larger fortunes, won greater victories, and held higher honors in their communities, than the so-called smarter class.

We see the same principles holding true in the life history of the man who determined to become a judge of the Supreme Court. What were his chances of succeeding? He had ability, not only in large degree, but in the very largest, and this must have followed from the fact that he kept himself constantly at work acquiring knowledge in his line. He had a judicial mind, which means that he could sift facts, dispel confusion, get at the pith of a controversy, and apply the logic of the law in such a way that its judgments were right. Some one has said that a judicial mind is the ability to discern what the law ought to be when it is not known by precedent decisions. At any rate, such a mind is acquired from habit and study, and it takes years of careful examination into the reasoning of courts to get at the true lines of logic. But it is attainable by him who wills.

Then he was quick to get at his knowledge. This was also an acquired talent. Over and far above all else, he was honest. This was publicly known. It could not have been concealed after a leading lawyer, tired and sick with the nauseating trickery of his profession, arose in court one day and made the following statement: 44 The facts in this case are agreed to; there remains nothing but the law to he settled. The learned counsel confronts me with an array of decisions that I am satisfied completely remove all doubt.

MYSTIC UTOPIAN SUPERMEN

I would not be true to myself, nor to the court, if I contended against them when I cannot do so in my own conscience. However, I am free to say that, when this cause was first brought to my attention by counsel, who came into it before I did, I advised my clients and their attorneys that they were in the right. I had found decisions that seemed to incline to that view; but what I did in a casual way my learned brother has done in another way not possible to counsellors who are rushed in their work by a practice that is far too extensive to be exact. I will submit what decisions I have found." There was no doubt he had done all he could for his clients; yet he seemed discouraged at the greater scope of investigation employed by the lawyer to whom he referred.

The end was now in sight. No judge has opportunity to read up on all the questions before him. He is wearied by court trials, but yet must study into the long hours of the night to keep within the plainest lines of duty owed to litigants, and here he stops in despair. Lawyers, by briefs and references, call his attention to precedents; but these must be read to ascertain the precise points on which former decisions of law courts have rested, and much reading and study are necessary. The lawyer whose history we are taking as an example was clearheaded enough to see that a general, indiscriminate practice of his profession would bar the way to the goal he desired. He said that he would earn less money, and confine himself to the larger cases which presented mooted legal propositions, for then he would keep in touch with the moods of the highest courts. To his surprise lie found himself employed by litigants who sought him for just such purpose, and the fees ^ere much larger than they would have been had he taken a greater number of clients. Lawyers feared him, for he was too thorough, too exact, too exhaustive in his researches to please them. They worked hard to place him on the bench of the trial courts, the jury courts as they are known. His aim was the Supreme Bench. When the appointment came, he declined it. His income was more than ten times its salary. Again it was offered him, after a lapse of years, and again he declined it. He had won the goal, and more beside. He will yet accept such a position if his views do not materially change.

Any person may accomplish that which the will dictates. If we had cited the case of the young man who sought to become a great lawyer, we might have shown by easier methods the certainty of winning such a goal. We went further, and presented the resolve of one who aimed at an office that is seemingly an impossible one, as it depends so much on the accident of fortune of elections and appointments. Let us see how much chance is involved. When a man has made his mind great with a knowledge of the law; when he is quick, ready, apt, clear, forcible and impregnable in his legal reasoning; when he can protect the interests of litigants by correct judgment; when he is feared by the great lawyers of the bar; when he is known to be honest; when, if he were judge, his decisions would save many protracted appeals to higher courts with their endless costs, how long do you think the profession or the great public will allow that man to remain in private life? A determined man may acquire all the qualities we have named; he is then sought after for the position on the bench. History has proved this to be always true; and there is today room waiting in every State and in the national courts for such men. The goal is attainable. Will what you will, it is yours if you are in earnest. Be in earnest in the exercise of good judgment when the goal is selected; do not choose the impossible, for that would dethrone your earnestness; go straight on to the end. It is yours.

MYSTIC UTOPIAN SUPERMEN

We come now back again to the young man who wished to rise to eminence in oratory. The person in question was in no wise adapted to that profession. His personal appearance was awkward, uncouth and in every way against him. Some elders told him that his face and shape of the head indicated some mechanical occupation as best suited to him. Still his heart was set on the idea that he did not belong to the laboring ranks for life; he had ambition for something higher, and knew nothing more to his taste than oratory. Under advice of a successful speaker, who said that the use of speech developed the art, he attended the meetings of a debating society with disastrous effects, not for the society, but for himself. He had not then learned of the fact that Daniel Webster, the greatest orator the world ever produced, had failed utterly in his first address; nor that Beaconsfield's first speech in Parliament was a dismal defeat. He had none of the elements of oratory, except the determination to be one.

It is surprising that with nothing to encourage him he ever kept his course on toward the goal, which in fact he had not fully selected. All his friends and family were against his plan; all his faults of body, of voice and of mind were barriers to success, and it seemed as if all the great orators of history were made of stuff quite different from his own nature. All this while he wisely kept at work earning a living, for the study of oratory does not much interfere with any other matter. One night, after listening to the burning words of a great speaker, and being thrilled as no other influence could do, realizing that nine-tenths of the power of a thought is in the way it is uttered rather than in its composition, he went out under the starlit sky, and walked through the fields far from the town, as if his nature needed the fullest breadth for the deciding of this momentous question, and there and then he selected his goal. He would become a great orator.

Once his mind was made up the power of magnetism was felt coursing through all his veins. This of itself surprised him. The next day he seemed a giant within himself. It was a novel experience. It made him see the world through larger glasses than the orbs of his own vision. He was to himself the central figure, and the map of the earth started from his feet and radiated in all directions to the farthermost limits. This was conceit, he thought, and began to fight it down; but it made him humbler toward his fellow beings, so he believed it to be rather a sense of responsibility under the great pledge he had made to his life. Still the magnetism that followed this concentration of his energies upon one focus was distinctly felt, and could not be deemed aught else than the force of his will. It was a grand experience. It seems strange to you who read this that magnetism does spring up from so simple an act; but when a person determines to reach a certain goal, and the willpower decrees it, the act is not simple. When the countless energies of human beings are whipped into one concentrated and concerted line of action, the result must of necessity be powerful; and this is what the will is capable of doing.

Now arose the influences described under our principles. His life, like that of every earnest person, was surrounded by thousands of details, from which his magnetism was to draw such as its interest might attract. He heard much of great orators, he read of them, he saw the essentials in part that went to make them impressive. Little things filled his mind, each of no value alone, but in combination they rounded out the structure of his thoughts. Then he caught ideas that shed rays of real light upon his purpose. It was easy to listen to speakers, for there were two or more opportunities for hearing pulpit orators on Sundays, and other occasions during the week. Then a majority of the lawyers of his county came to court sooner or later, and found it necessary to address juries, to which might he added the customary political harangues in which men tried to see who could outdo all the others in the elasticity of the truth.

To sum up in this part of his observation, he came to the conclusion that ninety-nine speakers out of every hundred were exceedingly tiresome and worse than useless. He saw juries writhing under the wearisome talks of attorneys; he saw congregations get sleepy under the dutiful regime that compelled them to listen to sermons that were altogether tiresome, lacking all charms of magnetism and gradually keeping would-be worshippers at home as the only means of defense; he found lecturers growing unpopular because they struggled to hold their influence over audiences, not by reason of their oratory, but by their sensational babyisms, their monkey-jokes and their exaggerated facts—the three ideas of modern lecturers who do not use the stereopticon for holding the interest of auditors (?) who see rather than hear. The false orator was a shouter. Small boys and timid women were induced to believe that noise was oratory, and they did not care for it.

Here were elements of discouragement enough to drown out the laudable ambition of any person, and they have kept most of the best men out of this most exalted profession, leaving the cheap talkers to prove to the public that oratory is not a pleasing art. Would he, or should he, refuse to follow out the line of his ambition because it was degraded by haranguers and maudlin shouters! This inquiry seemed like a stopping place; but lie did not bait long. What was true oratory! He asked himself over and over again. He did not dare to ask others, for be feared their ignorance, and knew they were not able to speak from a knowledge of the truth. The inquiry was an important one—What was true oratory!

He tried hard to secure such an answer as would give him the real facts, and these he very much desired as guides to his future conduct. He traveled to large cities to hear famous orators, and to analyze them; to listen to better lecturers than came to his town; to attend the great churches, where more successful speakers had drifted by the law of gravity; and in this way he obtained better ideas. One man was an elegant enunciator; he spoke his vowels, consonants, syllables, words, phrases, clauses and sentences with a polished and beautiful clearness that was charming, and it almost seemed as if this were the secret after all. He had read in books that humanity was distinguished from the lower animals by the power of articulated speech, and this particular speaker had developed such power to its highest art. Could it be that perfect enunciation made the orator! He reasoned it out, and suspended his judgment until he could go further in the analysis.

Next in the charms of speech came an orator who did not use the common run of voice so often heard among the less effective speakers. One man had a very high pitch, and although he varied to some extent, he made it his prevailing voice; and the more he shouted, the higher up the scale the voice went, until every ear was sore and every brain irritated by the harsh screech. Then came the resolution never to inflict such pain upon his audiences. Another speaker had a more agreeable pitch; it was located in the middle part of the range, and this was a tremendous relief from the other fellow who went so high. Still, when he got to shouting, as most of the failures do, the pitch would tend upward a little and was correspondingly tiresome, even painful. He asked himself, what use was it* to inflict soreness upon the sensitive nerves of the audience, when the chief purpose of oratory was to charm and to win. It would be just as reasonable to court a beautiful girl by thrusting pricking needles in her ears; such courting would not win her. He could see one reason why oratory was on the decline, why juries were uncertain factors in courts of justice, and why religion was suffering so terribly at the hands of modern preachers. He could easily guess why John Wesley and George Whitefield were able to make hundreds of thousands of converts, and change the history of all England by the magnetism of their voices.

One more speaker aroused his interest. It was one who had no note in his voice lower than the middle tone. He was more popular, for the voice was incapable of producing pain. Think of that in oratory! 'A man who causes the least pain is the most popular; or, in reality, the least unpopular. As long as churches endure and jury trials are ordered under constitutional law, so long will some portion of humanity be coerced into listening to speeches, and perhaps in daily life the monotony of duties will make even the lecture field a welcome change with all its pangs. This was the way he reasoned. Discouragement was the natural consequence of such discoveries. Men, bright in some of the matters that involved the exercise of judgment, lacked common sense enough to know that a harsh voice, a one-pitched voice, an unmodulated voice, or a shouting voice could not serve any of the legitimate uses of the mind. Most persons who fail in life, when expecting success, are blind to the essential fault.

There was one man who really charmed his hearers by the pleasant variations of his voice. It was not confined to the low register, like a lion growling in a cavern from which he could not get free; it was not kept in the middle realm of the scale; it used the upper notes rarely, but it played like a great organ through all the marvelous beauties of song, leaping from note to note as the meaning demanded, and blending the whole into one harmonious expression. This was one of the uses of modulation. He noted the fine effects of pleasure produced by the quiet touches of the lighter tones, the solid stamp of character in the sturdy timbres that required no shouting to make them impressive, the thunder peals in the occasional bursts of power, and the lightning of magnetism that sent its flashes over the whole structure; and this pleased him. So he began to think that enunciation, that perfect coinage of vowels, consonants, syllables, words, phrases, clauses, sentences, groups and paragraphs, each in the proper die, each set forth in place and proportion to suit the character of the thoughts with which they were burdened, was the first essential of oratory, especially as it stood for the best presentation of that one distinguishing gift that separated man from the brutes, while modulation was the second essential, carrying as it did the charm of variation in the music of speech.

By this time his attention was attracted to the tones of a voice in a man whose every note was peculiarly rich. Then he asked himself,—Is it possible that one human voice may be so different from another; so different from all others! Is it not made by the larynx, and is not every larynx made by the Creator! How, then, can one voice be harsh, crude, rough, raw, rasping, aspirate, breathy piping, twangy, scratchy, or something else, while another is rich, melodious, resonant, clear, fine, beautiful, exquisite, and silvery in tones!

This was a serious problem. It betokened an examination into the well-known art of voice-building, to see if such defects were curable. What was his own voice? It was unpleasant. No one cared to hear it. He attended still his debating society, but he was rarely ever sought for his powers of speech, and what he did say seemed to assist in thinning out the attendance.

He talked with some acquaintances who had been trained by teachers, and he learned enough to ascertain that a slight improvement had been made, but not as much as might have been had the pupils taken interest in themselves. Not one in a hundred make the progress that is possible under such help. He learned from good authority that a new voice could be built in two years, and he went to work upon it. The larynx changes its size, weight, strength, force and character with the training it receives; but the real nature of the voice is in the instrument as a whole that produces it, and this instrument is the pharynx and mouth, the hard palate or sounding board, the soft palate or muffler, the resonant chamber, and much else. He worked hard. Little by little he acquired a new voice; by changes so slight as to be unobserved, he took on another character in tone; he had an instrument of a million strings; he could use the timbres, the qualities, the stresses, the degrees of pitch, force and time; he found that there were mental colorings that gave meaning to sound, and emotional colorings that stamped the heart and soul upon his language, and the more he delved, the more he saw ahead of him to acquire. It was all wonderful.

Surely the art of speech was not one to be considered the birthright of every fellow who thought he could talk because he had a voice and something to say. When our would-be orator had discovered the value of the many acquisitions by which the thoughts are expressed, he believed that the secret was his; but, alas! he had a still longer road ahead of him. The arts and embellishments served to furnish the best channels for his thoughts, but what were the thoughts themselves worth? The merchant marine is best served in its carrying of goods by the most convenient and most effective means of transportation; canals, rivers, seas, lakes and oceans on which to journey, and every variety of ship in which to store the merchandise; but the real value of the latter, the source of its supply and the ports to which it is to be conveyed, are even as important as the means of conveyance. He found a parallel truth in oratory.

The question then arose, which was the better of the two? He studied orators, and analyzed their subject matter and its manner of delivery. In such cases as those of Edward Everett and Rufus Choate he found that the charm is entirely lost in the absence of the speakers, and this he attributed to the magnetism with which they presented their thoughts. Among living orators he found that some had very good matter but wretched manner; others had poor matter, and one only of the many effective means of delivery; yet all had the audacity to pose as representative speakers. He saw, he realized, he felt in every fibre of his being what a magnificent power that man would be who could combine the thoughts of highest value in sentences of transcendent skill, and utter them in those best uses of the voice that nature with a lavish hand would gladly bestow upon him who was willing to toil for the guerdon. Over all there was needed the inspiring force of magnetism that lighted up the man, the mind, the thought, the language and the graces of art, making them a combined power not to be resisted by any counter human energy.

Closing the mind injures it.

This is the Forty-ninth Principle. In a number of ways this law has been referred to in the present volume. The willpower is an active and aggressive energy, a throttle open with a guiding hand upon it, never relaxing its control. A closed mind may be pictured in one or two illustrations, either as a horse balky and moveless, or running away unguided, or else as a locomotive stalled and stationary against all efforts to start it, or sent out with steam on, and no person in the cab to control it. The closing of the mind is not a shutting of it up against all efforts to move it, but a set action or inaction that admits of no alteration.

The refusal to change an opinion is a closing of the mind, for it is not open to influences either of right or wrong. In exactly the same sense the determination to do a certain thing, or to pursue a certain course of action, closes the mind when it refuses to desist, stop or change its method of progress. In other words, it is equivalent to saying that this particular thing shall be done, even if I know it to be wrong, or the plan of action I have entered upon ceases to meet with my approval. "When I say a thing I mean it," says the shallow mind. "Everybody knows that what I promise to do I will fulfil," says another. Here is a vast difference. Nothing can be more praiseworthy than the fulfillment, of all proper pledges, promises and appointments. The business of life depends upon that.

The mind is excused from every improper loud agreement, contract, promise or threat. The law states as much. A large number of contracts are annulled by the courts. A note even, which is a commercial bank bill in some of its effects, is set aside as between the maker and payee, if made under mistake, in error, for lack of sufficient consideration, through deceit, or is obtained by other improper means. But the kind of mental closing to which we refer is that which takes away the continual watchfulness of the judgment and stops the motion of the will. A potentate said: "I will slay the first person I meet." He met his daughter, and slew her; not for any fault of hers, not to aid himself or his people, but simply because he had said he would. No pledge, however solemnly made, can rise to the dignity of even the smallest obligation when its purpose, its method of execution, or its effect is useless or wrong.

When the Roman lawmaker made death the penalty of an offence, and his son was the first offender, he was right in ordering his execution if the law was right and the penalty not too severe in any case; he should not exempt his son from a desert which some other man's son would have to meet, although he had the power to save him. We are now dealing in questions of abstract justice, but are free to say that the parent is always justified in saving the life of his offspring, no matter what the offense or how deep the shade of guilt. In blood there is no sin that merits death. The family ties are stronger than all laws of earth. Much less is it justifiable to keep a foolish pledge.

The fulfillment of any proper agreement, promise or appointment is a matter of necessity. None such must ever be broken if there is a possibility of preventing the breach. It often requires a constantly open mind to avoid disappointment in such matters. All persons should know what agreements are pending, what appointments remain to be fulfilled. It is wrong to make one, then shut the mind in forgetfulness and pay no further attention to it. Too many persons are careless in a matter of this kind. A promise is made to a friend; the time comes around when its execution is due, and the promiser is totally oblivious of the fact; the friend may know that the breach was unintentional, yet the same degree of respect and confidence will never be shown again. Weak it was to make the promise and close the mind to it, weaker still to show no concern over the loss of trust that must follow.

Parents are freely willing to make all sorts of promises to their children, but when they shut their minds to the keeping of them, an injury has been done to themselves and to the little ones. On the other hand, the continual making of threats is reducing the magnetic quality of the mind. Most threats made to children are abandoned. "If you do that I will surely whip you," says a parent. The child does the thing inhibited, but does not receive the whipping. Seeing that the threat has no potency, it goes on, day after day, defying its parents, and soon becomes unruly. The question of governing children has many phases. A proper threat of punishment should be fulfilled if the child merits it. An improper threat should be abandoned, as where the mother said: "If you touch that flower I will whip you until you cannot either stand or sit." The child did touch the flower, and did not reach that condition in which it was impossible to stand or sit. Another mother said: "If you speak one more word I will punish you." We cannot conceive of any situation where the utterance of a word requires punishment, and there is no necessity of keeping the terms of the threat. Better than these methods of governing children is that which employs magnetism and needs no penalties.

We trust that the difference between closing the mind against doing a thing and against ceasing to do it is clearly seen. The effect is the same in its injury, for it involves the same principle; and one is as stubborn as the other. Thus if a person refuses to consider a matter that requires attention, or if he will not look into it far enough to see whether it requires attention or not, he closes his mind; while, on the other hand, if he decides to do a thing and goes ahead blindly to the end, or persists against his judgment in the attempt to do it, he likewise closes his mind, though against the ceasing of it, which is in no way at variance with the principle.

Discretion is the magnetism of judgment.

This is the Fiftieth Principle. Most mistakes cause regret; some repentance, others remorse. All are detrimental to the union of the energies of life. The confusion and scattering of these powers necessarily bring disturbance in the forceful run of magnetism, especially if a reversal of action or a complete rearrangement is required. Discretion is a rare gift, but it is a magnetic one. It is often cultivated by the weighing of results under the standard of past experience, generally of others.

Nothing can be more satisfactory than the skilful judging of probable consequences; and few things give a man more confidence in his mental powers than to find he had formed correct opinions. It is not at all essential that the element of guesswork or the law of chance be depended upon, for they involve the flavor of lottery, and the more one indulges in that flavor, the less he will develop his powers of judgment and discretion. It is true that when these efforts come to a standstill, and all ahead is clouded and dark, there can be nothing done but to await the turning of the hand of fate. Here the skilful mind sees the alternative, and prepares to accept either without loss.

MYSTIC UTOPIAN SUPERMEN

In the anticipation of trouble the magnetic person uses all the discretion possible, looking at every kind of outcome. He says, or acts in effect as if to say, that he will do his best to avert the misfortune; but if it must come, he reasons thus: "It will occur in a certain way; or, if not so, in another way; or else in a third. If it should happen in the first way, I will act so and so to meet it; if in the second way, I will change my plans, and give it a welcome by doing thus and so; but if it comes in the third possibility, I shall meet that by such and such methods." It will be seen that he is not to be surprised. Every futurity has one, two or more chances of happening; and discretion reasons out what these are, how they will befall and the probable effects. This much being understood, the next thing is to learn what to do in any event, so as to meet the exigencies. Thus discretion not only teaches a man to avoid mistakes and troubles when they are merely portending or are unnecessary if due precaution is taken, but it teaches him to be prepared in advance for trouble that cannot be averted. When it arrives, it is generally too late to meet it with a minimum degree of annoyance. It is a stitch in time that saves nine.

The use of discretion is one of the bulwarks of success in the career of every man who rises in the world by reason of his native ability. This principle is seen with the lawyer in his practice. One of the keenest attorneys was answering the statement that the advocate who had the final argument in a case always had the advantage. The counsel for the plaintiff in a civil action, or the prosecuting officer in a criminal trial, addresses the jury last, at least of the lawyers. In some States the judge delivers his charge before the summing-up speeches of the lawyers are made; in other States he is required to follow them, so that the erroneous effects, if any, may be counteracted. The warmth of effort and of appeal must come from the men who strive to win for their clients. The lawyer for the defence does his best; all the surprises, all the strong points of the cause have been quietly conserved, and he makes mountains of them in his eloquent speech. Then the attorney on the other side proceeds to demolish the effect.

It has been frequently said of Daniel Webster and Rufus Choate, who were undoubtedly the giants of their day in the legal profession, that whichever side was in the right would win when these two advocates opposed each other in the same case. In one instance, Webster was on the wrong side, for the litigant who is at fault needs a strong lawyer to save him; but so hard did he fight that Rufus Choate declared it took him a whole day in his final speech to undo the effect of Webster's great address to the jury. This shows that the last speech is not always easier in a trial. But when a man is in the right; when his lawyer is not the abler of those engaged in the struggle; when he must sum up to the jury, and then be followed by an address of tremendous power, skill, adroitness and fallacy of such a nature that the common minds of the jury are unable to extricate the truth from this entanglement, then justice fails, unless the defendant's counsel is equal to the danger.

Solid men who are not accounted great or brilliant have, by their discretion, been able to thwart these influences. Said the lawyer to whom we have referred: "The advocate who speaks last to a jury has the advantage only when his opponent is careless in the preparation of the case; otherwise the defence is in the best position. I remember that the hardest victories I have won have been in cases where I appeared for the defence and had the most eminent lawyers against me. I borrowed trouble, as I call it, though I mean that I anticipated trouble, and prepared to meet it. I never allow myself to be surprised in a trial if I can avoid it. My plan is to go into my office at night and alone, and there address he jury aloud in my imagination. I take the opposite side of the case. Talking aloud excites thought, makes new ideas and gets the machinery of the mind in operation. I have a pencil and a writing pad. When an idea of force comes to me, I write it down at once. I do not wait a minute. The best thoughts come out of the everywhere and are evanescent. I secure many valuable things in this way. I tear the defence to pieces. I picture my client as the man who is wrong, and the plaintiff as the one who is right. I invent, by every kind of ingenuity, the points that must most impress the jury. Now, in an ordinary important trial, the summing up is limited to an hour on each side; yet I put in three or four hours, and out of the mass of points I make I find a certain number of strong ones that are really the most essential to that side. A new light comes to me; I see through the plaintiff's case, as though it were transparent. I see what must be the position, or at least what ought to be if the counsel for the plaintiff is thoroughly familiar. In the greatest of such causes I have talked to imaginary juries in my office a half a dozen nights or more, to get the other side exhausted of all its points. When the trial is reached in the courts, I know more about the plaintiff's case than his attorney does, as I have several times proved. I anticipate all his argument, and generally all his testimony, though some bits of evidence cannot be foreseen. Why, in that last cause, tried a month ago, I spoke for the defence three full hours, closing just as the court adjourned late in the afternoon, the worst time of all for a defendant to stop talking to the jury. I was forced to this by the strategy of the plaintiff's lawyer, who kept his dilatory arguments going till noon time. Yet in my speech, I covered all the ground of the defence; I anticipated all the points the very able advocate would make in his address of the next morning; I answered them very fully, even exhaustively, and I told the jury quite vividly the very points he would present to them; and although he had all night to get his offset to this, he could do nothing but go over the ground I had covered. He labored very hard to make the points appear new, but he failed utterly, and when the jury had retired he said to me, very savagely, 4 Which side of this case are you on, I would like to know,' meaning that I had argued both sides." The action of so keen a mind must be ascribed to his discretion in foreseeing events by analysis, and preparing to meet one alternative or the other.

The same results have been attained in matters not relating to court trials, although they present the story of life in all its forms. Edwin Booth found, on one of his tours, that his costumes and scenery had parted company on the way to a certain town, the former going in one car by a wrong train, and the latter in another car by another wrong train. He was assured that both would be on hand in time for the performance. Instead of worrying unnecessarily about the affair, he first ascertained what could be done to hurry them on. A number of telegrams were sent, and no stone left unturned; so all was done that could be accomplished in this direction. Then he imagined himself on the stage without scenery and without costumes suited to the character; or with the scenery, but with no costumes; or with the costumes but no scenery. Then he and his manager discussed these possible situations, and prepared to meet each in turn. In the town in question there were no costumers, and the theatre itself had but three regulation scenes. These things are known in advance. One of the regulation scenes was a wood or landscape consisting of some trees and a stretch of country; but nothing in the play called for that. Another was an ocean view, called an horizon by actors. The third was an interior, called a fancy chamber. Only this last could be of service in the play in question, which was the Merchant of Venice. The first act opens in a street in the city; the landscape scene and the ocean could not picture the canal or the street for them, and the fancy chamber did not suit either of them or the subsequent movement of the play. Here was a vexing problem. If no costumes came, it was decided that an explanation should be made to the audience, and the actors go on in their ordinary clothes, while the stage should be set in an exterior and the performance called al fresco , or in the open air. If the scenery came, and not the costumes, it was decided to allow the company to wear their ordinary clothes, while Mr. Booth appeared in a black gown, which he might easily borrow from a friend whom he knew, and who had one that had been worn there by a supernumerary on a previous occasion. By this planning in advance, all confusion was avoided on their arrival; all fussing, fuming and worry was laid aside. It so happened that the scenery did not arrive, but that the costumes came in time, and a beautiful al fresco performance was given with a delightful smoothness. Had the deciding of what to do been left till they arrived, the actors would have been worn out, and their magnetism would have been lost. As it was, Mr. Booth was at his best, and the audience seemed not to realize that the scenery was lacking. When the local manager made the announcement that the scenery had been delayed by the railroad, but that al fresco performances were in style among the elite, it pleased them.

The use of the will assists in developing the will.

This is the Fifty-first Principle. A good quality grows on itself by using. All the virtues gather strength by the earnest practice of them. Love is enhanced by true love; charity made a fixed habit by the act of judicious giving; hope is brightened by the upward gaze of faith, and what is worth improving is made better by the very act of improving them. The will is likewise developed by making many tests of its action, providing these efforts are discreet and founded in good judgment.

All unmagnetic persons lack energetic wills. Only those who are blessed with positive magnetism are able to exert the will at all. Others think they are showing willpower when they are merely exhibiting obstinacy under a closed mind. Thus a verdant fellow, who had once or more times tried to drive his father's hogs to the brook, only to have them go the other way, and who therefore drove them from the brook, and thereby got them to go to it, went to a large city. He was met by a lifelong friend, whom he never saw before, but who pretended to know him and his antecedents; and he took pleasure in correcting errors, and they parted company. Soon another friend came along, and explained to him that the foregoing stranger was a bunco steerer, who was pumping for further use. "Oh, I'll know him if I see him again," said the countryman. But the second friend really did know him after thinking it over; he told him who he was, asked him if his name was not so and so, his father such and such, and soon proved his title to his confidence. They then went around together for mutual protection, until the verdant fellow was robbed in a very quiet manner. He then saw through the trickery, though he required a policeman to explain to him that the first stranger had pumped the facts out of him and given them to the second stranger. Later on a cousin, whom he had never seen, met him by appointment, and was refused an audience, in the belief that it was a third stranger. In such ways the absence of discretion and willpower lead to disaster.

In contradistinction to this case was that of a green fellow from the country, who was told that he would be victimized if he went to the city. He liked the idea, took a hundred dollars in bank bills, and went. On his arrival he was met by a green fellow fully as much in need of protection as himself, and who told him that he was afraid to go about alone, as he was never in the city before. The first verdant seemed to sympathize fully with him, and stated that it was his first trip. "I have a hundred dollars here," he said, showing the amount. The eyes of the second verdant glistened, and the first one saw it. Intuition dwells in humble minds as well as the astute. He caught the idea at once, and proceeded to catechize his friend. The latter made every effort to get him into certain streets, but it was to no avail. At length they parted.

He inquired of policemen where to go, and found their information to coincide, so he deemed it trustworthy. Soon a very nice and pleasant faced young man met him, and called him by name; it was wrong as usual, and the stranger expected to be told the true name, but he got only the confirmation of the first name, Johnson. "I guess I have hit it by accident," he probably thought. "Silas Johnson is my name," said the country fellow; "and my father, Joshua, is a trader in horses up in —ville. His brothers are Peter Johnson, a blacksmith, and Henry Johnson, a farmer, six miles from town." So he went on, and they parted; but not before the hundred dollars had been displayed. Soon came stranger number two, a rather sedate man, with a hymn book under his arm and a drawl in his voice. He stopped, lifted his hands in surprise, looked for a moment, then rushed to the green fellow, saying, "Well, well, of all pleasant surprises this is the best. Delighted to see you. Don't know me? Well, you could not, but you are the perfect image of my father. Your father and mine were second cousins, if you are Silas Johnson, of-ville. If not, I have made a mistake. Let us see; your father's name was Josh Johnson. They called him Josh, but I know it was Joshua. Joshua was a good man in the old Bible days; and you had two uncles, Peter Johnson, a blacksmith, and Henry Johnson, a farmer, who lived some miles out from-ville; let me see, it must be six miles.

Well, how are you?" They chatted for a while. This verdant fellow had given false names to the first stranger, and had made them up on the spot; and as soon as he heard this invention he knew that the two men were in league to defraud him.

To him it was a pleasant experience. He showed the man the hundred dollars, and wondered how he could lose it. The first attempt was being led to a crowd and jolted; but he held his hand on his money and jolted back. When this experiment was repeated, he caught the hand of his aggressor, and found that it led to a third stranger two feet away and behind his hymn-book friend. This man he hung to like a vice, for he had a fearful power in his hand; and although the scuffle caused great commotion, he clung to the thief through thick and thin, and delivered him to a policeman. This occurrence puzzled the second stranger; he made a subterfuge attempt to trip the country fellow, who observed it and said nothing.

Matters proceeded in this way but with new attempts to decoy the fellow, until at last they got to the shells used in the game of monte, and this interested him exceedingly. The hymn-book man was quite unused to it, and wondered how it was done. He tried it though, for it was very plain that any bright mind could detect the plan of operation. The first time the stranger tried he won a dollar, then two, then five, then ten, and he never lost. The money was genuine, no doubt. The green fellow was asked each time to try it, but he replied, 4 'You try it once more." After the ten dollars were won by he hymn-book man, he ventured fifty cents and was successful; then a dollar, and equaled it. He got quite excited, and his friend, the hymn-book man, urged him to put up his hundred dollars all at once, and make another hundred on top of it. He said he would try five dollars first, which he did. All the crowd knew he had a hundred dollars, and those who knew the game expected that he would be permitted to win the five dollars and that the hundred would come out at once. He did win the five dollars, and he put them in his pocket. They expected him to rush out his full fortune, but he merely said, "Fellers, I come to this yere city to see if I could keep from bein' robbed. This yer feller with a hymn book has been showin' me about for the past few hours, a-doin' his damdest to rob me, but I hain't that sort." The bunco steerer slinked away. The case shows the power of the will as a means of protecting oneself from the deepest intrigues.

A young woman states a case that shows the effect of a constant practice of the will. She loved a young man, who had proposed marriage and been accepted. He seemed to regard her as a weak object in his hands, to be molded by him as he pleased; and she could hardly succeed in protecting herself from his aggressions. He meant to toy with her affections, and had the advantage of his superior will coupled by her ardent love for him. This was a combination that could hardly be resisted. One day she read of weak girls and the fate that generally befalls them; also a bit of advice, telling girls to exercise their willpower to the utmost. She did not propose to offend the young man, not to act in a severe and prudish manner, not to show petulance that might make him regard her as a bad dispositioned girl. On the contrary; she treated him graciously, and at times, when he seemed desirous of taking advantage of her, she looked him fully in the eye, and sweetly said "No."

Her account to a lady friend showed that as she uttered the word she exerted her willpower to the utmost, and the decisiveness was stamped on the tone of her voice.

A young man who was tempted to drink had been so far overcome by his companions as to be unable to resist the use of beer, which is the beginning of the drunkard's fate, and on one occasion he had taken a glass of wine, and later on a drink of whisky. As he had scoffed at the idea that beer would lead to the habit of fixed alcoholism, he was overwhelmed with grief at the thought of being so deceived. He sought advice, and a good friend told him that his willpower would save him, and explained the process of magnetism in its use. He resolved to test the matter. At the next temptation he said no, and acted no decisively, and won. Again he was tempted and sought the aid of his willpower. It grew stronger as he used it. He then went in the study of magnetism, and fortified his willpower to such an extent that he could repel all temptations and not offend his acquaintances. His whole life was revolutionized.

Intensity is the arousing of the vital centers first; whence their power travels to the whole body. When the will is at work, the mind usually starts the action. Where there are ganglia, or where gray matter is found, there the electric batteries exist. The brain is the central furnace of magnetism. The mind is either positive or negative. If the former, it sets the will going, if it does not close; but if its energy shuts up its operation into a fixed refusal or a fixed, unswerving course, it is obstinacy, and all magnetism is at a standstill. If the will keeps alive and active, becoming a moving progression of force, it is soon as powerful as the limit of magnetism allows. These laws are important ones and should be understood. The so-called iron will is as useless as a furnace of blazing fire when it ceases to give out its energies to some governed purpose. It may be observed in any person who is without doubt highly magnetic that he becomes tense as the power takes on strength. This is best seen in watching a speaker addressing an audience, or a person in conversation, who shows magnetism. Relaxation, or what is called the devitalizing of the body, is just the opposite; then every power drops; the vital centers are disconnected from the muscles; the mind even is languid, and there is no control over self or others, although the functions are in every way normal.

In watching persons who display magnetism, it may be seen that those who are obstinate, no matter how strong the will may be, are not tense nor warm in vitality. They are coarse, ugly, cold, stalled, and things of fixed and mindless strength. It is true that a person should be stubborn in the right rather than weak and overcome in the wrong; but he never gets on in the world. A horse that balks is perhaps better at the edge of a precipice than one whose knees are so fragile that he cannot keep from toppling over. The wishy-washy characters are objects of pitiable contempt, while the stiff and unreasoning rocks who cannot be moved except where they wish to go, and as far as they wish to go, are objects of disgust. We like not the silly fool from the country, who gave up his money to city sharks at the very first suggestion; we like not the stem fellow from verdant regions also, who locked up his money at home, and took but little with him for fear of the loss; but, rather, we like the greeny who carried the roll of bank bills in his trousers ' pocket, who told everybody he had the hundred dollars, who showed it to the sharks and sharpers, and who held on to it in spite of the deepest intrigues. That fellow was not obstinate; he was not afraid; he was strong, and conquered. That is true magnetism.

When the mind is sending forth its streams of energy, then the will is most dangerous, most effective and most far-reaching, for it is most active. To sustain the will, there must be a constant propulsive force, and this comes from tensing the mind, which imparts intensity to all the faculties. By this process we have the secret of success in the use of the will. The study of this one phase of magnetism is in itself important. As has been said, the best opportunities for observing the action and effect of intensity is when a person is speaking, either in a conversation or an address. The orator that wins furnishes an excellent illustration of this use.

We recall a session held one Sunday afternoon under the auspices of a certain church. A large audience had been attracted out by the promise of interesting speakers. The first address was brief and merely introductory. The second was made by a stranger, who talked smoothly, and what he said seemed to be freighted with information that aroused attention, but in twenty minutes this grew tiresome, owing to his personal lack of vitality. It was a relief when he sat down. The third speaker began in the same way. He was all devitalized. In muscles, in attitude, in the craning of the neck, in the languid flow of the mind's efforts, in every way he was lacking in energy. Four men made preparations to go home; the children were restless, and the pastor looked sorrowful. This man came from a distance, and had a reputation in a far off locality.

The four men looked at the door and measured the distance from their seats to the place of exit. They had their coats on their arms, their hats in their hands, but did not take the step that would start the journey home, for the speaker had shortened that craning of his neck, and was now becoming erect in attitude. Something in his legs raised him an inch higher; they were no longer languid. There was nothing sudden. All was quiet gradation. Once in a while a speaker who lacks magnetism is compelled to make a remark intended to shame his tired hearers. This results in needless enmities. On the occasion in question the man did not resort to such measures. He saw the four restless auditors, and knew that they would slip out at the first lull in the proceedings. He did not say, "I will wait until those who wish to retire have done so," but he gauged his own momentum, and knew that he would soon be well under way. He did not throw some intensely interesting remark to catch their minds as by a hook, nor did he promise great things as an inducement for his audience to remain.

Like a giant steamship getting momentum as she floats down the bay in the majesty of motion, he straightway swung into the channel of his power; yet without any evidence of change at any place of transition. His whole body became tense, in little gradations; his neck was now straight; his head rested upon a magnificent pair of shoulders, like a globe poised on the back of Atlas; he neither stormed, thundered, pealed, nor jerked. The floating palace was acquiring headway. The voice was so still in the quietude of its tones, now grew richly mellow. Ideas without effort flowed in an easy stream of power, while the arms rose in attitudes of expressive meaning. The man was becoming tenser in his body, though not by any means less active, for this quality does not mean mere rigidity. The four listeners, who were aiming to go out, ceased to gaze in side glances at the door; they turned around, and faced the speaker; the coats fell to the seats, and the hats got down under them by some sort of magic that was never explained.

Then the power of magnetism was more and more felt. The voice deepened at times in a wonderful descent to the rich mines that were beneath the surface; it flashed rarely, but with beautiful effect, in the glowing streams) of light that came across the horizon; it moved in irresistible floods of power toward its goal, the greater ocean beyond; yet at no moment did the orator appear to labor. All was majestic, all at ease; yet every fiber of his body was alive. The eyes took on a new glow as the flesh became intense, and one seemed to keep pace with the other, as though the laws of cause and effect were at work. The gleam of the eye is closest to the brain, and that is nearest to the seat of the will-power. Exertion or straining was not apparent.

The will is strongest when its intensity is smoothest.

This is the Fifty-second Principle. Some students have fallen into the belief that a physical, a nervous or a mental straining is necessary in order to produce the best results in the development of the will. Such struggling leads only to distraction and confusion; the very influences that are not advantageous. We have seen men of genius strive to send forth their magnetic powers by tearing their passions to tatters, as Hamlet would say; we have many and many a time noted the heroic storming of some amateur tragedian, as he attempted to impress the audience with the idea that he was the greatest actor of the world; yet they, the astonished beholders, merely studied his grotesque movements in amazement, wondering what he was really trying to do. Cicero wearied his hearers at first by his excessive vehemence of manner, and would have been buried in oblivion but for that excellent charm of common sense which told him of his errors. Genius thus may run away with itself.

The most splendid exhibitions of magnetism, and the greatest, have been those wherein there was no struggling to send forth the will, no straining of the voice, no fevered pulsing of the nerves, no tearing of the mind, no severity of gaze; but, on the other hand, that perfect smoothness that is the result of a consciousness of supreme power. Then is a man or woman most dangerous. Quietude is deceptive, and the world is not on the alert. Expectancy is wanting, and there is no preparation for the coming conquest; no method of resistance has been adopted. One hardly knows the volume of power that is accumulated by intensity when aiding the will, if magnetism is already acquired. The three furnish an irresistible combination. In the unusual quietude of Mr. Moody, the evangelist, is seen the almost contradictory force of human electricity, ever sending out its influence over those who come within the range of his voice. He himself grows tense as he proceeds, but never strong; what force of tone he has is lacking in those bursts of thunderpeal that made Spurgeon, Beecher and Whitefield greater than all contemporary orators. Mr. Moody had full willpower, a vast fund of magnetism, and a steady, quiet but giantlike intensity. The will is the strongest when it is smoothest in its power. We have seen what it is; in another realm we will learn how to accumulate it and use it.

THE ESTATE OF Personal Attainment AND THE CHARMS OF MAGNETISM

HARMS are embellishments of manner, of method, of thought, and even of feeling, that cannot fail to lend power and advantage to those who possess them. A face that is ugly may terrify, and even hypnotize, because of its frightful effect; but no person wishes to win the will of another by putting to sleep the faculties that make the personality a prize worth winning. Said a man who loved, or thought he loved, an excellent young lady: "I could not secure her heart, but I was unable to reason in my mind that she ought not to belong to me. For this end I hypnotized her, little by little, until I had her consent. But she was clay, nothing but clay. 'No enjoyment sprang from my conquest. A rag doll could yield to me as much. I turned about in my methods, told her the facts, and began the other way. By magnetism I climbed the ladder of success; by hypnotism I descended to the pool of remorse .' 9 The two directions are exactly the opposite of each other, and they lead to results that are antagonistic in every sense.

There is a physical magnetism that sometimes carries things by storm. It plunges forward in a flush of excitement, and all things crouch before it. The vitality of the lion, the tiger or the bully is of this sort; and a temporary paralysis of the willpower causes the poor victims of fright to remain powerless. In the same way a woman becomes speechless in the presence of a burglar, and many a man loses all control of himself under circumstances that overwhelm him with alarm. This is due to the fact that the suddenness as well as the force of the shock stops the breath, and holds the heart still, making a display of strength impossible. A man cannot be brave if his heart will not beat. These bullying methods are not magnetic. This is not an age of animalism or of force among the most civilized nations.

Leaving such brute energy out of the question we come down to the single fact that there is no way of securing control of individuals worth having, when secured, except through magnetism. This power uplifts each human being; it affects and brings him up to the standard of the person who exercises it, even though but temporarily. It wins, not subjects. It creates the impression that the superior being is one whom it is agreeable to know and to serve. The hypnotist charms as does the snake; the magnetic individual exerts a charm that is real. It produces pleasure because of its value. It supplies vitality and exuberance where these are lacking; it sustains them, where they are present.

Magnetism gives buoyancy to others and arouses vitality.

This is the Fifty-third Principle. What is meant by buoyancy is a lightness of feeling, as though the weights that have dragged down life are released, and the heart once more soars to realms of hope and radiance.

Many a time have we heard some weary person say that the presence of such an one had driven all sorrow away, for a while at least. " Why do I go to hear Mr. Gough lecture every time he comes? Because he lifts the heavy load of care from my heart; he fills me with life, and I am stronger for weeks after he has lectured." It is well-known that John B. Gough's magnetism was of the very highest order, and drew larger audiences at every renewed engagement. In one city he failed to attract a large number at the start, although his reputation had well preceded him, the difficulty being due to the fact that he was regarded as a temperance lecturer, when in reality he had a large repertory of other subjects; and the city was passing through the era of decay due to the general use of alcoholic beverages. The people spoke of him as one demented. The press published the statement that he had arrived in the place drunk.

His personality was an example of the power of magnetism. The lecture was slimly attended, but by his proofs he showed the perjury of the press, and held the editors and reporters up to such scorn that they never again received the confidence of the public. Those who were fortunate enough to listen to the lecture came away a stature higher. One lady said: "I never felt so grand as when I came out of that hall," and her sentiment was echoed by others. The magnetism of the man had overcome the first meeting of his enemies in that place; but he was destined to follow up the advantage. Later on he delivered another lecture in that city, in which he repeated his proofs of perjury against the press, and his reception showed that the people despised the papers, as after-events also corroborated, for the paying advertisements were withdrawn, and the papers suspended.

In another place he met something of the same experience, for the reporters and editors all came forward with the allegation that Mr. Gough had not been sober for a year, and that his nerves were unstrung from habitual drunkenness. It is well-known that a person who is in such condition could have none of that steadiness of nerves that is necessary in the self-control of magnetism. The public knew this. His enemies and his friends knew it well. So, to prove the absurdity of the charge, he took a goblet of water, adding more, until it was full to the top and almost ready to overflow; then, during the most impassioned part of his lecture, he held the goblet out at arm's length for fifteen minutes without so much as jarring off a single drop. The wonderful steadiness of nerves and the tremendous strength of his magnetism were marvels that enraptured his audience. Year after year he came to them, and lived to see his enemies, the editors and reporters, buried in the grave of oblivion that sooner or later closed over them.

There is a pleasurable satisfaction in the new vitality which we feel when we come under the influence of a great soul. Something is added to the force of our own faculties. There is strength in the contact. A man who suffered from a headache that his doctor could not cure, went to hear a speaker who possessed a large amount of magnetism, and came away without the headache. A young lady, who was subject to painful headaches, found that they would fly away whenever her aunt came into the room, as she believed the lady took them from her.

The evidence is very full and very thoroughly corroborated that all magnetic individuals exercise this happy influence over those who are weaker; sometimes all that is necessary is to enter a room, or to speak a word, or to give a glance of the eye, and the depression gives way to buoyancy and a feeling of stronger vitality.

A magnetic person may supply magnetism to another.

This is the Fifty-fourth Principle. In its application to the practice of hypnotism it has an important bearing, in that it furnishes the power to release a subject from sleep, and restore him to his normal consciousness. We have seen that the magnetism of the subject must be exhausted by the operator before such sleep can be induced, and it remains for the latter to again supply what has been withdrawn.

If this is not done the subject either falls into a condition of true catalepsy, or else wakes out of the condition as soon as his sleep brings back vitality enough to establish magnetism or nervous life, although only on the negative side. The question has been asked, if one who is powerfully magnetic is able to yield up his own magnetism enough to establish a positive fund in another individual. The idea that a person possessing this power obtains control over others by lessening their freedom of will is wrong. When magnetism produces an influence over another person it increases, for the time being, the power of that person's mind, and adds a volition or desire to agree with the views expressed by the person exerting such influence. It wins this agreement by fair means. In order, however, to do so, it is necessary to give such strength of mind to the person as will enable him to grasp and understand the ideas which are set forth. When the influence is of an emotional character, the whole nervous system of the person to be won is enlivened, strengthened and made responsive to the feelings which are expressed.

Persons whose magnetism is negative have been brought over to the positive side by the great power of some individual, as is often noted at the theatre. The stimulus for dramatic talent has been aroused under the influence of some very magnetic actor; and persons so affected have gone from the amusement hall firmly resolved to devote their lives to such art. It is said of actors who have become discouraged through their own waning abilities, that their power has been revived and a new lease of genius secured through such stimulus. Magnetism and vitality are associated under certain conditions, but each is an element in the makeup of the being. Vitality may be referred to as relating to health or physical strength although magnetism associates itself with the source of both; but the latter term is more familiarly recognized when it occurs in the operations of the nervous system, through the mind, in the emotions, or as some form of feeling. Through these channels it reaches similar conditions in others, and furnishes them with some share of its own power. It makes the vitality stronger, and sets in motion the currents of bodily health, without taking any of these qualities from the person who thus benefits others.

The best physicians are thus endowed with the ability to stimulate into health the depressed vital systems of their patients, and to buoy up their depleted magnetic state by the vigor and fullness of their own nervous life. "I felt better the moment the physician arrived," said a wealthy banker, who was suffering from nervous prostration. " Although I was very ill at the time, and lay in bed with my face from him, having no knowledge who was coming, I felt as if a strong influence was approaching me; and, somehow, I found that I had more strength and more of that quality which I had often known as personal magnetism. I turned over, and saw the doctor's great eyes shining upon me, and his features seemed to say that he proposed to bring me back again into health, even if he lost some of his own magnetism by so doing. His voice was decisive and told the same story. When he placed his hand upon my forehead, it seemed as though an empty shell was being filled from some large storage battery." The same kind of experience has been common with those who are ill and are fortunate enough to have the services of physicians who possess a large fund of magnetism.

Magnetism awakens and strengthens whatever faculty it affects.

This is the Fifty-fifth Principle. Not only does this power give its virtue to individuals toward whom it is directed, but also reacts upon the person exercising it. Let a man who is undergoing a system of training or culture for the purpose of enhancing his own value give his mind full scope of action, and he will soon discover that the brain and its operations have been benefited. If a student of magnetism, after making some headway in the acquisition of the power, devotes himself to cultivating the will so that it may be made an instrument of resistless energy, he will be pleasantly surprised to learn that this faculty has grown with great rapidity.

Man has so many faculties, and they are so varied in their uses, that it is only necessary to refer to them in a general way. We have known many students of dentistry, and many practitioners in that profession, who have taken up the art of magnetic culture as a means of assisting them in their work. Whether the old style of dental work is pursued or modern methods prevail, it is of the utmost importance that the nerves he strong and always under the most exact control; and it is their steadiness, coupled with good judgment, that determines the real skill of the dentist. The instruments he uses are small yet powerful in their effects; his hand should not allow them to slip nor should rough usage and unevenness of applied force cause pain to the patient. There is no difficulty in recognizing the hand of skill, or the more clumsy hand of unsteadiness; and many a person has refused to go a second time to a dentist who, no matter what his knowledge may he, lacks control of his nerve or has not that fineness of touch which lessens the suffering and gives a relative pleasure, if such is possible. From reports sent by dentists who have learned how efficacious the art of magnetism becomes in their profession, we are satisfied that no greater blessing could be secured, both for the practitioner and his patients. One very frankly stated that the study of magnetism has added thousands of dollars to his yearly income by reason of the greater skill acquired.

The lives of most doctors are so irregular that they are constantly subject to low states of vitality, from which their patients suffer fully as much as themselves. No man more than a physician needs the aid of magnetism; and it is our pleasure to know, from knowledge secured directly from them, that many physicians, reaping the advantages of this culture, have acquired magnetism where none was known before; and others have increased the stock already on hand. Lawyers have been slow to take advantage of anything that adds to their personal qualifications for rendering useful services to their clients, their chief aim being to extract as much money as possible, and to flatter themselves by occasional successes in litigation, no matter what the means employed. There are, however two or three lawyers in every hundred who believe that the greater their own personal attainments may become, the more useful they will be to those whose money makes it possible for them to live; and these few, numbering thousands in the aggregate, are finding out the truth of the matter. Wherever any attorney has entered earnestly into the study of magnetism he has added vastly to his ability, to his reputation and to his income.

Magnetism aids the lawyer by making his brain stronger and clearer; by enabling him to grasp the more difficult situations in a case; by leading him into the depths of the law without submerging him; by showing to him the salient facts in a cloud of disconnected testimony; by enabling him to explain everything clearly to his clients; by preventing him from the disadvantages of confusion and distraction during the heated conflict of trial; by giving him a better standing in court, both before the judge, the jury, his associates and opponents; by enhancing his power in argument, and, above all else, by quickening his keenness of insight in the examination of witnesses. The reason why most lawyers refrain from any means of self-improvement is a fixed belief in their own extraordinary powers, which is not borne out by the experience of after-years; still they keep on waiting and looking for that sudden blossoming which never comes, whose embryonic petals are mildewed in the infancy of their budding. Hence the unmagnetic lawyer is a failure.

A very valuable illustration of the change that this culture will produce in one life, comes from the statement of a lawyer, who undertook to improve himself at the age of twenty-five, after nearly four years of practice. He had commenced work in court before the close of his twenty-first year, being the youngest jury advocate in his country, and found himself favored by an extraordinary combination of circumstances, of which he was able to take full advantage. He lost case after case, and soon found that prospects, which had at first appeared splendid to him and his friends, were rapidly fading away. This condition of things discouraged and disheartened him; he saw that something was wrong, but what he could not tell. He was gifted in speech, was a good rhetorician, was keen in logic, and had depth of reasoning powers for one of his age; yet older and mightier lawyers awed him; the adverse ruling of judges made his mind a vacuity for the time being, and shrewd witnesses overmatched him. Cross-examination was something he could not understand.

At the age of twenty-five, when he was really about twenty-six, his prospects had practically vanished; his conceit had proved a bubble of thin vapor, and he cast about him to discover the cause of it all. After months of enforced idleness his mind perceived, in the efforts of the great advocates to whom he listened with rapt attention, that they possessed a quality which he utterly lacked. This was commonly known by the name of personal magnetism. People said it was born in men, and could not be acquired; and this he believed for a while. He took the trouble at least to analyze this quality, and he found that it was always attended by certain personal charms, which seemed to be the source of the power itself. Further examination showed that such charms were merely attendants upon it, necessary to it, but not originators of it. He was compelled to look further. He noticed that magnetic men were cool and always free from embarrassment; that they spoke deeply and from their souls rather than from the mind; that they derived their power from within, so far within that they seemed to speak with another self, and that they had warmth in their tones, a gleam of brightness in the eve and a tense condition of all their physical faculties ,

All these things gave evidence of an electrical or phosphorescent fire burning within. When a magnetic speaker began to exert an influence strong enough to affect others, a person sitting at a certain angle could always discern this electrical brightness of the eye. The lawyer to whom we have referred spent some time in the study of these forces, specially as applied to the human being, and he satisfied himself that they could be acquired. Books then told him so. He found that they came both by negative and by positive means; that in a negative way, by preventing waste and loss of vitality, the natural accumulation of nervous energy in a single day became enormous, and that this might be added to by exercises, training and regime. He was somewhat idle in his profession, and took plenty of time to discover the full truth of these new suggestions and to put them into practice.

Soon after he had become interested in these ideas, he had a court trial at hand, and herein he resolved to make some effort toward winning through the aid of the power of personal magnetism. He really trained himself specially for the handling of this case. By some very good luck the trial was delayed three weeks beyond the time first set, and he had a total of nearly three months in which he had devoted himself to this culture. He laid everything else aside, for he was thoroughly in earnest. He had not then studied the nature of the will as a magnetic force, but somehow made the mastery of himself in this particular trial the goal of a most determined resolution. Never before did he open a case so calmly and yet so firmly. Never did the members of the county bar see him so cool, and they said that he had the self-possession of one confident of victory. The first real and effective cross-examination that he had ever done he did at this time. He actually discovered errors in the statements of witnesses, and destroyed the value of the testimony offered against his client. In the various arguments that attend the offering of objections during the course of a trial he was clear, concise and effective, and almost uniformly successful in the positions which he maintained. His argument was the best he had ever delivered, and the first entitled to positive praise.

Four years later this lawyer had become a master adept in the use of magnetism. The only thing we care to specially note in this connection is his statement of the remarkable clearness of mind which attended him in the cross-examination of adverse witnesses. This clearness almost reached the realm of the subconscious faculty; and certainly many questions, which he was prompted to ask, and which brought answers that materially helped him in the winning of cases, must have sprung from the gift of intuition. In illustration of the same point, a very successful jury advocate once made this statement: "In probing the minds of witnesses opposed to me I often found myself impelled to ask questions that came to me by a sort of inspiration; and many an apparently lost cause has been won by the hazard of chance inquiries. It seemed as if the witnesses had these important things in mind, and thought of them so hard that my own mind must have caught them; and one case, I am sure, was lost until I saved it by a chance question." This experience has been confirmed by other attorneys similarly gifted.

Magnetism is enhanced by every physical and mental charm.

This is the Fifty-sixth Principle. Not only does magnetism benefit and improve in every way the faculties of those who employ it, but it also is improved by the charms of personality in the individual. It would not be reasonable to expect any power to win by the sheer force of its own energy, any more than we would expect an engine, without evenness of action and freedom from friction, to do effective work, even though the most powerful energy was driving it. Magnetism is the power in the individual; the charms of his personality are the channels, in part at least, through which that power acts.

Any method that will attract the favorable attention of others is of some service; and any thing that will repel makes the exercise of power so much the harder. No person has ever been successful in the use of magnetism who has not aided it in every possible way. Flattery from a shallow soul, uttered in display and without semblance of genuineness, is always repelled; even those who are pleased to be praised by the empty heads of sycophants become angry at the dead tones of such flatterers; but let it be charged with the warmth of magnetism, and it takes on a new life at once. In such a way have the aggressive natures of the world's famous personages won their way to the hearts of those who would otherwise have remained enemies. We do not mean to say that mere flattery is a charm; the fact really is that the fascination attending it lies in the politeness, the sympathy and the kindness of heart that magnetic men and women know well how to use with the greatest effect.

Nothing is more valuable in the study of human life than the close analysis of those methods by which successful persons capture the good opinions of others, whose aid is necessary to them. The lawyer, by his extraordinary success, may force the public to patronize him, but he cannot force the jury to believe in him simply because he has won other cases and has achieved a great reputation. To fall back upon such a belief, and to repel the jurors by unpleasant methods of procedure, would be foolhardy in the extreme. The clergyman might claim that he is charged with the power that is implied from the nature of his profession, and the great majority seem to rely upon nothing else; but if charms of manner, elegance of mind and effective beauties of voice were substituted for the loud and rasping notes of a discordant voice, the results attained would overwhelm the world. Many physicians pretend to believe that a knowledge of drugs is all that is necessary to bring their patients back to health, and so much vantage ground is lost in this profession. The same principle holds true in every department of life.

The personal habits of some individuals tend to repel those who would like to be their friends. Awkwardness may be endured in the seclusion of acquaintanceship, when unobserved by others; but no young lady takes pleasure in displaying to her choicest friends a lover who is constantly having a misunderstanding with his feet; who knocks things over by the angularity of his elbows, and who sits astride an imaginary war-horse when in their presence. In a well-balanced nature love is never blind to faults that invoke general ridicule; and many a genuine love match has come to an abrupt end because of the crudeness of the lover, and he has been left to infer that the cause was due solely to the fickleness of his sweetheart. She was too generous to wound him where he was most vulnerable.

The roughness of mind and heart, as well as those of the body, have stood in the way of success in thousands of instances, where ability would otherwise have carried men to the highest pinnacle of fame. It needs hardly be noted that many prominent men in recent American history have been obscured because of their lack of charms, both in mind and heart, although they have been gifted with genius in its grandest form. When a little success makes a man arrogant, overhearing and independent of the opinions of others, his ability is never great enough, nor his past triumphs brilliant enough, to prevent the decadence of his power. His career begins its downward course. If he succeeds at all after that, it is by compelling others to yield to him, and this enjoyment of power is bound to be short-lived.

Temperament is the result of magnetism, not the cause of it.

This is the Fifty-seventh Principle. The first step toward the attainment of those personal charms, which aid magnetism in winning, is to establish a fixed temperament; and this is done by the adoption of new habits. It is supposed by some, if not by most persons, that magnetism is the outgrowth of a natural temperament, the influences of which give it birth. There is no reason for this assumption. The analysis of the lives of men and women proves very conclusively that the magnetic temperament is developed by methods of living, regime or courses of conduct that tend to conserve the nervous energies; and those who are described as possessing this power by the gift of nature are entitled to the credit themselves, even though it has been unconsciously secured.

Experiments show that any person who is in earnest by emulating the examples of others, if he is able to ascertain what they include, can develop the same temperament in himself. If he waits for it to become established before he undertakes this line of study, he will wait in vain. The temperament is undoubtedly necessary, for it is a continual source of supply and stands him in good stead under all circumstances. He needs it in those hours of conflict or discouragement, when the very foundations of his nature seem to fly from under him; when enemies are strongest and friends weakest; when it is hard to assume an attitude of courage that his own position does not justify, and when a compromise with the soft terms of policy, at the expense of honor, will relax the tension of the strain under which he is held. No man can have a better friend, a more staunch and abiding supporter than such a temperament. No woman is better qualified to take care of herself in the world, to repel aggression without giving offence, or to show her superiority to the average man, than when she is aided by this temperament. Yet both sexes may acquire it at will. Like many other forms of riches which surround mankind on every side, it requires but intelligent effort to possess it abundantly.

Common lives that seem to lack all character in their temperament, have been revolutionized after the use of magnetism has commenced. It is not merely in the study, but essentially in the adoption and practice of this power that advantage arises. It may be adopted by a resolution of the will, founded upon a knowledge of the ways in which the native force is kept from wasting, and also upon the regime that drifts into lives without practice of any sort. Man is the daily creation of his own mind, and life is the accumulation of days. Young men are most ambitious in the years when they seek hardest to earn their own living; say from twenty-one to twenty-seven in many cases; and they most easily acquire new temperaments. Older men change at will, but are not as flexible. We have known women at every age lay down the coil of a badly-planned life, and take on the vesture of temperaments calculated to improve their conditions. In some the change is most rapid. We must see what steps are necessary to be taken.

Magnetism broadens the features.

This is the Fifty-eighth Principle. To one who reads carefully and repeatedly the requirements and regime that make and attend the change from a negative to a magnetic temperament, the first real surprise is the destroying of the "worry wrinkles" that are found on the brow in most persons. There are three kinds of these; the first and most common being the two indentations at the top of the nose, between the eyes, at the base of the forehead. In some persons there is but a single indentation; in others there are two, of about equal height, for they are always vertical; in others they are unequal, one being long and deep, the other quite short and thin, while the weakest of all nervous temperaments have three.

The strongest men and women, in a nervous sense, make one deep wrinkle and another shallow one, generally on each side of the nose, while a spray of very faint indentations will appear over each eye in rare instances. The life, or dramatic meaning of a vertical wrinkle is dislike; and this comes from the fact that occurrences of the day cause feelings that embody the mood of dislike. We never worry at what we like. Hatred, malice, revenge, and all the darker characteristics of the mind tend to produce these vertical indentations. In any event, they show a negative state of magnetism and a temperament not of the best. They do more than this; they mar the face, destroy its beauty and repel the admiration of those who would otherwise find pleasure in looking upon it.

Study the faces of those whom you meet, or of those with whom you are thrown in daily contact, and note the accuracy of this law. When the brow is knitted, something is wrong; some idea has passed through the mind that has caused dislike; or some fear, worry, fretful influence or other similar mood has detracted from the peace of the brain or nervous system. A mother shows this more than a father; for her cares are many, and she never is free from them; but a man in business, who cannot keep matters straightened out or always under control, will come home with the deep indentations at the brows. Speak an unkind word to one of your friends, and no matter how boldly it may be defied at the time, if it has sunk in you will note the deepening wrinkle hour by hour during the day. The sullen brow depresses the face and narrows it perceptibly.

If you wish to see how quickly the smoothness or beauty of the face may be destroyed, knit the brows and go about that way all day long. Your acquaintances will ask, "What is the matter?" Strange glances will be cast at you, and the remark may be made: "Something has gone wrong." This will not be so, if it is your custom to carry knitted brows, for they will not exhibit surprise. Many a beautiful woman has lost all her good looks by this deplorable custom. Young ladies, who have depended upon their faces for the retinue of admirers that have made life enjoyable, find at length that they are not so attractive as formerly, and wonder what has come over them. They see all the defects of skin and color, but not those of the muscles. Said a young man: "Here is the photograph of the girl I once loved. Look at its smoothness of face; and now, three years later, see how ugly it has become." It was ugly indeed; but the cause was in the muscles, as the general shape of the face showed the possibility of great beauty.

On inquiring the cause of his discarding her, which he had said he did, we found that it was due to an irritable temper. She had scolded him often for trifles, was fretful, and seemed to dislike most persons, for she rarely had a good word for any one. "Yet, when I met her, she was a very sweet girl and had a very beautiful face." The cause of her change of temperament was really the habit of fretting at little things. It grew on her, until it became a settled habit. This is true of very many persons. They fuss and fret, and give way to every little hit of irritation, until they no longer have any control of themselves. Then the face gets narrow, and the wrinkles come in.

We mention the case of the girl who had been discarded, because it arose in the midst of a circle of acquaintanceship well known to us. The young lady was aware of the ugliness of face that had come in so short a part of her life; she knew in time that it had driven her lover from her and was constantly ostracizing her from the friends whom she would secure, and she had just sense enough to inquire the cause. For three years she believed it was due to the meanness of the world in general, to the falsity of all mankind, to the fickleness and empty hearted pretenses of those who would fawn upon her if she would permit them. Then she became satisfied that it was due to herself.

This was a very wise conclusion, and few indeed are shrewd enough to catch the spirit of a fact so accurately. She took a mirror, and exclaimed, "What a face!" It was her good fortune to become a pupil in expression, where the phases of life are studied under the principles and fixed laws of nature. To her teacher she said frankly: "I am studying my own face under your theories of facial drift, and I wish to see if I can control it. In the first place, is it symmetrical?" It certainly was, in bone formation. There was no deformity of brow, cheekbone, nose or chin. No better shaped face could be found. The trouble was with the muscles only. The hideous ugliness was due to a contraction of those strings that move the flesh to suit the mind and disposition. Every ill-natured thought ploughs its small groove through the face; but this is really done by a contraction at the temple muscles, as a basis for facial drifts, followed by the narrowing of the brow.

The face is a bunch of strings, called flesh muscles. Each part is in two arrangements; one to pull the flesh one way, the other to pull it back again. These masses of flesh are capable of being moved up or down, right or left, and in any combination of these directions, as up to the right, up to the left, and so on. In fact, there is no direction in which some part of the face cannot be moved. The skin is a live leather, overlying the flesh beneath; it is controlled by an intricate interlacing of little muscles, and every thought sheds its influence one way or the other on this construction. The expressions of which the face is capable are more than two thousand millions in number, and they are all made by the multitudes of directions which each fine fibre may make.

It stands to reason that, if a skin is smooth when stretched, it would be wrinkled when collapsed, relaxed or contracted. Magnetism is a life of tensity which destroys all relaxation as indicative of weakness; it pulls the face out of its narrow shape into one of breadth. The mere sensation of pleasure does this, while gloom contracts the features. An examination of the process of change seems to prove that the broadening of the face begins at the back of the ears, and pulls the temples smooth; but the flesh at the temples plays its part at the same time. The forehead is also active, so that it cannot be said that the scalp at the back half or third of the head is the only motive-power at work.

In noting these important movements, no result is more satisfactory than that which comes from the bringing of a genuine pleasure to one who has been depressed. A gentleman was quite worried over the uncertainty of news in a certain business transaction. His usually serene countenance, which indicated self-control and magnetism, was now severely contracted, and deep indentations were noticeable between the eyes at the base of the brow. Two friends secured information of the brighter turn of affairs in the business matter, and came to him resolved to see what effect the news would have on his knitted face. It was agreed that these two men would sit, one on each side, and note the effect of the gradual introduction of the report which they were about to make. The conversation had been adroitly planned.

He greeted them as usual and then relaxed into some business matters that required attention. The two men began a cross-fire of remarks widely separated in point of time, but calculated to lead indirectly to the subject that was uppermost in their minds. The first referred to a third party who had become interested in a business deal of a similar nature, and he said of him, casually: "Mr. A. is likely to pull out after all." There was a long pause, when the second man said: "Yes, I saw him this morning. He was feeling very cheerful." Another wait of several minutes ensued. The man in the center of this group of three was listening, then went to his work again, as though he had not heard at all; but the effect was noticeable; there was a tightening of the muscles at the temples, and the scalp behind was somewhat tense. The first man continued: "I heard that A. was through with the matter." Another pause. The second man added at length: "Yes, he's through, and his bank account is fatter today." This was too much for the worried man. He swung around, and asked: "Have you heard anything definite!" "I merely got word that the deal was closed." "Which way!" "A. came out ahead." "This helps me." "Does it!" "Yes; I will phone up." The knitted brow was not yet smooth; there was a lingering doubt. He rang his telephone, and communicated with agents who had charge of the matter, and learned that the load had fallen off his shoulders. Success came, and in a very large measure. He sat down to go on with his other business, but it was too tame. The face had come out smoothly; the deep indentations were gone. They left their tiny scars, awaiting the deepening effect of some future worry, if it should perchance happen to come.

No face is so repulsive as that which is narrow. The lines at the sides of the mouth grow straighter in conditions of negative magnetism, and they become more curved and broader in cases of positive magnetism. The cheeks are thrown in against the nose, and the nostrils are pinched. Look at those little openings at the nose, and see how broad, how wide open, how distended they become under any phase of self-control; then note the pinching of the same features when the disposition is meaner. They say the dramatic meaning of closed nostrils is cruelty. It may be that the center of the face, which is in fact the seat of emotional intelligence, is indicative of the heart's moods, and that cruelty and its kindred meanings are found in such contractions, while generosity and sympathy are associated with the broadening of the face-center.

Then the forehead muscles play a very important part in the determination of moods that are the outgrowth of the reasoning faculties. Let a person think much on a subject, and his forehead will show lateral or horizontal wrinkles running over the nose and partly over the eyes. These are strangely produced in two ways. When the brows, or the little lines of hair over the eyes, are raised high, the forehead takes on horizontal wrinkles, the true meaning of which is doubt. Certainty tends to bring down these eyebrows, and firmness plants them squarely over the eyes. Uncertainty raises them; the greater the doubt, the higher up they go; and you have seen some men and many women who are unable to withhold this evidence of their worrying.

In one case a woman of generally calm face was seen to raise her eyebrows very frequently. In a week they were fixed at a quarter of an inch higher than before. The trouble was due to the fact that her husband had taken inventory of his goods at the store, and the account of stock showed a falling off in the last six months. This he told to his wife. The thought of poverty, of failure in business, of the anger of creditors, and the disgrace among neighbors when the report got out, filled her mind all the livelong day, and haunted her in dreams. In a month the eyebrows had risen a half inch, and in four weeks more she had them up close to the top of her forehead. No change could be more complete. It was amazing. Her brother called upon her from his far western home, and could not refrain from an exclamation of surprise when the uplifted face greeted his. He inquired the cause; but she, faithful to the promise made to her husband, refused to divulge it. The brother then went to the latter, who had not noticed the change in his wife; the gradation had been so little day by day. They discussed matters of business in confidence, and better success came. But it took as many years to restore that forehead to its normal shape as it took months to produce the former change. This is a common experience; a tendency the wrong way is not so easily remedied, for it soon fixes itself.

Trouble is the combined meanings of that uncontrol which instigates the expressions of doubt and that dislike which is shown in the knitting of the brow. In the making of this double meaning the vertical wrinkles pervade the lower half of the forehead, due to the contracting and narrowing of the face; while they are crossed by the horizontal wrinkles, making a display of broken skin. The forehead is truly clouded. Its meaning is trouble. The strange fact is that the horizontal lines are due to the forward movement of the scalp more than to the upward action of the eyebrows. This pushing down of the forehead by the scalp's action allows the brows to remain down also, as in sullenness; the latter having some element of firmness in it, as is seen in the closed mouth when the corners are down in the settled mood of discontent.

Magnetism tenses the face, as does any bright sensation, and this tensing opens the features. We have referred to a young lady, who allowed her peevish nature to so narrow her face that it became quite ugly, although it had been beautiful. This ugliness drove her lover away. She studied expression, and learned what were the causes and the meanings of all muscular changes of the face. Under advice she also studied advanced magnetism. Not by artificial methods, not by pretenses of a better disposition, not by massage and the mechanical means of smoothing her face, did she attempt to get back its beauty, but by a deeply rooted system of magnetism that went to the core of her feeing and revolutionized her mind, her heart and her nervous nature. She won back her loveliness and her lover. The same thing is true, or may be made true, in all lives; for magnetism broadens the features, as it also broadens the whole personality. It is the best of all personal attainments.

Cynicism weakens mind and heart.

This is the Fifty-ninth Principle. If we were dealing with nothing but physical magnetism, we might let this subject go without discussion. The best phase of this power is in its mental and emotional character. The beef is good enough, but there are departments of human life far above flesh, even though dependent upon that as a basis of existence. Our principle refers to the dark malice of the mind; the very thing that turned the sweet faced maiden to a hideous hater of her fellow mortals, and stamped its nature on her face.

Cynicism is a distrust of the motives of others; a looking for something sinister in every good deed; a berater of charity because of its possibility of intended display, and a snapper at everything and everybody from early morning to the last hours of the dreary day. Its first effect is seen in the features. The brow knits more and more deeply; the forehead has its wrinkles of doubt, as though all persons were objects of dire suspicion; the nose becomes pinched in cruelty, and the corners of the mouth drag down. Take a mirror, and try to change your face to such a condition; see if you deem the same beautiful, and try to catch the meanings that lurk in the disarrangement of those lines that may mark the sublime trend of grandest thoughts, or scrawl the hatred of the devil. Do not allow cynicism ever to possess you.

It is not because of its moral, so much as on account of its magnetic value that one should be free from the cynic's disposition. The cure is in the formation of a new habit, by the resolution of a determined will, which shall forbid the doubting, distrusting moods to come into the mind. Bad things grow first and fastest. When you look for flowers, the weeds are there. Uncanny habits take a strong hold on most natures, and resist to the last. The will alone can conquer them. Now, here is an opportunity for you to try your own value. What are you worth in willpower? We know you are cynical; just a little, perhaps; but it is the little out of which everything great grows. Eradicate it. It is better to hunt for good motives in every human life, and be deceived, than to hunt for the had ones and find them; better because of its reflex action on your mind, your heart and soul. If all men and women would cease searching for the ill in others, and set about finding the good, there would be much more of the latter in the world, for we can always find what we look for. Try it. Set the example. Get a hundred others to try it also. It will become infectious.

Adverse criticism is unmagnetic.

This is the Sixtieth Principle. It is true that all persons are free to pass judgment on the acts and thoughts of their fellow beings when any earthly good can be accomplished by so doing; but the criticism should be bright, sunny and generous, without being untrue and misleading. If you cannot say bright things of a person, keep silent. Few indeed are the individuals who are totally deprived of some affirmative quality; if you find such, you may pass them by. There are some people whom it is best to disregard.

Criticism is of two classes; the first applies to matters of which the public seek to be informed, the second to those in which individuals are interested. It is useless to speak of the methods employed by newspapers, as such methods are generally beyond the pale of civilization. As long as they attack evil, show fight to the devil, and cry down the bad in every form, they are the agents of good; but they do not do this. We believe that it is the duty of every man and woman who honors the truth to make war upon dishonesty. Criticism attacks the individual. War attacks a principle. Persons engaged in doing injury to their fellow beings should be suppressed, and their punishment should be intended to deter them and others from doing such injury. All these things come under the head of crimes.

So frail is the human heart that perfection is far from possible. The critics are always steeped in the poison they discover in others. From the tone of their language they seek to create the impression that they themselves are free from faults. They do not deal in crimes or penalties, but in weaknesses of life; picking out faults here and there, and holding them up to ridicule. They do not attack principles or methods, but persons. They avoid dealing in laws of operations, and confine themselves to characters which they choose to sully, because mud looks stronger on white. They prick human beings always in sore and tender spots, as though it were a sudden discovery of theirs that there were vulnerable defects in mankind.

What is gained by the general criticism of art, of professional work or public careers ? If a production of the artist is worthless, absolutely and entirely without merit, why not let it alone? The absence of notice will certainly not be construed into a favorable report. If it pleases the ignorant, let it stand for their sake; for the wise will not be deceived by it. If a picture or statue is so poor in taste and skill of execution that it repels the uninitiated, it is not worthy of notice; but if it gives pleasure to one mortal, let it go to him in peace. Critics have pronounced as daubs some of the masterpieces of creation; so the opinion is sometimes no better than the thoughts expressed. In professional work, singers, speakers and actors have been made the butt of ridicule by the cheapest of scribblers, the most ignorant of whom are found in the large cities. In New York it is so easy to bring favorable notices from certain critics that men, whose income from their papers is merely nominal, have become wealthy in bribery. In that city, and as well in any of the large centers of population, you never see a stinging, sarcastic or mean attack on a play, an actor, a singer, a musician or a speaker, unless the critic is bidding for money, and is making the notice as bitter as possible in order to secure a bribe against its repetition in that or other cases.

If professional work has merit, let that part of it be stated. If it is utterly lacking in merit, it is a wonder; but let it alone. Every time you turn on the mud faucet in your own brain, you daub yourself. You cannot besmirch another without getting spattered. If the work has but little merit, state that much, and there let the matter rest. No one will be deceived. It is much better to be silent, or to state a little and have it bright, than to turn the mind into a green scum simply to let loose some words of ill. Nor is it the harm that may be done to others that is to be considered; the moral side of the problem is not what we are presenting; it is the reaction on your own mind. To possess the charm of brightness, you need all the sunshine there is in life. You can get none so well as by shedding it, as though you were an original sun, throwing your rays to planets and their satellites.

MYSTIC UTOPIAN SUPERMEN

That class of criticism which interests the curious minds of the masses is in the line of personal malignity. There is so much devil in men and women that they enjoy the downfall of virtue. Even when the pale-faced and pious souls exclaim, 4 'Too bad!" they mean it not. Here is a man who has held up well for fifty years; the public has learned to place their confidence in him; the newsmongers get hold of some bit of gossip started by some "human gabber," and the story is distended and distorted till it is suitable for a column or more of print; the criminal papers start it with big headlines; the vilest of these take a whole page, with circus poster type running clear across, and it is given to the public. Now the men and women who say, "Too bad!" and who pretend to such sorrow because of the downfall of this man— well, what do those pale-faced, pious persons do? Do they feel the pangs of sorrow because of one more good man gone wrong? Not at all. They read every word of the account. They get other papers that contain the contortions, horribly stretched out; they call the attention of their friends and acquaintances to the affair; they scatter the news as widely as their morbid natures can, and they are totally lacking in the sense to see that the discrepancies of the sensation stamp it as an untruth on its face. What next do they do? We shall see how sincere is that expression of pity. The next day the less criminal of these scare-head papers come out with the statement, in a few lines on a back page of their issue, in an obscure corner, to the effect that the scandal was wholly without foundation; that it was made up out of whole cloth by some gossip, and that the man was innocent. What do the pious men and women do? They glance at the refutal with disgust. They never correct the lie to their friends and acquaintances. Such is human nature.

We present this scum of the heart because you must meet it everywhere, and you must not cater to it. You cannot afford to send such clouds across the sky of your own life. Disappoint the morbid greed for this scum by refusing to become a sewer through which any mud shall flow. Persons whom you meet may declare that they never indulge in gossip and scandal; that they do not care to hear it, and all that; but the fact is, they will prick up their ears to catch something ill, and will turn deaf at mention of something favorable. "I heard a certain thing of H.," said a man to an assemblage of acquaintances. "What is it?" chimed in every voice, in eager inquiry. "He gave a hundred dollars to some worthy poor," was the answer; and the assemblage said "Oh!" in tones of disgust. On another occasion, a man =said to the same group: "I heard a certain thing of D.," and they asked quickly, "What is it?" "Well, I heard that B. got into trouble last week." "What did he do?" "Out with it," "Tell us all about it." "Well, he borrowed fifty dollars of a friend—" "And never paid it back?" "Not exactly. He lost it." "Pretended to?" "He said he lost it." "Yes, yes; of course, he said so. He would say that." And so the conversation went on. Let any ill report start out concerning any man or woman, and the curiosity of the mind demands to know it, and to retail it. Let a suggestion of good, no matter how slight or how strong, be made concerning a person, and it dries up all curiosity. It is altogether uninteresting.

A very conclusive experiment was made with a woman who had professed to despise gossip. A gentleman friend took for the subject of his test an almost unknown personage, so that the question of interest in the individual might not enter into the problem. He then remarked to the lady: "I have been pleased to hear good reports of Mrs. J."

"Are you interested in bicycling?" "Somewhat. You know Mr. J. does not ride a bicycle." "I never heard so." "They speak very well of him, and I heard of a very excellent deed of his not long ago." "That is very good. Bicycling is coming into vogue very rapidly." "I believe it is already quite popular. I got hold of a piece of gossip about this same Mr. J. that does not put him in a good light." The woman swung around, directed her gaze from the open window toward the man, and asked: "What did he do?" "It was something that does not reflect credit on a man who pretends to be honorable." "Will it bear repeating?" "I think so." "Then tell me." "I interrupted you in your remark about bicycling. Are you learning to ride?" "Not yet. I may, however. But what was that about Mr. J.? You are very tantalizing. Tell me; you keep me in suspense." "Oh, yes; I forgot. Do you wish to know what it was he did that I mentioned as being very good?" "No, no. I don't care for that. You said something else." And this woman then saw the weakness of her nature; but she excused herself on the ground that her own heart was but a reflection of humanity in general. So it is.

There is a reason for it, but no excuse. The reason is a plain one. All human beings are defective. Not one is perfect. The best man and the best woman is morally vulnerable somewhere. When that weak spot is found, the human devils dance about it like a crowd of revelers, glad of its existence. You must not join in that crowd. You need and must get a better temperament, one that cannot endure the upholding of dark suspicions in this world of light. Be brave. Never see evil in another. See only the good. Never hint at the bad. Solicit the favors of sunshine, cheerfulness and loving kindness, and shower them broadcast wherever you go. It will pay you well. It is the magnetic temperament.

An unpleasant voice is unmagnetic.

This is the Sixty-first Principle. The voice is a reflection of the real person. No matter how we attempt to vary our tones, we cannot escape this law. Even the affected assumption of ease fails to conceal what is behind the voice. It has been common of late years for persons who realize that their words are harshly spoken to assume a certain style of utterance, which is known as affectation, such as we hear in the fop, or in the languid lady; but supposing the pretender to be ill, or discouraged, or envious, or malicious, or in whatever mood you please, the voice will betray such condition by mixing other qualities or colors with the affectation. On the same principle it is impossible for a good-natured man to assume a really disagreeable tone, although he purposely uses a constricted or throaty voice in the attempt.

There are fixed qualities in the human voice, and they are natural because they are the result of long continued use, which has developed into a fixed habit. If a person has seen too much of the ugly things of life, has developed enmities, sought revenge, or given vent in other ways to a disposition of dislike or hatred, he will have a voice that tells this story in spite of all he can do to conceal it. Ordinarily this is known as a guttural fault; the throat seems to be narrowed, as though he were attempting to growl at everybody and everything. We are sorry to say that a large majority are endowed with this harsh and unpleasant quality; and it is probably true that the same majority of the human race has experienced feelings of hatred or the desire of revenge to a greater or less extent. Another common fault is that of the aspirate voice, by which the tone is mixed with unvibrated air; and the meaning of this is a desire for secrecy, for it is the natural outcome of the universal gossiping habit. It is said that not one person in ten thousand, on an average, is free from this evil. An aspirate voice is unpleasant and irritating.

In order to cultivate a pleasant voice it is first essential to get at the root of the trouble, and this will be found in the temperament. By mechanical exercises the guttural and aspirate qualities may be eliminated, except for the purposes of art, where they do some service; but the only result attained is the acquisition of musical clearness and purity, which may be entirely lacking in interest. Still it is a fact that mechanically pure tones cannot be long kept from becoming harsh. It is by no means a difficult matter to overcome all impurities of voice, including the most serious defects as well as harshness, by magnetic exercises alone. This is the short road of the best of voices. Under the usual systems of voice culture it has required not less than two years to establish purity and brilliancy of tone, whereas the development of magnetism has accomplished as much in a shorter time, besides adding permanency of value that can never be attained by mere vocal practice. The voice is disagreeable in the quality of its structure, in the method of its use, and in what it seeks to convey. Everybody is agreed that harsh or unpleasant tones annoy those who are compelled to hear them, as scratching on glass with a nail irritates the ear.

Dead tones are unmagnetic.

This is the Sixty-second Principle. We have seen that the voice may be made mechanically pure by exercises in voice culture which are designed for producing that result. At first we wonder why a sound that is free from defects, as of harshness and a scraping roughness so often found in the speaking tones, should not be pleasant when the faults have been removed. So they are, by comparison. The note of an organ that had a cracked reed proved annoying to the church folks; when a new reed was put in the place of the defective one, the sound was pleasant by comparison. The note was clear, beautiful and perfect. To hear it once was charming; to hear it a thousand times was pleasant enough; but to hear it always was lacking in the charm that it first gave, for it was a dead sound.

All persons have live or dead voices, in the sense that they speak from the muscular system, or from the mind or heart. A young man said of a young lady, who had one of these mechanically perfect voices, "She has the most beautiful voice I ever heard." He followed her for several years as a friend, admirer and suitor. She was of a lovable disposition, as far as she was capable of loving, but had no malice or hatred in her heart, for she was too inactive; an example really of an undeveloped nature. This young man could not endure the emptiness of her tones after he had become better acquainted with her; their clearness and purity gave him no pleasure, although they did not produce that distress which the opposite qualities do, and were preferable to them. She had a dead voice, one that was completely lacking in magnetism, in emotional warmth or in mental strength.

Most voices are far from pleasant. They serve for a while as a means of communication in business or social use, then the hearer is glad when they cease.

We often meet this dead voice, and in a variety of forms. Sometimes it is coupled with aspiration in its worst condition; at other times it is gutteral, harsh and scraping; and in these combinations it repels all persons who come within its sound. These are those whom we dislike very much to listen to; they talk and say nothing; or, when their ideas are worth anything, the way they present them is wearying. "He is a very attractive looking gentleman," said a young lady, describing one whom she had been glad to meet; "but the moment he began to talk I was tired of him. His voice is nothing, just nothing." The supposition that an oral voice is a dead one is well founded, and it is generally true, but not always so. There has been life discovered in tones of the oral quality, but it is languid. In a few rare cases physical weakness has been the real cause of this unresonant voice. At all events, it should be turned into one of magnetic warmth, and this is the quickest and surest of all methods. The dead voice is overcome in no other way, no matter how hard one may try to force it out by culture of the mechanical sort.

Monotony of sound or action tends to hypnotize rather than magnetize.

This is the Sixty-third Principle. What is called range of pitch is variation up or down the musical scale. There are three registers in the voice, speaking in a general way, the highest being known as the head register, the middle as the throat register, and the lowest as the chest register. These divisions are made for convenience only. In each of these great divisions of the musical scale there are from eight to about eleven half notes, or actual singing tones. In other words, there are from twenty-four to thirty-three different degrees of pitch; in certain very remarkable voices there are more, in most persons less.

In spite of this possibility of change or variation, the ordinary individual uses but one or two of them. In conversation you will hear almost no modulation at all. The man with a harsh voice does not know it perhaps, yet he keeps it going, and in a monotony of sound at that. It is wonderfully distressing. By some good luck he learns that his unpleasant voice is repelling his friends, and he proceeds to cultivate it so as to sweeten it a little. This is not sufficient. He needs variation in the use of it, for everything monotonous tends to irritate the mind and nerves. He may never know why his more beautiful tone is not a full relief to his friends and acquaintances.

What is the value of one pretty note? Will you go to hear the most celebrated singer warble on one tone, say on C? It is a very excellent tone, and has all the exquisite charm of culture, and we will say some of the warmth of magnetism; but it is merely C. You purchase a piano, and it pleases you immensely. Your daughter likes some one note better than all others, say D, and she plays that a full hour. Do you like it, simply because it is perfect? Yet you are compelled to listen to one note only in some lovely individual, and it is in your presence all day long. It is monotonous; and monotony kills. It saps the life of one fibre of the brain, and one prick of a needle may produce insanity. All about you are one-note speakers, or one-note talkers, and they are failures. The human voice has the greatest opportunities of all the faculties, and is the most used, but the worst used.

All monotony is distressing. By it one may perhaps hypnotize. We have learned of this process being successful through the scheme of addressing the subject in one pitch of the voice, taking pains not to indulge in any modulation. To eat the same food is bad for the blood, as it seems to cloy the stomach and weaken the eagerness of hunger by deadening the action of digestion. To see the same things in the same way in your room is likewise wearying. The same foods, the same regime, the same habits, the same amusements, the same thoughts and monotony of life in general or in detail, is more or less exhausting. It does not do to take all the vitality out of one nerve or one class of nerves. In the same way a voice of one note does injury to a speaker, producing on his mind, by reflex action, an exhaustion that is dangerous to his own vigor of thought. It is always seen that a man or woman with a monotonous voice is correspondingly dull in brain and heart, when using the voice. Some excellent writers cannot express valuable thoughts offhand. Some of the best novelists are tiresome in conversation in speech. The attempt to make them lecturers has failed. Lacking magnetism, they have not acquired warm, rich voices; and to secure the value of their minds they have been compelled to write out their lectures, the delivery of which has destroyed the merits otherwise possessed.

Methods of speech should afford pleasure to others.

This is the Sixty-fourth Principle. By the word "methods" is meant not merely the quality and general characteristics of voice, but the many little arts that aid to give its tone pleasure. These are so numerous that it would be impracticable to consider them apart. We have already referred to the unpleasant qualities of the voice, also to its deadness in certain individuals, and to its monotonous use; but there are other things, called methods, that annoy. You would hardly think that there would be much else under this line; but we shall see.

Under the term methods we may include as much or as little as we please, and in whatever department we may choose to enter. Thus the use of force is a mistake, if it is employed under the idea that it has unusual value. Not many years ago, the proprietor of a large summer hotel lost nearly a hundred of his regular patrons before he discovered the cause. It seems that the hotel was surrounded on three sides by a very broad piazza, the front portion of which attracted the guests in the forenoon hours. These patrons generally remained in the month of August, and some for two months, and most of them had come year after year. In the season to which we have referred they began to leave in a few days, and refused to assign a reason. At length it was discovered that a man, who talked in a loud voice had made it impossible for the guests to enjoy themselves.

It was his custom to take a prominent place on the main piazza and talk on all subjects with equal facility, and thereby make his voice a constant source of annoyance. Force is physical, animal, mechanical. Magnetic voices are always powerful in their use of blows or peals =of sound; but these are not to be employed more frequently than the thunder itself in a storm. You never hear it thunder all the time. The least bit of interest or excitement tends to send the voice up the pitch, and our admiration for it is lost at once, no matter how beautiful the person. The voice naturally has three normal pitches, the normal high, the normal middle, and the normal low. A low pitch is not a soft voice, but simply low in the musical scale, and should be developed into strength.

The following natural principles will serve to guide you in the daily use of the voice:

1. A very high pitch with force is used by scolds, vixen and irritable people.

2. A high pitch, a note or two below the normal high, spoken with softness and slowly, is the most affectionate and tender of all tones.

3. A middle pitch is an indication of calmness of mind and heart.

4. A pitch a little below the middle adds earnestness and seriousness to a tender and

loving voice.

5. A low pitch spoken with force depicts strength of character, firmness of mind and heart, and a ruling spirit.

6. A low pitch spoken softly betrays solemnity.

7. Whispered tones, either composed of pure whisper or aspirated tones, indicate a suspicious, stealthy or deceptive nature. There should be no aspiration in any of the pitches.

Some of these little rules you already understand, but they have a special significance under this head, and should be kept constantly in mind until a new temperament has been acquired. An empty voice is the first great barrier in life; and, as it makes those around you nervous and irritable, the counter-purpose will become desperate and destroy your growth of influence. Somebody will be working to get you out of their circle of acquaintance. The remark of a man that he never traded at a certain store because be disliked to bear the proprietor talk, has a general significance. To frame pleasant sayings in the mind is not sufficient, for they may not sound pleasant when uttered. We can deceive our friends by writing, for then the voice is not beard; but spoken words are colored by the feeling that prompts them. A cross remark, when not intended, has often escaped the lips and made enemies. We do not know bow the words are going to sound until we open our mouths. A vixen is known by the voice. Irritability is so plainly marked in the manner of speaking that only strong self-control can eradicate it. It is not what we say, but bow it is said, that influences others. "No" can be said to mean "Yes." "I am glad to see you," may be intoned so as to mean "I am sorry you are here."

Study the effect of your speech over others. Remember that you cannot afford to drive away friends or to make enemies wantonly. You cannot shut your eyes to the fact that you are in competition with all mankind, and that others stand ready to push you one side when you are no longer able to bold your own. Personal attainments are powers that defeat, each in itself, some counter influence that seeks to put you down. This study involves a knowledge of the general rules of human nature; and an application of personal magnetism in dealing with such persons as mere acquaintances, ordinary friends, tradesmen, employes, agents, and all persons whom we meet in ordinary transactions. If we were alone in our desire of power, all persons would fall within the sway of our will. Purpose, however, is so strong in life, and in all animal life especially, that we are crossed at every turn by counter purposes. Their counter purposes are as numerous as the sands on the sea, as varied as the thoughts of man, and exist in every conceivable degree of strength. They are because of all crime and wickedness. When the desire is stronger than the power of execution, the natural consequence is agitation and broken lines of influence. As we will see later on, this leads to destruction of things, persons, self and soul. The counter influences to be met are worthy of your study. We do not now refer to those which come from special sources, but ask you to examine the great world at large, study its vagaries, customs, expectations and criticisms. Depend upon your willpower to meet them and hold them in mastery. This indomitable willpower is the genius of greatness, or the despair of the wretched. Either is for the time so much the superior of all counter purposes that the latter are completely controlled; in the one case they are swept into straight lines of greatness, or demolished by the energy of crime. You can meet and overpower the evil forces at work by your own strength; but they are best kept at a distance by a magnetic temperament; and this is built of the best things in life, teaching smoothness and avoiding whatever is rough and annoying.

Nothing automatic is magnetic.

This is the Sixty-fifth Principle. What are called automatics are the little movements that throw themselves off, so to speak; they are self-acting. All the world is full of them, and they originate in every conceivable way. They take the attention of others from your mind or purpose, and scatter your own influence. Did you ever watch your friend? What are his mannerisms, his individualities, his automatics? Individualities are character peculiarities. Mannerisms are physical peculiarities. Automatics are small and disagreeable movements that attract attention and detract from the usefulness and character of their possessor.

With the exception of those who have perfect self-control all persons possess automatics. Indeed, it is claimed that no person is free from them at one time or another. One person winks continually. Another squints the face into a constant contortion; this gentleman chews his mustache, this lady bites her fingernails, that girl nibbles at the ends of her fingers, this young man drums, or keeps his lips in motion, and so on through a long list of automatic motions. But sounds are very disagreeable when automatic. We can look away from the sight of the motions, but cannot close our ears to the person who drums, or taps the foot, or snaps the finger, or whistles, or hems at every pause, or says "uh" a thousand times an hour when struggling for the right word, or keeps some sound going to annoy those within hearing.

The persons who most indulge in these faults are sometimes those who most need the power which they are wantonly throwing away. These tiresome and irritating physical habits ruin a person's usefulness, and directly affect his success in the world. It is a pleasure to get away from the person possessing them. Many clergymen fail because of this difficulty. No friend is bold enough to criticize so small a point. It touches the sensitiveness too finely. Only this year we were called upon to criticize the leading clergyman in a town where he could have reaped a harvest of souls double that obtained. He felt that he was a failure, and asked for a frank opinion. We had seen him in the pulpit, and stated the cause of his indifferent success. "In the first place, you bob your head forward on every emphatic word, sometimes craning your neck, and sometimes pounding the atmosphere with your forehead. This of itself is tiresome. No one can endure to watch you long; for, even if the particular fault cannot be analyzed, the public feel the lack of your self-containment and control. You make many gestures, probably too many; but those you do make are meaningless and therefore irritating to the beholders. Your action is merely automatic; with the possibility of thousands of varied movements of the body, you make but one or two, and repeat them for three-quarters of an hour. " He wrote down these ideas, told them to his wife, and practiced at home to overcome them, if he could.

The claim that a person should not be conscious of self is not true in every sense. There is a consciousness required that is of the kind that a good grammarian uses; a knowledge of when a thing is wrong. "Did you notice the spelling of any words in the book you finished today?" was asked of a very accurate orthographer. He said he noticed nothing. This is consciousness. Had there been any bad spelling he would have noticed it. A good grammarian never notices correct usage, but is quickly cognizant of errors. In the same way a person should be conscious of self, and avoid automatics when they occur; not paying attention to what is free from such faults. This is effected by temperament.

Genuine frankness is magnetic.

This is the Sixty-sixth Principle. By this law the mind and heart speak so much as they need, and speak it openly. Subterfuge and concealment are never necessary. Nor is it proper to open the mind on all occasions or to every person. It is commendable to keep your most private thoughts to yourself; your plans, your ambition, your secret communings, if they seem to demand it; but of this you alone are the arbitrator and must decide. Ingeniousness is an art with some, a pretense with others.

There is an air of genial magnetism about one who is free from deception, Frankness does not mean to tell everything you know. On the other hand a careful person will keep many things to himself. Where it is unnecessary to tell, it is quite unnecessary to lie. Do not employ circumlocution to evade. Be frank enough to say you wish to refrain from telling. A magnetic person can refuse the request of another so completely and yet so delightfully that a pleasant sensation is left where a sting might have ensued. Do not have any uncertainty in your answer. Be brave in small things. Honesty of purpose is the best cornerstone of all magnetic lives; yet there are some persons, notably lawyers, who so work themselves up into the belief of the honesty of their own dishonest views that for the time being they experience genuine feelings of truthfulness. Rufus Choate was one of these men. He did not have faith in his clients; but he used the process of mental vision to summon before his mind his imaginary honest clients, for whom he pleaded with all the zeal and warmth of his generous and noble heart. The circumstances that looked suspicious in their connection with his real clients he made consistent with the lives of his imaginary ones, and showed to the jury how an honest man might commit deeds that, while appearing suspicious, were in fact innocently done. So mental vision is an aid to dishonesty, and it is to be regretted.

What a grand mail of manliness and womanliness is earnest frankness. In the privacy of your own family you may make an ape of yourself, if you wish, and it is generally a relief to an overwrought brain to do so. But out in the great, broad world, where the battle of life has to be fought, you should be in earnest. It is easy to joke, and you leave the impression of being a jolly good fellow; but your influence in life is much marred. A jovial disposition is always appreciated when proper if accompanied with dignity and reserve. Humorous illustrations are made more humorous if the speaker contrasts himself with the subject-matter of the joke.

One's life conduct should be about right. Courage is so important a factor in this great art that its absence at once detracts from one's personal power. A man who lacks courage is a coward; not always in the sense of conscience, and moral cowardice is its lowest form; but in the sense of embarrassment. Ignorance, in some persons, is the cause of this trouble; in others it kills embarrassment. Generally speaking, however, a lack of knowledge, a discovered mistake, or forgetfulness will give rise to embarrassment. If we know that we are pronouncing our words well, an affirmative courage is present. To be sure of being correct is always exhilarating and aids the development of magnetism.

If we know that our voices are good, and are easily controlled, the same result follows. If we know that we are awkward, we become embarrassed. To be awkward, and not to know it, mars our usefulness, for then our friends and audiences lose confidence in us. A graceful person, free from affectation, inspires the friendship and confidence of others. That saves embarrassment.

IF YOU ARE CAUGHT IN A MISTAKE, ADMIT IT.

This precept is nearly always a good one. No honest man need ever fear the result of admitting an error. If the error is unnoticed, do not call attention to it, if there is no possibility of harm arising from its concealment. If it is noticed, and you attempt to dodge it, the result will be disastrous. A ready, straightforward acknowledgment of the error has a breezy air of frankness about it that always charms and captivates. Dishonest people generally seek to circumlocute and explain away their errors.

Some persons run away from empty fears; some seek to dodge the irresistible; and all put off till the last moment the disagreeable duties of life. Such avoidance is unmagnetic.

DO THINGS THAT YOU DISLIKE TO DO.

Of course, this applies to things that are proper to do. It is human nature to shirk, to dodge, to evade, to put off. It is never magnetic, however. Such habits are easily formed. It is unnecessary to state that laziness is an enemy of this art, as it is of every art and every good thing in life; but there will he little laziness present in any pupil who masters the tension exercises. They will drive it away, and probably forever.

On arising in the morning you will think of some duty that should he performed. It may not exactly he disagreeable, but it is unattractive, and you feel that it can be put off for a day or two. Go about it at once! You wish to speak to your neighbor upon a matter that needs rectifying, but which he may be ignorant of. It may be slightly unpleasant. Do it at once. It is good training. You owe a man a bill. You meet him on the street. Speak to him about it frankly and honestly. If you can never pay him, say so. If in a year you may be able to cancel the debt, say so. Whatever the facts are, tell them. Do not hang your head, and merely nod as you go by. If you know he is in the habit of passing a certain street, do not dodge him or change your accustomed path, even though it is just as convenient. Such habits make a currish spirit and stamp the face badly. If your creditor asks you for the debt, do not be annoyed, even if he is angry. Dignity and manliness will make you supreme master of the situation.

All persons may be unfortunate enough to be insolvent debtors at times. It is a bad freak of human nature to spend ,your cash at most any other place than that of your creditor, simply because you are afraid to meet him. Persons who can no longer get credit will spend their cash at the store of one whom they do not owe. This is unmagnetic, because it is unmanly. Go to your creditor, and tell him that you cannot pay him the old debt, but that, as long as be will sell you at as low prices as others, you will give him the preference of your cash patronage. It builds up a manly and magnetic spirit to seek out and to perform things that you dislike to do.

If a person owes you do not be afraid to ask for it. Do not whine and beg, but come directly to the point; show him the exact position he occupies in the matter. Your magnetic directness may secure the claim, where threatening or peevishness would do no good. The mere presence and look of a creditor has made many a debtor feel glad to pay the debt.

If you owe a person an apology, make it; but always in a frank, honest and dignified manner; no matter whether you have offended the greatest or the meanest of earth, intentionally or unintentionally. It is not yielding to apologize where an apology is due. Never be profuse. A simple, earnest remark, coming from the heart, is always sufficient. Do this even if it is hard to do; that makes it better practice.

If you have a favor to ask of another, do not put it off. The more you dislike to do it, the sooner you should attempt it, for you should be thankful that such an opportunity presents itself for practicing this precept. And so we might go on citing the ways in which you can perform things that are not inviting. Many such opportunities present themselves constantly. Hail them as good omens, and never disregard this precept. It will make you manly, and that quality is essential to magnetism of the person.

Politeness is magnetic.

This is the Sixty-seventh Principle. To be polite is to be both skilled in the science of etiquette and polished in the art of good breeding. So important are these two great accomplishments that a special book, known as Ralston Culture, has devoted a large space to them. The laws of etiquette are founded upon natural rules in most instances, and no person is excusable who is ignorant of them. The fads and whims of artificial form are not worth learning. So that a person is correct, as far as good judgment and sense hold sway; he is cultured.

Politeness that is not natural, is generally insipid, flat and colorless. By natural politeness is meant that manner of tongue and action which is a part of ourselves at all times. Naturalness is merely habit. One habit can easily be changed for another. After the first struggle is over the new habit displaces the old. The tendency of mankind is to drift into barbarism. The cultivating hand of art checks this tendency and seeks at every opportunity to improve man.

Politeness should be studied as an art and practiced as such. It is sometimes practiced only before company, but the shallowness is soon discovered. A person naturally polite will be so before a beggar and before a king; before his own sister as well as in the presence of some other fellow's sister; before his mother, father, child, servant, dog; and he who is coarse at home, or boorish in his private life, can assume only the thinnest gauze of politeness when occasion demands it; and because it is mere assumption, he will become embarrassed, will blunder, halt, hem, and show either stupid reticence or a brassy boorishness under the guise of pretended felicitations conversation. The latter has the supreme satisfaction of feeling happy while making others miserable.

Success is worth attaining, whether it is forced by the command of a haughty will or invited by the dulcet tones of kindness. Polish is the fairest of accomplishments, for it attracts as the light draws a moth. Many a plain woman has won her way to the good opinion of others by nothing better than an elegance of manner and politeness. Society is a power in every locality. It is intended to draw the line between the coarse animal instincts of humanity and the higher hopes of refinement, and is undoubtedly the birthright of gentleness. How quickly a gentleman of reasonable ability might rise in life, if he were to give unmistakable evidence of the possession of this quality.

Sympathy is magnetic.

This is the Sixty-eighth Principle. It deals with a quality of the heart, as politeness is a quality of the mind and muscles. In the present existence men and women are always in need of sympathy and are always looking for it. No one is so strong that it is not accepted as a solace for the sufferings and disappointments of life. To be alone on the face of the globe would make man a brute, a soul of iron without a single pulsation of kindly interest in anything except the operations of crude nature. Humanity is based upon sympathy by which hearts are interwoven into the fabric of society.

This quality is an angel with wings outspread toward opposite poles. We cannot bear to witness the agony of others, even when they might have averted the condition their own wantonness has brought upon them; but it is as harmful to them as to us to encourage or even permit such wantonness to have free scope. This age is saturated with fraud and deceit, the practice of which destroys the magnetism of the possessor and may outflank the strength of the honest man. You cannot afford to use crooked methods; for magnetism is the doctrine of straightness. Nor can you afford to be ambushed by the trickery of others. The proudest army the world ever saw, the chosen array of men tried in battle and proven in bravery, could not withstand the treachery of the diabolical methods employed by savages. Strength must fight in the open.

This law is true in magnetism, and is one of its most important principles. Sympathy is needed for those who are attacked in ambush, and for yourself as well if you are unable to cope with this disadvantage; but it must be withheld from the classes that prey upon your honesty under the pretense of doing you a service. You may be as magnetic as you please; if you step into a trap that will catch you in its sharp clutches, you are defenseless. The sword that cut the tendon at the heel of Achilles laid him low. There is trickery at every hand, waiting to entrap you; and the age is now in the vortex of a whirlpool of deceit.

There is plenty of dishonesty in the world, but far more honesty. Because the former is so abundant it is no reason why you should distrust mankind generally. A confidence in those about you affords you more comfort, and draws the love of others to you. It is well to be on your guard, so as to save yourself from loss. You can rebuke dishonesty by a full, powerful glance of the eye.

We should take a kindly interest in everybody, where we have occasion to meet and talk with them. Make our tones pleasant and sincerely earnest. Pitch the voice at or below the middle register. Soften it if the occasion demands. Do not be sympathetic to bestow a favor, or to be patronizing. Do not be verbose. Do not "slop over." Say nothing of a sympathetic nature unless the heart prompts it, and there is thought behind the words; but make the heart prompt it. Educate it to kindness. Study faces; look into the eyes of those you meet, and read their lives. Mental vision will aid you to carry your study of men and women into their homes; and it rarely ever fails to tell true stories of their joys or sorrows, hopes or disappointments.

In your sympathy learn to discriminate between the classes that cause so much suffering to their fellow beings and those who are fighting the battle of honesty, and you will find both sides in array. Dishonesty is more active; one foxy man will, in a day, cover more ground than ten honest men, taking all the averages into consideration. This should not be true. It is the duty of those who possess a superior power to drive out of ambush the lurking outlaws; for fear is a detriment to courage, and the bravest cannot help fearing a tricky adversary. You can understand this principle better by putting yourself in the place of one who is willing to fight a foe openly, as man to man, but who would be foolhardy to submit himself to the sure dangers of subterfuge.

The preceding table of dishonesty was prepared some years ago, and has been before the public for a decade without adverse criticism. Those who are in a position to know agree fully with the percentages given, and some have offered suggestions tending to strengthen the positions given. Corporations are bodies in the aggregate designed to avoid responsibility, and to shield the official as well as the member behind the mass. This aggregation is controlled by one spirit only—policy. It is a spirit without a soul. The common law of England and America has for centuries maintained that corporations have no souls. All humanity is absent in their conduct, and without humanity there is no chance for the development of magnetism.

Politicians are dishonest to the core, in and out, from their hides to their centers. The so-called profession of politics is the lowest in the whole category of methods by which man seeks to get a living by his wits. It is the diametrical opposite of statesmanship. The latter refuses to be bound by party, but first demands the principle. All party ties are fetters of freedom; and there is no honest man who is willing to give up his freedom to a party, unless he is a stupid dupe. To think and to act in a certain rut is not liberty. The party man is a caged bird of songless voice. The statesman is an eagle, whose broad, expanding wings lift him out of the hollow dungeons into a plane far above, from which he is able to view a wide horizon.

Manufacturers are nearly all dishonest, especially in America. The race here is for money only. If a reliable brand of goods is established, it is only because there is value in the name of honesty; and this mere name must be paraded for the purposes of advertising. American manufacturers are the most unreliable in the world, and this is not necessarily a reflection upon the people, for most of the manufacturers are the off-scourings of the Old World. Many attempts have been made to expose them, but they combine with politicians, and have influence in legislation to such an extent that it is almost hopeless to dethrone them. When we state the lamentable fact that the white flour sold at this day is badly adulterated with injurious matter, such as white clay, earth, ground lime, terra alba, fertilizing material, as well as corn, corn husks, alum and other poisons, it tells the whole story; for when manufacturers are so dishonest as to imperil the lives of humanity by the invasion of the staff of life with their money-making diabolism, we can hope for nothing better in other directions.

The study of magnetism has everything to do with the question of honesty in food manufactures. The surest way of securing magnetism is by the natural funds in the vital system of the body, and these are directly supplied by the nutrition of the blood. Pure foods, if of a wholesome character, will of themselves generate more than nine-tenths of all the magnetism the body needs. It is the purpose of nature that they should do this.

MYSTIC UTOPIAN SUPERMEN

Pure foods tend toward the healing of all diseases; they drive away pain by substituting wholesome flesh in place of that which is imperfect. They supply power because their nutrition is turned into vitality. On the opposite hand, the use of dangerous foods will soon drive away all magnetism.

A very ready test was made of this fact in the case of a man who was acknowledged to be of the highest order of power in this line, but who, on attempting to address a meeting where much was expected of him, could not do more than deal in words. He was suffering from intestinal pains caused by the use of adulterated foods. An actor, who had held for years a power over his audiences, found his magnetism all gone, and he spent his weeks and months fighting to hold his own in the dramatic profession, while it was impossible to get vitality from the food he ate. At length he suspected that he was falling prey to the numberless food adulterations; he saw in the papers the statement that no food was pure, or at least that all kinds were adulterated, and he fell back upon the plainest of the wholesome foods, using those that he knew could not be tampered with; and lo! to his gratifying surprise his magnetism came back in full force. He said: "I now use a better class of foods, if simpler, than ever I used before, and I am correspondingly benefited.^ Herein is a secret worth learning, if you would get the best value from what you eat. And the best is much the cheapest.

We will not take the space to discuss all the list in the table of dishonesty. The chief importance is in the fact that we must avoid being waylaid by the trickery of these classes. A retail dealer says: "I am not one of those who pretend to be honest. I simply try to be when I can; and when I cannot, I do not try. I defy any man in my business line to be honest all the time. The trouble is principally with the wholesalers; they are up to new tricks all the time. Here is G., a retailer; he was convicted of selling chemically made vinegar that was rank poisonous. I had some of the same kind, and I would have sworn it was pure vinegar; but it was not. You see, I did not know. I cannot find out how to tell all these adulterations. I had bought the best grade of spices, cream tartar, peppers, and other goods; but they all turned out to be fraudulent. I paid the highest prices. What am I to do V 9 And he then went on to say that he could not look a man in the face to whom he had sold some of such poisons. It made a sort of sneak of him. The men who sold him the goods he never dealt with again, and he took the trouble to notify other retail dealers of the fact, which he persisted in until he had ruined the wholesalers. This was right. If other honest men would do as much, the enemies of humanity would be driven from ambush.

A judge of court once gave evidence of a keen knowledge of human nature. A business man purchased some guaranteed all-wool suitings, some guaranteed all-linen handkerchiefs, and other things from a peddler who had a regular route. The goods proved to be very inferior grades of cotton. The peddler was arrested and discharged. The judge said: "In this age of misrepresentation the courts cannot stop to correct the falsehoods told in business. The complaining witness certainly knew, or ought to have known, that peddlers are no more honest than other merchants. " In another case the judge ruled to the jury somewhat as follows: "The decisions of courts in the various States, particularly in what are termed leading cases, as far as they affect this cause, establish the right of a man selling goods to praise them to excess, even to overstep the bounds of truth. If he guarantees them in such language as would amount to a warranty of their nature, grade, etc., he may be liable in a civil action for a breach of such guarantee; but false statements are not of that character. There seems to be no penalty for them, unless it is a clear case of obtaining money or other value by false pretenses. A falsehood that overpraises the goods would not be construed as a ground for either a criminal or civil action." In other words, the courts hold that deceit is to be expected in trade, and that a purchaser should not find fault if he is victimized. This is an unpleasant assertion, but is born out in actual experience.

A man who had been in business thirty years and in politics for ten or more, said: "In the ten years of my political career, which is now as successful as at any previous time, I have never met an honest man in that profession, although a certain few have the reputation of being unsullied. When a Representative or Senator does not dare to accept a bribe from a corporation, he accepts a retainer to act as attorney, whether he is an attorney or not. Among my business acquaintances the only honest man I have ever met— that is, the only man who was probably honest all the time—was a retail grocer, who would not sell pure goods on the guarantee or reputation of a firm of makers or wholesalers, but who got at the knowledge of their contents in one way or another and gave the facts to his patrons. He was believed in by all his customers, and built up an immense trade. He and a few of his wealthy patrons combined in a little society, and hired chemists to analyze the goods. This became known . 9 ' We have received a large number of similar letters from the earliest students of our book on Advanced Magnetism.

If you are thinking of buying land or of otherwise engaging the services of a real estate agent, it is well to remember the remarks made by the judge of court. While most of them are dishonest at some time or other, about two in a hundred are honest at all times; but these two have not settled in your locality, it is quite probable. It is very humiliating and disheartening to be cheated in matters that relate to a home; so we advise you to inquire of all your friends and acquaintances who can give you light upon the facts that pertain to such transactions. Lawyers are not all honest at all times; some are honest part of the time, and some are never honest, as the effort would fracture their cheek. There is a class of counsellors who pride themselves on their knowledge, their chastity and their integrity; men who never take a small case, and who charge extortionate fees in large ones. They would not misrepresent a fact to court or jury, but they are thoroughly dishonest while satisfying themselves of their honesty; for it is fraudulent to accept a retainer that is worth more than all their services should be valued in the whole case; keep their clients in the dark as to the probable future charges, and finally extort an extra fee of enormous proportions. This is the practice of many white-featured lawyers. Perhaps their conceit makes them believe that they are honest. Extortion is always a crime, and any charge that exceeds the actual value of the services rendered is extortion. We believe you will agree with our logic here.

The greatest evidence of hypnotic contagion is the blind belief that the ignorant classes have in the statements made in the newspapers. In one of the largest American cities the "yellow " journals have a large following, the rankest of which are three in number in the morning and three in the evening; although most papers that use large type headlines, called scare-heads, are "yellow," sensational and debasing, as investigation will show. The enterprise (?) of such papers is emulated by all other dishonest editors; their syndicate Sunday falsehoods are copied far and wide; their concocted scientific (?) articles are eagerly caught up by the smaller press, who know better than to believe in them; and so much of the profession of journalism is saturated with the lowest stripe of dishonesty. How eagerly a fake interview with a prominent man, created out of nothing but the criminal brain of an editor or faraway ethereal correspondent (?), is caught up by all the papers of the country without exception, and paraded into the homes of those who are too busy to analyze the frauds of the press. Several years ago, the New York Liar pretended that its European correspondent (a myth that existed in the brain of the editor of the N. Y. L.) had seen Admiral Dewey, and had succeeded in making him talk in a very indiscreet manner; the whole thing being, of course, repudiated by him as an invention; yet every paper in America published that interview, as though it were true. We asked an editor if he believed it at the time he read it, and he quickly answered, "No; we all knew it was a lie. That New York paper is an unparalleled liar. But we published it because it was news, and the people do not care whether it was true or not." Another editor said: "Journalism of today in America is a sort of dime novel affair. It is mostly fiction of the cheapest grade. ' 7 And we have reports from many editors who would like to see it made an honest profession. That such lies do an incalculable injury is well known, from the fact that so many editors, reporters and correspondents are killed every year by those they have maligned, and juries have refused to convict the slayers. Reputation is dearer than life, and if a man may kill his would-be murderer, it is good logic to assume that juries are justified in acquitting those who have removed pests worse than murderers.

Beauty of thought is magnetic.

This is the Sixty-ninth Principle. Before this volume closes we shall show that true magnetism, that which wins and which ennobles the character that wins, is associated with a realm of which man knows but little. Assuming that there are opposite poles of existence somewhere, but not fully recognized as yet, and assuming that, for the sake of convenience, it would be proper to call one of them hell and the other heaven, we feel justified in asserting that negative magnetism tends toward the former condition and positive toward the latter; that hypnotism is at the lowest extremity of the basest form of subconsciousness, while magnetism is at the highest.

The more you examine these propositions the more you will be convinced of their truth.

Life has two main highways —one that ascends, the other that descends; one that invites everything that enhances the value of existence, the other that invites all the meanness of the universe into its pathway. A flower is an object of praise, a weed inspires contempt. A song awakens the memory of other days, and its swelling notes are fraught with the fragrant airs of youth and love; a discordant scratching on the windowpane is sound that distracts. Thoughts that are beautiful are born of heaven somewhere; whether it be on earth or in brighter skies, we know not. All power for ruling life is akin to the all prevailing scheme that is sending this planet on to a grander destiny.

A fountain can rise no higher than its source, and a mind can give no more than it has. Beautiful thoughts are pearls of life, and can never die. Well spoken words reflect their meaning on the soul. A thought read by the eye or coldly uttered by the voice appeals to the brain only, and is rarely ever fully absorbed. A thought feelingly spoken, with the full heart of the speaker back of it, is soon absorbed. Thus the grandest and most sublime experience of the world's past great men and women can be drawn into our natures.

The greatest characters of one generation have absorbed the thoughts of the greatest characters of the preceding generations. This accumulation has come down to us. A great character leaves behind him, in language, the very pith and essence of himself. The things a man says are himself. He at one time loved to quote the grandest thoughts of his predecessors, until, by absorption, they became a part of his character. Edward Everett declared this to be the surest and quickest means of building a strong character; and no great person has ever failed to follow the plan. Webster was full of Milton, Shakespeare and the Bible.

Flowers are the stars of the fields, the pearls of the garden, the jewels of home. They abound everywhere to please the eye with their beauty, and fill the air with their fragrance. They are to the substantial growth of vegetation what poetry is to prose. The sky is studded with them at night, when earth's flowers have gone to rest. The love of flowers should be cultivated. To look into the construction of the tiniest bud that blooms, and contemplate its world of life, its intricacy of growth, will awaken the heart to a desire for the purest things of life.

Music likewise touches the depths of the soul. The love for this can be increased by cultivation. It is not necessary to be able to sing or play. The author can do neither, but he can listen to both with intense enjoyment. The ballads of everyday life, and the profounder music of the thoughtful composers impress the mind and heart; but the common airs known as topical songs, and the "catchy" tunes that amuse merely, are to pure music what "slang" is to refinement. Character is not built up by cultivating a taste for "slangy" songs. Here the line should be drawn. The first experiences of childhood are stamped on a whole life. The earliest impulses of a day live and breathe into a strong and pure life all through the hours till night. We are affected in the daytime by the first mood of the morning.

Some persons in society never say a bright thing; they are clay. Some cannot open their mouths without saying a positively dull thing; they are useless earth. Their social position is to wear colors and fill in the background. There are many talkers in society who have a vocabulary as small as a kitchen maid's, yet who do most of the talking. The repetition of words, and the redundancy of thought furnish as much brightness as a meal of dried apples twenty-one times a week. Such persons are empty minded; and flippancy or morbid moroseness can be the only offspring. True brightness can be acquired by all who desire it, and then the mind will scintillate with the modesty of a diamond. The surest way to achieve this much-to-be-desired result is to repeat aloud, to yourself only, the thoughts which you would say to others, and to correct them as you hear them.

It is the habit of many to talk as though it was unimportant whether the ideas, or even the language, were understood or not. Those who lack the power of voice and enunciation bury their thoughts in an unintelligible mass of sound, thereby reacting on the creative talent of speech. All things born must have some means of communication with living beings. The orator is dead to himself even, if he cannot use his voice. The writer must know how to use pen and ink. The poets of ancient centuries sang their fancies, those of today frame them in written speech; yet these jeweled galaxies of the mind could only have been felt were language unknown. To him who would create, unfold, develop, and give to the world the priceless gems of thought, the glittering and flower-spangled beauties of that rarer realm of life, there must precede in gifts the means and methods of expression; there must come the art of making sentences easily, the flow of language and the clear coinage of enunciation. As one writer says: "Good fortune and good speech go hand in hand."

Persons who can say beautiful things in a beautiful manner, who are unable to make themselves heard or understood, shrink back on themselves and lose courage, as has been the experience with many a man and woman who would otherwise have proved themselves of untold value to mankind. It is not loudness of voice that enables one to be understood. If the vowels have no mouth action the utterances are not clearly made and not easily heard. It is not sufficient that the audience hear the sound of the voice—they should hear what is said. Language consists merely of syllables, syllables of vowels and consonants. One syllable differs from another merely in the fact that different vowels and consonants are employed, or combined differently.

If a speaker or reader with more voice than brains should endeavor merely to make himself heard, he could do it by shouting or yelling unintelligible sounds, as the street venders do; the voice is heard, and distressingly so. But a quiet tone, accompanied by a clear enunciation, will carry sense, in the form of intelligible words, farther than the shouter's voice. A strong voice is of no avail if the vowels and consonants are not well formed and made. The vowels should be formed as far forward in the mouth as possible, and be accompanied by full lip action. One vowel differs from another only in a change of the shape of the mouth. The consonants should be made by the firmest possible contact of two parts of the month.

Conversation is often made the channel of expression of beautiful thoughts. It is an avenue of opportunity that should be made much of, for it is not possible to develop the brain and its best realms unless the channels of communication are employed. A thought that has never winged its flight out of the mind is deadborn. No better means of testing your magnetism, your dignity, your power and self-control, can be found than in the opportunities of good conversation. Do not, of course, become a mere display, nor an arrogant consumer of the time and attention of the assembly or whomsoever you are engaged with, but use the highest discretion. When others talk, listen. When others are ready to listen, talk. It is an advantage to the wise to be heard. Remaining silent soon relegates you to a lower stratum. Between these two dangers you must steer your way with care and intelligence. In listening, throw your whole interest upon the thoughts of the talker; if you are as magnetic as you should be, you will be able to quietly silence an empty talker, and open the way to a more fruitful conversation.

It is excellent to seek society, to make it if you cannot find it otherwise, to extend your acquaintance with refined and worthy persons, so that the flowers of life may be cultivated as well as the flowers of the garden. Good society is the best school for both sexes. Where it does not exist humanity is barbarous. The best society is that wherein we find the best refinement, the best thought and the purest hearts. Etiquette is a code of conduct founded on common sense, and intended to establish refined customs among people who interchange social courtesies. But what is good etiquette in society is good at home.

Caste in social rank is the true law of life. If men and women openly refuse to cultivate those charms of mind and manner which are within easy reach of all, they should be relegated to their proper rank socially. It is true, and lamentably so, that what is called the best society is often a mixture of good and bad; but even here the good has its opportunities. A few people make the personnel of the whole, and the leaders are often magnetic rather than boorishly wealthy. No better ambition can be found in life than the desire to rule the drawing-room; and the history of the highest caste of all the cities and countries proves that brilliancy and merit, when magnetic, may lead the salon, even if wealth and ancestry are lacking.

The magnetism that charms must be developed on charmable lines. It is a mistake to think otherwise. A lady, who had opportunities but no desire to make herself refined, once sought the aid of these lessons. "I just want to charm people," she said. "But, madam, do you suppose that coarse features, foul breath, discolored teeth, a snappy voice and masculine tread will aid you to charm the persons whom you meet?" "Why not, if I acquire magnetism?" Well, why not? In the first place, the soul of pure magnetism, or the vital gift of pleasing and winning, has existed since the birth of the sky. All that pleases, and blesses while it pleases, is magnetic. The kind ways, the cultured voice, the smile, the poise of color, the harmony of music, the sympathy of love, are natural emanations from the soul of magnetism that permeates existence. For you, then, to be socially magnetic, the first step is to decree by act of your will that these charms shall be yours.

In the realm of attainment you acquire the temperament that makes your work, your efforts, your life even, a naturally magnetic success. Sudden adoption of habits must result in mere artifice, a thing that is pricked like a bubble when it is brought in contact with the real influence of strong men and women. You must be able to cope with the greatest. Do not depend upon the unreal. You need temperament; a fixed habit, a soul saturated with whatever is best, a character that is vital in its power; and these are the true magnetic temperament when they are charged.

EMPERORS have lived who have had no control whatever over their subjects. Plain men and women have lived who have ruled over emperors. To be furnished with the physical force of armament and willing executives is the highest ideal of power in the minds of most persons; yet from time immemorial it has been known that a glance of the eye, a pressure of the hand, a word from the lips, has had the charm to sway the potentates of earth, and many a wayfarer of lesser caste.

The art of controlling individuals is a many-sided study. It may consist of physical force, or of compulsion resulting from superior power or an advantage of position; or it may be the outcome of fear, policy or some mental calculation, or the desire to follow some leader in whom the highest confidence is placed. When Wellington crushed his greatest enemy, he did not do it by persuasion, but by the outpouring of fresh soldiers upon tired ones at a moment when both sides were exhausted. This was physical force. The police officer who is stronger than the man he arrests induces the latter to accompany him by sheer use of his muscular vitality; while many a smaller and weaker "knight of the baton," as he is erroneously called, has overpowered his victim by the energy of his will. This is physical magnetism. We well recall seeing a man of about a hundred pounds avoirdupois, hurrying a keeper out of a store, without laying hands upon him, although the keeper weighed much more and had strength sufficient to throw the little man out of the window. "The tiger, the pugilist, a Napoleon, crushes the prey to earth. The magnetic will achieves the greater success: it captures the will of its opponent."

In the cases cited we see the difference between the use of mere muscular energy and the use of physical magnetism. Then there are motives that are powerful instruments of influence between individuals. This play of motive is the most far reaching of all the agencies of control, as it brings two parties together in mind, or may do so, where all other attempts to come within reach of one another might have failed. We see it in trade more often than in other channels of communication. The seeking of an advantage over another is not magnetic, for it is not noble; and those who "squeeze" their fellow beings make lifelong enemies, humiliate and often break the spirit of others, all for no real gain. It is better to win than to press the good will or acquiescence of others.

Magnetic-control should begin in simple affinities.

This is the Seventieth Principle. By affinities is meant the likes or inclinations of another person that can be adopted or made to come into your own life for the time being. They are stepping-stones; and the simplest of them are the first flags of the pavement, if the homely figure may be allowed. It would be folly to antagonize in the start the person whom you sought to control. Human nature sets itself against any such challenge, and a consequent obstinacy or shutting-up of the mind might follow.

It is never necessary to humiliate oneself in yielding to the views of another. An affinity may be established where views are not the same; but an open antagonism should be avoided. A member of one political party should not bring up the question of politics to another, unless he seeks to change his views, in which case he should first establish other affinities. There should be some agreement to begin with. It may be assumed that a person of strong magnetic temperament sweeps all before him; but this is only true when his subjects are of the lesser grades of will; it is necessary to be the equal of giants in this art. You do not wish easy conquests. There may come times when superior wills are pitted against you, and you must at least hold your own, if not conquer. No man or woman should ever make you a subject. In an age of liberty, the body should be free; the mind should be freer, and the willpower freest. Let no one become your victor.

Simple affinities are found by a skilful management of conversation. Etiquette demands that matters of religion, politics and personalities should not be broached; but if the person to whom you are talking insists upon doing so, you may easily find his mind by allowing him to express himself for a brief while; then turn the interest to other subjects. A too apparent agreement in anything is not policy, for its purpose may be seen at once. Shrewd minds are deep and perceive the trend of a designed conversation. Very soon the process will become one of mental culture in which the superior diplomatist will make the moves as on a chessboard, and his opponent will be forced to suit his choice of objects to the desires of his more accomplished companion.

The best study of simple affinities is found in the methods of successful lawyers when they appear before juries; and the examples there seen may be learned and adopted in private life. The rules are the same, and the operations of one suit the requirements of the other condition. What a magnetic lawyer will do before a jury, any magnetic man or woman may do in exact principle before any other man or woman. Therefore the following illustrations are helpful in this study. It is not known that magnetic persons are the most careful, painstaking and thorough of all classes; they leave but little to chance, in fact nothing that may otherwise be controlled. So, when we see a lawyer looking up the private lives of jurors, we learn something of the care that may lead to success.

The following illustrations apply to cases that have been doubtful; so evenly balanced that a straw might almost have changed them one way or the other. In the outset we will mention a very trifling incident that undoubtedly led to victory. It so happened that the lawyer was of the same political persuasion that was embraced by ten of the panel of jurors, and he had two peremptory challenges at his disposal. By using these he filled out a jury of twelve party believers. In the course of the trial he lent a political color to his remarks, and even went so far as to attempt to draw the party line. The judge suggested that it might endanger the chance for agreement in the jury box, and the opposing lawyers were glad of the "bad mess" he was making. After a verdict they found to their amazement that the jurors were one and all of the same party as that of the counsel who had used his two challenges. His adroit movement was not the sole cause of winning; it merely brought the jurors into common ground of like and dislike, from which the magnetism of the lawyer could secure leverage and begin its work.

When one sees the long train of victories secured by a great advocate, he does not realize the kaleidoscopic changes necessary to establish such results, unless he follows him on his career. This is a profitable means of studying the origin and use of magnetic control through simple affinities. One such lawyer may be seen in a dozen different phases. We recall the case of a polished city attorney of the highest rank as an advocate, who had a very important trial before a jury of farmers in a distant part of his State. He had no knowledge of farming, nor of the character or methods of the tillers of the soil; and all the attorneys for the opposition were familiar with both, and able in argument, which had a telling effect in such trials. The city lawyer examined the case thoroughly, for large interests were at stake; he called his clients frequently to his office, and twice made a trip to them; he arrived at the county seat a few days before the case was put on the short lists, so that he might become acquainted with the atmosphere of life about him.

He did more and what every successful advocate ought to do; he took his witnesses in hand, gave them a very careful examination-in-chief, so that he might know what they were really worth in their knowledge, and he wrote down minutely all they said, even in the smallest details. Then he, unconsciously to them, cross-examined them, to see if they were telling the truth, or would contradict themselves. If he was satisfied that they were not honest, he discarded them altogether from the trial, and retained only those who could be believed. That is right. He then began a sort of side-examination as to their ways of living, their moods and thoughts, by which also he secured much of the vocabulary of that part of the country. Indeed, he became well fortified in the homely but forceful phases and idioms of the people. A keen mind gathers much and loses nothing worth keeping.

When the trial began the city lawyer had changed a little in his dress, but not so much as to produce surprise. One man in the box said: "He must be a country lawyer who has gone to the city to practice." So much was a breaking of the ice that separated them in caste. He had learned something of the crops that were raised in that locality, something of the hopes and prospects of the farmers for the coming season, and soon began to saturate the trial with bits of information that fell in like crumbs at a feast, giving comfort, if no more. When the argument came he was dressed like the foreman of the jury; and to this he had come by gradations during the two weeks' struggle.

The presentation of his side to the jury was a masterpiece of skill in establishing a simple affinity. He did not flatter the members by profuse compliments, but came among them as a lover of country life, as one interested in the farmer because his parents had known the hardships and uncertainties of securing a living in that profession; he called it a "profession," not a branch of labor. Without being coarse or common, he evinced a vivid love for this vocation, telling them that the first language of earth was the Aryan, and the first known men of civilization, if not of the whole race of humanity, were called Aryans, which meant noblemen, because the tilling of the soil was the noblest of all occupations. In his methods and phrases he spoke as a farmer, and the whole populace assembled in the room were heartily sorry when he got through. They liked him. They looked with glowing eyes of enthusiasm upon his manly form and sincere face. The jury were in accord with his views, and needed then nothing but his magnetism to win them.

The principle is a great one. It shows that a smooth, pleasant, agreeable way of approaching a person is far better than an angular or vinegary method. Now, we do not pretend that magnetism wins by securing of a friendly feeling, nor by the affinity; but it does find the way shorter and the victory more easily attainable when opposition is lacking and an affinity is established. Such a process is the sure harbinger of success, if there is magnetism. It is ever true that unmagnetic persons have won victories by the aid of affinities alone. We must not lose sight of the lawyer whom we have agreed to follow in his course. An important line of business took him to the Far West. Before he arrived he had discarded silk hat and starched shirt. He dressed as the best men there dressed.

The case was tried by the ablest of the lawyers in that section of the country, men who were immensely popular. He knew that his magnetism was to be tested to the utmost. He dropped way down to a rough style of talking, though serious and always dignified. He used idioms, slang and phrases that were new to him a month before. He tried to dress and look like the jury. He knew incidents of wonderful shooting; of the braggart tenderfeet that had come from the cultured East; of marvelous luck in gambling; of enormous capacities for whisky; of the meanness of Indians, the relics of barbarism, compared with which the saloon and poker-room of the present day were palaces of regal splendor; and he impressed the boys with the fact that they were in reality the kings of earth; free, fearless and plucky. Such a change in a lawyer was a transformation, a revolution; but it won the case.

Again in the culture of a metropolitan city, he shone as a man, a student, a polished speaker, unharmed by the rough usage of his cowboy experience, and free from the nasal twang of his bucolic career. If his metropolitan jury was composed of laborers, he knew them thoroughly, and could speak from their level; if mixed in character, he reached their sympathies, not by an undue display of the soft side of his case, but by a manly association with them in ideas. And so he went on, from success to success. Some lawyers think it wise to browbeat and terrorize a petty judge; or to appall him with a multitude of decisions the import of which is rammed home by taunts of ignorance. A few of the weaker justices are overcome by such methods; but the best success is always attained by making honest cases as clear as daylight, and showing the judges how much they know, not how much they never learned.

A skilful lady is able to give most men ideas of how to establish a simple or complex affinity, either with one of her sex or with a gentleman, if she is sufficiently, interested to undertake the task. Any conversation soon shows the likes and dislikes of the persons engaged in it; but you should be careful not to step upon a tender subject in such conferences. Be neutral, and let the other person do all the positive talking until you have made the discovery you seek; then establish the affinity, and handle it with the greatest care.

Motive is an easy channel of influence.

This is the Seventy-first Principle. Most persons are utterly lacking in motive, or have one in concealment if they are diplomatic. It is the first duty of every one who would maintain a superior position to ascertain if there is no motive, or if one exists in the purpose of the conversation or communication, whatever form it may take. If one really exists, the next step is to see if it is near the surface and can be easily discovered, or is hidden and will not appear until the time is ripe; or, which is more important than all, to see if the true motive is kept in the dark and a pretended one displayed for purposes of deception.

If it is perfectly clear that there is no motive at all, then allow the conversation to proceed along neutral lines until you choose to make such use of the meeting as you please. If the motive is near the surface, draw it in sight by encouraging the individual to talk on such matters as may occur to you, and keep yourself in the background. Sooner or later it will come out. If it is hidden, all you can do is to wait; but be as cordial and as encouraging as possible. In the course of the conversation there will be indications of what is coming, and your own keenness will be sharpened by dealing with them as though you were merely waiting for them. If the motives are concealed by the expression of others, the other person is probably dishonest and should be watched.

Yet it is not always true that the statement or presentation of one motive in place of the real one is dishonest. A. was to some extent in the power of B., and was being unduly oppressed by the latter. B. was unscrupulous, and had but one good trait in his character; he hated to see another person get the advantage of him or of any one else. A. took the trouble to show him that C. was securing such advantage over both A. and B. This was true. B. at once saw it; and, having the power, he became the antagonist of C., while strengthening the position of A. This was what the latter desired. His real motive won, but it has remained concealed even to this day. The false motive is the only one that became known. It was not false in the sense of being untrue, but merely as a blind.

The other side of the motive question is what is intended by our principle. Your motive is not a matter of so much importance in the process as that of the individual whom you wish to control. Most persons are influenced through a desire to accomplish a certain end. This is the root of evil in legislation. One man seeks to secure the passage of a bill that will place him in favor with his constituency; this is the first and most potent factor in politics. So that he accomplishes his end, he does not care what happens in other directions. Now comes along a certain member of the Legislature, who seeks the passage of a bill that every member would individually vote against; but he agrees to their separate matters, and proposes to throw in such favor the legislators who are behind him in his measure, thus appealing to their motives as reasons for aiding him; and they yield. This is common history in Congress as well as in State Legislatures, and is wrong.

In private life many a person has failed in seeking to control the minds or wills of others; and, to their surprise, some brighter mind has stepped in and won with ease. A certain man holds a piece of land which is needed by H., who has tried in vain to purchase it. The owner refuses to sell, as he has no reason to do so. By and by H. wakes up to the idea that men must have reasons for doing things; so he casts about for a motive in the owner which ought to prompt him to sell. Investigation shows that the town is being rapidly built up in another direction; that, following the history of other towns, it will soon leave this portion as a valueless suburb; that he, H., is interested in checking the advance of greed in the wrong part of the town. Soon the owner finds that H. is right, and sells him the land at a price much lower than he would have willingly paid. A better house is built, and the spirit of growth is partly attracted in that direction. H. really discovered this motive. This is an oft-repeated fact, and shows the lesson clearly.

There is an ether that fills all space.

This is the Seventy-second Principle. It is one of the most important of those that are connected with the study of magnetism. The proposition stated in this principle cannot be disputed. Even the densest solids are admitted to be composed of single particles, known as molecules, having space between them. This infinitesimally small space is filled with the universal ether. Until our readers accept this statement as an assured fact, it will be a waste of time to proceed with these studies. If any doubt exists, consult the best scientific works of the world. This ether brings us light and life from the sun. Without light there can be no origin of life, and no long continuance of it.

Sound is a mechanical vibration of the substance of the atmosphere; but any elastic solid, as steel, wood, etc., as well as water, will convey sound. A vacuum will not. Thought vibrations are ethereal, while sound vibrations are material. Light travels by the same medium as thought, goes as fast and as far, and its perception may be clouded or extinguished by opaque matter, as consciousness of thought may be clouded or extinguished by disease or by physical defects of the brain. Light vibrations are ethereal, and are so infinitesimally delicate that they are terminated by opaque matter. Light cannot die; its absorption is a step only to its escape as electricity. All scientists now concur in the theory that light is undulatory, and vibrates or waves as it is transmitted, thus abandoning the corpuscular theory which was advocated by Newton.

All scientists now agree that there is a universal ether, which fills all the space in the universe, and is also diffused among the molecules of which solids are composed. This ether is declared by A. Daniell, in his Principles of Physics, page 208, to be a medium for the transfer of heat through space; a medium for electrical phenomena, and a medium for the propagation of the waves of light; he therefore calls it the luminiferous ether. Maxwell (who is quoted by all scientists) has even measured the density of this ether, declaring it to be of water, or equal to the rarity of our atmosphere at a height of 210 miles.

This ether will permeate all solids and liquids with the speed of light, which travels at a rate of 186,000 miles per second. This ether passes through the bones, brain, flesh and liquids of the body with equal rapidity, and consists of active or absorbed light and electrical movement, constantly undulating. Thought and life are identical; light and life are identical; electric movement and thought are identical; electrical movement and light are associated. Some day the newest discoveries in electricity will show that man is merely an energy of this kind, as far as all his vital functions are concerned; he will be made a part of the system which is fast being recognized as the source of all the physical and so-called spiritual laws of the universe.

It is probable that the ether which pervades all things is intended as the great sea of communication between place and place. It is not at variance with the known plan of life, as far as man has ascertained it. Ears are made for air. Take air away, and you must take ears away, unless you can substitute some other means of communication between mind and mind through the natural senses. Nature is peculiarly simple, while being enormously inventive. Two human beings wish to exchange ideas; and there are just four ways in which they may do so. In the simplest of all four, they may convey messages by the sense of touch; a pressure of one finger many mean what it will; of two fingers, something else; of three fingers, still something else; of four fingers, another letter, word or idea; of all five on one hand, a still further idea. These may then be combined with themselves and with the other hand, until a full alphabet is formed, from which a system as accurate as that used in telegraphy may be made.

It will be seen that the touch method of communication does not employ any medium of passage. The ideas are expressed in the use of the flesh against the flesh, and the process is necessarily slow and cumbersome. This is the real principle involved in telegraphy, although the different touches are marked off by the interruptions of the electrical current. It is akin to that used by deaf-mutes; for what they say to the eye, they can state in the dark if they are close together. Thus two girls, who were afflicted by the loss of speech and of hearing, could talk to each other by the hour after retiring at night, their hands being under the bedclothes. Life is too full of opportunities that demand rapidity of action, for any system of communication without a medium that permits distance.

A little thinking will satisfy one that distance requires a means or medium, or else there can be no way of carrying the ideas. There never yet has existed a method that did not require such means, except that of touch. To have to place the hand on an individual whom we wish to address would necessitate contact, and there could be no general form of speaking to a number at a time. Nature realized the requirements of the situation, and proceeded to supply the needed means. She never introduces any superfluous matter; and if what is at hand can be made to suffice, she uses that. The atmosphere was placed around the globe dense enough at the surface to supply all needs for breathing, and to carry on the hundreds of processes that are essential to plant and animal life.

The atmosphere being already established, it was not necessary to create a new medium for communication. Had it been, there would have been one finished as soon as life was ready for it. The air was light, changeful, buoyant and capable of vibrating in mass. This was sufficient. It was then necessary to provide an instrument capable of producing vibrations rapid enough to make an impression as sound. A fan passing back and forth with speed may disturb the air, but we do not recognize it; we need something that will carry itself a mile away, and no ordinary number of vibrations will do this. Something is lacking. The speed of the fan is increased; still it is not enough; it goes faster, much faster than the eye can follow; still faster it goes, until there are vibrations enough in the second of time to produce what the ear can recognize as a tone. It is sound. It does not in fact exist, but is said to have existence because it seems to have, owing to the impression made on the brain. It seems to be a low base note at first; then, as more speed is added, it ascends the musical scale, and climbs to the higher notes, the top tone being the fastest. When the speed is too rapid, the ear cannot recognize it, for it blends away into nothingness.

This is the medium for speech. It requires in the human body an instrument that is capable of vibrating the air, and this is found in the throat at the head of the air passage, called the epiglottis. There, under that little tongue, are two lightly hung, top-heavy pieces of cartilage, which vibrate with great speed whenever they approach each other while the air is passing out of the lungs. It is a wonderful device. If it made but one sound, we could not talk, except by interrupting its tone, as in telegraphy. But its natural sound, when the mouth is wide open, is ah as in father; and, as the mouth closes part way, it turns to a as in mast; closer it makes a as in mat; a little closer it produces e as in met; then a as in mate; when most closed it produces % as in mit; and the flattest of all sounds is e as in meet, which is made when the mouth is nearly shut. To utter the round sounds, the mouth shapes itself to round positions, the closest of which is oo in boot; and so on to the most open. All this is marvelous; to think that a mouth needed for eating, with lips, teeth, tongue and palate required for mastication, could make the changes essential to human speech; added to which are the consonants or touch positions, whereby a vowel is given contact and a new effect is produced.

This is human speech, and its medium is the air. But this is not all. Sound, being merely the vibration of the body of the atmosphere, is not a reality. It is not a movement which you can feel, for its vibrations cannot be interpreted by the muscles. The nerves of the body are not sensitive to the fine action which is involved in sound. No finger can detect them, although the delicate fibres are able to find the lines of print on the smoothest paper. Nature makes sound live by reason of a still more delicate contrivance in the brain. The vibrations must be caught, and this is done at the drum of the ear by a little disc called the tympanum. It is connected by a nerve with the core of the brain. When the air, which is set in vibration by the voice of A., reaches the tympanum of B., it sets that to vibrating in exactly the same way, and the sounds that leave A.'s month strike B.'s ear. But they must be interpreted, or they will be empty, silent waves. In the head the nerve carries the vibrations in electric currents from the tympanum to the core of the brain, so that the sounds that leave A. 's mouth strike B.'s ear and travel over this nerve to his brain. There they produce agitation at a place where the least, the tiniest, the faintest of real motion is magnified into a world of noise. Of this much of the distance the real medium of air begins at the larynx in the throat, and stops at the tympanum. The rest is electrical, for nerves and brain are such.

MYSTIC UTOPIAN SUPERMEN

Had man been a fish he would have used the water as the medium of communication. It is not possible to speak in the volume of water itself, but one can hear very readily, and each sound seems louder and is audible a greater distance away, owing to the greater density. A blow is heard miles away. The voice is communicated to the water by a method which allows the speaker to be out of it. Man was not made to be a fish. The air is one of his means of speaking to others, but is not the only one. It is about him day and night, not only because he needs it in respiration, but also because he is dependent upon it for life itself. The air is not more than three or four miles deep as a useful envelope of this globe; even at a mile of depth it is too rare for some lungs · but it is more extensive in a highly elastic condition, some claiming a depth of two hundred miles, although it is likely that its characteristic composition as oxygen and nitrogen is not to be found much more than eight or ten miles from the surface of the earth.

Out somewhere in space it ceases to exist; but there is no place where all is void and empty. Men were not always conveniently near, so that their thoughts could be communicated by the touch of the hands; nor are they always within the sound of each others' voices. If A. wishes to send a message to B. some miles away, and there is no telegraph system, he must write it; but he could not see what he wrote, nor could the person read it, unless another medium were established. Air is present day and night. Light is absent when its source, or one of its agents, is withdrawn. We can hear, but not see in the dark. Light is an activity; air is a substance. Light may or may not be the medium in which it operates; but it certainly is a force; and being a force, it must have some means of passage.

One theory makes light a series of waves on the bosom of the universal ether; another makes it a substance in and of itself. If the latter is true, it is then its own medium; if the former is true, it is action, and not substance. It is of no consequence in this study whichever is correct. Its presence is action, and by this action the nerves of sight catch form; that is all. The shapes of things are cast in reflected waves against the great optic cable, and the vibrations of the latter go to the core of the brain, to be magnified, interpreted and made known. The action of light plays in waves along some medium; in waves such as we can catch from some far away star at night, whose tiny vibration has been millions of years on the way. Sound has limit. The universe is not large enough to limit sight. The broken, fragile ray comes struggling along to tell us that vast aeons ago its masterworld sent it forth across the sea of space to apprise us of its existence; yet that world, and all the distant stars whose light we see, may have been blotted out long before this planet came into being, for the rays go on forever.

Every influence has its means of communication.

This is the Seventy-third Principle. We know that thoughts and feelings are influences, just as sound and sight are influences; and magnetism is in, behind and the impulsive energy of them all. When the lightning plays along the cloud it takes its leap to earth as soon as the opportunity presents itself. When the electric current traverses the globe, it runs along the wires by which it is conducted, although it will not long stay pent up even in storage chambers. So, when the finer phosphorescence of thought impels its waves from mind to mind, it does not make a clear leap through void space.

Nothing passes from one place to another unless it has its medium of transfer. Not in all the universe has such an act been known. The chasm is not possible.. Nothing was known of the process by which sound was communicated until recent centuries; and light is yet being studied. So wise and so great a man as Sir Isaac Newton presented a theory that could not stand the test of modern examination; yet all who are familiar with the operation of light admit that it needs a medium of communication, either its own or some other, in order to reach the earth, and to pass through all the avenues of the day. And what is true of one influence is true of all.

That thought passes from mind to mind by channels other than those of the natural senses is too well known to be discussed at this place. Hardly an individual living is free from some experience that proves the truth of the claim; but the fact is that hundreds of ideas from other minds come to you each day, and you do not know it. Gray matter, wherever found, is capable of thinking. Thought and gray matter are identical; the latter being the result and subsequent cause of the former. Thought occurs not only in the head, but in all other parts of the body, where there is gray matter. Thought not only pulsates in the cerebrum, but when excessive affects the entire body, causing an abnormal increase of heart action, and sometimes fever heat ending in headache and loss of sleep.

The medium of thought is the universal ether, which fills all space in the universe, and is also diffused among the molecules of which solids are composed. This ether is declared to be a medium for the transfer of heat through space, a medium for electrical phenomena; and a thought is life and generates light by turning into electrical movement the absorbed light of the brain. This electrical movement vibrates wherever the universal ether exists, which is everywhere. Thought is an electrical movement originating in the brain or gray matter, and vibrating the ether.

Two persons are walking along the street, the brain is active in each, and one thinks of a subject just before the other utters it. "Why, I was about to speak of the very same thing myself. How queer we should both think of it." These experiences are common. The subject, too, is often one which is totally disconnected from any previous topic of conversation, and is in many instances quite remote in character from the surrounding circumstances of the conversation. Persons of constant association and general sympathy are reading each other's minds every minute of the day without knowing it.

Murat, the great Frenchman, standing on the edge of a precipice one day, in companionship with a supposed friend, suddenly read this person's intention of killing him by pushing him over the rocks. He turned, and saw the man preparing to do the deed. This man afterward confessed that such was his purpose. A witness, who had baffled the skill of a sharp lawyer on cross-examination, was about to leave the stand in triumph, when the lawyer was prompted by some mysterious influence to ask a very peculiar question. It was the one question which the witness had hoped to escape, and his thinking of it impressed itself upon the brain of the lawyer. A personal friend of the author owes his success at the bar to his skill in reading the mind of every witness. He has ferreted out more facts and terrified more knaves on the stand by hitting upon the true inwardness of the mind, than probably any other lawyer in America. His success is magical. He is a master in controlling the incidents of a trial; in presenting evidence clearly; in keen cross examination; in getting at the truth without fail; in potent argument before the judge and jury.

A well balanced magnetic brain will rarely ever lead a business man into error. Success depends upon the penetrating power of his judgment. All persons recognize the fact that mental impressions are conveyed from mind to mind; but how they are conveyed has hitherto been unexplained. It is not sufficient to know how they are conveyed. With a firm conviction of the truth of these principles well established in your mind, and a deep and lasting resolve to develop the magnetic wealth of the brain, you will make very marked progress in a study which has for its achievement the following great purposes:

1. An active brain of the most healthy type.

2. A growing mental activity.

3. An impressible brain, capable of receiving the thoughts of others at will.

4. A controlled brain, like that of all the grandest personages of the world's history, entirely subjugated to the decrees of the will; each department being opened and closed as desired.

5. A nobler, better, larger life.

Constant change and variation increase the magnetic vitality.

This is the Seventy-fourth Principle. When we consider the facts set forth under the last principle, we see at once the strong and urgent necessity for a vigorous and ever active brain; and there are many other reasons why our present law should be adopted. Activity is the right arm of strength, and variety the constant refreshment of all our faculties. Law after law crowds upon us as we proceed to look into the subject before us. In an earlier principle in another book we find that the faculties are best preserved by their constant use.

The employment of the faculties in any one direction a part of the time is strengthening and highly beneficial; all the time, it would lead to atrophy and breaking down; while to pass from one to the other would result in a shiftless career. What is meant, therefore, is that the faculties must be used so as to give them all the vigor possible, so as to prevent weakening by such change as leaves nothing completed, and yet so as not to hammer away at a single idea until the brain fails. Here are many laws, not in conflict, but, in the order of adjustment, working together. It seems on its face a contradiction to say that there must be eternal change, daily change; yet that nothing must be given up, nothing left incomplete, nothing allowed to displace other matters.

The meaning is clear if we look further into it. Change does not imply the abandonment of anything. To carry a plan through to its end requires the evolution of its details by the law of progress. An ambition that stands still has a worthless subject-matter for its goal. Life is a highway, and all roads lead somewhere. A man who stands still is not living. He may exist, but he is better off buried, if he cannot get started. Any plan in life is a series of change. Then it is not best to devote oneself altogether to one idea or one ambition. There should be a supreme goal in this life, but many minor ones also constantly being selected and attained. This is change multiplied. Nothing is deserted, nothing abandoned, nothing left to some shifting moods; but plans are carried to their ends in victories.

MYSTIC UTOPIAN SUPERMEN

Life itself is full of action in the small processes of the body; nature is busy in all she does in the growing period of the year, and tends to silence and rest in her frozen, unmagnetic period; and man should ally himself to her, in principle at least. When winter freezes the river and soil, when the clouds hang chilled with snow vapor, when there is a hush of bird and leaf through the forest, and stillness prevails everywhere, then the electrical vitalities of nature are at rest. The thunderstorms, heavily overcharged with lightning, are the offspring of summer, when all life is filled with excessive action.

The man who would be most magnetic must be most active; not in the sense of small, wasting motions, but active in the larger and fuller sense of mental and nervous employment. He who has the most to do, who really accomplishes the most, is the quietest in outward mien. He must conserve his expenditure in order to be able to do the work his greater schemes demand. The powerful machinery that sends its currents of life through thousands of wires of use could not withstand the leakage of its own storage, for the latter takes more energy than the former. When the electricity of the body has free waste through the nervous and restless movements, it is kept at low ebb, because accumulation is not possible; but when such leakage is stopped, and the power of life is piled up in force, the regular use only stimulates it to a greater accumulation. Hence action is of the highest importance. Men and women who have most to do, give the least outward evidence of it in the hurry and rush of the body; the mind is constantly employed, and the faculties are perhaps strained to their utmost; still they go on gathering greater power. Not only does much rest do injury to these faculties, but they are never at their best until the most is demanded. To accomplish much, it is necessary to have much to do; activity, change, variation—these are the impulses of life and of magnetic power.

Magnetism is a volume of electrical energy.

This is the Seventy-fifth Principle. When we seek to make our power felt in others, we must remember that a medium of communication is necessary; and this is the universal ether in the case of electrical power. But the medium is not alone sufficient. When the air was found to be an excellent means of communication for the voice, it did not do the speaking, nor could there have been the transmission of sounds unless there had been the energy somewhere to produce them. This is at the diaphragm, where the air, being collected by an inhalation, is thrown by this great muscle against the vocal cords, which resists it, giving almost any degree of force desired.

In setting up the electric systems which now abound everywhere, it is not enough to have the machinery and the wires; for they may be complete even to the acme of perfection; but there must be a volume of energy collected at the powerhouse and sent forth as needed. For one purpose this goes out in small quantities, for another in larger; or, for the greatest test of strength, the volume and the intensity are increased to their utmost. When a human being seeks to influence another, he cannot hope to do so with no force at his command. First there must exist the power, or at least the knowledge of how to get it at will; then it must be of sufficient strength not merely to do the ordinary work of the day, not merely to take care of the little influences that do counter-work in our lives, but to cope with the giants about us.

There is nothing in the present book that is intended to take the place of the mechanical acquisition of electricity. That must come from the volume that precedes, where the many exercises do in fact lead to the accumulation of magnetism in almost unlimited quantities, to use an everyday term. Our purpose in this work is to take that power in charge, and give it all its varied and marvelous uses; for these are many, and what they may accomplish is far above expectation. So, to start with, there must be the volume of electrical energy always in the body; we may think of it at the brain if we will, for there it is most abundant; and from that place it gives evidence of its presence by the glow of the eye, and of its activity by the dilation of the pupil. These two propositions are so important that we shall consider them in the next pages. Let us suppose that you are studying the accumulative exercises in personal magnetism, in conjunction with the present book, and that you are able at will to summon this force for use. We are then ready to proceed further.

The magnetic eye has a phosphorescent glow.

This is the Seventy-sixth Principle. In later pages, soon to be considered in the present realm, we shall see that there are different sources of electrical vitality in

the body; and there are variations of the eye-glow. Light is a reflection from outer influences, as when the day is thrown from the surface of the eyeball; or a candle, lamp or gas light is seen to shine thereon. It seems strange that the weaker the eye is, the more readily and the more brightly it reflects light, as in the case of sickness, when the surface of the ball is glazed and shines unduly; while the stronger it is, the less susceptible it is to light, and the more it glows from its own power within. This is easily proved by ordinary observation.

Self-glow, as we term it, when the light is generated from within, is one of the most important tests of health, as well as of vitality and electrical force. It is not light, but mental electricity, or phosphorescent thought. To cultivate this is your present purpose. Practice any of the tensing exercises of the first volume of Magnetism; rest from all magnetic practice a full day of twenty-four hours; then go into a room so dark that no object can be discovered, give one very slow, steady, smooth, earnest, but not too energetic tensing of the whole body. Immediately close the eyes. If you have developed any magnetism at all, you will perceive a dead light or still glow in the front of the brain. Some persons can throw this glow outward into the air; others see it in the eyeballs, whether open or shut; others can carry it to the inner brain. In either case the result is valuable. Follow the exact directions of this experiment for two weeks, if possible, always resting from magnetic practice for a whole day before the above is tried. Keep a record of the results, written on thin white leaves placed in this book.

The following experiment should only be made when the body is in good health and free from all depression. There must be a day's complete rest from all magnetic practice, preceded by a day of tensing exercises. This is required on the principle that all growth occurs during rest. The exercise that causes the growth does not itself bring it. No mistake is so common in magnetic practice as to keep continually exercising, in the hope that the magnetic exercise brings the growth into a higher magnetic state. In physical practice, as in a gymnasium, continual muscular labor may produce exhaustion. In unceasing magnetic practice the results are not seen, but rest develops them. Your good judgment will tell you whether you practice too long at any one time. The rule is to keep at it as long as it produces a pleasurable glow or lively sensation; then stop, and renew the practice, but on that day only. There should be but three magnetic practice days in a week, and no two successive. It will be found that the system is more magnetic on the next day after practice and rest.

EXPERIMENT.

At night after retiring, on a day of magnetic rest, tense the body, head, neck and brain, with the eyes closed; then strike each eyelid once lightly, so as to disturb the eyeball. The blow must not be strong enough to do injury to the eyeball. The effect seen is not light, nor any principle of fire, excepting the ordinary glow of dislodged atoms. This is the first step in discerning the magnetic fire of the eye. As a rule, it cannot be seen in the light, and is always most clearly observed in absolute darkness. Here may be noticed one of the incidental adjuncts of the exercise, aiding the larger experiments that are made. The eye, under excitement, in some rare cases has a magnifying power within the brain sufficient to show atoms, and in a greater number of cases it shows molecules and every kind of atomic combination.

The reason of this is clear to one who understands the nerve-life between the eye and that part of the brain which is excited by the optic nerve. A madman or a drunkard, in some instances, may labor under mental excitement sufficient to derange this nerve, in which case visions of a variety of molecular combinations follow. The author was told by one drunkard that a cartwheel, larger than himself, always chased him when the symptoms of delirium tremens were coming on; another drunkard was followed by some beast; another saw snakes, and so on through a vast catalogue of unusual objects; and several have given absolutely perfect descriptions of the atom, thus confirming certain theories.

In fever the eye, in a few instances, has magnified objects in the room to a wonderful increase of size. The brain interprets the objects revealed to it by the optic nerve, and this interpretation is called sight when the eye is the agent of transmission. Blind people are often able to interpret more than others dream of; they have a glow if they are magnetic; they derive a correct knowledge of things about them, and see by the sense of this inner light. Should you be possessed with a degree of magnetism sufficient to enable you to magnify the corpuscles within the brain into their atomic elements, you must not overdo the practice by too constant repetition. Something cannot be made out of nothing; whatever you see in the eyeball, in the brain or elsewhere, is there. It is a fact, and there are many millions of things displayed.

The power of the eye is increased by proper practice.

This is the Seventy-seventh Principal. It contains a truth, the importance of which has been rarely understood. The eye and brain act together. If you see a person about to strike you, his purpose will appear in the eye. The law of succession in the effect of thought over the body shows that the muscles of the flesh act last; the thought is seen in the pupil of the eye first; it shines there as it is being wrought in the brain itself; it then lights up the face, but there is an appreciable difference of time, say a full second, between its thinking and the expression on the features. When you notice the face aglow with the operation of the mind, it is not what is being thought, but what has been thought, that is seen there; and any one who is skilled in the interpreting the meaning of the lineaments, can quickly ascertain the difference between what is said and what is about to be said.

MYSTIC UTOPIAN SUPERMEN

In most cases the eye gives the cue to the change in the thought several seconds before the words are uttered. It is quite curious to note the travel or journey of the mind through the body; first, the eye; second, the features; third, the flesh; lastly, the voice. The speech never accompanies the thought; even where the reply comes quick as lightning, as they say, it is not as quick as the eye, and an appreciable space of time is apparent. The magnetism of the eye has power over the brain, and the two stimulate each other. We have often seen persons of the keenest mental force, who could not grasp a certain thought speedily enough, and who would excite the brain by quick, full movements of the eyeball, first to one side, then to the other. It was like waking up the mind.

The value of a quick and powerful eye cannot be understood until it has been acquired. It is of many-sided use. The speed of a gaze is of itself most important at certain times, and this is obtained by following out the exercises to be given in the next few pages. It is possible to attain a most remarkable rapidity of action by such practice, and some day you may need it. We recall the case of a man who could not read an ordinary page of a book faster than a child of ten would do, who spent two years on the eye exercises given herein, and acquired such quickness and energy of glance as to be able to read a whole page of difficult writing in a second of time. In another case a business man was able to do the same thing, although he never possessed the power previous to the practice of these exercises; and he turned it to good account in a number of instances. A lawyer, by the same practice, was able, on a certain occasion, to detect the contents of a letter in the hands of the opposing counsel. It was a letter that the other side proposed to conceal or withhold; and this lawyer caught its contents when his opponent, in lifting up other papers, looked at this to see its purport. He had less than three seconds' gaze at it, yet caught the whole importance of it, after which he turned it to account by cross-examination. The opposing attorney does not believe to this day that the contents were acquired by these quick glances of the eye.

Nothing will stimulate the magnetism of the brain so much as the excited action of the eye. A single glance from a madman will freeze the beholder with terror. As all the eye movements of insane or frenzied people, which so appall us, can be produced with equally terrifying results by a little practice, it enables us to at once grasp the simpler methods of beginning our control over others. The steps now to be taken are not difficult. The first thing necessary is to strengthen the eye in its three directions :

1. The eyelids and surrounding muscular formation of the face.

2. The inward muscles which control the eyeball.

3. The eyeball itself.

This lesson will be devoted to acquiring the true eye position. No. 1—Take a hand mirror, and sit facing the gentle light of the window. Look into the mirror, watching the upper eyelid of either eye, and note its location relative to the pupil and the iris. Everybody, of course, knows that the pupil is the central part of the eyeball, and is sometimes very small. The iris is the larger circle in which the pupil is located. The white of the eye surrounds the entire iris.

The movement of the upper lid over a small space affects the entire appearance and meaning of the face. While these movements are slight, they are easily discerned in the mind of the person making them, even though a mirror be not used.

MOVEMENTS OF UPPER LID WHICH PRODUCE EYE POSITIONS.

First Eye Position.—Locate the edge of the upper eyelid half way between the pupil and the top of the iris. This means calmness.

Second Eye Position.—Locate the edge of the upper eyelid at the top of the pupil. This means indifference.

Third Eye Position.—Locate the edge of the upper eyelid at the top of the iris. This means strong interest.

Fourth Eye Position.—Locate the edge of the upper eyelid half way over the pupil. This means deep thought.

Fifth Eye Position.—Locate the edge of the upper eyelid above the iris, so as to show a narrow line of white above the iris. This means excitement.

Sixth Eye Position.—Locate the edge of the upper eyelid above the iris, so as to show as much of the white as possible. This means uncontrolled excitement.

All above movements may be easily performed excepting the last two. There is not one person in a hundred who can assume a look of uncontrolled excitement without practice; nor is there one in ten thousand who cannot do it after a reasonable amount of practice. The use to be made of these movements will be explained later on. At the present time it will suffice to say that all the movements may be acquired by practice, the only thing to do is to find the time to spend in the practice. It is necessary to become so familiar with them that you may know without the aid of a hand-mirror just what position the upper eyelid is in. When these have been mastered, the final eye position may be undertaken. Before trying it, however, the fifth and sixth movements must bo acquired. In cases of difficulty the better way is to open the eyes as widely as possible, and stare very hard at a hand-mirror, putting all the intensity possible into the muscles of the eyelids. If this at first hurts the eyes, desist for a while. In time the exercise of hard and intense staring, if made ferocious, will strengthen all the muscles of the eyes. I have known many cases of weak eyes completely cured by a careful and judicious method of staring in the way described above. The better and safer plan is to devote one minute in each hour to this strengthening process of staring. In so doing, do not contract the brows too much; these should be normal in position.

Seventh Eye Position.—Locate the edge of the upper eyelid at the top of the iris, as in strong interest, and at the same time bring the lower eyelid to the under edge of the pupil. This signifies scrutiny.

Having learned certain movements of lids, the next step is to strengthen the framework of the eye, or that part of the face which surrounds the eye. Too many human beings are weak-eyed. There is no case of this kind which cannot be cured. To prove this, test the value of the exercises in this and the next two lessons. Too many persons lack control of the upper eyelid. They appear sleepy or lifeless at home, in company and before audiences. Too many persons pinch the face between the eyes, on either side of the temples, and underneath as well as above them. For this defect the chief cure is the open face.

It is probable that some difficulty will be experienced in making the student understand the meaning of the open face; and perhaps still greater difficulty will be encountered in giving directions for acquiring it. The benefits to be derived from an open face may be stated as follows:

1. The features absorb great quantities of light for the brain within.

2. This face indicates to others the calm control of the passions.

3. It smoothens the wrinkles.

4. It beautifies the countenance.

5. A closed face is repellant, and its nerves are not in an absorbent condition.

Closed faces are those which seem to be shut up, and are generally wrinkled and knitted, but not always. Persons with weak eyes cannot endure the ordinary light of day. To go about "squinting" their faces into a closed condition. Some strong men and women of good eyesight form a habit of doing this, entirely without cause. Persons who fret or worry, soon show it in their "pinched" faces. Care, poverty and suffering leave their marks on the countenance, but the hand of art can remove them all. By the term art we do not refer to the adornment and paints or balms placed upon the skin. These do not remove, but merely cover up the defects.

If the student will, without the aid of a mirror, attempt to move the muscles that lie at the temple near the brows, he will find he can knit the forehead just above the nose between the brows. This is the closed condition of the brows. In our unpleasant moods the scalp comes down over the forehead and produces the wrinkles which are generally supposed to be brought about by raising the brows. Low foreheads are the result of this scalp movement, over which few persons have any control. In order to understand how to open the face, we must get hold of the muscles, and must move them by their own efforts, not by any extraneous aids. To do this the better ' way is to shut up the face first.

EXERCISE FOR MOVING THE FOREHEAD.

Contract the brows and wrinkle the forehead as much as possible by bringing the scalp forward; then, by a reverse action, smooth the brows and forehead as far as possible.

Always carry the face open; keep the mind upon it constantly until a new habit is formed, and then it will take care of itself.

We will conclude this section with two remarks:

First.—An open face indicates emotional supremacy, and is magnetic.

Second.—A closed face indicates the lack of control of the emotional nature, and is unmagnetic.

Balanced eye-movements preserve the sight.

This is the Seventy-eighth Principle. It is of more than ordinary importance to protect the eyes from loss of vision, for we do not find weak-eyed persons very magnetic. When we meet a man or woman of ability we expect to find one who at least has been able to prevent the wearing of glasses. It is our candid belief that all glasses are unnecessary; and we say this after years of investigation of the subject. We may be pardoned for repeating the following facts. It was our own work of many years ago that first suggested the cure of farsightedness, nearsightedness and weakness of the eyes, from which most other local afflictions arose, by preserving the shape of the eyeball on the one hand and stimulating its magnetism on the other. Yet the movements to be given here do both.

We have had reports from every variety of source stating the results of our methods, and we shall select a very few of them as means of encouragement to others. Here are two rather recent statements, both similar to one which we published some years ago. A woman writes: "I commenced the study of advanced magnetism solely because a lady friend of mine had studied it for years, and found that her general health was improved by it. She liked the help it gave to her vitality, and especially the strength she gained in the action of her heart. She wore glasses, but never cared for the eye movements. I took to that practice at once, and my eyes became regular, or what you call normal in shape; and then I could not use the glasses, as I saw perfectly well without. I then said to the lady who called my attention to the book: 'What would you give if you were to have your eyesight restored so as to get along without glasses?' and she said she would gladly give twenty thousand dollars. I asked what the book of Universal Magnetism (referring to the earlier edition of this volume) had been worth to her, and she thought a great many thousands of dollars. Then I said: 'You may add twenty thousand to that, whatever it is, for the department on eye movement has restored my sight to me as perfectly as when I was a girl.' She found it true, and today she does without her glasses." The means of cure may be open to you, as the whole process is presented in this volume.

Quite in line with this letter, is the statement of another woman, who simply wrote: "The exercises of your high-priced book have cured my eyes. They were very weak, and I wore glasses continually. I had spent two thousand dollars on my eyes with specialists, who made them worse; that is, they got worse all the time. Then, for three years, I struggled along with no medical aid and no treatment. I had a friend, whose eyesight was restored by your book; my husband would not pay the price, as he said it was too high for a single book; but he paid many times more for much less information than can be found on two pages of the book. I saved the money, and sent for the volume, as you know. He now encloses the price for the same work for his brother. Actions speak louder than words.' ' That was all, except the names. It spoke mighty volumes. A very terse letter reached us, enclosing remittance for the book, and simply saying: "My glasses are discarded. Send the book to my son; his eyes are very weak." We gathered from the missive what the result had been in the case of the person writing.

Let us proceed to these exercises and see what they are. It is well known that the nerves that move the eye muscles are directly connected with the electric batteries of the brain. Nothing shows so quickly the mind's intent as the human eye. It is moved by every mental feeling. In return it excites the brain by its own action. The student will begin to understand how little he controls his own eyes when the exercises of this section have been attempted. His inability to perform them should not deter him from persisting in practice. If we refuse to try to do a thing because we cannot do it at all, many great accomplishments in life would be denied us.

First Eye Movement.—Open the eyes as widely as possible, and hold them open by the principle of tenseness mentioned in the Mechanics of Personal Magnetism. Do not raise or contract the eyebrows; keep them normal. Look hard at a hand-mirror held on a level with the head, directly in front of the eyes. While looking at this, try to open the eyes even more widely and at the same time tensely.

Second Eye Movement.—Open the eyes as tensely and as widely as possible. Look at the little fingers of both hands held about, but not quite, an arm's length from the body, a little below the shoulders, so that the eyes must look downward a little. The palms of the hands must be toward the face. Now separate the hands, still keeping them on the same height as before. Do not move the head, but move the eyeballs only, first to the right and then to the left, looking at each hand alternately. The hands should be placed as far apart as possible, and yet not far enough to prevent a focus of the eye upon each hand, without having to move the head. This eye movement should be performed with the third eye position, or strong interest.

Third Eye Movement.—Repeat the second eye movement, accompanied by the fifth eye position, or excitement.

Fourth Eye Movement.—Repeat the second eye movement, accompanied by the sixth eye position, or uncontrolled excitement.

Fifth Eye Movement.—Repeat the second eye movement, accompanied by the seventh eye position, or scrutiny.

Sixth Eye Movement.—Opening the eyes as widely and as tensely as possible, tip the head slightly backward, and without moving either the head or the eyelids, raise the eyeballs upward until the eye is focused on the ceiling as nearly overhead as practicable. Now move the eyeball downward without moving the head or eyelids in the least, and focus the gaze upon the floor as near the feet as practicable.

Seventh Eye Movement.—Repeat the sixth eye movement, with the following variations: Look upward to the right and downward to the left. This requires an oblique movement of the eyeball.

Eighth Eye Movement.—Repeat the sixth eye movement, with the following variations: Look upward to the left and downward to the right.

The great value of these eye movements will become apparent only after long and severe practice. It has been proved conclusively that they accomplish three things perfectly:

1. They create brain magnetism.

2. They strengthen the eyes.

3. They brighten the eyes and beautify the countenance.

The following questions from pupils are anticipated and answered:

Question 1.—Is there any danger likely to result to the eyes from a practice of the foregoing eye movement?

Answer.—It is safer to practice about ten seconds at a time, and not more than ten times a day, for the first three days. Afterward increase ten seconds daily, and preserve the same number of times, unless the eyes water badly. The only danger is in straining the nerves of vision or the muscles about the eyes. When the eyes get strong, as they will in time, the pupil ought to practice five minutes at a time, twelve times a day, distributing the time evenly through the day.

Question 2.—Is artificial light dangerous in these exercises ?

Answer.—It is immaterial whether the light be natural or artificial, so that the student is not in it. The light should never shine upon the eyeball at any time. As will be seen in another lesson, light is not absorbed into the brain through the eyes, but through the features. It can never be too dark for these exercises, and a strong light in time will be easily borne if it is not allowed to shine into the eyes. It is therefore better to have the light fall upon the back of the head.

Question 3.—Should the student form a habit of carrying the eyes tensely open?

Answer.—Yes; it is better to do so, providing the upper eyelid is not raised into the realm of excitement.

The health of the eyeball is increased by special outward exercises.

This is the Seventy-ninth Principle. A few very valuable ideas may be compressed in a brief space. It is, of course, known that disuse and dark rooms are great causes of disease and change of shape in the eyeball. In caves the eyes grow totally blind. In dark cities the eyes are quickly affected. The natural rotundity of the ball denotes health of the eye and correctness of sight.

The eyes should not face a strong light, but they should be in it, as their strength depends upon their activity, just as muscular strength depends upon exercise. The overuse of the eyes strains their muscles, just as any other muscles may be strained and injured. Reading in the twilight or in a dim light is not good, if the eyes resent such use. Using weak eyes against the atmosphere when too cold, as at sea, has resulted in blindness. A change of the shape of the eyeball injures the natural sight. If it is too round or too flat, the use of glasses is necessary to restore the focus or range of vision. All this may be avoided. All the exercises thus far given in this stage lead to a restoration of the natural shape of the ball. In addition to such exercises, the following movements should be practiced until the assurance of perfect health of the eyeball has been reached:

First Movement.—Place the palm of each hand against the side of the face, as near the eye as possible. The hand will extend the entire length of the face, the fingers just touching the top of the forehead over the temples. Move both hands up and down one hundred times. The skin must not be rubbed, it simply moves up and down with the hand as though fastened to it.

Second Movement.—In the same position as just described, move the skin of the temples forward and backward one hundred times.

Third Movement.—Repeat the first movement one hundred times, except that the right hand moves upward, while the left hand moves downward. This alteration must be carefully done.

Fourth Movement.—Repeat the second movement, but move the skin of the right temple forward, while that of the left temple is moved back; and thus alternate for one hundred times.

Fifth Movement.—Move the skin of the brows over the eyes, upward at the same time, for one hundred times.

Sixth Movement.—Repeat the fifth movement by alternating, that is, move the skin above the right eye upward, while the skin above the left eye is moved downward.

Seventh Movement.—Move the skin below the eyes upward together, passing over the cheekbones one hundred times.

Eighth Movement.—Repeat the seventh movement by alternating.

Ninth Movement.—Move the skin in circles in the positions given in all the preceding eight exercises.

Tenth Movement.—Pinch the skin as lightly as possible, but sufficiently to hold it between the thumb and two fingers, while lifting it from the bony structure of the face, including all the directions heretofore given in this lesson.

Eleventh Movement.—Close the eyes, and, while closed, take hold of the eyeball with the thumb and fingers. Move it about in every possible direction, but do not use the eyeball roughly. It may be moved in any direction, no less than eight distinct movements being in use. One hundred times will be sufficient.

Twelfth Movement.—Vary the last exercise by pinching and flattening the eyeball alternately. This movement alone has been known to restore the normal shape of the ball, causing wearers of glasses to discard them. Nearsighted and farsighted people should practice these things.

Of all the literature upon the unnumbered subjects of human health and life, not one line has ever before been written upon the gymnastics of the eye. It is more than valuable to man, and it quickly fades under our common system of neglect. You can attain brightness of eye, clearness of sight, quickness of glance and beauty of expression by constantly and faithfully practicing the exercises of this and the preceding lessons.

How long shall they be continued?

As long as life lasts.

We must eat and drink, and exercise daily for health, or sickness follows. Why not devote a few minutes three days in the week to the better care of the brain and eyes?

Accept our assurance that no better beauty of the face and eyes can be acquired than that which follows the steady practice of these exercises.

The activity of personal magnetism is indicated by the dilation of the eye-pupil.

This is the Eightieth Principle. As will be presently seen, there are several kinds of electricity in the body, which appear as varieties of magnetism, although the same original force may be the prime cause of them all. The eyeball is an irregular shaped globe, the front of which is marked off by circles. Of these the outer line is the limit of the white, so-called, although it is blue, brown or muddy, as the temperament may determine. Next to the white is seen the iris, or color band. It is a circle that carries the hue of the general eye; some are blue, some brown, and others shade from these to darker and lighter; but all colors of the eye, when derived from the iris, are either blue or brown; when known as jet black, it comes from a distension of the pupil.

The pupil is a hole or aperture within the band of the iris, through which the light passes from without, and in which the magnetic glow of the brain comes from within. The old argument, as to whether the eye itself has expression, is always an interesting one; the claim of expressionists being that the lids convey all meaning of even the moods, passions and emotions. This is true. The upper lid expresses a range of such meanings, while the lower lid conveys the idea of scrutiny when raised evenly, of malice when raised inwardly, and of laughter or merriment when raised outwardly. We are of opinion that the eyeball at its white is the key to health, and in the books of the Health Club we have outlined all such meanings. We are also of the opinion that the pupil is the key of the magnetic condition.

When the magnetic vitality is low, the pupil of the eye is contracted and uninteresting; when it is high and active, the pupil shows a corresponding distension, and varies as the condition alters. To this rule there is the exception of the abnormal expansion of the pupil, due to disease or to a highly nervous temperament; and such eyes appear black because the pupil covers much of the iris; and, being an aperture, like all holes, it looks black. Many of these abnormal distensions are due to excess of magnetism, left unused, and a fixed iris has resulted. Such eyes should be trained until the pupil will distend or contract at will, and until this is done there is no assurance of healthy eyesight. Blindness has often ensued from neglect in this matter.

Another apparent exception should be considered at this time. The amount of light in front of the eyes has something to do with the opening and shutting of the band of iris. This is best seen when watching a cat. Let her face a dark corner, and the great pupils will open and almost fill the eye itself; let in a flood of strong light, and the iris will come over like two parts of a curtain and shield the optic nerve. The pupil then appears like a perpendicular slit in the iris. Now, a cat is instinctively on the alert for the sound of prey. Let her face such a light as will shut up the pupils; then say to yourself that, after all, she cannot open the pupils except in a dark room if it is true that light alone controls the movement of the iris; and, while wondering if this is true, imitate the scratching sound of mice. If the cat is deceived, she will expand the pupils, even in the strongest light, showing that there is animal vitality within that dilates them under due excitement. It is not uncommon to see a cat dozing on a porch in the sunlight, with eyes closed, or half open. Attract her attention, and she will look at you with pupils almost invisible; yet, let a bird come near, and in the same light, the pupils will expand enormously.

No doubt you have observed this fact many times. In human beings the same law holds good, whether the magnetism is physical, mental or emotional. A young lady becomes alive in her conversation; and as the interest or excitement increases, the pupils of her eyes expand. As the orator warms up to his work, if he is not magnetic, he will use more action and more noise of voice; but, if he is magnetic, his voice will steadily grow richer, while the pupils of his eyes expand little by little. Blue eyes, gray eyes, and all light shades, come to look black when the speaker, the orator, the singer, or the converser is swayed by the action of personal magnetism. This law is so valuable that it should be followed up; and, for this reason, we append exercises that help to increase the special magnetism of the eye. The work to be given in this lesson is of more than ordinary importance, for it opens the way to much of the success that may follow.

Sit alone in a room. Make the body tense. Look at a spot on the wall some eight or ten feet away. Increase the tension of the muscles of the brain as you fix your eye upon the spot. Look away, and rest the eye.

First Exercise.—Again look at the object before you, at the same time exercising the willpower of the brain upon an imaginary line leading directly from the center of your brain to the spot on the wall. Cause this imaginary line to revolve to the right while tensing the brain easily, though energetically. Increase the speed of the revolution of this imaginary line to the right, while using willpower as much as possible with tension. As you succeed in transferring the strength of the tension to the dominant force of the will, you will recognize a new power in your being. Careless, hasty, ill-prepared practice will be useless. The pupils who succeed in this, the grandest of all training, must come to the classroom with thoughtful, earnest minds, free from other cares, determined to win the full measure of gain from every minute spent in the pleasant task.

Second Exercise.—Repeat the last exercise, and continue the revolving energy of the imaginary line toward the left. In both these exercises do not proceed farther than the eye can watch the object easily; and in case a blur comes over the object, withdraw the gaze at once and rest.

Third Exercise.—Repeat the first exercise by commencing with the revolution of the imaginary line at its greatest speed, and gradually lessen it, until you bring this line into a slower speed.

Fourth Exercise.—Repeat the third exercise with the line revolving to the left.

Fifth Exercise.—Commence the first exercise, and cause the revolving line to commence as slowly as possible; then, without the slightest activity of even the smallest part of the body, gradually increase the speed of the revolving imaginary line, until the minute spot on the wall is lost in a blur, and a faint white line of phosphorescent glow is seen extending from the eye to the spot.

Sixth Exercise.—Repeat the same to the left.

In the highest magnetic degree the eye gives forth lightning.

This is the Eighty-first Principle. When the lights of the hall or room are favorable to the view of the eyes of a magnetic speaker, it is possible to see lines of glowing phosphorescence streaming forth from the pupils. This more often becomes visible during the performance of tragedy, when the footlights are lowered. Phosphorescence is not strong enough to withstand competition, unless the speaker is full of electrical vitality. We have seen, and have heard of others who report the same experience, the flash of the eye in many a person under due force of thought or magnetism; and it is not by any means uncommon.

Practice of the right kind always brings results in the shape of strength and greater accumulation of power. The exercises now introduced have been instrumental in effecting such end. The eye itself is capable of magnetic movements, executed with lightning-like rapidity. These stimulate a most needed vitality in the optic nerve, as you will soon realize.

First Practice.—Place the eye in any one of the following positions:

a. Right level; that is, the eye is to pass as far as possible to a right position on its level, without turning the head.

b. Left level.

c. Right ascending.

d. Left ascending.

e. Right descending.

f. Left descending.

g. Direct ascending.

h. Direct descending.

Pass from any one of these to any other of them in a straight line. Then take all of them in turn.

Second Practice.—Place the eye in any one of the foregoing positions, pass as quickly as possible to another, and return to the one first taken. This double movement must be made with lightning rapidity, with no waiting at the first point reached. Then proceed to make double movements in all the positions.

Third Practice.—Place the eye in any one of the foregoing positions, pass with lightning rapidity to any other one, and on to a third, and then back to the second and to the first all in one movement. Then proceed to make quadruple movements in all the positions.

Fourth Practice.—Imagine a streak of lightning passing from point to point in one flash. Involve at least six different directions in one such flash.

Fifth Practice.—Take two books, one on the right and one on the left of the table; throw the eye to a single word on the page of the right-hand book, and, as soon as it is seen distinctly, glance to a single word on the page of the left-hand book; as soon as it is seen distinctly, pass the eye with lightning rapidity to the first word, and if it is not easily found, compel the eye to hunt for it until it is seen; then pass the eye back to the word on the left-hand page, and proceed as just described.

The purpose of this exercise is to compel exact lightning movements. This may require a day, a week, a month, or a year. The exercise must be persisted in until perfectly accomplished. It is the most useful accomplishment which any person can acquire.

The following exercises have achieved the most remarkable results in magnetizing the eye. The first set will be partial review.

LEVEL EYE MOVEMENT.

Take a standing or sitting position, and remain dead still during the entire exercise. Look at some object as far to the left as possible, without moving the head from a front attitude; then follow an imaginary line slowly and steadily to the right as far as possible, without moving the head. To be performed correctly, the eye should move very smoothly and change its focus without jerks.

Repeat the same movement very slowly, and with a tense movement of the muscles of the eyes.

Repeat the same exercise as last described, excepting as to the movement, which should be slow, but not quite as slow as before.

Repeat the same with a normal movement—that is, neither slow nor fast.

Repeat the same with a rather fast movement of the eyes as intensely as possible.

Repeat the same with as rapid a movement as possible, very intensely; move the eyes back and forth repeatedly, following the imaginary line. This line should be about three feet from the floor, although the height is immaterial, so that it remains of a uniform elevation.

MYSTIC UTOPIAN SUPERMEN

THE PENETRATING GLANCE

It is better for the student not to practice this until he feels a consciousness of his growing personal magnetism. To be practiced at its best, it is necessary for two pupils who are engaged in this study to meet solely for the purpose of engaging in the counterpart work of the Fourth Peculiar Exercise. Only two persons must meet for this purpose. If both of them are students of Personal Magnetism, the result will be much more satisfactory; but if such is not the case, some other means should be adopted.

The two persons who are to engage in this exercise should select some room where the light is mild, neither very bright, nor very dim, and where there is no moving air. The light need not shine in the face of either party; if it should, that person will find some difficulty in maintaining his own glance. Sit facing each other, with the knees touching, both feet fully on the floor and the palms of both hands on the legs near the knees. Put the eyes in the position of Strong Interest; the brows normal; that is, neither raised nor lowered, and the face open. All these are essential requirements. Sit upright.

Look straight into the pupil of the eye of your colleague; whichever eye you look into first, look into all the time that glance is being maintained. There must be no winking, no resting of the eye, nor any movement of the body. All must be dead still. It is a most important magnetic principle that we should never perform an act of any kind unless there is thought behind it directing it; therefore it is necessary to keep the mind active while the glance is being maintained. Make an effort to say mentally these words:

"I CAN AND WILL OUT-LOOK YOU!"

Say them to your colleague, not to yourself. Say them constantly. Mean them. Throw your whole character into them. If at any time you should find supremacy waning, very gradually close the hands into the Increasing Tension. This will cause the glance after a while to absorb a like nervous intensity.

At the first attempt at the Penetrating Glance, repeat the above line only twice, and lower or remove the eyes slowly without moving the lids. At the second attempt repeat mentally the above line four times, and so on, until by adding two repetitions to each successive trial, you have been able to repeat the line thirty times, slowly and with nervous energy. If in the exercise the air becomes dark, it is better to stop, although no ill has ever been known to accrue from that sensation.

Take a favorite dog, one that can be trusted, and, look him straight in the eye in the same manner, constantly repeating the line: "you are afraid of me."

Accompany this by the eye in the position of Strong Interest, sometimes varied into excitement, in which case the brow will be raised slightly. Feel the meaning of the line. Make it tense as a thought, and accompany it by the Gradually Increasing Tension Exercise. The author has driven a dog into insanity by the glance of the eye, and could subdue the most ferocious beast in the same way.

Take a boy or girl younger than yourself, say of the age of from ten to seventeen, and talk vigorously, while glancing steadily into the child's eye. Do not talk nonsense but make some sensible remarks of interest. Note the result, and forward the same to the publishers of this work. Some persons are able to keep a child from looking into the eye; others can hold the glance of a child, and prevent it from looking away. Repeat the same exercise, without words, and report the result.

Such practices should be frequent; but the glance must have some powerful living thought behind it; if it does not, it is a mere stare and empty. Think in looking; think in talking; think in moving. Nothing must be done without thought behind it, directing it.

THE WALKING EYE MOVEMENTS.

The importance of the present exercise will never be appreciated until time has proven the thoroughness of the practice. It ranks as one of the very best.

The pupil must walk in the magnetic step described in the first volume. Walk in a straight line. Before starting, look straight ahead, and, keeping the face and head still, turn the eyes as far as possible to the right. Take three steps, and turn the eyes to the left as far as possible, the face still looking ahead. After the next three steps, move the eyes to the right, keeping them there until they are to be moved to the left. The walking must be continuous; that is, do not halt at every third step. The eyes should be in the position of Strong Interest, the face open, and the brows normal. In walking bear the weight firmly on the ball of each foot, the heel touching the floor, but not carrying the weight.

The exercise may be varied by moving the eyes very rapidly while walking very slowly.

Be sure that the muscles of the eyes are very tense all the time.

The brain is the engine of magnetic energy.

This is the Eighty-second Principle. The human brain is an organ of great and mysterious power. In its activity it controls our intellectual, moral and physical forces. After death, or after an accident, and before death has ensued, when the substance of the brain is exposed so that it can be examined, we find nothing that impresses us with the awful vastness of its power. In the present part of this work it is unnecessary for the student to enter into a physiological investigation of the anatomy, action strength or weakness of the brain. While it is well to know all these, yet such knowledge is neither a help nor a disadvantage in the performance of the exercises to be given in this phase of the work.

Until the system of magnetic analysis was introduced no man in the world has been able to tell what thought is; nor can he attempt a description of the process of mental action, even in its intellectual state, much less in its workings, as the originator of the will; and still less in its emotional condition. No human eye will ever see the brain at work; and even if the skull could be raised during life, the aid of the most powerful microscope would probably disclose only the following conditions during activity:

1. The flow of an acidulous fluid over the convoluted brain.

2. A contractile action producing something like fine wrinkles in the surface of the brain.

3. A fiery glow or fire, permeating the whole brain, and more particularly that part which is at work, and resembling the so-called phosphorescence of the sea.

While, therefore, it may be unnecessary to attempt to acquire too much science in this work, it is essential to keep in mind the three following divisions of the human being:

1. The intellectual.

2. The emotional.

3. The will.

The last named is the most important, for the reason that in the magnetic control of others it is the direct agency of success. The will may be cultivated to a remarkable degree in every person who has the patience to perform the exercises devoted to that work in another part of these advanced lessons.

Without cultivating, developing and strengthening the will, the other two divisions of our being are useless in our contact with mankind; without it the emotional tends towards insanity, and the intellectual dries up the magnetism of the body; or, to quote from another, too much intellectual development without a corresponding growth of the will-power makes "a bilious skin, brittle hones, large joints, heavy eyes, and a skull full of wrinkled brains that rattle like dry beans in a pod." The world contains thousands of very intellectual people who will always remain in obscurity, for the reason that their development has been one-sided.

Many a person of strong willpower has achieved the highest success in life without the aid of intellect. Probably every student of these lessons knows of this fact in his own community. The will, united with the emotional, makes a combination of still greater value, and the union of the three is the greatest possible power. Whatever the combination may be, the first is essential. The conventional division of the being into the mind, soul and body is correct, except when other terms have been substituted for them, as for instance, the mental, moral, physical and will. The term will has often been used as a synonym for physical. This is quite incorrect. The willpower is "the power behind the throne," controlling the mental, moral and physical, or in proportion to the development of each.

In the magnetic control of others, the will is much exercised. There must, however, be in the body and in the brain an accumulated quantity of magnetism, and the power to create an unlimited supply for use when desired. The first volume of exercises is designated to partially effect this purpose, and is therefore either a precursor or a companion of the present series of lessons. If the student has completely mastered the first book, he should, nevertheless, use it in connection with this. "Habitual Regime" must be insisted upon most rigidly. The lessons in personal magnetism teach the pupil how to accumulate great quantities of magnetism in the body; but the work of creating it in the brain and exciting it there for action, is left to the present series of lessons.

The activity to which the brain will be subjected must not be regarded as exhausting. The contrary will be demonstrated to be the fact before this work is completed. There are no exceptions to the assertion that all practice in the art of personal magnetism builds up splendid brain power, fortifying it against mental derangement, preparing it for hard study, and giving to it the best life of which it is capable. Remembering that the habit-making exercises of the preceding volume must be constantly practiced, and that the whole work should be a companion to this, we will proceed to furnish a series of exercises for creating magnetism in the brain, and will explain the mode in which this influential power may be excited into action. To possess personal magnetism is one thing; to know how to use it is another.

MYSTIC UTOPIAN SUPERMEN

Magnetic influence is driven forth upon the ether-sea in waves of energy.

This is the Eighty-third Principle. The ether-sea is a medium of communication, like air or water; excepting that it goes among solids as though they were worlds of orbs separated by great chasms of space. If a man could stand upon a molecule of the most dense and compact solid, as small in proportion to that as he is in proportion to this globe, the nearest molecule might be as far away as are the planets of our system. It has for thousands of years been supposed that all matter is held in such control, and that mind and magnetism sway molecules at times out of their relation to their fellows in structure.

It used to be said of the will that it was capable, like faith, of controlling all atoms, particles and molecules. An old but respected writer says: "The will is the spontaneous power of the mind to make particles swerve without variation of their vis viva" and another says, in reply: "This doctrine of controlling particles without changing their vital energy is untenable.'' In dealing with the brain-energy, therefore, it is essential that we ascertain first the nature of these particles which may be controlled by the mental operations, if indeed they can be; and this question is entitled to some attention here.

Take a drop of water and look at it through a powerful microscope; we see an aggregation of life and motion. A stronger microscope is applied; the drop of water has now assumed an immensity that is marvelous; yet its component parts are so small that the most searching magnifying power cannot produce them for the eye to behold. If a man were to collect a million of small shot, he would have but a few quarts in bulk. A mountain contains so many millions of small shot that, if the figure 1 were written down but once for each million times a million of them, the mind would be dazed in contemplating the repetitions of the figure 1. How many small shot would be contained in the massive earth?

A drop of water is thus composed of infinitely small particles. Sir William Thomas said: " If a drop of water were magnified to the size of the earth, the molecules which compose it would appear no greater than small shot. A molecule is said to be the smallest mass of any substance which is capable of existing in a separate form; that is, the smallest part into which it could be divided without losing its chemical identity. When a molecule is divided into its parts, these are called atoms. Thus a drop of water, if it were magnified to the size of the earth, would present the vast number of molecules referred to, and yet this would be capable of further division into atoms. This is the old theory; let us examine it. A microscope is helpless, and only by effect does it disclose a few of the facts which are hidden from the brain.

Science tells us that "an atom is the unit of matter;" "the smallest mass of an element which exists in any molecule;" "a hypothetical particle of matter so minute as to be incapable of further division." The great and good men of modern times, in and out of religion, are accustomed to make use of the word "atom" as a convenience in the study of life; while all have considered the theory as purely hypothetical. No man has said that he knows there is an ultimate indivisible particle.

Tennyson, in "Lucretius," cries:

"The gods, the gods! If all be atoms, how then should the gods, Being atomic, not be dissoluble, Not follow the great law?"

MYSTIC UTOPIAN SUPERMEN

As far as our universe is concerned all parts of it are dissoluble, and no particle of the human body is intact. But in this general dissolution is there a limit—a stopping place? If not, then we must face the monstrous assertion that particles, by constantly subdividing, become finer than nothing, and this is hopelessly untrue. Yet, be this true or not, it is a fact that the greater the subdivision, the more the atoms of matter must expand their bulk into space; a drop of water reaching possibly a rarity equal to the distance from the earth to the moon in a single straight line. This extended bulk is connected and associated. It is the ether-sea, and along its tides the waves of thought, of feeling and of magnetism speed with a rapidity greater than the flight of the sunray. Nothing is so swift as thought. Thought-force is essentially magnetic, because it signifies a state of intense atomic vibrations in the nervous organism.

Ether is composed of elemental atoms.

This is the Eighty-fourth Principle. It is not a theory, but a law and a fact combined, of which much more is to be said in our book of profound philosophy, "Future Seeing." Nature is economical to the last degree; and out of her wonderful simplicity she accomplishes results that man in his deepest inventions could never dream of. Matter needs but one atomic structure to make all that exists. Let that single particle be endowed with a trinity of three laws, attraction at one end, repulsion at the other, and revolution at its center, and every chemical element, every law, every force, every form may be accounted for without the slightest difficulty.

This trinity of three endowments is essential; two will not suffice, and four are unnecessary. Even so difficult a subject as that of light becomes easy when these three laws are applied. Nature needs no other in the sky than that which is composed of elemental atoms; and with this she can build the sun and the planets, besides endowing them with life of every kind. Chemical action, from its explosion to its quietude, may be accounted for by these three laws. Adhesion, with its variations from the least to the greatest, is likewise explained; as is also the law of gravity and electricity, together with every known thing or operation. How this is done is considered in the philosophical work we have already mentioned, '4 Future Seeing." If nature is able to build all existence from a single atomic structure, it may be set down as certain that she will do so, and has done so. In all her prodigality there cannot be found a wasted piece of matter or a wasted principle.

When it is kept in mind that this ether-sea is universal; that it penetrates solids as though they were not present; that it glides between the molecules of matter as light passes between the stars in the sky; then we can get an idea of the all-pervading activity of this ether. A sea that lashes its waves upon the shore of an island, far inland, will carry to that island, and take from it, such messages as are borne upon that sea, whether from distant or from closer ports. So the mind, being in part a solid, is touched by the currents that play against its life, and needs only the knowledge of such vibrations and the vocabulary of their meanings, in order to interpret them. It requires time to catch the sounds of vowels and consonants in words; and few persons today are able to distinguish a in mast from a in mat or a in mar; so time and expression are necessary to the understanding of ether waves. But intuition has already made this possible.

The physical energy throws the white fire of force.

This is the Eighty-fifth Principle. It relates to the muscular system as the predominant feature of the exercise of power which is displayed. It is not claimed that the mental or the nervous energies may be absent in the use of the muscular activity. The parts of the body cannot he separated from each other. It is true that the mental brain may have only an automatic consciousness of what is done by the muscles; but this apparent separation is due to the fact that nature has purposely provided a separate brain to direct the habitual movements of the body, for no person could remain long active who had to think about each motion of the muscles. It is fortunate that the cerebellum is entrusted with that duty. For instance, no person could play the piano, using the fingers in exact touch on the multitude of keys, unless the consciousness of each individual action of the ten fingers were assumed by a secondary brain.

The magnetic energy of the body differs in many ways because of variations of use; while probably originating in the same general source. As the standpoint of observation may be changed, the consideration of the subject may likewise undergo change; and, in this series of principles, we propose to adopt the use of colors merely for convenience of description. The hardest variety of willpower comes from the muscles. These are found not only in the so-called muscular system, but also in the tissue structure of the body, whereby the flesh is built and held together. This department of life is typical of force. While it cannot be separated from other parts of the body, and is dependent upon the nervous system as well as upon the mental, it is capable of predominating at times. So may the nervous power predominate in the exercise of the will; and the same is true of the mind. All are interwoven in the acts of life; yet each may, under certain conditions, lead the others in the expression of energy.

When the physical energy is at work without magnetism, we see it presented in the form of ordinary toil. The woman goes about her household duties, her many steps and movements counting a vast expenditure during the day; the man may walk, run, jump, lift, strike, or engage in the various details that constitute labor; yet there is no magnetism, perhaps. The mind is needed, but it is secondary to the muscles. The nerves guide the action, but very soon they are automatic in what they do. The mind learns its lessons, and quickly teaches them to the muscles; then the strain is principally upon the latter. A man who has never used a saw or plane will not be able to accomplish anything at first; but after the mental part has been acquired, the muscles become skilful with experience, and they then predominate.

We have thus far dealt with this principle as apart from the consideration of the use of the will in muscular effort. Our chief purpose has been to show that there is such a condition as the supremacy of one system over the others; that, although the faculties are inseparable from mind, nerve and muscle, there may be such a thing; one leading another in the expression of magnetic or other energy. Nearly all such expression is devoid of magnetism, for the reason that it is directed by the latent will.

The latent will cannot vibrate the ether-sea.

This is the Eighty-sixth Principle. In an almost informal manner we have referred to the two wills, without so much as stating them. This was done to leave them for the present discussion of their nature. There are two wills, the latent and the active. Each has its share in every physical, nervous and mental energy; for which reason it might be stated that there were six wills: The latent physical, the active physical, the latent nervous, the active nervous, the latent mental and the active mental; but these divisions are of no use. They might serve to fill out a textbook for some college.

The latent will has continued possession of all our faculties for the greater part of the time; and few persons are aware of the duties that are relegated to it. This will performs many things that we are not aware of. Common habit is one of the familiar illustrations of latent will. Thus a person whistles at first by an exercise of his active will; again by the same direction, but at length he finds himself whistling unconsciously. Drum with the fingers on the table five minutes daily for two weeks, and at the end of that time you will find yourself drumming by habit, by an exercise of the latent will. Anything that we do repeatedly in the same way soon comes to be done mechanically. Many persons sing in this way, for the temptation to do so is very great. It would seem quite improbable that a speaker would employ so listless a method, yet nine out of ten of our public speakers lapse into this habit. Whoever will carefully analyze himself will soon come to appreciate the difference between the latent and the active will in every kind of utterance. In all manner of conversation this destroying agency is present. The thoughts come to the mind, the words to the tongue, the two connect, and so pass out on their empty mission. It is well enough for the commonplace things of life to be performed by the latent will; the acts of eating, dressing, walking, and other things; but if we wish to control others we should train the will always to be active when in the association of others. The active will leads; the passive will follows.

The vast network of atomic rays, when considered as a whole, should be referred to as the universal ether. Only the active will is capable of vibrating this ether; the latent will has no effect whatever upon it. A few propositions in explanation of this principle will be given. They should be carefully thought over and understood. Any obscurity in the mind of the pupil as to their meaning should be cleared away as soon as possible.

1. The ether-sea connects the nervous system of one person with the nervous system of another.

2. The nervous system is the seat of the emotional nature, or the passions.

3. The emotional nature moves, charms, fascinates another when magnetic, and may irritate when unmagnetic.

4. The mental nature convinces; the physical overpowers.

5. The active will may direct any one or all of these three natures.

6. The latent will cannot affect the ether-sea as an agent of the emotional nature.

In the magnetic control of others the operation of the will simply commands the accumulated magnetism of the body to vibrate the ether-sea according to its dictates.

This command could not be obeyed, if the accumulated magnetism were not present to obey it. Therefore the magnetism must first be accumulated. The will consists of internal energy, which a person within reach of your voice, touch or eye, if he has greater magnetism accumulated than you have, will charm, attract, and use to overpower you when he employs his active will. If he has less magnetism accumulated, he cannot help but yield to your influences when you choose to employ your active will. It is immaterial whose will may be the stronger, as the will without the agent can never reach the emotional or yielding portion of another. Two persons possessing an equal amount of magnetic force will be congenial to each other. When considered in this way, the will seems to be separated from the energy which we call magnetism; in other pages we have treated the two as constituting a united force, which is more accurate, although analysis separates them as we are now doing. We might liken the matter to charioteers who are equally determined to win, but who possess horses of unequal merit; neither can go faster than the horses are capable of traveling. So the will cannot execute its purpose apart from the magnetic energy. But let both be present on a grand scale and we have the great men and women of the ages.

The active will is a conscious determination to accomplish a fixed purpose.

This is the Eighty-seventh Principle. It is not possible to separate will from magnetism. It is an old saying that the man of the strongest will is generally the man who gets the advantage over another. This is not true; nor is it true that in the magnetic control over others one will is any better than another. To be sure, one may be stronger than another, but it has no advantage from so being. The amount of accumulated magnetism on hand quickly settles the question of supremacy, if the active will is used and it means what it says.

Many a man of a strong will has ended his life on the gallows. Obstinacy, a bulldog disposition, and all kinds of self-will are found in this class of natures. Personal magnetism never requires the aid of strength, never appears obstinate, and wins, instead of compelling. A strong-willed man on a jury will "hang" it, or prevent an agreement. A magnetic man will win over the other eleven. The former goes out of the jury room hated and suspected; the latter is considered a man who saw the right side of the case before any of his eleven fellow jurymen had carefully sifted the testimony in their efforts to arrive at the evidence. To put into daily use the accumulated magnetism of the body it is necessary to form a habit of connecting the active will with this wonderful influence; and for such purpose the exercises which are given in subsequent pages of this realm will prove beneficial.

Having seen that the will is both active and latent, we will now revert to the principle previously stated, which says that the physical energy throws the white fire of force. By this is meant that the muscular faculties, when they predominate, are capable of accomplishing in a physical way the purpose set by the body. Remember that the mental faculties are not withdrawn; that the nervous system still has its functions to perform; but that the muscular energy is leading the others. To this should be coupled the active will and magnetism, the latter being supposed to be already accumulated.

Many illustrations of such combined power may be found in the animal kingdom; not so frequently with man as with the brute species. When the tiger springs toward his prey there is but small likelihood of his missing it. Having measured the distance, and knowing his own ability from previous use of the muscles in play, he needs only to catch the victim unawares. The force of the plunge and the terrific energy of his presence suffice to overwhelm the will of the animal to be caught. Under such a spell the cat holds the mouse enthralled; it stands less chance of escaping when the eyes of its tyrant are upon it, and many a time it seems as if it were fixed on the floor, unable to move.

Human beings exhibit at times this exuberance or excess of energy, and it counts to good purpose under many circumstances. The man who ran twice as fast as he ever ran before, to save his child from a train, gave an example of the force of which we speak. In contests, the same physical will often determines the victory; something stronger than the muscles helps out. Bedridden persons have shown the same intensity of force, and sickly women have resisted the combined power of several men who sought to control them. A mother, who sees her child in danger, will get an almost superhuman strength, which is really a volume of reserve magnetism which is soon exhausted, leaving her in collapse; a condition that should never occur in the use of this power.

We might cite case after case of the white fire of force, and yet distinguish it from brute strength without taking it from the physical class; as in the work of gifted pianists, artists with the brush, sculptors, and others, whose muscular skill is charged with magnetic valor. The difference between physical energy and magnetism is seen in the use of the violin. One player is capable of making a loud noise by the employment of his muscular energy; another player, a virtuoso, will extract from the same instrument the most thrilling sounds, and charm even the untrained ear. So in the speaking or singing voice, there is an immense chasm between mere loudness and feeling; but here the nerves have play, which is not true in instrumental music.

The mental energy throws the blue fire of thought.

This is the Eighty-eighth Principle. We now tread on loftier ground, and come to some of the direct practice in this splendid art. Nothing can be more beneficial, and nothing more ennobling, than the work before us, when considered in connection with the principles involved. These laws are magnificent. They must not only be known, but should be absorbed into the character and very being of every individual; they should walk with us by day, and sleep in our hearts by night. In every age of the world's history some agency has been employed to uplift life; at one time it was mechanical; later on it became physical; now it is mental; and in the immediate future it must be magnetic, making use of the preceding systems as its base.

The true description of thought must include the phosphorescence and electric energy that attend the production of it. Thought is a power. It is a collection of organized groups of intelligence, each made up of lesser activities; and, wherever they are manifest, whether in the least or the greatest exhibitions of force, they show a dependence on electricity as a source, and on phosphorescence as a means of expression. The latter is evidence of energy in use. It is the inherent energy of living or of being. Thought pulsated in the tiny cell long before it united with its fellows to produce any organism, even that of the microscopic bacterium, and its throbbing has gone on to the limit of the highest creation.

When an attempt was made to describe the nature of a telephonic transmission, the most popular definition was that which compared it to the waves of a line of sound, commencing at the larynx in the throat, where the vibration is started; then carrying these waves in the air as merely pulsations of that body to the disc of the telephone, which is like the tympanum or drum of the ear; this film is so delicate that it vibrates with the air and to the same extent in force and in all characteristics; its vibrations, passing rapidly back and forth, interrupt the electrical current, and these interruptions reach the disc at the other end of the line, giving it the same pulsations that were imparted at the beginning. They lack power to move the mass of the general atmosphere; but the ear, when placed near the disc, is able to catch these vibrations and carry them along the nerve to the brain. The peculiar fact is that the brain is made a receptacle of the throbbings, which it turns into meaning and accepts as thought. So light also, which is a wave movement, is interpreted in the brain as ideas or thought.

The strength of the wave is determined by the intensity of the thought.

This is the Eighty-ninth Principle. The brain is not affected by every sound it hears, nor by every thought that comes its way. If it were, the result would be unpleasant. Thousands of sounds, from large to small, are thrown upon the ear every day, and they naturally vibrate the nerve within; but the brain knows nothing of them. You hear what is going on, it is true; but you have no consciousness of it, unless the sound is unusual, or it makes a demand upon your attention. The ticking of a clock will keep you awake at night, if you are not accustomed to hearing it by day. If, however, you hear it always, you cannot even catch its sound by an effort, for the commonness of it has deadened your consciousness of its presence. So an instrument made to record all sound impressions that occurred from sunrise to sunset, gave evidence of an enormous number that affected it mechanically, while they were unable to reach the mind at all.

The brain is so constituted that remarks roll off without attracting its attention, as criticism rolls off unsensitive natures. We listen, and yet do not catch the thought in the sound. This is experienced in the effort to follow the sermon of the ordinary preacher. He may shout for an hour in tones loud enough to be heard a mile away, yet few persons receive the ideas, for they listen without hearing. There have been many attempts to account for this double nature of the brain, as some have called it. "You are not listening to what I am saying," says an impatient person to another; and the other finds the last few words still vibrating on the nerve. He repeats them. "What did I say prior to that? What have I said during the last five minutes f" He did not know. The fact that the last idea can be caught on the yet vibrating nerve of hearing shows that the brain may go back a little way and extract the idea out of the last uttered sounds.

Where an unusual noise has been introduced in a locality, everybody notices it for a few days or weeks; then it is not heard at all in the brain, though it is really heard in the ear. A visitor is annoyed by it, and you cannot even hear it by trying. This is also true of sounds not continuous, as the passing of street cars or railway trains, and even the screeching of locomotives. "How can your babies sleep when the whistles blow so loud and shrill ?" asked a woman. "They are used to it," was the reply. City people in the country are annoyed for a while by the universal din of the night amid the generally profound silence; but very soon they are unable to hear the noises.

Thought may be separated from voice.

This is the Ninetieth Principle. The more interest you feel in what you say, the more likely you are to reach the minds of others. Your voice may have no difficulty in reaching the ears of thousands as well as of one; but to be heard is one thing, to be understood is another; and to have your thought received is still more. You are heard when your voice is loud enough to reach the person addressed; you are understood when you enunciate distinctly; but your thoughts may not be received at all. This failure need not be ascribed to the obscurity of the ideas, which might prevent a comprehension of them; it is the commonest of all failures.

MYSTIC UTOPIAN SUPERMEN

It is possible to read for an hour to a listener, expressing only the simplest thoughts, and yet not be able to reach the conscious attention of the individual. In such a case the thought was not in the voice; the reader was not thinking of the ideas; or, allowing that he was, the listener was engaged in ruminations of a different character or of things far away. "I heard every word that was said," remarked the person addressed, "but I was not paying attention; so I did not catch a single idea." How is it possible to hear what is said, and not know what is said? That the sound lingers is well known from the fact that it can be picked up and carried into the mind and there interpreted.

This shows that the thought is separable from the sound itself, and that a voice laden with ideas may fail to place them in the brain of another. Of course it is true that a dead sentence may be revived and interpreted, as where it is read by the eye, or heard by the ear, and revived just as it is about to pass into nothingness. In such manner the voice, spoken in the phonograph, is taken out at any time and read into the conscious brain. Such methods are of value next to nothing, and lack all life; they certainly serve no usefulness, except in the merest mechanical way. That which appeals to the eye goes directly to the brain; that which appeals to the ear may die in transit. We look at what interests us, and can concentrate our attention at will; but we are compelled to hear all the ten thousand sounds that till the air in the course of the day, and nature is kind enough to relieve the brain from the tax of knowing what they are or what ideas they represent.

There are two sides to the separation of the thought from the voice. On one we see the inability of the hearer to give due attention; on the other we see the inability of the speaker to think in his voice. It is a common occurrence to find these two sides represented in a single conversation more common among women than men; although both sexes are given to the habit. Two young ladies are talking together; one speaks a hundred words or so, and the other starts in at the first pause for breath, saying, "Yes," or something as light, and going off at a rapid rate on a theme in no way connected with the subject first introduced by her friend. They proceed in this manner until there is something of specific interest mentioned, when the listeners catch the idea. It is generally scandal or a love affair. That the one who speaks, when the subject is not of vital interest, is not thinking of what is said, may be known from the fact that there is no tensity of ideas, and the train of thought, when interpreted, is not resumed unless it has something of unusual moment to keep it alive.

Similar to this most useless way of employing so great a faculty as the voice, is the tiresome style of orators, especially those in the pulpit. A majority of preachers, who read their sermons, do not connect their thoughts with their voices; in fact, their minds are far away. An actor who spoke his lines with vigor of sound, but with his whole attention on an outside matter, was told by a friend and admirer that he produced only a muddle in the minds of the audience. "Your voice was excellent, loud, strong and clear; you spoke distinctly; your enunciation and modulation were as good as ever; but the force of your voice was offered evidently as a substitute for your magnetism. How do you account for it?" "I can easily explain the difference. Usually my mind is on what I am saying. I know the lines perfectly. I need not think of them to speak them. Tonight I was brooding over a little trouble, and I am sure that I did not utter an idea of the play; I spoke the words only." By his statement and that of his friend it seemed that magnetism is lacking when the thought is separated from the voice.

No more vital question can arise than that which relates to the usefulness of oratory in the pulpit. In some churches the officials prefer that the sermons be read from carefully prepared manuscript, thus securing better structure of the sermon at the expense of native force and freedom of self in the delivery. A certain bishop issued a similar order to his ministers, and gave as a reason for it that they came to the pulpit on Sundays without a full preparation; they depended upon their ability to say what was in their minds, regardless of whether there was anything tangible there or not. This confession of the bishop was an admission that the clergy under him were either unable or unwilling to think out their sermons, to plan their structure in advance, to make outlines and notes, and to commit these to memory or to preserve them in a form for easy reference. The true art of extempore speech requires as careful a preparation as if the address were to be written and read. The bishop said that the sermons had been growing more and more rambling, some of them containing injudicious and carelessly formulated statements, showing lack of preparation and study.

When this disposition is analyzed it is found that a lazy person may speak better by having his manuscript before him, already written; that a lazier person will write down a few notes, and depend on the luck of finding ideas and language at the time of speaking, and that the laziest of all will come before his audience without advance thought, notes, outlines or anything else. Despite cleverness, natural ability, eloquence and everything that experience might add to his chances of success, he is bound to be a failure. Such a habit is injurious to the personal power of the speaker, as time soon proves. Not to be confounded with such slack methods, is the fullness of thought that comes when a theme has taken complete possession of the person; when he is so thoroughly charged with his subject that a mind brimful of ideas is but waiting for the occasion to give them utterance; for the best of all means of getting ready is to live in the atmosphere of the subject until identities are lost by merging together. Such instances are very rare, however.

The principle is a vital one, and has its place in every magnetic life, though in lesser degree. What is called an all-around knowledge is too diffusive to be effective. Only a gaseous matter diffuses itself widely. A general education is of the highest importance; but he who would throw the blue fire must be full of his subject. No person can be diffusively magnetic. This does not imply that he is to be of one idea, but merely of one at a time. He may wield the power all day long, controlling one individual after another, yet largely in the line of his mental operations. If he proposes to throw the red fire, the rule changes, and there he may hold sway over a greater number; for feeling, and not thought, is attempting the mastery of those who come within the domain of his influence.

The nervous energy throws the red fire of passion.

This is the Ninety-first Principle. In speaking of this law we shall revert to others that have been but partly discussed; for this will save repetition where several principles relate to different lines of control. By nervous energy we refer to the power, and not to the weakness, of the nervous system. A person is spoken of as "nervous," implying that he lacks control of that part of himself, or is fidgety, embarrassed easily, or cannot endure distracting things; he jumps a little when a book falls to the floor, or shrinks at the screeching of an engine; a small boy with a drum annoys him; the young lady who practices the five-finger exercises on the piano over his head distresses him three hours every night, and so on. Or there may be a frail woman, like the womanish man, who is simply nervous regardless of outside occurrences; who broods over trouble, and magnifies it till the perspiration runs cold sweat down the spinal column; while another type is all unrest within, having the constant desire to fly out of the skin, as a little gentleman once put it.

True nervous energy is an accumulation of power; not the erratic action of weakness. It differs from physical and mental vitality in that it represents the passions; 'and these are here intended to include the moods and emotions as well. It is here that true magnetism shows itself. An explanation of what is meant by an emotion should be made at this place. The popular idea clothes it in tears or sadness; but there is no more sorrow in the emotion of laughter than there is in the emotion of malice. Whatever proceeds from the nervous system and is colored by its interest is an emotion. We cannot separate the muscles from the nerves when the physical expression predominates, but we can make the physical a representation of mere force, and so subdue the mind altogether as well as conceal all appearance of nervous interest; yet it is perfectly true that these three departments of our life are always associated. We all know what is meant by the predominance of muscles over mind and over feeling; we all know what is meant by the predominance of mind over the physical and nervous; and it remains to be seen what is meant by the sway of the feelings over the mind and muscles.

A person who is very much in earnest in saying a thing, creates a far different impression from one who shows merely a mental interest or a physical interest. The very same ideas, uttered from the fire of force, appear to have a different weight, a different meaning from that which is imparted by the fire of the mind or the fire of the passions. "Let him beware who offers insult to our flag," shouts the ranting orator in a volume of force that might be grand if it came from a Setting of quietude; but, as most speakers yell from beginning to finish, the noise they make with their mouths is always deplorable. "Let him beware who offers insult to our flag," says the argumentative speaker, and his glides and modulation, coupled with the peculiar emphasis which the mind alone can give, tell that his thought holds sway. Such a method cannot rant. It may hold true to the line of mental magnetism; it may unite force with thought; but as long as the latter predominates there can be no mere shouting. At such a time, and in such an expression the union of the two is most powerful. It needs only the third to make it irresistible.

The use of the red fire changes the effect, and the utterance is no more what it seemed at first. "Let him beware who offers insult to our flag." The force may not be lacking, but the voice is mellowed by the richness of magnetism; the nerves are on fire, the eyes aglow, the body is tense, the tones ring out with a solidity of strength that is manifest even in the quieter efforts; and all present can see a transformation in the man. The features are not the same. There is no dragging down of the head and chest in obedience to the law of gravity, but the body stands erect, firm, impressive. All these evidences of energy can be easily traced to the nervous system. What are its offices?

Whenever the interest is expressed by the nerves, it may properly be referred to as feeling. To say that a person speaks feelingly need not imply the use of tears or the drooping of the features. Joy is the outcome of feeling. It is not true that magnetism is created by such use; but it is the fact that it employs this method as the best channel of delivering itself. The word passion is a stronger term than feeling, as it presents more the idea of intensity; for which reason we refer to the leading emotions as passions. Of these there are the bright and the dark. As night and day make the completed diem; as summer and winter for the year; as the good passions are rounded out by the bad.

As the emotions and passions spring from the moods and feelings of the nervous system, and as words come out of the mind, it is not easy to express the former by the agents of the latter. We all know that love is the reigning queen of this department; yet there are so many kinds of love that it is necessary here to adopt a technical definition. In the dictionary, and by popular use, a person may love husband or wife, father, mother, sister, brother, son, daughter, fruit, flowers, birds, cats, dogs, oysters, clams, dry weather, lettuce, cheese, the poor, the sinner, and a heterogeneous mass of everything and any-thing, all without sense in the use of the word, except in a few instances. "I love steamed oysters, but I hate fried oysters," is a common mode of saying two things, neither of which is really meant. Hate, and even dislike, are affirmative attitudes; to dislike a thing is to have a positive reason for so doing; while most persons merely do not like certain things, yet cannot properly say they dislike them.

The distinction between the love that may be felt for a person and for an inanimate object is as wide as affection may go. The woman who loves her pet bulldog has nothing more than an affection for the beast; and, because it has life and responsive intelligence, she would mourn its absence or its death. A man may love his companions in the brute world, his dog or his horse; he may love his gun, a tree, or a brook, if pleasant associa-tions are called up by them; he may love his library, his favorite volume, a portrait; but all these emotions are properly classed under the term affection. The holiest of all earthly loves ought to be that which the child bears for the mother; perhaps it is the holiest; but the most enduring, the most faithful, the deepest and best, is that of the parent for the child. It cannot reason, for it does not proceed from the brain. It is blind to faults in a remarkable degree, for it sees beyond the source of all faults.

Yet while it is proper to refer to parental and filial endearment as love, we are com-pelled to put them with others under the term affection; and, in our limited technical use, we include nothing in the word love except that strange influence which brings two hearts together under the command of the marriage passion. Of this we will speak later, as it is the mainspring of life. Opposed to this love is the dark passion of hate. These are the two poles of all animal existence, from the least to the greatest. Stepping aside from them, we come to the second group, in which hope is the bright star and grief its shadow. It is because of hope that we all continue to live, and because of grief that we seek to hope again. Shadows tempt us to the light.

It would seem as if these passions included all others; but there are classes yet to be considered. Pride is a bright, a lofty and an exalting passion, taking us where hope points the way. Its opposite is shame. Then comes resolution, the fourth of the bright class, with fear as its other pole. Excitement, the flame of labor, whereby the impulse of energy stamps genuineness on love, on hope, on pride and on resolution, is a bright passion. Its technical meaning is not the same as that popularly given it. Depression is its dark oppo-site. Here are the ten passions; five of them are bright, five are dark; and they include in their subdivisions and associate emotions all the colorable feelings of which the wonderful nervous system is capable of experiencing or expressing. In fact, most persons really experience the hundred emotions, while they cannot express more than a half dozen of them.

So important and so satisfying is it to an ambitious soul to develop the ability to recognize and to give true color to these variable moods, that we strongly urge every reader of this volume, every true student of life, to spend six months in a school of expression, taking the whole art very thoroughly, and devoting the time solely to the professional course. By this is meant a balanced study and training, wherein every detail of objective expression is taken at the same time with every detail of subjective expression. Besides making the man or woman more useful in life to others, and besides finding it the very best means of acquiring culture that the world affords today if truly taught, it is the best aid to the study of magnetism. Many persons take the training in expression for these purposes only.

We will look at a few of these emotions, such as arise from the ten great passions or are associated with them, for the purpose of obtaining a better understanding of what is meant by the predominance of the nervous system in the expression of magnetism. In the family of emotions connected with love we find kindred feelings, the closest of which is affection. This differs as the objects vary on which it is lavished. Then such a mood as respect is well understood as belonging to the steps that lead up to affection and love, some claiming that it is a necessary basis for both these tributes, although such claim is not always sustained in the facts. Fancy is distantly akin to the general idea, and goodness also has association; but the attempt to show that all these emotions are interrelated would be profitless. They may exist in an harmonious group without actual kinship.

We can see why mirth, joy, flattery and ecstasy are rightly placed in the group of love, as harmonious with it; and thrill or animal passion of marital love may, under its technical name, stand in the same class also. The great passion that holds the pole opposite that of love is hate. In a group harmonizing with it are such emotions as those of defiance, disdain, contempt, scorn, jealousy, anger, treachery, revenge and rage; the last being the climacteric motion of hate. Passing to the bright passion of hope, called a passion simply because it is the central life of its group, and not because it makes its owner passionate, we see the harmonic colors of peace, mercy, reverence, ambition which inspires hope, prayer, longing, wishing, trust and faith. The opposite pole of this passion is grief, and it is grouped with disappointment, regret, sadness, sympathy, melancholy, disconsolation, desolation, despair and frenzy. Each is different; each comes from a fixed color; and it is in the predominance of the nervous system that each is possible. For the highest magnetism you must eliminate the dark passions.

Another of the bright passions is pride. In its group are sacrifice, dignity, triumph, nobility, patriotism, eloquence, solemnity, sublimity and grandeur. The opposite of pride is shame, with its harmonic group of anxiety, petulance, humility, repentance, guilt, murder, remorse, agony and desperation. The fourth of the bright passions is resolution, and its colors include resentment, warning, threatening, challenge, courage, recklessness, daring and intensity. These are opposed by the passion of fear, the group of which includes the emotions of superstition, stealth, apprehension, alarm, fright, awe, terror, horror and frantic fear. The last of the bright passions is excitement; in its group are doubt, wonder, perturbation, surprise, bewilderment, amazement, embarrassment, insanity and madness. These are bright in their activities only, being a series of unsettled conditions through which the better is struggling with the worse, and thus feeding the flame of existence. All fire and all light is the result of chaotic excitement of particles. We would think that this passion had no opposite pole; but an examination of life shows that depression is the exact opponent of excitement and is always its reaction. With it, in an harmonious group, are the decrepitude of age, the willingness of resignation, the falling to sleep, dizziness, fainting, the physical color of pain affecting the nerves, the cataleptic state called trance, the purpose of parting with life as in suicide, and the fading away of the world in death. Here, in these one hundred emotions, are all the moods of human life, running the awful gamut from the sweet temper of peace to the black mystery of death.

If you will look into these many expressions of the nervous system, you will find all of them free from the control of either mind or body. They are peculiarly the progeny of the feelings, and come out of a different department of the body from thought or force. They are powerful enough to control the physical life, for by their influence the latter may pine away into sickness and emaciation. They are rarely ever subdued by the mind. The man in love will hardly think of other things; he certainly could not reason himself out of it if he were sincere. Facts may awaken one out of a thin dream. Even the emotion of goodness is free from all mental calculation when it is abiding and honest; for if a person is good because the judgment decrees that it is the best policy, the goodness may fly away when it is no longer politic to preserve it.

The action of a passion or an emotion may spring out of the mind; but then it is a piece of acting, creating a delusion. This is the method of the hypocrite, the dissembler and the actor. Some feign goodness, respect, affection, love, joy, reverence, trust, faith, regret, sadness, sympathy, despair, sacrifice, dignity, nobility, patriotism, anxiety, humility, repentance, warning, threatening, courage, surprise, insanity, sleep, fainting, and no doubt many others; while the professional actor is in duty bound to assume all moods as the occasion demands. So long as the assumption is mental, it must lack naturalness; but it is true that magnetism enables a person to step from the pretense to the fact. Herein arises the question as to how much the lack of honesty is liable to defeat the power of magnetism.

It is true that dishonesty is unmagnetic. This cannot be denied. The lawyer who utters an untruth to the jury may shout it, declaim it, pound it at them; yet he cannot charge the assertion with any true fire. It is false, and as such is a discord. He must believe in himself and in the fact before he can hurl the bolt of fire that shall burn its way into other men's hearts. He may step into the role of the actor, and thereby win himself over to the conviction. The character of the drama is a reality in the realm of fancy; it lives, moves, acts, talks, feels, and takes on humanity; and this the actor must realize. He first studies the part as something separate; but little by little he enters into it, until it has no separate existence; the two are one, and what the character feels, the actor also feels in full reality. This fact does not involve the old discussion as to whether he can act without feeling the effect of his powers. Some claim that the emotion may sway the audience and not the actor; others, that it must sway both alike. Either of these propositions may be separated from the one we have made; our claim being that no actor can express magnetism until the character he portrays is fully absorbed and made a part of himself, so that what the character feels the actor feels. It seems to be a fact that the stronger he is, the less he, as an individual, is affected by the portrayal; that the more smoothly and perfectly he is blended into the character, the less wear and tear is produced on his own system; while, on the contrary, the weaker he is, the more he is upset by his portrayal, and the more credit he obtains for his efforts.

From these associate considerations it would seem impossible to discuss the present principle without becoming involved in other matters. It is important, however, to come back to the question of the assumption of an emotion that is not in reality honest. The lawyer may know that his client is guilty. Rufus Choate, who won all, or practically all of his jury cases, was in the habit of compelling his clients to tell him the truth, so that he might be better prepared to meet the dangers that would arise at the trial. Choate was the most magnetic man at the bar, excepting Daniel Webster. When they met as opposing advocates in a case, it was decided on its merits; otherwise it was decided by the magnetism of the counsel. In the preparation of a trial, Choate gave it much thought; he idealized his guilty client into one who was innocent; and, throwing away the bad for the unreal, he made the former cease to exist, and the latter he changed into the real. He was the consummate actor, who could compel himself to believe with a fervid sincerity in the character which he assumed. On the same principle, the minister who wins the public by his magnetism, yet who is a consummate rascal, possesses the power of stepping into a character not himself. He becomes the advocate of a goodness that is not his own, but dwells only in the life of the fancy.

Magnetism creates a double life.

This is the Ninety-second Principle. It would seem at first as if the tendency of this power in a duplex direction would be pronounced a most serious fault, and relegate it to the ranks of evil agencies. But the fact is just the other way. The power to step out of one's self into another being, that is, into an ideal assumption, is always applied to a self that is bad. The ideal is always better than the real. We have in mind a clergyman who had a wonderful fund of magnetic energy, who preached effective sermons, who won many converts, most of whom remained true to their profession of faith even after they knew this preacher was not honest; yet, in spite of these merits, this man was a gambler and a debauchee.

In analyzing his history as compared with his character, we find that he had always been going wrong from earliest boyhood, having set fire to a barn on one occasion, stolen tools on another, and committed numerous thefts. At the age of eighteen he ruined a girl of fifteen; moved to another State, where he repeated the offense with a girl of fourteen, and married her out of respect for her father's demands, on whom he threw himself for support. He was not lazy. The father-in-law actually stimulated him to think better of his conduct, but saw that his whole character was saturated with evil. Then came to the young man, as has come to others of the same mold, the desire to enter the ministry. He thought it over for a year or two, but an unexpected affair attracted him to the ocean, which he followed for several years, leaving his child-wife with her parents. While at sea, he arose out of his lower self through the pretense that he was an evangelist preacher.

This statement was made to the captain who said that he seemed like a runaway criminal. Then came the thorough duplicity of his nature. He practiced continually the art of coolly preserving his nervous forces, and found himself magnetic. He conceived the idea of becoming a great preacher in a faraway land, under an assumed name. More and more he calmed his wild energies, and gained self-control as well as power over others. He assumed the attitude and carriage of a preacher, spoke to men in groups on Sundays, and actually impressed them with his sincerity. Knowing that his earlier conduct was a contradiction of this pretense, he was shrewd enough to account for it by remarks of the following tenor: "Boys, I am not the good man I wish to be.

I was born in sin; as a boy I lived in sin, and now, as a young man, I feel that there is a devil in me seeking to drag me down. If I let this evil propensity control me, you know what I would be like. I believe that every man has two angels in his life; he can follow one or the other. I want to follow my better angel; but, boys, I cannot at all times. The fight is harder for me than for you, because your evil nature is not so bad as mine. He unintentionally hit the truth.

So impressive and convincing was this confession that he received the credit of being sincere. The captain believed in him; and, at ports where they could find books, the two made purchases, in order to assist in the young man's sea education. In writing to a friend, the captain declared that this "preacher" had made his crew into new men, and that he never had such good government on board ship. Later on he gave him a letter of introduction to a friend in Australia, vouching for his honesty of purpose and his ability to influence his hearers. As the pretender afterwards confessed, this was the great thing he most desired; it opened to him his future. All he now needed was faithful work, study, and a lofty ambition to reach the topmost round of the ladder of fame. He failed because he lacked breadth of mind, and was not honest.

But the point of importance is the temporary genuineness that his magnetism gave him. In that faraway land he entirely subdued, or covered over, his evil side; then, finding it impossible to get out of a rut that prevented his further rise, he came back to America after being ordained. He was now unknown, and his name was new, for he entered the service of the ship under an assumed name, and this was adopted ever after. In Australia he gave evidence of sincerity in his ministry; so much so, that he was loaded with credentials from men of influence; and, as a test of the force of these, it soon became known that be was missed there. A larger salary was promised him to return. He was restless, and sought greater opportunities for rising, hence came to America, where he hoped to realize his ambition. He argued that he might evade meeting the persons whom he had wronged, if he kept out of their communities, and that when his fame and usefulness were very great, his youthful errors would be overlooked. This was true, for a man of force might master the indiscretions that stand out against him in a remote past. But what about the cauldron of evil that was seething within him?

He was still a man of pretense relying on the duplex nature which magnetism gave him; therefore he was the creature of an influence that must fade when the influences waned. He was unsafe. Soon the magnetism was neglected. He ceased to try to maintain it. He believed that the ability he had shown was due to an inherent power born in his evil self; and he fell back upon it. Then he was ruined, exposed, arrested and sent to the penitentiary, all without having his name and former identity discovered. In speaking of his career and fall, he said: "I was a different man when preaching. The power within me drove out my evil self, and made me another being. So much was I impressed by this fact that I came to believe that some good man had come to me, and was doing the talking. It was not till I got home from the services that I realized how bad I was, and what a pretender I had been." It is on the same principle that the actor is enabled to step into a character far different from himself; yet he can do so only through magnetism.

In the case of Dr. Jekyll and Mr. Hyde the evil character is hypnotic; and this must not be confounded with the duplex life to which our principle refers. A man may at times step into an evil role, through the process of hypnotic change; and this change may be superinduced by an idea, a fear, an influence or a mechanical agency; all of which we have fully considered in a preceding realm of this volume. So much of duplicity in the life of Jekyll and Hyde as is unreal, or is dependent upon the notions of alchemy, we have nothing to do with, as that phase of the case must be read with Jules Verne's trip to the moon. The world has many really double lives. When the normal is of average purity, and a drop ensues, or the duality is normal good and assumed bad, the assumption is not due to magnetism, but to hypnotism. Magnetism never lowers a human being.

The distinction is one of importance, and is worth looking at. We see a good life suddenly fallen. It has been in reality a good life; not a pretense, nor a piece of acting. It is changed to one of a duplex nature. The most common case is that of a business man, living at some distance from his place of business. A woman throws over him an hypnotic influence. He may have met her very probably, or she may be in his employ, possibly his typewriter or stenographer. He becomes infatuated by the hypnotic idea, which may emanate from her or may arise from his own thinking of her, either of which would lead him away from his good judgment. Now begins the double life; the normal is a pretense; the abnormal is evil and real. He will soon need magnetism, or the pretense must fall.

On the other hand, a man who is of a diabolical character often wins a fair reputation by the aid of magnetism. This is because the pretense does not cause a departure toward the bad, but toward the good. Magnetism in duplex lives never aids the real, but always the pretended. The real is never good, the pretended is always an assumption of good; therefore magnetism in duplex lives is the ally of the better side. Remember this, and do not blame the power. Its drift is always heavenward. Not a case can be cited where magnetism has even allured a human being downward; and, on the other hand, never a case has been known where hypnotism has allured a man upward. We refer to the semi-hypnotic state which does not pass into sleep or into stupor of any kind, but merely dazes the faculties or suspends the judgment. The cure for this is found only in the study of magnetism, which, if anything can, will destroy the meaner self.

Intermittent stress is the carrying power of feeling.

This is the Ninety-third Principle. We seemingly step aside to examine a law that is generally unknown in the study of magnetism. It is not entirely new, having been personally taught for many years as one of the secret exercises in the most potent form of this art; but this is the first time it has been published. We must take the matter up as from the beginning; and, even if you are familiar with it, others may not be; so that a full explanation is essential.

By stress is meant the use of the voice under some impulse of feeling. In conversation that is uninteresting there is no stress in the voice; it is then called a dead voice in the art of expression. But when the converser wakes up to some feeling he cannot help the use of stress, of which there are eight. If the sentiment of beauty predominates, the voice will instinctively fill out the syllables giving them a fullness suggestive of richness. This refers to flexible voices coupled with minds that have words at command ready and fit to use. It does not embrace such cases as are met in the commonplaces of life, where there are no tools of the mind in the voice. Wealth cannot give these tools, nor can it impart stress to voice. The daughter of the millionaire, who has seen the vale of Chamouni in the Alps, could say no more than that "It was perfectly splendid, you know; the peaks were awfully high, you see; and I just thought how fearfully nice it was.' * Her voice could have no stress. The style of delivery must have been broken and jerky as the chop sea of a bay.

It seems then that there must be at least the ordinary means of expressing one's feelings, before stress comes in. It is easily cultivated, as are most all the tools of expression. He who would say grand things must have words to picture the ideas; but they fall short of their effectiveness if not accompanied by stress suitable to the stature of the mind. So these variations of the voice go on through the eight elementary stresses, and then their endless variations come into play, giving new faculties to the mind and body. It is on this, as on other accounts, that the full art of expression should be specifically studied in a six months' course in some reliable institution.

But the only stress that concerns us at this place is the intermittent; and this we will proceed to explain and to illustrate. Feeling of every kind affects the diaphragm, that large muscle that constitutes the floor of the lungs. Under great excitement this organ, for it is so termed, is violently agitated. In weeping, it not only causes the whole chest-frame to heave, but gives the voice its trembling sound, from the jumps to the finer runs that indicate suffering. An imitation of weeping is the quickest means of ascertaining what is meant. This is a strong intermittent action, too strong to be called stress. It is rather distress.

Let the mood be changed to the other side of our nature, and the agitation of the diaphragm will give vent to laughter. The great muscle rises and falls with considerable force, while its effect upon the lungs is to cause the chest to rise and fall also, and the voice has a rhythmical sound, due to the same vibration. We mention these extremes because they are easily analyzed. In listening to an unmagnetic voice, we notice its deadness, and particularly its lack of stress. Again, in listening to a voice that is known to be magnetic, we perceive a sensation as of vibrations too fine to be caught by ordinary observation. Anatomy tells us that the diaphragm is active in proportion to the strength of the feeling which takes possession of the body. From this fact there is no escape, nor has it any exception.

Any general reading upon the subject will confirm the statement that the diaphragm expresses the degree of feeling that controls the body. A very important event will cause it to vibrate, not violently, but in a fine though intense action that is powerful even in its minuteness. The voice shows a strong degree of the intermittent stress, but not so much as appears in the tremolo, which is an affectation of some singers. There is really considerable agitation at the diaphragm. Its fine but decided movement reaches the abdomen, and vibrates its contents so that, in a majority of cases, it results in looseness of the bowels. This tendency to diarrhoea is chargeable solely to the churning of the intestines by the motion of the diaphragm. This experience has been frequently noted by nearly everybody; and some persons have accounted at last for their proneness to this disorder when excited.

The magnetic person is tense from center to surface of the body. A tense, muscle is vibrant. It does not shake or tremble, but it vibrates in a measure so small as to be noted only in effect. Such a condition involves the whole body. The diaphragm is the first part to catch the sensation; it takes it up, and sends it to all extremes. The voice is supported on the diaphragm, for it is a solid air column in effect, having its base on this great muscle, and changing from air to tone as it passes the edges of the vocal cords, the glottis lips of the larynx. The difference between the voice and stress is a plain one. Both are vibrations; but those of the larynx are exceedingly small, fine and close together, the slowest of them in the ordinary pitch reaching an enormous number per minute; while the vibrations of the diaphragm are very much less. In weeping they do not average one to a second; in laughter, not more than five; in the tremolo, not more than five to eight, and in the fine stress, when magnetic, not more than ten to twenty.

The learning of the intermittent stress, so as to adopt it readily, is always an excitement to the diaphragm and through that organ to the whole nervous system; just as the quick action of the tense eye will excite the 'magnetism of the brain, and invigorate both the eye and the brain. Some exercises are like a match applied to a magazine of gunpowder, needing but little to produce much. The artificial use of the intermittent stress is of value because it enriches the voice to a very high order of beauty, and it sooner connects the tones with magnetism than if it were forced to come naturally. It quickly becomes natural in use when habitual.

The right degree of the intermittent stress should be acquired by practice. This is brought about by reading any line in a tremulous tone until the nerves, by their vibration, bring tears to the eyes. This is, of course, artificial. It may require days or weeks to vibrate the tone until the tears start. If you cannot start the vibrations, then adopt the following drill exercise: Fill the lungs full of air; open the mouth about half an inch at the lips; let the air out slowly and steadily in the sound of "Oh!" prolonged, say ten or twenty seconds in time; place the flat of the hand on the lowest bone in the middle of the lungs, in front of the lower chest, just over the stomach, and with the fist of the other hand pound the back of the first as rapidly as possible while making the tone "Oh!" The result will be a wavy vibration of the sound as in the tremolo.

The purpose now is to connect the wave-movement with the voice while omitting the use of the hands. This is done by continuing the former assistance for a while, starting the tone with it, then removing the hands. It will be found that the voice will go on by itself. Then the tremulo must be reduced to that point where the ear can hardly catch it as a vibration. Adopt this into your voice on all occasions, ordinary as well as special. Never allow a person to suspect that your tones are vibratory, or that there is any change in them, for the affectation will defeat the purpose, besides being foreign to the true intermittent stress.

The nervous system must be in harmony with the emotion.

This is the Ninety-fourth Principle. It is of the highest importance in the effort to control another or others. We have named one hundred emotions, in groups of ten each, under ten great passions. Each emotion is a vital and preponderating condition, capable of taking supreme charge of all the faculties to such an extent as to lead them, though not necessarily to divert them out of the channels of their best usefulness. All magnetism should be captained. Every mood should have leadership.

It is then of very great importance that the emotion to be impressed should be fully understood, and that the nervous system should be brought into harmony with it. This is really the work of magnetic coloring, and can be acquired only by practice in cases where it is unknown. It is a rule that when a color has once been acquired it cannot be lost; or at least may be readily summoned at any time when the person is able to concentrate his whole attention upon it. Without this complete interest in what you are doing or saying, you could not be fully in earnest. No lover can win the object of his adoration if his interest in her is dulled and weakened. He may ask her the pivotal question at a time when she is so much in love with him that she will lose no time in delivering the affirmative reply; but this is not winning her; it is merely taking what is offered.

Of all questions that are asked more frequently than the whole remaining categories combined, is that which seeks to know if a woman may be won without love, or if a man may likewise be caught. In other words: Is it possible for a man to win a woman who does not love him, or whom he does not love? Is it possible for a woman to win a man who does not love her, or whom she does not love ? Here are really four conditions, for a woman's love is unlike a man's. A harder question than all is this: Is it possible to win the love of one whom you do not frequently meet; or, can magnetism reach beyond the glance of the eye or the tones of the voice?

We are coming more closely to the solution of these problems as we progress, page by page. There are laws yet to be presented and understood before the question can be answered. We mentioned love as the most common of all the emotions, and the greatest of all the passions. It is quite clear that no person can hope to win who is not in earnest; but that earnestness may be actual or magnetic. The latter idealizes an assumption until it is felt as an honest fact. Take any of the everyday emotions, as they are named, in expectation at least. Goodness is one of them; affection is another, pride another, and so on. If the magnetic mood must pass through one of these, there must be a harmony between the nervous system and the emotion.

At first glance it would seem as if it were not possible to employ more than a half dozen of the one hundred emotions which we have named; but, when they are understood in their technical bearings upon this question, it will be seen that nearly all of the dark ones must be avoided by careful study to that end, while a majority of the bright ones are necessary channels of magnetic influence. Of course, if your life is limited to a few common emotions, you must work in those, or else set about getting others within the range of your powers.

A mental assertion should accompany the energy of the will.

MYSTIC UTOPIAN SUPERMEN

This is the Ninety-fifth Principle. It is not easy to find words for this principle, as it includes something not translatable into language while retaining its true meaning. The will is an agent of great energy when magnetized. Let any man or woman acquire magnetism by mechanical exercises; then place behind it a living determination, and few persons can escape feeling the influence that is directly wielded. The only deterrent in getting results is because of the fact that the power is not given form. The wish of the mind is of the chief importance, and speech is necessary for its expression.

If a ghost were to come to you and chatter unintelligible noises, you would not know what it said simply from seeing or hearing it talk. Ideas to you are not ideas in any language that you cannot understand. Even the voice of a presentiment, the meaning of intuition, or the motive of subconsciousness is wasted if not put in words that you are familiar with. Many a person, talking and understanding but one language, has caught the ideas that were formulated in the brain of another who could not use or even have knowledge of the language of the former, as though an English speaking person divined the meaning in the mind of a Russian, while neither knew the language of the other. This is explained on the ground that the Russian tongue is known by some one who speaks English, and subconsciousness is able to connect the two with wonderful swiftness and keenness. It may be explained on the other ground that all ideas live regardless of words, and pass as ideas, each having form as words in individual minds; meaning that if one person could send his thoughts into the brains of a Russian, German, Frenchman and Italian, whose language he knew nothing of, the ideas would resolve themselves into the several tongues as needed for interpretation. Thus, if an Englishman were to send the idea of a chair covered with plush of red color into the heads mentioned, he would see clearly in his own mind the form of the chair, the quality and nature of the goods and the color; which, being ideas, are given life in the respective brains where they find suitable words according to the language of each. This is not difficult. If persons of four nationalities enter a room and actually see such a chair, they will not be at a loss to find the suitable words for expressing the details.

A mental assertion takes just the shape we have endeavored to describe. It prevents a wild presence of energy and determination, uncoined and unshaped. The gold has value because it is given form and carries its meaning on its face. Let it be a shapeless mass, and no merchant will receive it for money until its value is given the certainty it requires. Willpower is most powerful when it is most definite and most defined. We often meet persons who do not have the slightest idea what they wish, or what they intend even. The aimless speaker is the most tiresome of all. Not only does he drift and wander to and fro, but he scatters his energies to the winds. Some are magnetic in the sense that they have a vital energy at the start, which has been accumulated from previous habits; so the first few minutes of their address ring in the genuine tone, and the warmth of magnetism is distinctly felt; then they either forget what they are driving at, or are confused in its conception, and the effort fails. This is a common experience; and what is true in speech is true in every other use of the faculties.

The mental assertion is the formulating of the purpose into exact language; in brief phrases, if possible, and adhering to the form until it is accomplished, or until the greater end can be achieved by substitution of something better in effective power. "What I will to be done, I speak mentally over and over again, with all the energy, the fire and the determination of my whole nature, " says a man who rarely ever fails where he considers the attempt worth the effort. The fact is, very few persons really know what they wish; and fewer still have the power to formulate a determination into fixed language. "Call on him, and ask him to subscribe for this fund," says the chairman of the committee to the member who is charged with the duty or privilege of raising a certain proportion of the funds needed. The effort is unsuccessful. The man was asked, that is all. The solicitor did not at any time determine to succeed; nor was there either magnetism or a formulated purpose to win.

Contrasted with this failure is the effort of another who calls upon the same man. There is magnetism to start with; there is a knowledge of how to use it; there is the will-power; there is the diplomacy which seeks to reach the man by the channel of motive; there is the fixed determination to win, and there is the mental assertion behind the magnetism, the will and the determination. The man said afterward: "I knew by the look in the face and the tones of the voice that I was to be overcome. I saw at once a determination to obtain my subscription, which was lacking in the first member who called on me for the same purpose. I realized the hopelessness of obstinacy, and gave in speedily." Here we learn that fixed magnetic determination, taking full possession of the person, may change the face and alter the voice. These are effective weapons, if they reduce the opposition early in the conflict.

The language used when the mental assertion is behind it may be of interest to our students, and we will try to reproduce a few conversations at those vital points where the forces of the superior party are doing their best work. Let us compare the two sides. One has acquired magnetism by mechanical practice and by conserving his energies, instead of allowing them to run to waste; he has learned by principles or laws the use of this power; he has marshalled his warring forces into one army of united energy; he has formed a tremendous will; he knows how to fix the goal of an irresistible determination; he speaks the purpose of each act by a mental assertion which is a flame of intense fire; and then he goes in to win. Against this array there is nothing; there is possibly no magnetism, no determination, no union of energies; only the scattered forces, perhaps, of an obstinate mind, or a set will that cannot withstand an appeal to motive. Still it is better that giants meet and impart more skill by requiring its use.

Let us look at the conversation by which the subscription was secured. In this and other conversations the chief movements only are preserved:

Solicitor (entering, determining to obtain the subscription): am glad to see you, Mr. F. I have come to see you on a matter of importance.

F.—"Of importance to me!"

S.—"I think you will agree with me that it is." (Mental assertion: "I know you will agree with me that it is.") [Had the mental assertion been made openly, the claim that it was known to be of importance to him would have at once challenged his obstinacy; and this should be avoided if possible.]

F.—"A subscription, I presume."

S.—"That is it. We expected something from Mr. H., but be does not like music, and says it is better for the people to get along without concerts. The young folks soon go astray if something is not done for them. They find it hard work to amuse themselves. The band has generously offered to give two concerts a week for the price of one."

F.—"Why does he decline to subscribe?"

S.—"He gave as a reason that he could not afford it, as his business was not as prosperous as usual."

F.—"Do you think I can afford it any better than he can?"

S.—"We all know that times are hard, and that many of our best business men are running behind. Some will undoubtedly have to suspend. Report classes you with the more successful class." [This reply was not forced in. It very cleverly took advantage of the opening offered by F. when he asked if it was thought that he could better afford to give than could H. He was sensitive on the question of public opinion as to his prosperity in business. S. was waiting for a motive to develop, and saw the opportunity here.]

F. "How much do you want?"

S.—"No more than you feel you can easily afford to give." (Mental assertion: "You are able to give twenty dollars. I know this.") [Whenever a magnetic person suggests an idea to one who is seeking to settle a matter to which it relates, the idea is always conveyed to the mind of the latter. This is very clear proof of the fact that impressions are sent from one person to another by the waves of the ether-sea. In genuine cases no failure ever occurs in this experiment.]

F.—"I did not intend to subscribe for this object."

S.—"But you did not fully understand its import." (Mental assertion: "You will subscribe for it.")

F.—(Takes paper, and puts his name down for twenty dollars): "There; I judge from what you say that it is money well invested."

In discussing this matter with a friend, F. said that S. was full of magnetism at the time of coming in. Both were very much interested in the study of this art; S. having been engaged in developing its culture for two years, while F. was taking it up at about the time of the above meeting of the two; though neither was aware that the other was interested in the subject. F. had personally known S. for several years, and had noted the change that had transpired both in personality and force of character since the study of magnetism began.

After the success in the foregoing case, S. went to H., who had previously refused to subscribe for the fund, as already stated. But it is also true that F. had similarly refused, a detail that escaped his mind in the conversation with S. The solicitor now took the place of one who had employed no method at all in seeking the contribution. It was a statement of the purpose, the asking of whatever amount he would be pleased to give; a refusal, a continued begging, and a disagreeable termination of the interview, in which H. hinted that he was busy and would like to be left alone. S. now called upon him to go over the same ground. The difficulty was that H. naturally had some magnetism, but had no knowledge of how to use it or how to marshal his energies; so they ran to waste, and his business was really running down.

S. (Entering with a fixed determination to secure the contribution)—"I am engaged in the unpleasant task of asking our citizens to assist in maintaining a series of concerts this summer."

H.—"Yes, I know. I won't give anything. I have been called upon before, and have flatly declined. Giving is a voluntary act, not one of compulsion."

S. (Looking H. in the eye with mental assertion: "You will not flatly decline this time.")—"I have not said that I called to ask you to contribute to this fund; I only said that I am engaged in the unpleasant task of asking our citizens who are able to assist us in accomplishing this end. Some may give us money; but occasionally there are business men who have felt the depression of the times so severely that they ought not to be asked for money. One of our committee called upon you some time ago, and we owe you an apology."

H.—"An apology? For what?"

S.—"For asking money. We know that you are interested in the concerts, not for yourself, but because they lessen the evil among the young folks by lessening the opportunity for temptation. We know that you are, and always have been, public-spirited, and that your sympathy is always extended toward any movement that will benefit the rising generation." (Mental assertion: "You know the concerts will be of great advantage to the public.") [If the remarks had gone further, and accused H. of not being able to pay out money, it would have angered him and spoiled the whole interview. It left the idea suggested but not stated, and it was sufficiently in doubt to afford a puzzle to H., who was disposed to follow it up.]

H.—"I do not require an apology. What do you expect me to do?"

S.—"I thought I would call and let you know how I am getting along. I was sure you would be interested."

H.—"Do you mean to say you called for no other object?" [Here H. was exerting magnetism in the doubt he stated, for he came quickly to a focus in challenging the absurd idea that S. called for no purpose other than to convey an apology. S. saw the disadvantage under which he was placed; he realized the magnetic force of the emotion of a doubt, when genuine, and it was his duty to shift the mood.]

S.—"My object in calling was to see you, to confer with you, to ask your advice, if you will give it, and further to ask your aid in reaching M., who is either about to suspend in business or who uses the idea to keep us away." [Here S. came back to the hint of nonprosperity, but struck at H. without appearing to do so. He hit H., for the latter squirmed, remembering that he had given it as an excuse for not subscribing that he could not afford to do so.]

H.—"What advice can I give you?"

S.—"Well, we need a certain amount of money, but are thirty dollars short after exhausting the goodwill and the resources of the community. There is but one other person on whom we can call, and that is M.; but he refused us so flatly that no one dares call on him now. " H.— "He won't give thirty dollars ? What is the largest subscription?"

S.—" I believe F. gave twenty dollars."

H.—"Are you sure?"

S.—"Yes. Here is his name."

H.—"How did he come to give so much as that?"

S.—"He thought the object a good one. It is a sad thing to allow our young men and young women to go about with every temptation alluring them away from home. The absence of some form of public pleasure or private assembly creates a void and makes the town dull. Then it is that the devil suggests evil. Two concerts a week in the open air would become occasions of importance and fill this void of utter restlessness." (Mental assertion: "This you know to be strictly true. Money could not be better invested.") [It will be seen that S. was careful to avoid giving offense to H. by conveying too broad a hint that F. was prosperous in business, and offering this as a reason for his willingness to subscribe. It would have been too direct a charge that those who did not contribute were too poor to do so.

The utmost care must be taken to please. S. thus far has succeeded in keeping the prosperity question before the mind of H., while appearing to ignore it. The inquiry of H., as to why F. came to give so much as twenty dollars was a trap to see if S. would hint that F. was sufficiently prosperous in business to admit of his contributing the amount.]

H.—"If F. gave but twenty dollars, how can you expect M. to give thirty, when M. has refused to give anything at all?"

S.—"Most men who refuse to give money to worthy causes are likely to change their minds. I am not able to convince M., and have not attempted to do so. Instead of calling upon him myself, I thought you would be willing to see him, as you know him better than I do."

H.—"If I called on him I would make him subscribe, but he would not give thirty dollars. I think fifteen is his limit. I will tell you what I will do. If you will let me put my name down for fifteen, that will leave a similar amount for him. You would stand a better chance of getting half of thirty than all of it."

He did as he said, and then asked in a voice tinged somewhat with pride: "Now, suppose you fail to get the last fifteen dollars out of M., what will you do?" S. could not say, but hoped to win from M. H. was sufficiently interested to ask him to send him word how the interview terminated. It seems that S. had enough knowledge of the use of magnetism to realize the importance of working through a motive, as stated under one of our principles. He did not go blindly at M., but ascertained what he could of his motives, his wishes and general disposition. He found that M. was an ardent believer in the temperance of young men, and on this idea the interview was managed.

He spoke of the balance needed, and asked M. to assist him in thinking up the way of getting it. He then said that, when public concerts were given, it did great injury to the business of the saloons, and also kept young men from being tempted to questionable resorts. He hinted that the saloonkeepers were angry at the prospect of the concerts doing harm to their trade. With adroit skill and magnetism, S. succeeded in obtaining the fifteen dollars. Of his victory he notified H., and afterwards F. But he took greater pride in reporting to the chairman of the committee. It was a triumph for magnetism. There was no chance to doubt the usefulness of the special power which he had acquired. Above all was the peculiar effectiveness of the mental assertion, which seemed to live in his mind, not always in words; for it springs more from feeling than from thought.

MYSTIC UTOPIAN SUPERMEN

Magnetism in repose does not seek the eye of another.

This is the Ninety-sixth Principle. The old notion that honesty seeks the eye of another, and dishonesty avoids it, is not so true as it might seem. The farmer who had read in an almanac that it is not safe to deal with a person who could not look you in the eye, lost a large sum of money by pinning his faith to one who could look at him all day long. The question involves a number of considerations. In the first place, the more honest of two persons may have weak eyes, and the more dishonest may have strong ones. Then, the former may be facing a strong light, while the latter may have his back to it.

Whether for purposes of magnetism, or otherwise, it is a good idea to sit or stand with your back to the light, thus saving your eyes. This is good advice when alone, for neuralgia, headache and weakness of the sight are often due to an attempt to read or work with a strong glare directly in front of the eyes. Some sharpers, in conversation, make a great deal of this point; they work around the individuals whom they are addressing until the latter are at a disadvantage. We saw a canvasser, a bright, talkative young man, out in the cornfield one morning, so placed that the farmer to whom he was talking had the light in his face and was blinking like an owl that comes suddenly upon the glare of a lamp.

It is true that the practice and use of magnetism will give strength to the eye. Every student of this art should become perfect in the various movements provided in the earlier pages of this volume, in the Realm of Attainment. Then the eyes may withstand every glare, and any position may be taken with reference to the light; although we recommend always to secure that which avoids facing the light if possible. Little advantages help. It would not do to allow the individual to know what your purpose is in taking any particular position. If you are unfavorably placed, let some detail of the conversation act to cause a shifting about, which may be done quietly.

It is rude and unmannerly to stare at another person. It often attracts attention; and when it does, the criticism is unfavorable. If you look into the eyes of A. without cessation, he may think you one of those ultra-honest creatures who can always prove their integrity in this way; but to entertain such an opinion, A. must be very verdant. A little practice at gazing will soon enable you to look at anything or anybody with the most unflinching stares. In good society, what would be thought of it? More than one case of insult to women has been charged to the impudence of the fixed gaze. In the South, some years ago, a father challenged to a duel a young man who had looked continually at his daughter, although the latter was unconscious of it. A French comedy is founded upon the same plot, except that the offender was looking at an object near a lady at the farther end of a drawing-room, and the irate father mistook the point on which the gaze made its focus.

Let a man look steadily at another man, and the latter would invariably ask what was the matter; was anything wrong? A husband, who cast a magnetic stare, as he thought it was, toward his wife, was met by a look of wonderment and the query: "Is my hat on straight?" The following "guides" should be committed to memory for immediate application at all times:

1. Never open your mouth, except for a well-defined purpose.

2. Never speak to a person unless your active will is behind the words.

3. Never touch a person, unless in so doing you think some thought pertinent to the occasion and applicable to him. Direct that thought to him, and connect it with the touch.

4. Never look a person in the eye, unless you are thinking of something which you are mentally saying to that person, or unless you are speaking aloud to that person.

5. Gazing, when the mind is not saying anything, is mere staring.

6. When being addressed by a person whose magnetism you fear, always look toward him, but not directly into his eyes.

7. Looking into the eye of a person whose mind (either orally or mentally merely) is saying something to your mind, while your mind is saying nothing in return, subjects you to his power temporarily, and deadens the magnetic action of your brain.

8. If being addressed by a person whose magnetism you fear, and you wish to test your magnetic strength, look him directly in the eye, and while he is talking, repeat after him (mentally, of course) the thoughts he is expressing. During any pause, repeat mentally, "My willpower is stronger than yours," always gazing firmly into the pupil of the eye.

9. A person while talking has the advantage, if the magnetic forces of each are nearly equal. But the glance of the eye of a magnetic person may quickly scatter to the four winds all the thoughts, ideas and arguments of the person speaking.

10. Keep the mouth closed, the teeth touching. Any other condition denotes a relaxed, unmagnetic state, unless the jaw is in use in eating or you are talking. Practice this.

11. Never waste remarks. Have a purpose in what you say, and direct the will to drive home that purpose well.

The eye may vibrate the waves of the ether-sea.

This is the Ninety-seventh Principle. One reason for knowing the truth of the principle is its certainty under various kinds of experiments. The empty staring eye is not only useless, but renders the person liable to the influence of another. It seems that one theory of light makes the transmission of its ray merely a movement of the ether-sea, as it is well known that sound is a similar wave movement of the atmospheric sea. All forces make use of some agencies.

If the same ether-sea is vibrated in waves both for light and for magnetic influences, it must be then that there are two or more uses of the same agency. Nature does this in all her works. The atmosphere is used for scores of purposes, many of them being so common that it were idle to refer to them. Among the larger uses is that action by which power is furnished through morning air. It is sometimes the zephyr, sometimes the gale, or the ordinary blowing of the winds. In all such activity the same air may be vibrated in another way, carrying the sound of the voice. We may talk to a friend in moving wind or in still air. If the wind blows, and no sound is in it, there is one action without the other; if it is calm even to absolute stillness, there is another action without the former; if we talk in a blowing atmosphere, there are the two actions of the air at one and the same time. So it may he with light and with magnetic influences; one may exist without the other, or both may he found at work at one and the same time.

MYSTIC UTOPIAN SUPERMEN

The claim that one kind of waves would interfere with another, and each become impaired, is not a valid one. In the midst of daily life we hear sounds without number, of all kinds and degrees of force and quality. Out of what ought to be a jumble in theory, we select such sounds as interest us in fact, and pay no attention to the others. Even in the deathly quietude of country residence, we sit upon the piazza in conversation with friends, while the brook is running rhythmically in the near forest, the windmill is clicking on the tower, the trees are whispering their secrets to the sleeping birds, the tree toads are trilling their shrill lay at the stars, the katydids are out of tune with the crickets, and the frogs swallow great lumps of sound as though it were distressful to live at all; yet these are not all the noises that send their wavelets along the atmosphere on an August evening in the country. Amid what might he termed a chaos in theory, we talk on without losing a single word we care to hear; and, when a piano is thrummed at some remote house, a violin squeaks in another, a song comes up the valley, wheels rattle over the road, or voices are faintly heard at a distance, these added sounds do not affect us; they produce no waves that cut into ours. Even in a group of a dozen or twenty shouters, two persons may hear each other and catch nothing of more vigorous tones. In the stock exchange, the din of voices is unintelligible to those who are not in it, or who do not understand its meaning.

The law of selection has something to do with the choice of hearing and of discarding what we do not wish to hear. We select what is intended for us or what we are interested in; generally we can reject the rest. We cannot, however, reject what some person may purpose that we shall hear; for a voice may he sent to us against our will. Yet the sounds that do actually come to us are very limited, and form a small proportion of those that are constantly transpiring about us. The same law is true of the ether-waves. Light is ever varied and varying. It is of all degrees of brightness, intensity and hue. We give heed to what we will, and let the rest go where they will. In magnetic influences we know but little of the waves that are passing to and fro; those that are intended for us we may receive or not, as the conditions permit; those that we intend for others may go to their destiny only when our magnetism is capable of impelling them to such end.

The eye is the organ of light; it feeds upon light; what it cannot see, it cannot know; it thrives in the light, and shrinks in the dark. Cave dwellers become blind in time, and are born blind when their ancestors have dwelt in dark places continually. If you shut yourself up in an unlighted room, you will lose your eyesight, and possibly the eyeballs. On the other hand, the magnetism of the brain shines in the eye, and by a light of its own, being brightest in absolute darkness. It is connected with the fires of thought, of force and of passion. A thoroughly determined will shows itself in this organ, and many a man has quailed before it.

It is true that the eye conquers in nearly all exhibitions of magnetism. A simple request, accompanied by a glance or a look, has won all the victory desired. Magnetism transforms the features, but only when it is at work. The photograph of a person in repose of mood shows a different face, different lineaments, and different expression of the eyes from one taken when magnetism is active. Of Sarah Bernhardt, whose histrionic ability was due solely to her wonderful magnetism which has inspired all her culture, it is said that she had the face of a devil when she is in repose or lacking animation, but that she has the face of an angel when under the sway of emotions. One person described her as beautiful, and was taken to task for it by another who had never seen her; but in less than fifteen minutes after the curtain went up, the latter agreed that she was indeed beautiful. A man married an actress because of her beauty. In her home life she was neutral, homely and even ugly in face. He could not believe his eyes, and proclaimed that love was blinder than an old horse. This aroused her to anger, and she opened on him with a broadside of magnetism. He saw her face lighted up, and was the lover once more, though not to be satisfied. The excitement and thrill of approaching wedlock have fired many homely women with a temporary magnetism, which has lighted the face into beauty. This art never fails to enrich the voice or to lend charm to the features. Could it always remain alive in the individual, there would be no undulations of effect.

The point before us is the fact that the mere appearance of the face may carry conviction without the use of other agency; but this appearance must be the result of an accumulated magnetism. This much is accomplished by mechanical practice. Yet more is needed. There should be established, as soon as possible, a magnetic temperament, under the guidance of the principle relating to that acquisition. More yet is needed. The willpower should be cultivated; and the principles that assist to that end are many and effective. Then the fixed determination should take thorough possession of the mind, the nerves and the body. This, of itself, shows fully in the face, and has done more to win victories than all else combined.

We recall the cases of women who now rule their husbands, who had no control whatever over them a few years ago. It is not improper for a woman to hold such sway, for the influence is not hypnotic; it is magnetic and inspiring. These cases are numerous, and the women are graduates of this method. In nearly every instance they acquired the power solely by reading or by hearing the laws of the art stated by teachers. These laws have remained the same, although their language has been more or less extended until we placed them in the form of principles. Let us look further into the cases referred to.

The eye should be used with the mental assertion.

This is the Ninety-eighth Principle. It should not be inferred that the eye is to be always used. The law means that, if used, the mental assertion should accompany it. We are satisfied that it is wrong to use the eyes when there is a strong influence about you, and yours is latent or quiescent. "I was in the midst of a very lucid explanation of a certain matter to some friends of mine, when Mr.-entered the room, and raised his eyes to mine. In the instant I caught his burning gaze, and my thoughts went everywhere. I was the more surprised because it was the first time I had ever seen him." It seems that the person who entered had been challenged to divert the thoughts of the other individual, and formulated the mental assertion: "You cannot think what you wish to say." This was brought with him into the room. Before entering, he stood for ten minutes in an adjoining room, making the effort to accomplish the same end without using the eyes; but, as the other person had some magnetism, this failed. He then entered the room, caught the eye as stated, and succeeded. This showed that the wave influence was communicated through the eye.

Just prior to the statement of this principle we had referred to women who formerly had no control over their husbands, but who secured it through the use of this method.

MYSTIC UTOPIAN SUPERMEN

Our reports are so numerous that it would be impracticable to state them all, or even many of them. It seems that some of the most satisfactory cases of the acquisition of magnetism came out of nothing but the influence of reading the laws, or hearing them stated in private lessons. As set forth in the present work, it is now a complete system, and private teaching would be of no use; nor do we think a student would make half the progress under a teacher, whether publicly in lectures or privately in personal talks that would be made by the use of the book. We do believe, however, that a course in expression will be of vast help, especially in the specific ways mentioned, and in broadening the mind and character besides.

If reading is able to change the current of one's life, it is a grand thing. It is well known that biography has done this. Indeed, it is the hearing, reading or otherwise knowing that one man has achieved greatness through certain propensities that has inspired many a man to cultivate those very qualities that are needed. No person can possibly read the principles of magnetism, and their attendant explanations, without being benefited. A simple illustration is seen in other things. A man learns that thin shoes and a damp ground will quickly draw from his body all the vitality that can be freed, and that severe colds will follow, as well as loss of buoyancy that is needed in order to establish health. He does not go to practicing, nor does he take anything to regulate the conditions about him. He simply wears thicker shoes, and escapes further colds. This is the influence of reading, perhaps. So another person, who suffered from weak lungs, learned that to add a very little to every inhalation would soon strengthen the lungs; he did not go to practicing, nor did he take any time from his duties or his pleasures; he had to breathe, and it was as easy to "add a little inch" to each breath as not to do it, and soon a new habit was established. He never lost a minute of time in this attainment. Nearly all the substantial improvements of life are secured in such ways.

Let us look at some of these instances, and see what help they may be to us. One woman says:. "I was unable to induce my husband to give attention to his home. I scolded him for a year, and had coaxed him for a year before that. I tried to shame him. He spent his evenings away from me, and merely provided for his family. A friend of mine, who had the same trouble with her husband, told me that I could stop this by the study of magnetism. I did not practice regularly. I suppose I may say I did not do any real practice, for I took up an exercise from time to time as I saw the chance. The little I did was improving. The best was in the advanced method. These I read, and I repeated my reading over and over again, until I could understand. This plan suited me best. I became more careful of my energies; and it was most gratifying to know that I could acquire a great amount of magnetism by just saving myself all the time. It took me away from no duties whatever. It was living, and one must live. I think it easier to live right than wrong in this way. My husband knew nothing of the course I was taking. I could see day by day that he had greater respect for me. Soon he found excuses for not going away so much. After a while I had complete control of him. My home has been completely reformed in every way, and I am grateful for this blessed change." Her story is not the same as the others in its details, but it contains the keynote of the whole series of reports.

A few specific accounts may prove more interesting. Those given here are taken from portions of reports. The first lot are from the wives we have referred to in the pages immediately preceding. One writes as follows: "My husband was able to support me in better fashion than he did. I told him so; but to get ten dollars from him was like pulling teeth. I resolved to go without new clothes, so as to get the books on magnetism. I studied what I could, but my time was taken up with duties that prevented my practicing. What I learned of the willpower was worth many times the large amount of money I paid for the work. I was a different woman. One evening I asked my husband for a hundred dollars. He laughed. It was a sickly laugh, and faded away under my gaze. I said to myself while looking at him so earnestly that he quailed: * You will give me one hundred dollars.' I had learned not to say or think the mental assertion, but to feel it. He asked why I had asked for more money than I ever sought before, and I told him to make up for lost time, as I had been without so long. I did not beg, or plead, or cry, or tease, or threaten, as I used to do; but I requested the money. He saw that I was in earnest, and I got it, the amount in full." It appeared also that he could afford to part with it. In subsequent reports she said that he had squandered money away from home that belonged with his family; and she completely reformed him in this and other respects.

Another case is fully as important. A wife writes this in a very long statement: "I wished my husband to accompany me on a little trip one evening. He said he could not. I looked at him, and made the mental assertion, "You will go," and he went. On the way home he said I had never looked at him like that before, and it made him feel strange. Had I told him what the power was, I do not believe that I could have succeeded again. He is now completely and contentedly under my control." In still another case a woman writes: "My husband, who is in his twenties, took a fondness for my sister, who is eight years younger than I am. I endured this for two years. We live all in the same house, but in separated apartments. I studied this course for the one purpose of conquering him without offending either him or her. I did it solely by use of the magnetic eye." In some stated conversations which follow, the essential principles of other cases are fully presented.

A man who married a woman far more intellectual than he, was soon aware of the chasm between her and himself. He writes: "Under your advice I went into the advanced course, and am well satisfied with what I have done. I took your further advice to omit practice if I could gather magnetism by preserving my powers or energies. This I succeeded well in doing. I have not the happy possession of a wise intellect, and I could not hope to win my wife's respect by that. I tried to convince her of my devotion to her. This amused her for a while. Then she began to take advantage of it in a way that I cannot disclose at this time. It was on one of these occasions that I cowed her, and brought her to her senses. I have not written, nor told this to any person. I make this report to you for the good of this science." From other persons we learned that the woman was highspirited, arrogant and domineering. She lost all these faults to her husband, and toned them down before others.

One more triumph for the art of Magnetism!

Some brief conversations are given here in a rather mixed arrangement; but they will be understood without trouble. They are selected because of their difficulty, not one being an easy conquest.

"I wish you to buy a book."

"I have all the books I want."

"Not all you need. This is an important one." (Naming it.)

"What is the price?"

"It is very high for a book." (Stating it.)

"Shocking! It is absurd. Is any one fool enough to buy it?"

"It is sold freely. It is a necessity in all lives."

"How can a book be worth so much?"

"A book's value does not come from its paper and covers, but from its contents or associations. There are books that have sold for many thousands of dollars a copy, owing to some special reason. This book is like a gold mine; it will bring you wealth and power."

"Why do you not get a copy? Have you wealth and power?"

"I got a copy two years ago, and since then I have made more money than I ever had in all my previous years. Then I was in debt; now I have twenty-thousand dollars."

"Whew! It must be a book and a gold mine combined. But have you power?"

"I am sure I have. I now am able to control myself and others as well."

After an interval of explanation the book was sold, but there was no copy to deliver. Permission was given to forward the amount to the publishers. When the volume had been received and well studied, the purchaser agreed that it was of extraordinary value, and asked what interest the other party had in making the sale. He replied:

"Not any; not the slightest. I simply wanted to see if I had the power to induce you to buy it. I selected you as the hardest case I knew of; and I selected the most costly and most valuable of books."

It was a victory without doubt. The mental assertion was constantly made during the dialogue: "The book is a gold mine," and the idea of financial reward seemed most apparent. Here is another case. A young lady, who had been introduced to a gentleman whom she very much disliked, had the audacity to tell him so. The introduction was brought about by a trick which she soon discovered.

"I wish you to dance with me this evening. I am sure you will."

"I am sure I won't. I dance with gentlemen."

"Well," he said, looking at her severely, "I am aware of that. I have noticed that your acquaintances are all worthy of you and worthy of a queen, though I do not claim rank with them. You despise me because I am a plebeian, while you move in the rank of nobility."

"There are no nobility in America. We are judged by other standards."

"Some women are queens by nature. I know that you do not believe me a flatterer." The eyes spoke volumes. Such eyes! She looked into them, and they were the pleasantest fires that ever warmed her heart.

A young man lost the love of his sweetheart, and her warmed-over affection was nursed for a year by another, lie could not endure the loss, and took up the study of magnetism as a means of winning it back. One evening he called upon the young lady by arrangement with her father, who was averse to lover number two. She had declined to receive him. The father brought number one into the room where the daughter was reading. She proposed in her mind to excuse herself at the first opportunity, but the father got out first. She opened fire.

"Why do you call upon me?"

"Your father brought me here."

"But at your request. You have been very persistent of late. Do you see this ring?"

"Yes, plainly. You are engaged to another. It was because of that engagement that I came to see you. I do not propose to lose you. I will not lose you." He was quiet and free from excitement. She saw a look in his face that she never had seen before.

"Am I worth all this bother? What is there in my disposition that attracts you? Are there not other girls better than I am?"

"I love you."

"But I do not love you."

"You did once."

"Yes, I did love you."

"Love cannot change."

"But it has. See this ring. We are to be married in four months."

"No; I am sure you will never marry the giver of that ring." He did not seem to threaten. He was not defiant. He was merely in earnest, and she knew it.

"How will you prevent it? Will you use force? Will you steal me and run away?"

"No. You will decide that you love me, and this will awaken you to your duty. If you marry him, and then find that you are mine by the law of the heart, three lives will be wrecked." During the conversation he had never taken his eyes from hers. She looked down occasionally, and then up again into his face. This last remark was followed by silence. She cast her eyes upon the floor, and wished that he would say something further. She looked up again, and there was that gaze still devouring her. He had changed. The old love came back in an instant and flooded her heart. Once more she was lost in meditation; then she raised her eyes to his, and they were full, large, lustrous eyes, suffused with tears. As in a trance she came to him, threw away the ring, and knelt on the floor, with her face upon his knees. The father returned, and took her in his arms. The covenant there sealed was never broken, and they are happy even to this day. Magnetism had won in this case as it has in thousands of others.

Experiments are made at times in the use of the eye with or without the aid of the voice, to see how much influence may be secured over others. One set of these experiments deals with interruptions intended to divert the mind of some one who is speaking. A few extracts will serve to show what is meant.

"I will now proceed to tell you what occurred. I have already said there were four interests involved—"

"You have lost track of them," was the mental assertion of one who was looking straight at the speaker, and who caught his eye at this point. This assertion was continually repeated as the speaker showed signs of hesitation.

"These four interests are somewhat as follows. If you catch my meaning, which I trust you do."

"You have forgotten what you were to say," was the mental assertion of the interrupter.

"I was about to state what these four interests are; but I find that they are not of sufficient importance to take your time for them now. So I will pass on."

The bewilderment was confusing to the speaker as well as to the hearers, and it was some time before the interruption was smoothed over. In another case a person of powerful magnetism resolved to make the effort to substitute a word in the speech of a man who was accustomed to repeat himself too much for ease of diction. In the experiment to which we refer, he was using the word "institution" very frequently, in language somewhat as follows. The person influenced him to say constitution.

"I have said, ladies and gentlemen, that this institution is of the highest rank in its line. It is not too much to say that we are all proud of—"

"Say constitution," was the mental assertion as the eyes of both persons met.

"This—institution. It has fought its way up from the humblest of beginnings, and is now without a peer in our land. I do not say this idly. Some of you, whom I am addressing, are graduates of this con—this institution, and you bear me out in all I say. We have watched its growth, year by year, up to this moment, and our hearts are full of pride for our constitution." A general laughter followed. It was the opinion of many that the speaker had been drinking.

The following case is typical of so many similar experiences, if the drama and the novel are to be believed, that it may not be ascribed to magnetism. A young lady had been annoyed by the attentions of a gentleman whom she wished to repulse without offending. She had been a student of advanced lessons for two years, and knew how to use the power. One evening, which was the crucial, he called with the full intention of proposing. Little by little, as time wore on, he drew himself nearer to her, and was at his best. She felt that he was somewhat imbued with magnetism, due no doubt to the earnestness of his intentions.

"Miss Y., I have come to tell you something this evening."

"Are you sure?" she asked. (" No, you are not sure," was her mental assertion as she looked fully into his face.) He did not wince; he was too full of his subject. But she did not dare to remove her gaze from his eyes, as is was a contest of unusual strength. She found that she was not to win an easy victory.

"l am quite sure," he said, fervently. "I wish to say something."

"You are not sure that you should do so, even if you are sure you will," she replied aloud, while saying mentally: "You are mixed. Yes, you are. You know you are." He looked at her in wonderment.

"If I am sure I will, I am sure I should. Oh, Miss Y., I am positive."

"I am afraid you are not feeling well. Shall I ring for the servant? You are so pale." ("So very pale, so deadly pale," was the mental assertion.) Now his eyes lost some of, their intensity, while hers assumed greater brightness, and she felt sure of winning, if she could but keep him from actually mentioning the subject of marriage. She knew better than to challenge him by a hint at it. Her purpose was to keep his mind on his condition.

"I am perfectly well," he said, "but agitated. It is proper that one of my sex should be agitated when he has something important to say to the woman he adores."

"No doubt it is proper for every true gentleman to adore every true lady, but the agitation is uncalled for. You are sure that the matter is as important as you think?" She was being defeated, and had temporarily lost the mastery.

"I said I was sure."

"But you are not. If you were sure, you would have said it ere this. I have waited for you, and you are still talking about being sure." ("You are mixed," was the mental assertion once more.)

"I cannot think why I should be mixed, can you?"

"You look quite pale. Now let us turn the subject, and soon you will be yourself again." ("It will relieve you to turn the subject," was the mental assertion.)

"I must say what I intended to. The room is very warm."

"So it is out at last. I knew you would be able to tell it. It is important, and I feel the effects of the high temperature. I will have some fresh air." The man was completely cowed, and gave up the struggle.

A young lady of plain face and lack of pleasing accomplishments met a young man in a social gathering of her church. She was a working girl, and he the son of a wealthy merchant. They were widely apart in every respect. She fell in love with him, and wrote to us to inquire if such a girl could, by the study and use of magnetism, win such a man. We said that it was possible if they met occasionally. He was somewhat of a flirt and not disposed to settle down right away. She realized the almost utter hopelessness of the situation, but loved him, and went to work upon the studies. Among other things she learned that charms of person are avenues of approach in securing control over others, and she did whatever her means permitted. Soon it happened that her face brightened very much, and her manner was interesting. Other gentlemen began to notice her.

She took advantage of every means of seeing the man she loved, and of being seen by him; but never in any way that was not naturally within the course of ordinary events, as at church, at the Sunday-school, at the meeting of young folks so-called, at the social gatherings, and occasionally at other places. She kept her gaze upon him when he did not know it, and once in a while their eyes met. Her mental assertion was not, "I love you," for that would not have won him, but "You love me," which was her aim. He once said to a friend of his, when he came away from one of these magnetic fights: "There's a poor girl that sets me on edge whenever I come into the room where she is. I wish to get acquainted with her." This he did, and asked her to go driving with him. She declined, but told him that she would be pleased to have him call upon her.

"Why will you not go with me in my carriage? Other ladies have done so. Do you not like driving?"

"Oh, yes; I do very much."

"Do you object to me?"

"No. If I did, I should not have asked you to call. I would be pleased to go driving with you if my mother could go with us."

MYSTIC UTOPIAN SUPERMEN

"Then she shall."

This was the beginning. Both the mother and daughter were plainly but neatly dressed; yet he felt that their poverty humiliated him, and the remarks of his friends added to his chagrin. He did not call, and did not invite her to further drives. This was the end as well as the beginning of the first chapter. She yet maintained her fixed determination to win him. Her face followed him everywhere for days after they had met. Winter came and went. Summer was around once more. One evening a shower burst suddenly over the land, and found her at a sociable, or social, as sometimes called, without the aid of an umbrella. He offered his aid as an escort, which she accepted. On the way home he told her that he was glad to be able to talk with her once more, and continued:

"I was saying to a friend only a few weeks ago that I always felt happy when in the room where you were."

"But you were happy elsewhere."

"Not in the sense I mean. One evening I was waiting for a train at a railway station. My mother was with me. I did not look about, but soon experienced the same sensation, and I said to myself that Miss-is here also. I found it true, but did not let you know it."

This convinced her that she was able to exert an influence over him, and the only remaining question was whether he could be induced to love her or not. She knew that there was a vast difference in their stations in life. She was poor and a working girl; he was not only rich by his parents' wealth, but had come into the possession of a fortune by other inheritance. Magnetism to her was a religion. It made her sweet and lovable at home and in the little society that she entered, thanks to the church.

A few days after the rainy evening episode, she was offered a much better position under another employment, with salary out of proportion to the value of the services rendered. In her spare evenings at home she had studied bookkeeping with the aid of a girl friend, so that she was able to do considerable in that line. She and her mother were all that remained of a family of four, the father and sister having died. Her mother had done sewing, and had succeeded in supporting herself with the aid of the daughter.

Something in her heart told her that the young man had been instrumental in the change of her employment. Magnetism makes a good business man and a smart woman even out of humble material. As soon as she was satisfied that she could do the work required, she surprised her mother by renting a very neat and stylish cottage in an excellent locality, at a price not as low as' good judgment would otherwise have dictated. She had the parlor beautifully furnished on the installment plan, and went into debt in other ways. Then she dressed herself better, did as much for her mother, and forbade the latter taking in work, as her home duties were enough for one woman. This stroke of business policy in home affairs is mentioned as an evidence of the value that judgment renders to magnetism, and both to each other. He saw her as frequently as before, but bided his time, for his parents would be bitterly opposed to the idea of such a match. In a period of mental suffering he confided his love to a woman of commanding position in society, and she at once agreed to open the way for him. One day the girl's mother was surprised to receive a call from this lady. Then followed the girl's entrance into society, and the rest may be surmised. The young man's parents consented to the wedding. The love seems mutual in every respect, and the marriage is still a happy one.

The papers have referred to certain captures of wealthy sons by the influence of women; and there are several cases that might be mentioned. One of the most recent may explain the others. A young man in the twenties came into the possession of more than a million dollars. It was agreed between the brother, the sister and the mother of a pretty miss that she should make the effort to win him by magnetism. The papers have called it hypnotism; but this error is explained on the theory that the public are not familiar with the fact that hypnotism is a negative influence, and magnetism is positive. We are familiar with the facts, and know that no attempt was made to hypnotize the young man.

This family of four remained in the best society of a large city after their finances were waning, and they knew that their elegant home must soon be lost to them if some good fortune did not intervene to save them. Each had a separate book of advanced magnetism, and put it to good use. They were not forward in their efforts to influence the millionaire, but soon brought about a marriage with the pretty miss. The strange thing in this affair is the fact that, when his relatives undertook to save him from the impending alliance, he left his home, and took up his residence with the family of the prospective bride, where he remained for two years after the marriage. The claim was made that he had been kept under hypnotic influences for all the time, and that he was of unsound mind in consequence. This was not sustained. He built a large house to which he moved, and where he is living today. That he is mentally bright is known from the fact of his success in business, wherein he has added considerably to the fortune which he inherited.

In another case, a young man of poverty, by which is meant of humble earnings, fell in love with a young woman two years his senior. In his first letter to us he wrote: "I love her with all my soul and body. Can I win her? Can advanced magnetism help me!" We wrote that it would surely help him, but as to winning her, he could only decide at some future time. The fact was that magnetism was the only thing that could win, and it might do so even in cases where the circumstances made it seem impossible. This bit of history, like some others we have cited, is selected because of the disparagement between the persons involved.

The young man began the study of the art, and could not grasp the requirements, owing to a slight mental dullness; so he laid it aside. Then came the renewed longing to win the young lady. She was about twenty-one years now, and he about nineteen. She was the only child of well-to-do parents, and seemed to be destined to become an old maid, for she had refused to consider the proposals of men who were in every way qualified to make her happy. The young man in question was unknown to her. He wished she had brothers with whom he could affiliate and through them reach her. There was a cousin of hers, who was eighteen years old, and he was selected for the purpose. This was magnetism. It is proper to make everything aid in its work, so far as it may properly be done.

The study of magnetism was resumed, but too much was expected of it, and it was again abandoned. Still something had been gained each time. A year later he began in earnest, and kept up his zeal till he felt the power of a tremendous purpose coming into his life. His nature underwent a change that surprised his friends. The cousin was glad to know him and to be with him. In his capacity of wage earner he rose to that of superintendent by the time he was twenty-one, and then he embodied this remark in his report: "If I am not able to win the lady whom I love, and who is far above me, I can truly say that magnetism has accomplished wonders for me in other ways. I know positively that it has raised me from the common ranks of labor to a position far greater than any I ever had hoped to reach." He was at last an appreciative admirer and student of magnetism.

Omitting the processes whereby he reached an acquaintance with the lady, we append a conversation which he had with her at an opportune moment, when circumstances placed them alone at her home for a brief period one evening:

"You are much interested in our sex, I should judge from the way you talk of them."

"I am interested in one of them. She is so far above me socially that I do not know if I could win her even if she loved me."

"Does she love you?"

"Not a bit."

"Does she know of your love for her?"

"She does not even suspect. If she did she would hate herself for ever having talked with me."

"Are you sure she is not playing the part of an ingenuous maiden?"

I know she is not. She is too plain, too practical for that."

"Is she of a lovable disposition?"

"Her disposition is lovable; she never loved, and is said to be of a cold heart toward men."

"Don't you believe all you think. Girls are not old maids from choice, but from necessity. Some do not meet the men they love, and are too honest to marry those they do not love."

"This girl is an exception."

"Who is she?"

"I cannot tell. I respect her too much. She is far beyond my reach."

"Well, who is she?"

"I am afraid I would offend her if I should tell."

"How can you offend her by telling me? I promise to keep your secret. Confide in me as you would in a sister." She extended her hand, and gave him that confidence which her superior nature made a lavish expenditure.

"Now tell me."

"You will hate me."

"Why?"

"You are cold in heart, and do not like to hear of love."

"But I can hear what you have to say. Who is the very fortunate lady whom you love so much?"

"She is very unfortunate."

"No. I would congratulate her with all my heart."

"You are trifling. What hope can a young man have who loves a lady far above him in social rank and fortune ?"

"The hope that she will love him. Now who is it?" Her eyes rested full upon his. He sent the final shaft of love into her heart; he threw the red fire of passion, and the trophy lay upon his breast. She had no suspicion of the lady's name when the conversation opened. It was a complete victory, won under the subterfuge of embarrassment, during which she believed that he had lost all control of himself.

These conversations are not in the identical words in which they were spoken. We have required reports in the utmost minuteness of detail, and what is not clearly stated we have put in our own language, without disturbing the principle involved. No essential has been omitted, and none added. These remarks apply to what has preceded and what will follow in these descriptions of experiments. Some of the dialogue is presented word for word as it has been sent to us, with assurances that it was noted down immediately after the occurrences stated. Whatever variance there may be in language or diction, the only matter that really concerns the student of magnetism is the victory and the progress whereby it was attained.

One brief account may prove of interest in this connection. A man met what he considered his match in the art of control. He was forty years of age, and met a beautiful woman of thirty, who was possessed of great wealth. She had declined a man far handsomer than the hero of this account, and one who had more wealth than she, while the man in question was comparatively poor. He received an income of less than fifteen hundred dollars per year at the time he undertook the study of advanced magnetism, and about four thousand dollars annually at the period when the following experiment was made, two years later. The two were conversing together one winter's evening, when he suddenly changed the subject, and said:

"You should be married."

"What for?"

"To be happier."

"No woman is happier than I. Marriage would not improve my contentment. I am responsible to no one but myself; then I would be the slave of another."

"Not a slave, I assure you. Your qualities are too commanding for even an equal rank with the best of men."

"As a flatterer you are not successful. Your words do not impress me. Men are nothing to me; nor can they ever win one spark of love from me, since I have it not."

"Then you are a beautiful outlaw of creation. Love is the mainspring of existence. You are not in earnest. I see by your eyes that you are in love."

She drooped her head like a stricken rose, and when she raised it again, the story was told in words. It was to her as much of a surprise as to him, and more so; for she had never given him one tender thought. If some one had suggested his name to her an hour before as a possible lover, she would have treated the idea with railery; if some one bad hinted that she might become his wife, she would have been indignant to the highest degree. Yet she fell in love with him so desperately that there was no escape. For weeks she fought the idea as monstrous, and found that there could be no peace of mind, no happiness of heart, except by an alliance with him, and she became his wife. He had sent into her life the shaft that fells; he had thrown the red fire of passion.

Children are controlled by their parents through magnetism better than by any other process. Punishment is an appeal to the lowest of physical forces; the threat of punishment carries with it more influence, if the threat is known by the child to be always fulfilled. It should not be made carelessly, for then there is no faith in it, as the element of certainty is taken out. Let any child be so trained that it can depend on what its parents say, and let them avoid saying what is not meant or what is not necessary to the situation, and the government of children will be less difficult. But above all such measures is the use of magnetism.

This implies that the parent possesses the power mechanically; that is, it has been collected either by practicing exercises or by conserving the energies of the body; either or both of these methods will give a great fund of magnetism. This is the starting point. Next is the knowledge of how to use the power; the fixed determination, the will-energy, the goal of purpose, and the mental assertion, together with all those means of help that easily blend into one action of the magnetic centres. A glance of the eye conveys all to the child. It is the channel of communication, and is irresistible. There is no parent who need use any other means of obtaining obedience. Most unruly children are made so by the condoning of their faults under the sentiment of indulgence. This is harder for the child in the years to come.

The mental assertion in all cases of control must be used with intelligence. It is said to be mental because it is formulated in the mind, and there receives shape in language capable of interpretation; but it is in reality born in the energy of magnetism, and its source of origin should be treated as deeper than the mind. We think in our feelings, and feel in our thinkings. Practice of the most elementary character serves to develop this power. You meet a friend, and say: 11 Good morning." This is one of the simplest and commonest of sayings, and in almost every case comes from the latent will. Put back of it, now, the active will, and the result will be quite different. How are you to do this? There must be thought behind the words, "Good morning." Thought flashes quickly. Many extended thoughts can be called into existence while a very short sentence is being spoken. It takes time to shape the thoughts into words even in the mind. This framing of mental sentences is not necessary. In saying "Good morning," speak it with the accompanying thought of "I intend that you shall believe this is a good morning."

"How do you do?" Accompanying such a remark by the thought, "I intend that you shall tell me how you do."

"Will you come with me?" To be accompanied by the thought "You must come with me."

"I am sorry, but I am unable to do so." To be accompanied by the thought "I will not do so, and you cannot compel me."

These easy illustrations may be adopted by practicing them sufficiently. At first the thought will not accompany, but will follow the words. Familiarity with the method will soon unite the two. In this, as in the exercises following, observe two things.

1. Employ the active will earnestly; that is, mean what you say.

2. Excite the nerve centers into a magnetic state by the employment of the internal energy.

You look a person in the eye. It must be for a purpose; never allow it to be purposeless. Try the following occasionally with your friends. Avoid doing it in a way to attract too much attention. As soon as your eyes meet the pupil of the one of the eyes of a person you are looking at, repeat mentally, thoroughly meaning and believing everything you say:

"I am looking at you."

"I am looking through your eyes into your brain."

"My willpower is stronger than yours."

"You are under my control."

"I will compel you to do what I wish."

"Look away from me."

"Do as I tell you."

This series, repeated several times with a thorough faith in what you say, will have its effect, if combined with the nervous intensity which incites magnetism. The last mental thought, "Look away from me," may be made oral, and changed into any request you may desire.

Your child refuses to do a certain thing requested of him. You say mentally:

"I am your father."

"You must do what I say."

And then orally to the child:

"You will do this. Do it at once."

Force of the voice is physical, and therefore incapable of winning. It may compel. Any pitch of the voice above the middle pitch is physical in its tendency, especially if made on the bright side of the voice. Any pitch below the middle is emotional in its tendency. From this it will be seen that force in the high pitch is generally disastrous. The child at first is frightened at it, but soon gets used to its unemotional nature. The experience of the world has shown that disobedient children have parents whose voices are high pitched and loud, or who are weaklings.

The school teacher who requires force to keep discipline, answers to the same description. The minister, the lawyer, the orator, who cannot hold the attention of an audience, is likewise classed. The best voices, therefore, have

1. A strong low pitch.

2. Nervous intensity predominating over force.

3. The intermittent stress.

You have been insulted. If you can catch the eye of the person, throw your eyes at once into the gaze of scrutiny, and make their tensity very great; call up within you all the internal energy possible while holding a dead still attitude, and, looking directly into the pupil of his eye, say mentally:

"You have insulted me."

"You will answer for that."

"You are a coward."

This may be repeated over and over again. You must feel and believe each and every remark which you make. It does not require the presence of another, nor the commission of the insult to make this an excellent exercise. It may be practiced alone, and in that case the voice may be used, employing intensity, a low pitch and no force. The imagination must be very powerful. Can you stand in a room at growing dusk in the presence of an imagined but august personage, whose insult you would rebuke? The flash of the eye, the courageous demeanor, the haughty attitude, all should be assumed by you. Make the mental remarks, above given, as dignified and as fierce as possible. Say them over and over again for fifty times, endeavoring to add greater nerve-power each time. Any movement, however slight, will destroy the magnetic influence.

If you cannot perceive in your mind this being who stands in front of you, shut the eyes, and listen. A faint movement will be beard, very faint indeed. It is the magnetic current flowing past the nerves of the ear, which produces the resemblance to steps, so easily is the imagination worked upon. At the hour of growing dusk the currents are very sensitive in their movements along the nerves, and create in the brain many sensations of a physical and nervous nature, which lead some persons to believe them to be supernatural.

A truly magnetic individual will be able at will to throw the whole body into a tense or sensitive condition, without the aid of any outside movement, except, perhaps, the dilating of the pupil. This is called the ecstatic condition. It should be cultivated and practiced continually.

To resume let us impress upon the student the desirability of strictly following the directions given in this volume. Remember that the will may be latent or active; that the latter alone directs the controlling influence, and that the accumulated magnetism is the controlling influence. Faith alone, or the will alone, cannot be relied upon. This seems to be the deficiency in many so-called faith methods. Magnetism alone often exerts itself even when we do not seek to use it. Thus we sometimes find ourselves, when in the presence of a magnetic person, yielding homage to him, though no thought of his is directed toward us. This is merely the recognized superiority of the magnetic state.

Mental assertions should be practiced until they act as by a habit. That this can be accomplished is now known to be true, for many persons have acquired the use of the willpower in all they say and through first connecting every important remark with a mental assertion, and they have found that the habit is not only quickly formed, but is also a permanent one if properly sought. This may be said to be a temperament when it is made part of one's nature, and it seems more natural then than otherwise. The following are elementary exercises that have been used with success:

First Oral Remark.—"I am very glad to see you."

Mental Assertion.—"I am in fact glad to see you."

Second 0. R.—" This is a gloomy day."

M. A.—"I know you feel that it is gloomy."

Third 0. R.—"I appreciate what you have done."

M. A.—"I do in fact appreciate it."

Fourth O. R.—"I wish you to do this."

M. A.—"I propose that you shall do it."

Fifth O. R.—"Give me that watch."

M. A.—"You know well that you must give it to me."

Sixth O. R.—"I like you very much."

M. A.—"I am sincere when I say I like you."

Seventh O. R.—"I think a great deal of you."

M. A.—"I believe thoroughly that I do think a great deal of you."

Eighth O. R.—"I love you."

M. A.—"As Heaven is my witness I am in earnest."

Ninth O. R.—"Lend me one hundred dollars."

M. A.—"I in fact believe that you are willing to lend it to me."

Tenth O. R.—"This is only one dollar."

M. A.—"You know it is only one dollar."

And so we might go on for pages. The student may invent hundreds of examples of his own. Whatever he asserts mentally with a firm belief in the fact stated, or a firm confidence in his own mind that the person addressed believes the fact stated to be true, will in reality be so accepted if the nervous intensity of either voice or eye accompany it. It will then be seen that there must be belief in the student's mind; a firm and abiding faith, which is conveyed to another by the vibrations of the universal ether, which are originated only from the accumulated magnetism of the body. In the foregoing examples let the word in capitals in each sentence receive the greatest nervous intensity. Force is unnecessary and wrong.

Cords of influence are convenient terms that enable the mind to grasp an idea and a purpose, and wield them as powers with much greater energy. These helps are by no means small; they cannot be ignored. While they are creatures of the fancy, they have the same all-potent life that comes from the strongest children of the imagination. To their use add the intensity of magnetic lives, and the willpower is certainly an engine of fearful strength. The normal lines make their changes felt both in the user and the object toward which they are directed; and this feeling is so strong that it may be classed among the material forces of existence.

Magnetic lines execute the mandates of the will.

This is the Ninety-ninth Principle. One of the essential laws of the life and energy of the soul is the common fluctuation between the principles of attraction and repulsion. Brain activity directed to no purpose is of little value, as it effects nothing. Any energy of the soul, or conscious mind, set at work to attract or repel, throws into terrible use the engine of a magnetic brain. Why this is so is easily understood when the laws of existence are known.

In using your magnetic lines, everything must be done in a flash of speed. The will must act as though it were directing a lightning bolt. This speed is impossible at first. It may require discouraging practice. If not clearly understood, all will be made plain as the lessons are read and reread. The magnetic lines have two movements:

1. Repulsion. This movement proceeds from the normal line to a straight line.

2. Attraction. This movement proceeds from a straight line to a normal line.

A magnetic line may be referred to as having three parts; First, the nearer end, which is supposed to be at the center of the cerebrum, or brain; second, the farther end, which reaches the object of a wish, thought or purpose; third, the median part, which is supposed to be that part of a normal magnetic line midway between the points, or ends.

A normal magnetic line is one in which the median part is not on a straight line with the two ends. Imagine a bow with the nearer end in the brain, the farther end reaching to the object, and the median part at the middle or bend of the bow. If such a bow were to be straightened, the farther end would be placed still more distant; but if the ends of a straight line were to be brought nearer, the line would bend in proportion to the movement. The willpower must pass with lightning rapidity from the brain, through the median part to the farther end, immediately after which use the law of attraction or repulsion, as stated above. If you are not thoroughly familiar with every word of this full course of training, there will be a lack of clearness in understanding your lines.

EXPERIMENT

We have dealt with the subject of magnetic lines through figures and actual lines drawn on paper; but the difficulty of understanding them has been so great among careless students that the only safe course is in the use of experiments. In the first place it must be clearly understood that the only object sought after is brain energy, turning itself into magnetic energy. To begin with, we will assume that you have no magnetism; or,

if you have, that it is uncontrolled. Did you ever see a bale of cotton, all loose and fluffy? In it are possibilities of strength. They must be made into threads, cords and ropes.

Your body consists of tissue-cells, so many millions in number that you could not count them in ten thousand years. Each cell is an organized life, having a complete existence, and capable of supporting itself alone. It can eat, digest and multiply. It has intelligence, as can be easily proved. It has energy! Your body is a collection of energies, but in the form of a mass, as uncontrolled for magnetic purposes as a bale of fluffy cotton. The possibilities are there, but no more. Let us see if you can turn them into lines, into concentration, into a dangerous force. You well understand the power of union; but what may be the power of a concentrated union of energies, each great in itself and capable of a multimillion force, as the world has often seen, is a problem that can be solved only by experiment. Surprising results will be uncovered by students who delve into this field.

We must commence with the mind, for it represents will. Some wills are lax, others are firm; but, among the strongest, very few are able to weave their energies into a concentrated line. Thus the obstinate man is full of willpower, but it is generalized, as in the mule; and obstinacy is unmagnetic. Assuming that you have no will, that power must be first cultivated. No better attempt can be made than to adopt the regime, or any unusual part of it, stated in the first volume of Magnetism. The next step is concentration, or the weaving of all your millions of energies in one powerful line. This must be done solely by the imagination, for the force of this agency is able to overcome matter. We do not refer to that nothingness which people scoff at when they say "it is only imagination"; but to the power of the mind to summon an ideal to its assistance. This is the secret of genius in poet, author, orator, actor and warrior; for even the general wins his victories in his mind before the plans of battle are made.

The difficult part of our experiment is now at hand.

The better way is to train the will at home and alone; always basing it upon some principle in the study of magnetism. With this in view, seclude yourself so as to be free from disturbing influences, and proceed as follows:

1. Sit at one side of your room, so as to get as great a distance as possible between you and the object.

2. Place any small object on the table as far away as the size of the room permits.

3. Draw in your mind a straight line between the core of your brain and the object.

4. It is well understood that intense thinking about any matter will produce an affirmative or negative effect. Try this, and see; let the matter be what it will, a wish, an object, or a fact. You will either master it or be mastered by it. Success in life is secured, often unconsciously, by concentration of attention. The tissue-cells are being lined up into ropes of energy. Every great life is based on this one principle, and it is ninety per cent, of the full source of power.

5. But intense thinking is not our chief purpose at this place.

6. The straight line between the core of your brain and the object should be designated in the imagination as a silver cord. A magnetic brain has no difficulty in creating this silver line as a seeming reality. A poet sees his ideal, an actor his counterpart, as a thing of existence; so all great men behold the goal of their ambition in perspective.

7. The normal line is always a departure from a straight line, yet passes from the core of your brain to the object. It should be designated in your imagination as a golden cord.

8. A magnetic exercise of the will may be made in one of two ways: Attraction and repulsion.

9. Attraction changes the silver line into a golden line, and in doing this the angle or curve of the golden line is taken, not the line itself.

10. Repulsion changes the golden line into a silver one; or, in other words, the curved line becomes straight.

11. The change summons magnetism; the concentration marshals the energies; the rapidity of the change denotes the heat of the magnetism.

12. If you can imagine the silver line to be attached to the object on the table, and then raised in the middle to an altitude half its length, or nearly to the ceiling, you will at once realize that the object is brought nearer to you by changing the silver line to a golden line. Let us suppose this brings it half way. Again imagine a silver line to connect it, and let it be raised to a golden line the center of which is raised to half the length. Thus the object comes nearer in the mind. A few more repetitions, and it is yours. If the process is hard to understand, attach a cord to a chair at one end and to a spool at the other, then raise the cord in the middle. The spool moves toward the chair. Cut the cord to

make it shorter, and repeat. Soon the spool will be close to the chair.

13. Repulsion is simply the reverse. The bent line is straightened out, and the object is driven off. While all this appeals to the imagination, it is powerful. A number of great results have been attained in this simple use of concentrated energy. A strong instance is that of the man who could not drive a certain temptation from his life until he used the repellant lines. He said: "My mind was on the shifting of the curved line to the straight one, and I gradually saw the evil being driven from my life. It was imagination while it was going on, but stern reality when it was accomplished. The magnetic lines furnished a leverage by which to work, a something for the mind to do."

14. To test the efficacy of mental concentration, apply the magnetic powers of changing the silver lines to golden for attraction, and the golden lines to silver for repulsion, to any object of the affections or to any hope, quality, wish, ambition or person. That you may win friendship and ward off enmities is a matter of absolute certainty.

15. Before the lines may be used successfully in a general way, they must be developed in the workshops of privacy and in the way described herein. Time is required to secure a mental grasp of them, and weeks of trial may be needed. The result is never in doubt.

16. Lightning movements, and a lightning succession of movements, must be learned by practice and acquired by use under varying circumstances. The habit is weak at first; the apprenticeship must be served, and time and experience only produce the adept.

17. At least one principle in this volume must be studied before any experiment is made in the use of your magnetic lines.

The first influence of magnetism should be directed toward the members of your family. We have had many little histories of dissensions between parents and children, or between brothers and sisters, and these we have been instrumental in healing through the laws of magnetism. As an aid to outer living the affection of family ties should be seconded by devotion to friendship. Do not make this journey alone. Seek friends sparingly but successfully. Make yourself worthy of what they should be, and make them worthy of your new self. Let each January sun look down on twelve good friends and true, won during the year just fallen. Of these a record should be kept.

Love is golden when it attracts two hearts toward each other for the purpose of establishing a home on this planet. Every male being of developed growth stamps upon his heart in early life the flower of an ideal son. Every female likewise pictures in her sweetest nature an ideal hero. The ideals never change, never vanish, although often obscured by clouds for years at a time. It is not necessary that they be definite in feature or fixed in outlines or contour. The man loves his ideal always and ever, and the woman hers.

Ideals are of the soul, not of the body. When a woman loves a man with all the passionate warmth of her sunny heart she does not throw her adoration at his body, but at the soul of the ideal which was coined from the choicest blood of her youth, and stamped forever on the soul life of her nature. Now all soul-life must be interpreted by the agencies of the flesh, which are unreliable under excitement; and in consequence, many a woman has jumped into the arms of the wrong man. Her waking moments are filled with disappointment and repentance. Of course something must be done. Some prefer to sew a patch of tinsel over the gap in the affections, and deceive the world. Some separate, and never meet again. Some lead a drifting life, quarreling and caressing, until endurance is beyond question, and then the separation comes. Some make their headquarters at the so-called "home," and wander back and forth on wanton wings. Yet all this while the one ideal of early youth is loved by both.

There is no such thing in all the universe as the love of one person for one person. Two lovers are said to be "mated" for each other; if so, the mating is of the physical or mental endowments, not the loving parts. The same lovers could be equally as well, or better, mated to ten thousand others on this globe, if search were made. Fondness of association, and loneliness during absence, are common conditions of all created life, and these too often pass for love. It is excellent; encourage it; but it is not the love of ideal for ideal. It is time in the history of mankind for a more accurate analysis of this mischievous power which has swayed the world, ruined hearts and homes, and blasted many a tine brain by its insidious deception.

The study of love under the never failing eye of magnetism shows that it exists in two phases: First, as the ideal worship of a co-ideal; second, as perverted passion seeking only sex for sex, and taking the best available. This passion is a crime against the fiat of creation, and ill-fortune haunts the hearts and hovers over the heads of the guilty men and women who indulge in it. The ideal worship is the only love. Let us lay aside sentiment and cant, and accept the matter in its naked reality. No one person ever fills the measure of the great ideal. Some, when unveiled, shrink to nothingness in comparison with the haloed picture. But a serious duty rests upon our loves. There is a power, God-given, which enables us to take the miserable carcass of our shattered hope, and in it set the angel-soul of what we loved, nursing it until hope and ideal are one. You may make your ideal.

First make yourself worthy of the best inheritance of the human race; then throw the red fire; the golden cord will bind your lives together, and your opportunity will come for making your loved one your ideal. This triumph over the human heart has been many times achieved to our certain knowledge. It requires worthiness on your part; a never diminishing picture of your great ideal carried by your magnetic power upon the visage of your loved one; an evenness of nature, and always the same true, confiding, unhasting and unresting resolve to win and keep.

ESTATE OF THE CRYSTAL MIND

BROADENING rivers sweep to the ocean by the inevitable law of progress. We have serious work ahead. Our scope widens as the powers of living grow more potent and acquire greater value. We take on a new estate in the realm now before us. The cry is everywhere, "Reward and riches" not alone financial, but also mental and physical. Once the human family knew nothing but brute force; with claws they held their prey, and with tusks they tore the flesh from the victim's bones. A few tribes now remain that are animal in this sense; they tell us of the age in which we live, while geology brings to light the story intensified in remote eras.

The epoch of brute force is nearly gone; remnants are yet with us in uncivilized lands. Mind has for a long while been supreme, and its dizzy height is reached and passed. The subconscious faculty, revealed by magnetism and stripped of its baseness, is about to open the gateway to a larger wealth and grander rewards. In as far as mind has been master of the physical powers, so far will magnetism exceed the highest attainments of the mind. It is not new; it existed ere matter was rolled out into space; it is simply forging to the front by the law of value, and must soon take its place in the forerank of authority, capable of uplifting man to the magnificent estate of largesse. Reward is right. Munificence is everywhere promised, and nowhere fulfilled, unless through this estate.

Magnetism is an attainment that is not designed solely for the purpose of affording pleasure in reading. This volume should satisfy the mind's desire; but that is not enough. Its pages have not been written with that as the only end in view. The scholar loves his books, but he never expresses them; after he has read and learned a world of science, he is smaller than when he began. Law, to a lawyer, is valueless unless he can put its principles into operation; to know all the legal lore of the centuries is of itself nothing. The physician must heal, or his wisdom is a bauble. The minister must save souls; and he who is possessed of the forceful energy to uplift humanity, though his book-learning is scanty, is a greater power than the college-bred preacher who talks over the heads of the hungry multitude. We must express what we know, or the knowledge is a collection of dry bones. Talking is not such expression; we must live and act. The wisdom, the acquisitions and the attainments of magnetism should yield substance in every form; in mind, in bodily perfection, in riches and in rewards for our hopes beyond the realm of mystery.

The Crystal Mind is the climax of human supremacy.

This is the One Hundredth Principle. The power involved is the means of attaining everything within reach of mortal man; and, when magnetism shall be better understood, it will be seen that it is the chief representative force of the life that follows this career. Men have been deified in almost all ages; but the qualities that make them heroes are found in the realm of this power, whether their renown has come in deeds of valor, in generalship, or in the great republic of letters. Centuries ago, if one were to ask a man what line of conduct would bring him the most satisfying fame, he would reply, the career of a successful warrior. A woman would say, to be the mother of a victorious general would be considered the acme of earthly bliss.

A hundred years ago, or perhaps at any time within the past thirty decades, the love of fame sought expression in many other ways than through the arts of war. Position was at one time thought impossible of attainment, except by force of arms; today it comes in time of peace by the wielding of social or financial power, and the latter generally wins the way to the former. Genius has always been the child of magnetism, whether it was displayed in the stern profession of war, the exacting demands of science, or the flights of fancy. The more magnetism a man has, the more likely he is to follow correct impulses. The truest judgment cannot measure results. In the next few hours of every life there are occurrences that follow no mathematical law; they shift as the winds vary, true to some succession of happenings that no one can foresee. It is like the variations of wind, temperature and humidity. The laws that are at work are natural, it is true, but their full purposes cannot be known, except under the chance of probability, and this misleads the wisest at times.

MYSTIC UTOPIAN SUPERMEN

What to do and what not to do, excepting the routine of existence, must appeal to the judgment on the one hand, and to intuition on the other; and, standing on the apex of dilemma, many a man has gone down on the wrong side through the exercise of his best judgment, while many another man has been led by the power of magnetism through intuition into the fullest measure of success. Here genius leads the way. Cold calculation never made the Alexander, the Caesar, the Peter, the Frederick, the Napoleon or the Dewey. Genius is not reckless blindness; it is the impulse that tells a man how to do a great thing grandly. It opens the mind to an idea that cannot he understood by others until it is executed. When the first emperor of France, by cold calculation, figured out that the Austrians would join the Russians in their combined attack against him, he saw at what point the meeting would take place. Arithmetic told him that an army, marching at the recognized pace, must travel the distance in a certain time; and, furthermore, that the total number of his enemies united could overwhelm him. By no method known to war could he reach either army. Now genius stepped in, and told him that unprecedented speed could place his soldiers between these two hostile hordes. He obeyed. He met one before it had reached the other; he conquered and scattered that one, then turned around and dealt the same fate to the other!

There is no exception to the rule that magnetism creates genius by giving it quickness and clearness of sight, always aided by the best skill and truest judgment; but the latter cannot accomplish great ends alone. Every important life has its crisis, or its series of crises. What is called perfect judgment cannot be ascertained until all the after-events have occurred; then the loss, if any, will be accounted for; and what a man might have done, not what he ought to have known, will be proved by analysis. The wisest scientist can tell why the hail followed the excessive heat of a July day; but, seated in his observatory, and watching the haze of the atmosphere as it steams beneath the torrid sun, he cannot say whether the lower currents now tending from the south will pass east or west, or rise to the middle-upper or far-upper airs, and here, there or elsewhere exchange places with the colder currents, nor whether clouds, rain, hail or dry weather will follow this or that change, nor what will blow, whether blasts, gales, hurricanes or zephyrs. You ask him, and he will say: If this goes this way, that will go that; if the hot air can get above the surface of the earth, it will let the north wind down. But what will follow he cannot foresee. Even with the reports of all the continent telling him the weather elsewhere, he is not even then sure of it here. A change underway is the foreteller of its immediate results, in part at least; but before that change begins all science is helpless. What is true of wind and weather, is equally true of human life.

The animal is the victim of chance; while man's vicissitudes are controlled by two agents—judgment and genius. The latter is the child of magnetism, and the former is always helped by it. This power clears the brain, strengthens the mind, quickens intuition, and leads men and women up into the brighter realms of life. It is the largesse of mortal existence and immortal hope. Its greatest friendship appears in every crisis, when one of two acts must determine whether we rise or fall. There is no certain guide without its help. Its right hand may be called intuition; its left, judgment; and the two together, genius. The fruits of this combination may properly be termed largesse. And in this realm we find ourselves at this time. The first direct fruition is called the magnetic temperament, and this is never a missing or absent friend. Not only in the crises of life, but in every way and at every place, magnetism should bring its bounty to men and women.

It is taught by our principle that the Crystal Mind is the climax of human supremacy. Power that controls the intentions and shapes the purposes of other men and women, is an attainment of the highest value; but no power is equal to that which can look into the mind of a man, woman or child at will, and know what is there. As we climb higher and higher in the study of Universal Magnetism, if we are able to acquire this climacteric goal as the topmost summit of our progress, we shall have won a prize that reaches out beyond the gifts of Nature and partakes of the sublime beneficence of the Creator.

To know what is in the mind of every man, woman and child.

This knowledge of itself is a far more potent force of control than any phase of magnetism; but, coupled with that gift, it becomes the absolute ruler of men and women.

Let us approach this new condition understandingly.

The brain is to be regarded as merely the tool of the mind. The processes of thought are carried on in the brain, but the master director of every thought is not in the brain but in the source of brain action,—the meninges of the brain.

The brain is the storehouse of experiences and therefore of knowledge.

Thinking, while performed by the brain, is directed and wholly controlled by the triple lining, or three membranes, surrounding the brain.

The character of the thinking and the whole fabric of the mental powers are no better and no worse than the physical condition of these triple membranes. What they are, the mind thinks. What they suffer in injury the mind suffers. Here are a few illustrations of these facts given at this time in order to show to the reader the importance of studying this phase of life:

1. When congestion from the stomach reaches these membranes, irritation follows, often attended by profanity.

2. When alcohol taken in the stomach inflames the blood and the blood inflames this triple lining of the brain, thought is erratic, silliness of speech often results, and the inebriate does things that are unmanly and even unpardonable at times.

3. Anger sends venous or poisonous blood to these membranes, and the irate man is beside himself and loses control of his mental balance.

4. Typhoid delirium inflames these membranes that surround the brain causing the patient to take life, as has been too often the case.

5. In the milder malady known as the grippe, these membranes are slightly swollen, and the brain and head seem to be floating in the air; or else the objects in the room assume a floating and enlarging condition.

6. These membranes are normal when they are supplied with pure blood based on wholesome foods; but science has demonstrated that the continued use of abnormal foods or an unfit diet will poison this triple lining of the brain to such an extent that insanity will follow. In fact there are classified cases of mental breakdown that have been proved beyond a doubt to be due wholly to the use of improper foods which poison the blood and attack the brain powers through these membranes. These instances are merely en-

larged forms of the same results that attend the use of alcohol. Viewed in the light of these facts there is nothing strange in the assertion that insanity will result from continued abuse of this organ through the stomach.

7. Some persons are born with a slight intrusion of part of the skull bone against some part of the brain, with the result that criminal tendencies attend such persons all through life; and freedom from such tendencies has been obtained in many cases by operations that remove the intruding bone; or in some instances where there is only bone pressure. Criminals have been made good citizens by such operations. The pressure of the bone or its intrusion is against the membranes, forcing them against the brain.

8. Poison from an infected tooth, entering the circulation of the blood, has been found in a large number of cases to cause forms of insanity by irritating the membranes, and through them the brain itself. Criminal tendencies in children and young folks have been traced to such cause, and cured by operations. Recent experiments and discoveries along this line have given a vast amount of new knowledge on this subject of the influence of the membranes over the moral and criminal nature of human beings.

It must not be supposed that the brain itself is not the most important agency in the activities of existence; but it holds the same relation to existence that the motor vehicle does to its accomplishments; the responsible and controlling power being the driver at the wheel.

THE STORY OF THE WONDERFUL MEMBRANES.

It is right that we should investigate that part of life that directs its activities and that determines what place is occupied by every man and woman in the scale of civilization. And here we find ourselves studying the wonderful membranes that surround the organ of thought.

This book is written in a vocabulary that can be understood by every person who is able to read a newspaper. Intelligent and sensible people are found in the ranks of the so-called humbly educated classes; they are not able to grasp the meaning of technical terms. Yet it is possible to please and instruct even presidents and professors of great universities in the same simple language that can be readily understood by the nonliterary classes.

Let us illustrate what we mean.

A scientific man will tell you that the three membranes referred to are known by the following names:

The dura mater is the lining that clings to the skull. The word mater means mother. The word dura means hard. The two together mean hard mother. Two of these linings were called mothers from a fanciful idea that they were the nurses of the parts contained in them.

The pia mater is the lining that clings to the brain itself. The word pia means tender in this case. The two together mean tender mother. It is the most vascular membrane in the whole body, which means that it is the most active mass of blood vessels, and contains more such vessels for its area than any other part of the body.

One more word from the man of science. He will now speak of the arachnoid, which is the middle membrane. It is called arachnoid because it resembles a spider's web.

Thus we have Latin names for the three membranes, and such names alone guide the scientist; but translated into English they are hard mother, tender mother, and spider's web.

Surely we can afford to lay aside the technical terms that cloud the minds of the lay students; and that is what we will do in this book. Instead of such terms we will call them what they are, the three membranes that surround the thinking organ of life.

Two important facts now must be considered:

Between these membranes there is a body of fluid that comes directly out of the circulation of the blood; and from this fluid there run many millions of fine streams through the innermost lining, which we have described as the most vascular membrane in the whole body; meaning that it has more blood vessels for the transmission of blood than any other part in proportion to its area.

When a person thinks, studies, or otherwise uses the brain, this fluid flows with great force and activity. While thought is the operation of the brain, it cannot occur except by the active flowing of the fluid through the membranes as stated.

1. Thought cannot take place unless this fluid flows through the membranes into the brain.

2. When any part of the membrane is pressed by a bone or fragment of bone from the skull, the thinking is defective, and may result in crime on the one hand, or loss of some part of a faculty on the other hand.

8. When the blood that furnishes the fluid is impure, or diseased, the character of the thought is changed accordingly.

4. In perfect sleep the fluid referred to ceases wholly to flow. This permits the function-section of the brain to carry on the work of repairing the body; and it explains why repair takes place in the body only when sleep is perfect. Repair rebuilds nerves, nerve-vitality, tissue, organ structure, blood composition, and all parts of the body; none of which can take place when the brain fluid is flowing into that organ. Even the brain itself depends on cessation from thinking in order to be repaired and kept in health.

5. It has been proved by a vast number of experiments that the flow of brain fluid from the membranes into the brain in any quantity beyond the normal, interferes with or stops the other functions of the body.

6. . In hard thinking the flow of this liquid is excessive; and in all cases it keeps exact pace with the degree or severity of the thinking. This fact is not new, as it has been known to investigators for many years. In every act of thinking the membranes throw into the brain a continual stream of mucus highly charged with electrical acids; and in this way only is thought possible.

7. Whatever disturbs this condition during sleep, will set up the act of thinking during slumber, with the result that a person dreams; or when the disturbance is violent as after eating indigestible food, nightmare may follow. Dreams and nightmare have been shown in all cases to be caused, not by the brain itself, but by the action of the membranes sending this stream of mucus into the brain and arousing in that organ the work of thinking; and all the emotions that are touched by the fluid are subject to this awakening.

8. The hallucinations of fever, as in delirium, are due to this same flow of mucus which

the inflamed membranes rush into the organ of thought and feeling. The imaginings of drunken men are likewise due to the inflammation that ensues from the use of alcohol, affecting the membranes.

9. Brain fever, and similar forms of disease, cannot be traced farther than the membranes; the brain itself seems to remain merely the organ under attack from the outside inflammation. There are other maladies that involve its own tissue, but they are not in this class.

10. One of the most common epidemics in cities at times is that of meningitis; or cerebro-spinal-meningitis, as it is called. As its name implies, it relates to the meninges which are the membranes that we are discussing. It begins with congestion due to a wrong diet, and extends from the spine area to the brain area; the technical name of the brain being cerebrum for the larger section, and cerebellum for the smaller section. We make this explanation to show the origin and meaning of the name of this fatal malady. Translated into everyday words, it is the disease of the membranes running from the spine to the brain; we have included all three parts of the name and have not been compelled to resort to technical terms. Yet almost every person, no matter how humble in education, knows the disease by the common name of cerebro-spinal-meningitis.

11. The question arises, where shall we look for the seat of the mind; and, possibly, for the seat of the immortal soul? Shall we look to the brain; or to the membranes? The brain is the storehouse of all that life contains in each human being. This much is certain. It is also the machinery of thought, the engine that carries on the work. But it is not the engineer. It may be compared to the motor-vehicle; of itself it can give only the results that the driver commands. Left to itself it is useless, perhaps dangerous. Only as long as a competent engineer is at the wheel, will it respond intelligently. If the driver is sick, or drunk, or reckless, or unfit from any cause, it will produce results that are erratic and possibly violent.

12. A diseased membrane driving a normal brain will come into disaster and mishap; just as an unfit driver handling a perfect motor vehicle will not be able to make it do proper work. On the other hand a normal membrane driving a diseased brain will accomplish no more than the latter can perform; just as a perfect driver handling a faulty car will not do more than the car itself is able to do. These facts show that the brain and the meninges are interrelated; but does not lead to a solution of the question, which one is the seat of the mind? Perhaps both hold that honor. Let us see.

13. When a babe is born, to review well known facts, the brain is said to be smooth. It is not a perfectly polished ball, for its parts have shapes and sections all ready for being developed. But from the standpoint of intelligence it is in fact smooth. These facts are well known to all students of the human mind. But the outstanding fact that is most important of all is this: There is no evidence of the existence of the mind until the brain is developed by experiences by which it is enabled to interpret the purposes and desires of its superior officer and master force, the MENINGES.

The clairvoyant must pass into a degrading condition in order to see facts that are hidden from the ordinary intelligence. When the mind that dwells in the meninges finds its interpreter in the human brain, and makes its own knowledge manifest by that agency, it does not create what it discloses, but passes on from a source beyond itself, and through itself, knowledge that is lying all around its own abode.

The air is filled with ether; this ether is crowded with knowledge that needs only the right kind of instrument to give it interpretation and thereby make it known far and wide. Ten or twenty years ago this great law would have been laughed at. Today the receiving instruments are drawing into the lives of the world myriad waves, some of which are converted into words and intelligible sounds, but most of which are passing on to an eternity that may reveal them for what they represent. The knowledge is all about us.

A sound may be so fine that the human ear cannot interpret it as word or musical note; but it may be there nevertheless. Waves of song or speech are coming into the house without the aid of instruments, that are never interpreted. They need no broadcasting. From the beginning of time this invasion of Nature by a power beyond Nature has been in progress. Recently we entered a home where no aerial invited the radial waves; where an ingenious boy attached his receiving wire to the corner of the wall inside the room, and the instrument took up the work of producing the meaning of the waves that passed through the solid stone wall with the speed of light from the sun, and the knowledge that was crowding the air became known facts.

What metal wires and tiny machinery can do, the brain of a man or woman can do better. Two generations before the radio system was discovered and long before it was even dreamed of, we wrote and taught the principle that the human brain is akin to the interpreting instrument and the meninges akin to the receiving part, while all the universe is akin to what is now called the broadcasting stations.

The mind of every man and woman is broadcasting.

This fact is easily proved; and is fully acknowledged by every student of life. Your head is in the midst of thought waves and ether waves, and all the knowledge of all things that exist here or elsewhere; nor is it necessary to be developed into a psychic in order to acquire clairvoyant knowledge.

A defective brain will not furnish the qualifications of a correct interpreting machine.

Meninges that are muddy, lacking in clearness, or abnormal, will not receive this universally broadcasted knowledge. To make these two great organs of life effective we must bring them up to a state of perfection, as near as can be done with anything human.

Let us now seek the TRUTH.

THE WONDERFUL MEMBRANES.

The life within the body is nervous, which means electrical.

It is emotional, which means nervous.

It is mental, which means electrical and nervous.

No muscle can move without an electrical impulse.

No thought can come into being or take action without an electrical impulse.

The MEMBRANES are the collectors and distributors of every electrical impulse in the body. That which is called the spark of life is spread out all over the membranes of the body; and while these agencies do it to perform the work of living, they originate it, direct it, and control it. The membranes that encase the heart, furnish to that organ the power as well as the character of its work; for we all know that, while its tissue is given the mission of pulsating, the engine force that has been declared the greatest for its size and scope in the world, is furnished by the vitality of its surrounding case; by the flowing mucus that generates and discharges its flood of vital energy.

The stomach membranes do similar work, but must be stimulated by electrical juices. The saliva of the mouth that begins the work of perfect digestion flows through membranes. Not only is it a digestive power, but its healing qualities are of great value. The kidneys likewise are controlled by membranes which, when they are diseased, bring on the familiar maladies that are most feared. To be able to separate the poisoned liquid from the blood and thus to fight the battle of life, is the mysterious but effective duty of these membranes. There is nothing automatic or haphazard in this performance; it is the marvel of marvels, that so intelligent a function should be possible. How it learned to do its work, or by what kind of intelligence it carries on this necessary operation day and night without ceasing is the mystery of mysteries.

In fact the greatest inventive genius of the world could never invent a process like that. And what is true of one organ, is true of all.

The seat of life is in the membranes; never in the brain.

The seat of intelligence is in the membranes, never in the brain.

What is immortal in a human being, whether soul, spirit, or mind, is seated wholly in the membranes that surround the brain. These cannot fade, or become a blank.

While the work of thinking consists in making use of the storehouse of experiences in the brain, and while the actual work is done by that organ, as is the case with all other organs, the control and mastery should always be in the membranes themselves.

The best illustration of what is meant by the intelligence and directing action of a membrane, and one that is most readily grasped, is that of the kidneys. When their membranes are diseased, they cannot separate the poison from the blood, and the kidneys cannot do their work. The intelligence that directs this important function is located wholly in the membranes. And it is a most wonderful intelligence.

In the same way, but for still more remarkable uses, the meninges that surround the brain are charged with a supreme intelligence that directs the work of that organ in every avenue of thinking. The brain is the engine, or the machine, and the surrounding case is the engineer. Both are necessary. The driver of the locomotive is not the power, but controls that power, without whose mind the power would be wasted. If he were to fail to drive his engine, it would rust in time, and decay.

So with the human brain.

The neglect of the meninges, their disease or congestion, their warping and atrophying, or whatever else lessens their power of maintaining control over the brain, leaves the latter to rust, or weaken, or to fade back to the smoothness of infancy, and in time to become a blank, or semi-blank. There are a thousand ways in which the organ of thought may be injured or weakened. There are a thousand misuses of its activities, and a thousand forms of neglect of its functions; all of which pave the way for the loss of its keenness in old age, if not its stored up knowledge.

Therefore we have before us two achievements in this study:

1. To develop and maintain the RIGHT USE OF THE BRAIN.

2. To develop and increase THE INTELLIGENCE OF THE MEMBRANES.

As these achievements open the way to the only existence that is worth having in this world, and as they revolutionize the whole purpose of living, they must of necessity be acknowledged to furnish the most important study that can engage the attention of thoughtful people.

The first step is to shift the mastery from the brain to its meninges.

Too long have people been ruled by the knowledge that is stored away in the organ of thought. A locomotive engineer cannot perform the work of his engine, but he can make himself its master. The chauffeur cannot do the tasks that his car is made to do, but the moment that he loses control of it he is in danger. The mind is in the meninges; it cannot do the work of the brain, but it should become master of that organ, should drive it, and should never permit it to assume the power of ruler over life.

Therefore the first step to be taken is to shift the mastery from the brain to the meninges.

This mastery has come about by the weak or inferior condition of the membranes due to many causes which we shall consider. Before doing so, let us compare these membranes to the seed of man in order to understand what they are and what they contain. The seed of a tree contains in a tiny cell that is too small to be seen under an ordinary microscope, the whole history of all the trees from which it is descended; the fruit, leaves, wood, bark and texture with the influences of an endless ancestry, all compressed into a dot so small that its details escape the most searching glass.

The seed of man is a mere microscopic dot, a cell within a cell, and yet within another cell. It has never been opened to the eye of the highest magnifying powder known; but it is a matter of certainty that it contains all the form and all the details of the form that it is to bring into being; the head, eyes, ears, face, hair, lungs, heart, all the organs, the body in every characteristic, color of skin, color of hair and eyes, mental qualities, ancestral influences for many generations back, diseases that can be transmitted, blood taint, and endless peculiarities from a long past; all shut up within this dot, and carried in its tiny prison until the day when it shall be called upon to reproduce. For every cell that is so called upon, millions are made and meet their end unused; yet every one of those millions contains the same history and the same wealth of details; each is a replica of the one that is favored with the duty of bringing a new being into the world.

If we could see with eyes powerful enough to dissect the whole interior structure of one of those cells, we would behold the entire life of the man spread out within the walls of the cell, arranged and classified for the work of building a human body. A dot smaller than the point of the finest cambric needle is yet large enough to contain every bit of the future history of the man, and every bit of the past history of his ancestry. Not alone are the physical characteristics reproduced, but even the disposition, the mental value, and the nervous qualities are held in abeyance to come forth when that new life is growing.

Now if so small a cell can hold so much, what shall be said of the meninges that surround the brain?

They contain the mind, the spirit, the spark of life and all that constitutes the immortal part of the human body. These attributes could not reside in the brain, for that begins life a blank, and often so ends; while the membranes do not require development; they are there from eternity; they had their existence from the long past. In the seed of man they dwelt and sustained the whole history of the generations that have come and gone.

A great physiologist said: "The seat of life is in the membranes in all parts of the body."

A great mental expert said: "The seat of the mind is in the meninges attached to the brain, not in the brain itself."

One of the world's greatest doctors said: "If there is an immortal soul in a human body, it can he contained in no part except the vital membranes which are charged with an intelligence that surpasses all our understanding."

A surgeon of wide fame said, "When I see spread before me the pia mater I feel that if I had an eye powerful enough to probe into its secrets, I could read written there the history of mankind from the remotest past; for such history is undoubtedly a part of its structure." The pia mater is the membrane that rests upon the brain itself. Through its surface during thought, a continual stream of mucus highly charged with electrical acids, is poured upon that part of the brain that is excited into action. Just as the vital flow of electricity moves the muscles into action, so the vital flow of this electrically charged mucus excites the brain into action.

The work that the brain is able to do depends on its own powers and accumulated experiences; but what it is directed to do depends on the commands issued by the mind that dwells in the meninges. Every man and woman is in one kind of activity or another:

1. Either following the random and haphazard action of the brain;

2. Or directing the activities of the brain by the mastery of the mind.

In the former case the results are human and at random, because there is no true leader driving the engine of thought.

In the latter case the results depend on the condition physically of the organ of the mind, the meninges. These membranes are weakened or injured by any one or more of the following causes:

1. Inherited disease.

2. Chronic disease.

3. Acute lesions.

4. Inflammation.

5. Poison from excess of food elements.

6. Insufficient food elements.

7. Non-foods in the diet.

8. Improperly cooked foods.

9. Intestinal poisoning.

10. Teeth abscesses.

11. Diseased tonsils.

12. Bone pressure inherited or accidental.

13. Excitement.

14. Grief.

15. Sexual Excesses.

Autopsies show that inherited conditions keep pace with the place in the scale of civilization occupied by a person, tribe, or nation. There has never yet been found meninges that were normal in a savage; and this condition seems due to generations of food deficiency, or food lacking in proper nutrition or free from poison elements. The lower down in the scale of barbarism, the more abnormal were the meninges. An expert studying these membranes is able to determine the degree of savagery displayed by their deficient structure. Crime of all kinds involving cruelty and murder, may be seen depicted as plainly as if written in history.

There have been few American Indians that have been gentle, honest and peace loving; nearly all have been warlike and brutal; and these traits are not only found plainly indicated on the membranes, but are known to have been caused by the abnormal conditions present in them, driving the brain to originate and plan the execution of the diabolical deeds in which they gloried.

It is known that there are many foods eaten that are not suited to the needs of the body; and these act directly on these membranes; almost from the time they enter the stomach. A people or even a nation is known by its diet, and is controlled by its diet. It has been asserted many times that the nations that are called civilized are wheat-eating nations; that no people that were deprived of wheat ever rose high in the scale of civilization. This is not always true; for the facts are that wheat contains all the elements needed by the human body, and in the exact proportions required, and when a people or nation can find a food that meets these requirements they rise high in the scale of civilization.

But wheat was on earth before man arrived, and was waiting for his coming; so it was clearly intended as his food. Containing as it does all the elements needed, and in exact proportions, it undoubtedly was created by special design for his benefit. Yet if we look over the nations of the world we will be surprised to learn that those that are wheat-eating are the ones that stand highest in the scale of civilization. We also find that the lower the character of the general food eaten by a people, the lower that people will stand in the same scale. These facts cannot be ignored.

It is impossible for the membranes to become normal when the food is abnormal; and when generations of abnormal food have dealt injury to these vital parts, the result is savagery fixed and permanent.

Experiments have shown clearly that it is not the brain, but the meninges that suffer from poison, or poison food, or inflammatory drinks. A man was recently killed in a drunken brawl; and the autopsy showed the brain to be wholly free from injury, but the meninges were inflamed to an excessive degree from alcohol. In discussing the case the surgeon said, "This is the usual condition, the brain normal, the meninges highly inflamed from alcohol." It was not the normal brain that inspired the drunken brawl; it was the abnormal membranes that took charge of the brain action at a time when they were not fit to direct either the thoughts or the conduct of the man.

The same is true when the foods are unfit for the needs of the body; they irritate the entire membranous system, and set up inflammation in all parts, but first affect those that control the brain. "When a loving couple have returned from their honeymoon with never a sign of a quarrel in the horizon, and the gentle wife prepares or orders his first meals in their own domicile, and indigestion fells him day after day, the inflammation that climbs up into his dome soon makes itself felt in the erratic use of language and the exasperating irritability of his conduct towards her. A change has come over Harold.

A young man who had been brought up in the country migrated to the city and ate what was obtainable; he soon was the victim of congestion of the stomach; later on he became insane much to the surprise of those who had known him. The autopsy showed a perfectly normal brain, but highly inflamed meninges; and experts did not hesitate to declare that it was a case of food poisoning acting exactly as alcohol acts. A man suffering from typhoid fever, slew himself while in a delirium, and the autopsy showed a perfectly normal brain, but highly inflamed meninges due to the fever. Practically all victims of typhoid have delirium, and lose their reason for a while.

A man suffering from delirium tremens following a career of drunken debauchery, saw more animal life than was ever contained in the largest menagerie on earth; dragons, snakes, vermin, flying demons, and countless other specimens of an exotic character never described in any hook of authority on the animal kingdom. The autopsy showed a badly poisoned brain, but the meninges were of almost blackish purple color and inflamed to a degree hardly ever witnessed before. The surgeon made the statement that the forms of animal life that had brought terror to his last hours were imbedded in the membranes, and had come down from an era in the history of the earth when this man's ancestors actually lived among such life and beheld it; and he added these words; "I have not the slightest doubt that the meninges contain written in their tissue-cells the whole history of the past; and if we could read that history we would solve every problem of creation."

Delirium is known not to he seated in the brain itself, but in its surrounding envelope; therefore the strange forms that are seen during moments or periods of mental aberration are not produced by the brain, but by its envelope. If these strange forms differ from any things or any kinds of life that are not contemporaneous, it is fair to assume that they are, as the surgeon said, imbedded in the meninges and have come down from a past so remote that no account has been made of them by races now on earth. If man lived a hundred thousand years ago, he may have seen strange demons, dragons, reptiles and horrible forms of life, for they must have dwelt then on the globe; and if nothing is lost in the tissue-cells of these membranes, then those sights are still recorded there, and all we lack is the knowledge and power to read them. Some day, not far distant, this knowledge and power may be given the race.

This view is sustained by the best opinions of men of science; but it also is necessary to account for the strange , sights that are thrown into the brain during any form of delirium or fright. Something cannot come from nothing. If a man sees dragons and reptiles, it is safe to assert that they are pictured in some part of his head; and as the brain itself is a vanishing organ, they can come only from the membranes.

The seed of man is smaller than the point of the finest cambric needle; infinitely smaller; yet if there could be made a magnifying power sufficient to show the contents of that tiny seed, it would be made to appear as large as a mountain; and in its billions of parts would be found the whole history of the ancestry of man from the beginning of creation. Likewise if we could magnify the smallest dot on the meninges we doubtless would see the whole history of the human race from the earliest birth of man; we would read as in millions of photographs the visions that every ancestor witnessed as he beheld life and activities around him.

There is not the slightest doubt that the meninges contain and retain throughout all eternity the impressions encountered by all the ancestors that preceded them in the long past. Note how much of the world that embraces. One man had two parents; four grandparents; eight great grandparents; and so on until in about twenty-one generations back he had over one million ancestors and probably was related to every human being on earth in that stretch of time.

If the envelope that surrounds the brain contains microscopic photographs of all the experiences of the past, just as we know positively that the seed of man contains all the characteristics of the whole past, then it is true that this envelope is a written history of the whole race. What our ancestors saw as they looked out on the life about them, especially in those prehistoric eras when all life differed entirely from that of today, must account for the strange visions and experiences that come in dreams and in delirium. The habit of indulging in opium for the purpose of living in a world not like that of today, has been productive of dreams that can never be explained except on the theory there must be stored up in the brain meninges the photographs and experiences of a long prehistoric past.

What you see in a dream, what you behold in a delirium, what you encounter in the reverie, or what forms of inspiration come to you in the sudden flights of fancy known as genius, what secrets are disclosed to you when in an inventive mood, are all written on the envelope that surrounds your brain.

This brings us to the two grand divisions of this subject:

1. The visions disclosed by the membranes when in perfectly normal condition are orderly and true; and become a safe guide in life.

2. The visions disclosed by the membranes when in an abnormal, congested or inflamed condition are distorted, frightful at times, disordered at their best and always an unsafe guide in life.

Come now into the laboratory and look into the microscopic atom that is the seed of man. It is much smaller than the point of the finest cambric needle. When magnified it is a large world, a globe much greater in size than our earth, but we can know this fact only by inference. What is the inference that tells us the fact? This seed will grow, or might have grown into a child's body, and afterwards into the form of a mature man. The man would have possessed the vastly complex system that constitutes human life. If he were a Caucasian, that fact was locked up in that atom so small that the most powerful microscope could not discern its millions of details; for the tiny atom holds many millions of details. If as an atom it is magnified into a world of immense size, with countless and endless varieties of contents, and if as an atom-whole it is too small to be seen through the instrument of great magnifying power, how small must be the contents of this hidden world.

MYSTIC UTOPIAN SUPERMEN

That seed-atom will be born a Caucasian if the details of a Caucasian are locked up in its mass. No accident of Nature could make it produce a Mongol or other race. Moreover if the ancestors of that seed-atom had certain characteristics, some in the preceding generation, and others in far away generations, the seed-atom would contain the whole history, in addition to holding the complete and complex form of man, with all organs, all parts of the body, hair, skin, eyes, mouth, alimentary canal, and every trait, feature, faculty and function prepared in advance; all under instructions of the Master Mind to do their work faithfully when life has begun on earth. It is a proved condition that makes such facts sure and certain.

There are millions of details gathered from a history of the race reaching back farther than the geological birth of this globe, that are locked up in an atom so small that it cannot be seen except as a tiny speck, even by the most powerful microscope ever invented.

Our reason for elaborating this fact is to show that the smallest atom of any form of life is, relatively speaking, as large as our entire earth, as large as our great sun, beside which the earth is a mere dot; as large as the mightiest world that floats in space beside which our sun is a mere dot. Size means nothing; large or small. A germ that cannot be seen with the eye, may contain a world of human beings, all struggling to win a livelihood, all subject to the vicissitudes of the seasons and the uncertainties of existence, many of them worrying about the coming winter, or warring on enemies, or engaging in bitter fights and feuds, or holding up the nation's business while investigating oil scandals for political advantage through methods of chicanery and trickery, or otherwise passing the span of life in efforts to avoid staleness of daily drudgery, until the grave resolves the forms back to the general fund. And such life in its tiny microscopic world may be as large as ours to those who live it.

On the other hand the cycle of the heavens in which whole solar systems are born and die, may be reckoned as merely one heartbeat in the pulsation of the universe, requiring billions of years for that single action; while in the tiny microscope world, whole generations may be born, pass through their full measure of life and die, all in the ticking of a single second on our kitchen clock. So vast, swift, and mysterious is the small life about us; and so gigantic and slow is the great machinery of the sky!

What is true of the seed-atom, is true of every atom that composes the tissue of the meninges of the brain.

To the Omnipotent Eye the millions of infinitesimal details that are enclosed in the tiny microscope seed of man, are the written and recorded history of all the infinite past from the beginning of creation; and this must be true because every step that preceded the making of that seed was the result of a next preceding step, and so on without limit.

This million-form and myriad-form history is passed on from the seed of man to the meninges of his brain when he becomes a human being. Every tiniest atom of tissue that enters into the weaving and construction of the meninges of the brain is filled with the whole story of the past; and carries also the records of all knowledge that exists about humanity; including even the thoughts, plans and designs of every other human being in the word of contact with each and every one of us, Pause and consider the tremendous weight of this fact.

MYSTIC UTOPIAN SUPERMEN

Do you think for a minute that the zoological display that parades before the mind of men in delirium, is born of that disordered condition known as illusion? You cannot get something from nothing. You cannot get species of life into shape and form by the creative power of a mere fiat. It is true that there is disorder in the brain; and it is this very disorder that excites into activity the dormant past of the meninges; otherwise you would make something out of nothing, which is not humanly possible.

Certain investigators have listed the many forms of life that have come into the vision of men suffering from delirium tremens; because that erratic mental state is prolific to the highest degree, and productive of more and better specimens of the forms of life that have existed somewhere in the past, probably on earth. From this source have come the richest supplies of ancient animal existence; not always dragons and reptiles, but sometimes beautiful birds of shape and plumage never seen in our era; fish that outshine the most wonderful kinds in the sea; worms and crawling things that glow and glisten with phosphorescent light unknown to modern science; and so many other magnificent visitations that we stand beholden to the men who have sacrificed themselves and their honor and everything else worth living for in this world, to furnish us this knowledge that the meninges, once opened by inflammation and distorted, release from out the far distant past.

If what is ugly and uncanny can be thus revealed, something better may be secured by processes that do not invite the aid of delirium; and this is the work before us.

But rest assured that man is not a creator; that something cannot be made out of nothing; and that whatever the brain sees, whether in delirium or in dreams, has once existed or now exists in fact. This law is necessarily true, for it is self-evident.

The past and present are there, broadcast we will say, and ready to be interpreted; but not under a rational scheme by distortion and delirium. There are men and women living now who honestly believe they have had other existences on this earth; some professing to know who they were and their former address. If there is any basis for this belief it depends solely on revelations made through the meninges. The prophets of old saw visions, and received messages from heaven; there could be no other channel of communication except the meninges. St. John's Revelations must have come by this same process. All miracles that were not physical could easily have been the result of the same process.

The Crystal Mind is an open window.

This is the One Hundred and First Principle. But while the mind resides in the meninges and the thought operations are conducted by the brain itself, it does not follow that the condition of crystal clearness is easily attainable. It is the result of two causes; and these we will state in the most practical manner possible:

1. There must be a normal brain and normal meninges.

2. New tissue must be woven in the construction of the meninges.

The latter may seem a difficult thing to accomplish, but as every act of daily life weaves new tissue all through the body, the difficulty lies not in the weaving, but in using the right methods of weaving.

By experiments and tests that have been going on for many years, it has been proved that these desirable results are within the reach of almost every intelligent man and woman. By looking back several pages in this part of the book, you will note a list of the causes that weaken the meninges and make them abnormal. Any good general could marshal his forces of combat and reduce these enemies of the mind and in reality of life itself, by a wise campaign against them. You are a good general.

Then you will come to the law of One Hundred Percent Right in the daily making of the body. You create some part of your entire body each day by weaving new nutrition into the old structure; and as the body requires only fourteen elements in fixed combinations, the prevailing custom of using more elements in many other useless and poisonous combinations, results in creating an abnormal body either in whole or part. We cannot here write a book on these physical facts. You know what they are. The only rule to follow is this:

Put into the body each day only the food elements that are used in making a perfect body. A sound mind in a sound body means that the health of the latter controls the health of the former.

The greater work is under the second method which says:

New tissue must be woven in the construction of the meninges.

This is done by the activity that weaves; and in this case it is the activity of thinking. Every thought breaks down millions of cells; this is a fact that is taught in the school books. The new cells are woven in a haphazard fashion, and this is the basic reason why a human being is only a human being.

Look at what the microscope reveals: A small piece of the tissue of the heart, separated and placed under the glass, and fed with perfect blood, goes on weaving and pulsating as long as the conditions are favorable. Every heartbeat breaks down cells; the perfect blood supplies the material for the new cells; Nature adopts them and builds them; and for a while all is well. Now a whiff of tobacco smoke so fine as not to be noticeable ordinarily, reaches the blood and curdles it; the tissue that is built is erratic and abnormal; and cancer is the result.

We have said that every thought breaks down millions of cells in the meninges; and the same thought invites the weaving of new tissue. The brain of the student weaves better than the brain of the tramp or coarse idler. It is HOW YOU THINK that determines HOW YOUR MIND IS BUILT.

Assuming that you have made your brain and meninges normal physically by the processes stated in the preceding page, all that remains is to think along lines that will build strong, clear, perfect tissue, free from distortion and abnormal influences. The haphazard methods of thinking today and of using the mind, are constantly WEAVING MIND-CANCERS; for any cancer is merely erratically woven tissue whether of the body or any of its parts. Crime, insanity, evil tendencies, vice, gambling, prostitution, political partisanship, and similar monstrous phases of life are examples of MIND CANCERS, due to wrong methods of thinking.

A wrong belief will weave a MIND-CANCER; it may be bigotry, or an obsession leading to murder; but it is due to a morbid line of thinking.

Hard thought processes, backed by a supply of perfect blood built out of the fourteen body elements, will weave the OPEN WINDOW tissue of the Crystal Mind. This has been done successfully, but in a limited number of cases to a high degree; but every man or woman who has entered in the work required has made satisfactory progress so that they report that they have been and are gainers to a large degree. Like everything else that is comparatively new, like the radio discovery, the future will evolve greater triumphs. We provide here three lines of HARD THOUGHT PROCESSES, as something worth while to think about, and to give the mind the severest kind of labor. We will briefly summarize them.

First hard thought process. If you can think long enough and deep enough, you will think yourself back to God, is an old saying of the philosopher. If you can take the following law and think long enough and deep enough to catch the inspiration of its truth, you will have made one-third of the progress required: The universal belief and hope of immortality is self-evident proof of immortality. There are more than twenty ways of analyzing this law, any one of which will in time become the harbinger of a clear mind. Try to find one way if not more.

Second hard thought process. Another test of the operation of the mind is found in thinking out the truth of the following law: As no human being is gifted with the power of a creator, no thought, deed or impulse, plan or hope, can come into existence except as the result of some step that preceded it; and so on through chains of causation back to a beginning too remote to be considered; the result being that no human being is the creator of any deed, thought or other episode of life. Of course side influences and deterrents are constantly shifting these claims of causation, as would naturally be the control exerted by the knowledge that is sent by the channel of the meninges; seen in the inventions of geniuses, or the works of great men like Shakespeare and others, none of which can be of human origin though of human agency. When the truth of this law is perfectly apparent, you have made the second third of the progress required.

Third hard thought process. By the route of an inverted climax we come to the most important influence in the life of humanity as individuals and as nations; for we deal now with the actual cause of the misery and suffering that are everywhere sapping the vitality of the race. This is the universal belief in the necessity of political parties. This belief keeps crime on the increase, sustains all forms of gambling than which no more horrible mental degradation could be found, makes partnership with vice in every form, pollutes the courts of justice, robs the people of more than three-quarters of their prosperity through agitations that disturb the flow of business activities, and over-taxation that maintains the most vicious systems of theft and plunder that can be conceived, and rends apart and tears into shreds that national unity and harmony that are needed to secure the onward march of civilization. When your mind is able to see the truth in the following law, you will have reached the third and final stage in mental clearness: The business of the nation should be transacted like the business of any great concern, without splitting apart the groups of employees, or dividing the house against itself.

That there is a complete cure for the evils of partisanship, has been proved, and is being proved, by what is known as the No-Party Movement.

But the purpose of this law now is to test your mental ability to discover the truth stated; and to see if you are able to throw off the slavery of the mind that subjects you to the tyranny of party influence, which is not only a dangerous obsession when you cannot free yourself from its clutches, but leads to insanity by a short route.

These three groups of hard thinking weave new and perfect tissue which escapes all the mind-cancers referred to in a previous page.

The method is simple and effective, as well as logical and true; for it begins with the building of a perfect body, which is the Temple of the Mind and of the Soul. If a man is commanded to construct a house of gold he is expected to use gold; if a house of silver, he is expected to use silver; if a house of marble, he is expected to use marble; then why attempt to build the human body of other material than that which Nature and Nature's God decree, which are the fourteen chemical elements that have been created and set apart for that purpose? The defiance of this decree has brought into our times millions of doctors, mountains of pills, oceans of medicines and endless acres of instruments awaiting the hand activities of armies of surgeons. Obey the decree, and these things will pass away.

Then will follow the perfect health that makes the Crystal Mind possible and an abiding blessing; needing only the weaving of new tissue as the old falls to pieces in each day's uses of the organ of intelligence; and this is provided by the three stages of hard thinking.

Delirium breaks open some portions of this window by distortion, as will excesses, which account for the fact that some of the world's greatest geniuses have been wrecks in body through abuses that have inflamed the meninges. Or such followers of Thomas De Quincey, the opium eater, as have been transported into worlds of new beauties and delights, represent the power of insight into other realms of knowledge through abnormal and erratic openings of the Crystal Mind.

In place of the psychic, or the drugged brain, or the agency of delirium, we teach the normal development and the true unfolding of this new power over life and death. As one of our great adherents says, there is no harm and much good possible in becoming normal in this manner.

NATURAL DETECTIVES

THERE are living today in America a half dozen men and as many women who are natural detectives. The great Pinkerton of two generations ago was probably the best example this country has ever produced. Scotland Yard, England, has its scouts out at all times for some new recruit to this class. Of every one thousand good detectives fifty may be unusually effective because of this quality, while ten may be supereffective; and it is this latter number who are assigned to the most difficult cases. It is said of them that they possess an uncanny gift of catching the true facts from clues and trifling circumstances that escape the general attention of others in their profession.

Not long ago the Police Department of New York City employed a talented clairvoyant, or psychic, to shed light on certain mysteries and crimes that had never been solved. It is claimed that she rendered some service, but to what extent is not known; at least we have no knowledge other than some sensational articles in the newspapers, which are never safe guides. We endeavored to ascertain through helpers what was accomplished; and to this end we had access to the Department; but learned only that they were repaid for their efforts, although they were not disposed to make public some facts that had come to their knowledge. They justified the employment of a clairvoyant as a last resort; but admitted that there were very few indeed of the profession that were genuinely endowed with this power.

It is important that we make clear the difference between a cataleptic detective and a natural detective.

It is the same difference that has been following us all through this book; the positive and the negative; the hypnotic and the magnetic. The recipe for making a clairvoyant is simple, if it works. Investigators admit that there are less than one in a hundred, or about eight in a thousand who are genuinely gifted. The vast majority of them are mere tricksters, but a few of these have some real power in this line, although in very small amount. The first essential is the inborn tendency to nervous disease of the phase known as catalepsy. The second essential is the inborn possibility of self-hypnotism, of the possibility of being made the subject of another person who is known as the operator. It is abundantly true that there are countless thousands of men and women who can become subjects of other persons' will in this respect; with the result that there follows a cataleptic sleep often referred to as the hypnotic state. It is not always as true as claimed that the professional clairvoyant or psychic is able to induce self-hypnotism; most of the trances being pretenses.

But no matter by what method the condition is brought about, it then follows that in one case in a thousand or perhaps more, the mind of the psychic passes out of the realm of the individual and witnesses facts and conditions by the aid of some sense not ordinary or normal. True clairvoyancy cannot see what does not exist and what never did exist; for which reason it is impossible to predict the future, or to look ahead, by such a method. There are possibilities in another direction.

By the methods which constitute this section of our work, the normal building of the Crystal Mind produces in greater or less degree the qualities that result in making a man or woman a natural detective. Many very interesting and useful experiments have been made of this power, and they confirm the law as stated in the preceding pages.

All persons do not succeed alike; some forge ahead, while others keep in the background all the while advancing; but we have never known a person who applied these methods who did not show a decided gain in this valuable trait. Every day there are more incidents arising, more than one would believe offhand, which serve to give opportunity for testing this law that the Crystal Mind gives clearness to all mental operations so that it becomes a matter of great difficulty for another person to deceive and injure or wrong a student of Universal Magnetism.

OPPORTUNITIES for progress and self-improvement are never lacking in the study of advanced magnetism. As we enter upon another realm we find ourselves confronted by many new phases of the subject. Here we come to consider the special powers that are acquired through this art. Some of them may be classified as follows:

Power over audiences.

Power in the ministry.

Power over juries.

Power in the medical profession.

Power in business.

Power in statesmanship.

Power in social relations.

Power over the opposite sex.

Power in temptation.

Power in self-cures.

Power in certain cures of other persons.

Power over the imagination.

These subjects will receive attention in this realm; and, in an incidental way, others also will be discussed, for there is no limit to the extent and variations of the influence which is derived from magnetism. In the outset it is well to bear certain points in mind. In the first place, the power referred to in each phase is not derived from this realm, but is founded upon the general fund of magnetism which is obtained by the use of the first volume, and is further enlarged by the preceding realms of the present book. Nothing stands alone in this art. You should already be well endowed with the power if you hope to test the uses of it in this realm. Much of the matter is descriptive, and is intended to explain uses.

Much importance is given to the study of oratory, and the reasons therefor are partly stated. They are so numerous as to be almost without limit; so we content ourselves with presenting those that seem to possess the chief power. The meaning of the word oratory is certainly misunderstood by the public. The common idea is that any person who has something to say can say it. This is far from being true. It is not the fact in more than one case in a hundred; and in that case the chances are that the individual will fail to gain his point because of his inability to say what he had to say in the most effective way. If any person who has something to say can say it, the fact might remain that he would not know how to say it. The same thing spoken by one person may have a thousandfold more weight if uttered by another.

Human speech is the faculty that most distinguishes mankind from lesser creation.

This is the One Hundred and Second Principle. Under this law we propose to come directly to the subject of power over audiences. Speech is articulation, when we refer to it as a faculty not possessed by animals. The latter are able to make all vowels, simple and compound, but do not have the power of expressing consonants. What connection there is between mere consonants and mind, is not easily seen; but as these articulations enable sound to be marked off into syllables and words, it is very likely that they concur with the development of thought.

It is when speech rises to its height in oratory that its effectiveness is seen. The uselessness of attempting to measure its value by reading it may be found by comparing the occasion with the report made of it. It is not language, nor words, nor phrases, nor felicitations that give greatness to oratory; it is the manner of delivery. The addresses of Rufus Choate are very dry reading, but their effect when spoken was marvelous, charming and fascinating; so much so that no person could resist his persuasive power. The same is true of Edward Everett and all others who have been great as orators. Biography makes this point clear in the life of every such man. The claim that the press is mightier than the orator is true as far as the rank and file of the public speakers are concerned; but, as between the most powerful influence of the greatest newspapers and the tremendous sway of the true orator, there is as much difference as between a mass of mud and a sun of diamonds.

This disparaging discrepancy has been seen illustrated in the recent history of America. In one issue the combined influence of all the New York papers was exerted in one direction, while four speeches of ringing magnetism were personally delivered to less than twenty thousand voters; yet the power was felt in them, was transmitted to their friends and to the public, until the press was snubbed and ignored in settling the issue. One speech in Boston, some years ago, so aroused the public mind that the united shouts of the excited press could do nothing but call down derisive laughter on the editors' heads. This has been proved true in similar tests in every city and locality where the public have had an opportunity to measure the two values. At its best, the press never commands the respect of any portion of the public; and, now that its office is on a par with the dime novel, it is foolhardy to undertake any comparison with true oratory. We do not include in this term the ranting efforts of the multitude of speakers who believe themselves gifted, as they are not really orators.

The true orator speaks from the subconscious faculty.

This is the One Hundred and Third Principle. Not one person in a thousand is gifted in true oratory. He must not only be qualified in vocabulary, mind and fluency of composition to address his audience, but he must possess a large fund of magnetism; and this fund must be great enough to open up the subconscious faculty for him, so that his ideas may be there created and flow out of that realm.

When such a speaker is addressing an audience it is very easy to tell when he passes over the line that separates the conscious from the subconscious mind. A peculiar sensation is felt among the listeners; something that is real while it lasts, and soon becomes evanescent like a dream after the occasion has passed away. Many things that seem clear while being stated, are lost to memory a few hours later. The pencil is the best preserver of them. Some speakers open their addresses with the subconscious faculty, and hold their audience from the very moment of beginning, while others gradually approach this faculty, and pass into it in the course of a few minutes. Such an orator as Gough would require about ten or fifteen minutes before entering the realm; his harsh, husky, uninteresting voice would then become rich, resonant and mellow, holding his auditors for two hours on an average, while an ordinary sermon would tire in fifteen or twenty minutes. Beecher generally began in the subconscious faculty, so that his first few minutes were as interesting as the middle of his speech. Gladstone sometimes failed to enter this realm, and, when out of it, his efforts were often ridiculed; when in it, he was able to convince his enemies. Disraeli had similar unevenness of power. Daniel Webster, in his later days, was totally unable to speak from this faculty, and his appearance in Boston was described as that of a "magnificent wreck." There is a lesson to be learned in this law.

In a subsequent principle we shall show that the grade of this faculty is far above that which is aroused by hypnotic influences. The speaker is not only in any sense in a subjective or trance condition, but is openly outspoken, frank, free and magnetic. He is not uttering the thoughts of others, but the ideas of his own brain, although from the realm of the sixth sense. There have been no successful orators in all history who have not possessed and used this faculty, and the lack of power in the present era is due to the fact that men speak from mere mind and thought, without seeking the driving home impulse that makes ideas irresistible. There will be no great orator in any era, except as this power makes him great.

The orator must go with and not beyond his audience.

This is the One Hundred and Fourth Principle. A careful study of its meaning may lead to a higher degree of success in this great art. Most speakers commence by talking at the audience. It is doubtful if even the habit of talking to them is best. While the exordium, or careful opening, is a help, it is always desirable to make it simple and effective, and not too strong. Display of personal powers never accomplishes much; nor can such exhibitions be understood or realized as genuine, even if they are, until the audience has been carried up to the plane from which they appear to emanate.

Great endings are assisted by small beginnings. Lack of ostentation should accompany a humane sympathy and fellow-feeling between the orator and his audience, without familiarity. Terms of address should be dignified, and should be avoided wherever they can. To be constantly saying, "My brethren" "My sisters," "My hearers," "My beloved hearers," "Friends," "Fellow citizens," "Ladies and gentlemen," etc., is undignified. If once used at the beginning, that should suffice, and no further personal reference should be made, except in addressing the judge or the jury in a trial. Outside of these instances, the opening may be simple, sympathetic, and yet full of dignity. In order to go with the audience, it is not necessary to descend to undignified familiarity.

Listeners as a rule are fond of an appearance of association and sociability in a speaker. Some of the most successful orators, after a line or two of exordium, or polished opening that serves as a framework of beauty or strength, pass into a pleasant reference to something that is sure to arouse interest and pleasure at the same time. One refers to the beauty of the town, another to the time of the year with its fascinations, another to some familiar topic that is on everybody's tongue, another to some recent public occurrence, and so on, as circumstances will permit. A very eloquent lecturer undertook to handle the dry subject of astronomy, and render it interesting by reducing its principles to the plane of popularity and opened in the following vein: "Ladies and gentlemen, I am surprised to see so many of you out this evening. I wish I could say that the subject is as interesting as it is important. It is not of a kind to amuse the public, and if you should decide to get up out of your seats, and go home at any time during this lecture, do not for a moment think I would blame you. It is your right to leave anything you do not like. I would do the same thing, and would take pride in the spirit of independence that prompted it. Stronger influences are at work in this age of brightness to keep the mind interested; as our old familiar meteors are tempted away from their region in the sky, which astronomers had come to regard as their home until Saturn and Jupiter began their work of inducing them to stray away. '9 The lecturer went on to describe what he meant, and ere the audience had caught his idea, he was in the midst of an interesting talk which grew into a very eloquent lecture. He took his audience with him by first going among them, and at no time getting them beyond their depth.

The uselessness of speaking to hearers who are not on the same plane of association with the orator may be seen by watching the failures that are made, and which seem to throw the veil of obscurity over the work. Clearness should exist even before magnetism is attempted. The latter must have as its basis the greatest value that can be inspired by clearness, interest and importance of statement. Then it is that this power is able to drive facts home with unerring aim. But, as charms enhance all values, so the plane of association must always be maintained. No audience is so lowly that it cannot be uplifted. Even Father Taylor, in his Seaman's Bethel at Boston, speaking to ignorant sailors, was able to take them with him to heights of grandeur. But he took them with him. He did not perch on the dizzy heights, and attempt to pull them up; he went down to them, used the language and the simile of the sailor, and gradually carried them wheresoever he chose. No great orator ever gets beyond the depth of his audience. Webster used great words at times, but kept his meaning clear even in its ponderous weight; his large terms were not crowded together like the phrases of the average college professor.

Many a speaker has said in effect: "I am a scholar, my work is scholarly; I cannot descend to the level of my audience, because I would degrade my profession. They must come up to me." Such speakers are failures as orators; if they succeed, it is because they are mere readers of facts, and herein the press is their superior. Perhaps the greatest exordium in oratory is in Webster's reply to Hayne; yet, in all its elaboration, the most lowly mind would be entranced by its simplicity. No scholar need descend an inch from his dignity to put himself on a plane with his audience. They are human beings, and as such are worthy of some association; they cannot be outlawed by the methods of oratory. The grandest words of English speech are monosyllables, and no one suffers in dignity by calling them words of one syllable. Shakespeare, in his heights of sublimity, depends on such words for producing the masterly effects of his genius; effects that the greatest minds since his day have never equaled. If you will study his works, you will see in every instance that, as he rises to those heights, the words of two or more syllables gradually fall away, and unusual terms are no longer employed.

What can any orator hope to gain who will go beyond his audience? Let his theory be right; of what use is it to take his hearers into depths they cannot tread, or on heights where their footing fails and their wings cannot sustain them? "If they cannot understand me, it is their fault. I do not furnish them with brains/' is the belief of modern oratory. No great speaker ever acted upon such theory. "I must win," is the cry of genius. "I will measure my audience in the start; I will go ahead no faster than they can travel; I will never distance them." Soon he touches them through his magnetism, and establishes a cord of influence so powerful that he lifts them to any height where he chooses. His plane is theirs for the time being, and they are together.

The successful speaker studies his audience moment by moment.

This is the One Hundred and Fifth Principle. The art of succeeding in oratory is the art of knowing moment by moment the temper, the mood and the interest of the audience. It is the acme of absurdity to ask a close friend, after the effort is ended, "How did I do? Did they appreciate me?" Imagine Demosthenes, Cicero, Burke, Beaconsfield, or any of the thousand brilliant speakers of history, seeking information as to whether they succeeded in swaying their audiences. Such private testimony is of no value. The speech receives its answer in the conduct of the auditors. The orator knows, if he is at all in touch with them, just how much power he wields and what its effect is worth.

A minute study is necessary, if failure would be averted. This does not occur to more than one speaker in a thousand, and these nine hundred and ninety-nine prove that the press is of greater power than such oratory. "I never realize the presence of my audience, I am so full of my subject," says the fly-away talker, who is mastered by his own energies. "I know the mind and disposition of every man on the jury," said Rufus Choate; and in those days, when a lawyer could talk without being limited in time, he would keep at the jury until the last man yielded. Seeing this, he brought his magnetic oratory to a graceful close. In ordinary cases, the advocate of today is usually limited to one hour in his closing address; but in cases of such importance as many of those in which Choate appeared, the courts of today allow as much time as he had. He played to the twelve men in the box, and primarily to the judge. If their faces told the story of a victory already won, he was brief in his argument, unless he feared a speech to follow him.

The same rule applies to all methods of speech, whether in conversation, in acting, entertaining or oratory. There should be no conversation, even of the trivial sort, that does not meet the ends intended; if for pleasure, let it be measured by that standard, and not cause weariness; if for instruction, let it convey information in a way that will not bore while it edifies; if for a transaction, let the purpose be attained, and this requires a measurement of the effect of every word. This can be done without the appearance of doing it. The actor is accustomed by the very art of his profession to know how far the audience is for or against him. In general entertaining, it is a good idea to ask always mentally, "What is this worth to the audience?" The orator should, of all others, keep informed of every effect, for his duty is to convince, to control, persuade and win; a very different office from that usually performed.

When auditors show lapse of mind the orator is hypnotizing and not magnetizing them.

This is the One Hundred and Sixth Principle. No condition on the part of an audience is more fatal to the success of the speaker than that called lapse. What this is may be ascertained by reference to the other principle under which it is fully discussed, and you are requested to study that carefully in connection with this.

He who, in addressing an audience, is so carried away by his own enthusiasm or admiration of his efforts, that he cannot study each and every phase of the occasion and the effect, moment by moment, which his speech is producing, cannot hope for a high degree of success. Some speakers imagine that noise is the chief essential of oratory; and the theory on which they proceed is akin to that of a man beating a drum violently and blowing at random through a megaphone. Noise plays a very small part in the true expression of mind and heart; it deadens the nerves of hearing; the louder your voice becomes, the less easily it is heard, and the more it distresses those who are compelled to hear it.

The disregard of the ordinary rules of conduct, as set forth in this volume, in addressing an audience, will drive away their inclination to be led by you. Until that much is insisted upon as a basis, it is useless to hope for more. The speaker who talks along one plane of pitch is sure to produce weariness, the next step to which is sleepiness, hypnotism or disgust. An evenness of force is just as bad, and the result is the same, whether the force is weak or strong; a slow and dull voice is slightly better than a rapid and loud one. The pounding in a boiler factory does not awaken, but, on the other hand, stupifies. A harsh voice, or any presentation of the personality that annoys, cannot fail to defeat the magnetism that might be put forth, no matter how powerful might be its intended effect. These facts must be borne in mind at all times.

The first evidence of a lack of interest on the part of the audience is seen in some of them passing into the lapse state. This should be detected at once, for the tendency toward hypnotizing them is just the opposite of magnetizing them. You may hold them spellbound, but you cannot convince them, and win them to your standard of belief if you drag them along on this negative side. Says a woman: "I love to hear Mr. M. preach, for he always puts me into a peaceful feeling, almost as gentle as an afternoon nap." The monotone of Mr. K. seemed to destroy all opposition among the jury, for they sat calmly through it all for a full hour; but their verdict was given in favor of the other side. Says a juror: "I listened to every word he said, but I'll be blowed if I can recall a single idea, although every one of us decided that he talked beautifully." Too many speakers believe in the methods that depress their auditors ; they swing along in a regular rhythm, tell stories that sadden, and are satisfied to soothe their hearers into an hypnotic daze.

A constant recurrence of the same style of voice or delivery tends to produce this sleepy feeling, that while it holds the attention, does not secure the mind, and has no usefulness whatever, either at the meeting or beyond its walls. Thus we are compelled to listen to the singsong style that favors an unvarying recurrence of force and cadence. Even those who modulate, do so sometimes with a rising and falling regularity that invite sleep. If you rock a baby rapidly at one moment, slowly at another, jerk the cradle about a bit, kick it from underneath, and let one end come down on the floor with a bang, you will not put the little one to sleep right away; the tendency is to the opposite result. But let the motion be uniform and even throughout, and the baby will drop into a gentle slumber, unless some other cause is operating to keep it awake. So you may induce audiences to drop oft into a doze by the rhythmic swings of the voice.

Clergymen who cannot arouse by magnetism, try to do so by force of sound, yelling and pounding; but this is the boiler factory style. When they fail in such efforts, they seek the hypnotic plan of soothing their hearers into a dazed condition. It is a sad reflection on the usefulness possible among the clergy, that ninety-five out of every hundred are totally lacking in the positive power of magnetism, yet that all might acquire such power if they were enterprising and godly enough to choose to do so. You may go into most any church; the preacher is shouting, and the auditors have a faraway look; or he is soothing, and they are dreaming. Those who are pillars of the church, and who therefore consider it a duty to keep wide awake, do so with visibly painful efforts. Where is the good of such preaching? How long will it take to convert the world when the ministers of the gospel cannot hold the ordinary interest of their hearers, to say nothing of winning them over to the cause?

There are energetic men in the pulpit who are gifted with the insight required by the condition that confronts their profession. They have learned that the value of the thing said may be overwhelmed in the manner of saying it; that a weak truth well uttered and driven home is more potent than one of power if ineffectually presented; that the tricks of oratory are useless when apparent; that the best speaking is that which comes from the heart, well clothed in the graces of mind and body; that, while modulation and natural expression are far better than clumsy monotony and crude articulation, they are empty in the presence of magnetic fires, and that he who would succeed in convincing must elevate as he proceeds, and win as he elevates. Depression is the art of hypnotism; ennobling and arousing are the arts of magnetism.

Study your audiences in their every mood. Be on the lookout for evidence of the lapse. You will see it in the parallel gaze, wherein the eyeball is fixed in a far-off look and its pupil seems distended, while the face shows something like a dream. Such a countenance may stare at you, yet not see you. It is not uncommon to find your hearer looking you in the eye, directly and honestly as you suppose; but he is thinking of nothing, absolutely nothing. More often, however, his gaze is aside, but he is still attentive in appearance; you have driven all thought out of his head. You ask, "What did I just say?" and he replies "I did not catch it." "But were you thinking of something else?" "I must have been." "Do you recall what you were thinking of?" "No, it was nothing important, for I cannot remember anything of it." Here your words established a perfect vacuity in his mind. He was your subject, but you won nothing.

Working hard to conquer your hearers is not magnetic. The more effort you make, the more they will feel that you are at a disadvantage. A river that foams and tosses about is not so mighty as one whose still waters, running deep, bear great burdens along. There is majesty and strength in repose of manner. Two laws seem to work counterwise, that in fact are harmonious. The weaker you are, the harder you must strive to convince others of your power; yet the less you are agitated, the more power you will accumulate. Your audience will admire the conscious quietude with which you maintain your supremacy over them. When you see a speaker storming and raging like a lion at bay, you behold one whose vitality is running to waste; he is throwing off force and possible magnetism to the four winds of heaven. Let him concentrate it and drive it with a steady hand, and he might bear along with him his entire audience; instead of giving them the exhibition of a runaway team, with the driver oblivious of his plight.

A lawyer advocating a case found that the jurors went off into a doze at a time when he thought he was most interesting and effective. He imagined that they were tired out, probably on account of their excessive labors on the case; and, to keep them awake, he began to shout and make every kind of vocal and physical demonstration that seemed to be permissible in cheap oratory. Some of the jurors opened their eyes, gave him a look of wonderment, much as a dozer in a railway car might do when the train passed a brass band, then lapsed off again. "I shouted louder," he afterward said, "but they recalled the more. Noise could not interest them. I knew that I had the justice of the case on my side, and yet I felt that it was oozing out of my hands. My client could not afford to lose. I glanced at him and saw a look of agony on his face; I instantly put myself in his place; I ceased to be the lawyer; I was the man; all my inner feeling awoke, sympathy, hope, zeal, determination, and, then and there, as I stood on my feet before that jury, I resolved to win that case or pay for its loss in cash to my client. I know if every lawyer who realizes that he is on the right side, would make such a resolve, justice would triumph more often. Gradually I passed out of my previous methods, and found myself drifting along for a few moments in a transition mood; then my inner magnetism began to show itself. Twenty-four eyes were focused upon mine; the jurors sat up, they leaned forward, and soon I saw the pupils of their eye-halls grow larger; what I said they believed; and I stopped as soon as I knew that the case was won. All that the eloquent lawyer who followed me could say or do, could not wrest the victory from me. In two hours later we heard the verdict. I did not smile. I took my client by the hand, and realized, as I studied his face, what obligations rest on the shoulders of lawyers who hold in their power the rights, the property and the happiness of their clients. Thence forward I studied magnetism, and placed my dependence on its efficacy."

Good cases are lost because of the inability of attorneys to reach the jurors. They believe in two things, and disaster is charged to the stupidity of juries instead of placing it at the door of their own neglect. They can see no further than to believe that, if a person has something to say, he will say it; and if he is in earnest he cannot go astray. Neither of these propositions is true, standing alone. There are millions who have much to say, who, when they open their mouths, are unable to give it utterance. The great mines and funds of feelings and thought, go to the grave unused, because they are not clothed with the vesture of expression. Man is a creature of environments, hemmed in by a shell of limitations through which he rarely ever breaks his way. Genius lurks within most persons, but goes through life fettered, simply because it cannot set its wings free for flight.

By reference to another principle it will be seen that a magnetic person is able to pass at will from one of his estates into another. As long as he is in command of himself, he can always do this, and it is only when he is mastered by circumstances or by the superior magnetism of another, that he will fail to step out of one estate into another. Therefore, in connection with this line of study, it is necessary to glance at the meaning of other principles in this volume, so as to apply them to the one now under consideration. There is no one lesson that is to be the sole guide of the successful orator. His work must be based on all that precedes and all that follows in the teachings of this book. Even the negative side of the study, as presented under the realm of hypnotism, is valuable as showing what is to be avoided. It is not enough that we pursue the true course; for, even if we drift, as we may at times, we should know the rocks and shoals that threaten our voyage. With these remarks, let us now glance at a vital doctrine.

To destroy a lapse the speaker should pass into the realms of peace and intensity.

This is the One Hundred and Seventh Principle. If his hearers are in a vacuity of mind, it is due solely to the fact that he himself is in the realm of confusion. What this means may be seen by reference to the full descriptions which are given under other principles. Confusion may be lack of mental clearness, or it may be the unmarshalled condition of the ranks of magnetic vitality, like forces of magnificent power wandering about aimlessly without leadership or organization. Such was Cicero in the early days of his career.

Many a genius knows nothing of the laws of marshaling his hosts of energy. He comes wild, furious, erratic and useless. He estranges all his followers and pains his dearest friends. They recognize in him the possibilities of great leadership, the hope of success for him and them; but they see his army, the magnetic forces within, straying off without guide, and all his energy going with no purpose. It is necessary to have such ranks; for, when united, they become an irresistible power; but, without organization and singleness of leadership, they are no more useful than would have been the brigades of our greatest warrior if each soldier had been allowed to command himself. This is confusion; not necessarily of mind, but surely of magnetism.

We have told how the speaker may detect the lapse in his audience. The cure is in getting away from the cause and adopting the only effective means of awakening and not putting to sleep the minds of those who listen. The subject-matter must be valuable. Many speakers hunt for facts, anecdotes, stories, illustrations, and other things that will probably create great interest. When all these seem likely to fail, the weakest orators resort to the use of pictures which are placed on the canvas with the aid of the stereopticon. Minds and opinions are not won in any such way. If the lecture or address must be interlarded with items of mere interest, and of no other value, there is a wake of froth that follows the effort. The subject-matter should be great in all its details; interesting of course, but all this and much more.

The tools of expression must be the very best that can be procured. These are the coinage of perfect consonants, the enunciation of perfect vowels, the accurate delivery of language, the pleasing changes of voice by which meaning and feeling may be rendered in the sound that harmonize with the mind and heart, and the grace of modulation through which relief from monotony is always assured. Never in any case in the past, nor ever in any instance of the future, have or will the tools of expression come to a person naturally. Voice itself is not born in the body. The larynx is in the throat, but that is merely a tool by which air is vibrated. The tongue and lips are ready at the mouth, but they are useful for other purposes than shaping vowels and consonants. Let the larynx remain unused, and there would be no voice. All such faculties are developed in the way, to the extent, and for the purposes in which they are employed, and lack of employment would obliterate them.

The greatest mistake made by any author is the belief that the voice is born in him. It is true that sounds, crying, shrieking, screeching, shouting and the like, are produced in the earliest moments of life and are depended upon in after years by the public speaker; but the voice as a million-stringed instrument of the mind and heart, is a thing of development through use and training; and no orator ever stepped full-fledged into the arena with this instrument waiting for him to merely touch and play it. The biography of every great speaker tells us that he has studied and practiced certain definite methods until the voice has been built up to the standard needed.

Of every one thousand orators nine hundred and ninety-nine are failures to a greater or less extent; and most of them are decided nuisances. The tedious part of a law trial is the talk of the lawyer. The most tiresome part of church services is the sermon. Yet the guilty parties will not admit it. They consider themselves exceptions; and even go so far as to "know" that they are exceptions. With aspirate, or harsh, throaty voices, with mannerisms of body that only tend to irritate their audiences, they hold on to these false ideas with a certainty that is not to be shaken and that is understood only by a study of our principle relating to stubbornness. They refuse to acquire the tools of expression. Some are changing their views now; suggestions are being received and adopted, and speakers are making their work worth more money value through the use of the teachings of magnetism.

Assuming that the tools of expression are being used, the magnetic speaker will be able to quickly dispel the lapse of his audience. He must come out of the realm of confusion, and enter those of peace and intensity. There is no mistaking when one is in either of these estates. To pass into the realm of confusion he lets himself go, as though the boat, not being rowed up stream, would drift downward by its own impulses. To come into the estate of peace he must pursue the course of training as given under that department in this volume; and the same is true of the other estate of intensity, which is acquired under the study of the Will in this volume. The greater the determination of magnetism, the greater is the intensity.

In speaking, the deeper the feeling the less the body expresses it.

This is the One Hundred and Eighth Principle. It is a part of the law of intensity. The feeling is centered in the innermost part of the body; physically speaking, in the chest at that part where the life of the body is created by the union of the oxygen of the air with the blood. This is farthest away from the extremities. The more the energies run wild, the more active will be the feet, carrying the body about; the arms and hands in gesticulation; and the head in its sympathetic movements. It is also true that the less effective a speaker becomes the more action there is in the extremities of feet, hands and head. Again it is true that the less magnetism and the greater weakness he possesses, the more active he becomes in this way. The probable cause of the association of weakness and action is found in the attempt to accomplish a certain end; which, being unattainable in the use of vital power, must be sought by extraordinary effort.

These activities lead to failure. In the first place they tire the body and use up its physical and nervous vitality, leaving it floundering like a drowning man buffeting the waves. The experienced swimmer loses not one unnecessary motion; in danger he is strong because he is steady. The weakling in the trough of the sea, as on its calm bosom, strikes about in a wild ferocity. So in oratory. In the second place these activities detract from the efforts of the speaker by calling attention to his movements. In the third place they worry, irritate and unnerve the audience; rendering the value of the address as little as possible. No one can long endure the sight of so much distracted action. The worst of it is, the voice is colored by the motions of the body, and the mind thinks no better and no more smoothly than the muscles do their work.

While gestures are necessary they should proceed from the intensity of the power within, from which they receive their temper and by which they are controlled. Such action, representing and speaking from the central fire of life is always magnetic, it is never peripheral, never centrifugal, but is ever held to the force that gives it expression. It is very bad to walk about on the platform; the few changes of the feet within a compass of change will yield all the variations needed. In proportion as the power of self-control is lost the temptation becomes stronger to walk about, to pace the floor, to stride up and down the stage, and become a moving machine, or sort of locomotive. This does not apply to the actor who must suit his movements to the general action of the drama, and whose entrances and exits, as well as crossings, are made a part of the story which is being enacted. And there are times when the speaker must pass to other parts of the platform.

The orator should make no unintended movement, great or small.

This is the One Hundred and Ninth Principle. It is of the highest importance in the art of controlling an audience, that this law should be always kept in mind and acted upon. It includes every motion that can be made, commencing with the eyelids in one direction and passing to the fingers and toes as objective points of control. It is a very faulty habit to be constantly winking while speaking. "I have tried to stop it, but I cannot," says a weakling. Yes, you can. You have not half tried. If you really make up your mind to stop it, you will succeed. Another trial brings success. The persons who cannot do what they try to do, are childish in magnetism. Whatever any person resolves to do will be done to a finish if the resolution comes from a strong will.

It is not alone because the movements of nervousness or of runaway energy lessen the stock of magnetism on hand; but also because they weary the audience and produce an irritable condition in them that such action should be avoided. They are guilty of this double offense. We do not hesitate to affirm that no magnetic speaker can long hold control over others, and no unmagnetic speaker can win this power who indulges in unintended movements. The reasons why intention makes all the difference are two; in the first place, such motions become fewer all the time; in the second place, they are directed by the conscious will when intended, and are thus connected with the fund of power which they strengthen; while unintended motions grow in number all the time, and are offshoots that rob the body of its life. Then, again, they indicate a lack of self-control, which is everything.

A speaker who is so far lost in his subject as to be controlled by it is in the realm of confusion. We recall one who thought he had reached the realm of peace; but he nodded his head at every emphatic word in a sermon an hour long; there were never less than twenty such words a minute, or twelve hundred in the hour; and these twelve hundred nods prove exhaustive to himself and to his audiences. Mentally he is a success; magnetically he is a failure; his congregations are not increasing; he does not draw a single listener, for duty to religion compels his faithful members to attend church; and so his life is comparatively a wasted one. He cannot learn the lesson of success. His case is typical of others. Every step taken, every gesture made, every nod of the head, every act, large or small, should be intended and executed as such. It need not be slow at all times. The flash of lightning is not an accident of nature.

As speakers study audiences so the latter study the former. When the orator loses any of his magnetism, the listeners cease to follow him; they are restless and fidgety, and this broken influence they give back to him. He gets what he imparts. His own nature travels in a circle. When a power has been temporarily obtained in his address, and is lost, he is seen to carry his hand to his face and attempt to alleviate some itching sensation. This is the almost universal symptom of nervousness. Then his fingers seek something else, as a button, a part of the clothing, or a means of relief by going behind the body out of sight, in the trouser's pocket, or in the coat front. His next exhibition of loss of power is an irresistible desire to walk about, or to move the feet. Not only is he at a disadvantage with reference to himself, but he has confused his audience.

Magnetism, in creating vitality in others, receives back more than it gives.

This is the One Hundred and Tenth Principle. The law is one of more than ordinary importance to the orator. The question arises, whether the audience inspires the speaker, or the reverse is true. It sometimes happens that the applause will frighten a speaker; and it must be borne in mind that such demonstration is far different from the responsive feeling that results from magnetism. The latter is present only when the feeling runs deep. The occasion, the purpose for which the meeting is held, the general atmosphere of importance, all serve to give to the orator a degree of vital interest which he does not experience when the audience is cold and the whole work of arousing enthusiasm devolves upon him. He must furnish magnetism or fail.

Under such circumstances it devolves upon him to commence by taking the exact measure of his audience, and proceeding by easy stages to secure control of them. He must not challenge them by an assumption of power, nor by an early exhibition of it. If he allows his energies to run wild, the performance will fall flat ere it has gone far. Oratorical display is fatal. The well trained orator is taught to secure his effect by concealing all appearances of display, as the skilled actor knows how to avoid the stagey demeanor. The speaker always arouses antagonism if he seems to believe himself greater than his audience; he may be so in fact; he may show his superior manliness if it is safe to do so; but he must never parade his belief in himself.

Small beginnings with evidences of an inability to cope with the requirements of the occasion, in case the speaker is at all interesting, are certain to arouse sympathetic hearing, which becomes intensified as soon as the audience begins to believe in the man. Then his magnetism, coming slowly into play, will send a thrill, quiet, deep and strong, through the hearers; this he feels in the instant; it goes to him in greater quantity because it comes from a greater supply if active; and he now has more to give. As long as he handles himself carefully the exchange goes on, yielding him new life each time. The horripilation of the skin, which accompanies his recognition of this power, is felt equally by his auditors as by himself. What he experiences, they experience. This thrill tells him that he and they are en rapport. He is in touch with his audience. This is a great victory, and should be maintained throughout the occasion. By care in controlling himself he may not only hold this power, but may increase it by the very use.

What a magnetic person sees clearly in his own mind is photographed on the tones of the voice.

This is the One Hundred and Eleventh Principle. This law has no relation to the subconscious faculty. By reading this book it will be seen that the latter power is in two parts, a low realm faculty of morbid sight beyond the use of the brain in its ordinary senses, and a high realm faculty which constitutes the last estates of the volume. But, aside from either of these gifts, is the well-known ability of the mind to so clearly stamp its own pictures on its nerves that they take part in the vibrations of the thoughts and travel out to other minds with them.

The use of this power is so necessary to the talker, the orator, the actor and to all persons who wish to clearly convey their meanings to others, that it should be understood and cultivated by every man and woman. We must first see what it is, and then ascertain how it may be acquired and increased. The telephone conveys along the wire in electrical currents that affect the air, the tones, intonations, glides, stresses and even the overtones of voice by which almost any speaker may be recognized from all others. The phonograph receives such sounds and talks them back again at will. That either process could transmit words, syllables, vowels, consonants, and qualities of tone, is certainly wonderful, and a generation or two ago the power to do so would have been challenged.

In a similar way, but by a different medium of communication, the thoughts of one person may be sent to the brain of another, and there be felt and interpreted. They vibrate the ether-sea, just as sound vibrates the atmospheric sea, or waves vibrate the ocean. This ether-sea is a well established fact. The transfer of thought by channels other than the senses, is also too well established to be argued. Thought felt intensely in one mind and directed to another will strike in waves upon that other, and, if the latter is in a responsive condition, the meaning will be interpreted. Neither person may see the other, and no sound may be uttered or heard. Third persons may be oblivious of the transfer.

The photographic power of the mind is established by a clearly defined thought, an intense thinking and an irresistible determination to send it to another mind. All human beings feel before they learn to think. Every thought can be traced to its origin in some passion. The experience which we have while feeling a passion is the source of some subsequent thought, or train of thought. By analyzing a train of thought we will find its parts and processes made up of mental experiences, each traceable to some distinct passion. Instincts and passions are not identical. The former are capable of developing only the latter, and that in crude form; while the latter alone are capable of developing thought. The lowest forms of creation possess strong instincts, and no real passion. The higher types of animals, next to man, possess but few instincts, and feel many of the passions. Man's instincts are very limited, while he is capable of running the whole gamut of the passions. A passion must have results. These results pass into our lives and make up existence. The results of the passions are certain kindred feelings, known as emotions, which, as they are developed, show themselves in very marked convolutions of the brain. The results of the emotions are thoughts; or that succession of feelings, which, because of the natural movement of cause and effect, we call the process of reasoning. The reasoning faculties are located in the nervous system, and are merely a succession of emotional results; they are coextensive with the life of the nerves. The passions have not been established at haphazard by the Creator, but are placed in the brain-system with careful exactness. The nerve system is capable of thinking, and is not confined to the head, although thoughts as well as nerve-force arise in the head. Every system must have its center or source of intelligent control.

Words are sounds that appeal to the ear, or characters that appeal to the eye; and represent something which we have experienced through the emotions directly or indirectly by the avenues of the senses; as something we have seen, heard, felt, smelt, or tasted. Between the word and the real thought which it represents there is a connecting link. All persons are more or less impressed. It is a cultivatable habit. The present lessons explain this fact. Your thought is excited by one thought section of the brain; and excites a corresponding section of all other brains. This is a universal law. But in the general transmission of conflicting thoughts your brain is excited in many sections at once.

Therefore in order to receive a strong thought, which comes to you always as an impression, it is necessary to cultivate two habits. Once let the mind be placed on its proper training as to divisions and recognition of the divisions and their separate activities, and ever after the power of receiving and understanding impressions will abide with you. An impression is a feeling of something about to happen, or something that is happening. If it is something about to happen, then the thought of it is already well fixed in some mind, and that mind is directed toward you. In the far West the desperadoes, by years of intuitive acquisition, will feel the presence of immediate danger, and this feeling is so acute that it becomes a living fact to each. They never make a mistake, when sober.

In spite of the evils of gambling, the expert gambler has attained to one degree of excellence; he knows the mind of his companion in the game. A very expert poker player can only be thwarted by a man who can throw his mind off to opposite moods. To study these men as they sit studying the faces of others, and thereby learning the condition of their hands, will repay one for the loss of morality which may be suffered. What is thus turned to a bad use may be made far more valuable in a good use. It is a fact that merchants in trading, or great capitalists in dealing with men lesser than themselves, have gained their advantages by knowing the minds of those with whom they came in contact. The gambler is forced to the habit by necessity, as any criminal may be forced to follow some high moral law at times in order to keep out of jail. Keen uses make keen faculties. The man who seeks to know what is in the minds of others, comes in time into a habit of gaining access by the use of methods which necessity tells him must be adopted if he would succeed. These methods should receive our attention at this place, as they are always dependent upon magnetism for the force that makes them vital.

Magnetism may open and close the mind at will, for waking, sleeping or thinking.

This is the One Hundred and Twelfth Principle. The foundation of its power is in the accumulation of magnetism under the mechanical practice of the first volume. Having done this, the next step is in the study of the two great estates of this book; namely, the realms of peace and will. It would at first seem true that the greater the magnetism, the easier it is to close the mind, especially for going to sleep; but the less magnetism a person possesses, the more confused are his energies. These must be supposed as wild powers, for it is their uncontrolled state that leads to wakefulness. The fact has been tested over and over again. One of the hardest working and most magnetic physicians this country has ever produced was able to put himself to sleep while waiting for an engagement with a patient; if the latter came late, the doctor had improved the few minutes by a sound sleep, from which he would awaken as easily as he fell into it, yet would derive full benefit from the repose.

Insomnia has been completely cured in any case, however severe, when the sufferer has acquired magnetism under these advanced lessons; of course, using the first volume as a basis for the culture. We have had occasion to recommend this power to many who could get no relief from other treatments, and the result has always been the same, a complete cure. The reason is told in the realm of peace and its predecessor; for scattered energies, like engines running wild, are dangers to the body and confusion to the mind. These are held under control by magnetism. More than that; a person possessing this power is able to fix the length of time for a nap, and awaken at the moment indicated.

Experiments are very conclusive in this respect, and we will suggest the following as the best: Close the mind, or at least attempt to do so. The first twenty trials may result in no progress; one trial a day being sufficient, and from thirty minutes to an hour being devoted to it. Thought flows in a succession of waves, like a swell across the sea. In the course of three weeks of daily practice, directed under the principles stated in the realm of the will, you should catch the recognition of a flow of thought. As soon as you recognize the thought-flow, which must result from faithful practice, you will know just what is operating in your brain, after which it will be an easy task to shut off the flow of thinking. Try it, and be convinced. The proof of a thing is in what it does. Scientists differ as to theories, but when they come to facts they are often dumbfounded to see their pretty theories demolished. Take, for illustration, the splendid systems of psychology taught in the great universities of the world; they fall and crumble before the great facts of life.

When the outgoing flow of thought is recognized, it is easy to control it at will. It may be shut off, or turned on in smaller or larger currents, like some stream over which a check is maintained. The reverse should now be attempted. Allow no thoughts to come into your mind, as you allow none to get out. Those persons who are susceptible possess no power over the impressions which they receive from others, and they are often distracted by outer influences. You should close your mind at will against intrusions, or open it at will to catch others' thoughts. The reception of ideas or of impressions, which are feelings, from another, is easy if the other is at hand or in sight. Think of that person with the constant mental assertion: "I am passively listening to your mind." Of all the mental sentences capable of being used this has proved the most efficacious. Try it. But if the person is away, or if there is no person in mind, and you desire to draw into your brain some strong or distinct thought, as an impression, it is necessary first to stop the outflow and the inflow of thought from general sources, and absorb that which comes from the distance.

The ordinary senses convey something of the moods, thoughts and purposes of others, as the student of facial expression has ascertained; but the finer, more delicate, and yet more certain way to be felt, is through the ether. Imagine for a moment a person sitting in your presence. If he is thinking of any subject, that subject is transmitted to the ether about him, which fills the entire room, until the subject itself occupies all the space. His thoughts are as much out and around him as they are within him. They vibrate in every nerve of the body. Now, any person who is constituted or developed as to be able to feel the influence of the thought-waves upon the ether, would read his thoughts clearly and distinctly.

This resolves the matter down to the single question: How shall we put ourselves in a condition to receive and feel the thought-waves which are vibrating all about us? The reply is to be had in the maintenance of the four following rules, which are summed up as four acquisitions: 1. An indomitable will. 2. Large magnetic life. 3. A persistent thinking of, and yearning for, the object desired. 4. The throwing out of the magnetic lines toward that object or wish. Any person, no matter how weak, may acquire all these conditions, even if none of them are present in the least degree. To this great end the art tends.

But for the purpose of this power we need the four conditions to affect the distance about us; that is, to give us control over facts occurring on earth, though not in our presence. To do this we need all the aid of the long course of training found in the estates that lead up to this lesson—to enable us to control our outgoing thoughts, or, for the while, to prevent our originating any ideas or thoughts. Herein lies the greatest cure of mental troubles. Only men and women of great magnetism are able to stop thinking. Lesser mortals worry at every trifle. Worry kills more people than all other causes combined. Worry is agitated thinking. It operates to mar the free action of the medulla oblongata, or the third brain, from which spring the nerves that give vitality to the vegetable body and the three functions thereof; namely, respiration, digestion and circulation.

When a person worries the large brain absorbs all the vitality of the nervous system and general strength; little vitality is left for the medulla. Consequently, the respiration almost ceases; the heart becomes fitful and ultimately deranged in its effort to meet the unusual demand upon it, and digestion is very feeble. We sit at the table in good spirits, eating heartily in response to a lively appetite, when bad news arrives. The gastric juice stops flowing into the stomach, digestion ceases, and appetite is lost. Likewise a person who carries one thought too long, or who is pinioned by an uncontrollable activity of the brain, cannot digest food readily.

No more useful lesson in life can be learned than this which is taught under the present principles. It is gratifying to recognize results in the many experiments which have been made by our students. To be controlled by one's own wandering and of these erratic feelings, is to be at the mercy of a stormy sea without rudder, oars or sail to guide and direct the boat of life; but to be the constant prey of others' moods, and to be the tool of every passing influence, is still worse. We know of nothing so important as the magnetic control of the mind, for this organ is a world in itself, and controls all else that belongs to human existence. It is the moral agent as well as the mental and physical. Life is one long series of activities impelled by this organ.

Magnetism perfects the brain power.

This is the One Hundred and Thirteenth Principle. The brain is an engine that feeds on electricity, phosphorus and magnetism, the latter being the directing agent and master as well, while the former are means of obeying its dictates. It is not possible to think without phosphorus and electricity; yet these are not sufficient. Add to them the power of magnetism, and the engines may run wild. An engineer is needed; the will must drive the forces that tell for man's ruin or supremacy. This will must come to recognize the thought-flows, the incoming and outgoing ideas, and must direct them at all times.

Having gained this much of the mastery, the will must adopt the photographic clearness of thought and feeling that is referred to under a preceding principle. What the mind of a magnetic person sees or feels clearly will be photographed in the tones of his voice. Speech is the most common means of communication, and the man or woman whose brain is so clear that every utterance is perceived and understood by those to whom it may be directed, is already a great power. This skill is acquired by magnetism, and has been explained. The use of a faculty strengthens it, and, in fact, preserves it against disease. The brain should be tested by hard work daily ; not all the time, but for a while each day.

Memorizing magnetizes the brain by its activity, if the thought is fully felt and appreciated. As the memory is strengthened with wonderful rapidity, it a sin to permit it to remain weak. Its use or nonuse quickly affects it either way. A breaking down of the brain-power first appears in the difficulty of remembering names and events; and, while it is not true that the cultivation of memory would restore the brain, it would nevertheless help it some, and prevent mental disease. As we owe many duties to those with whom we deal in business and social life, we have no right to forget them, for our forgetfulness often causes annoyance and loss to them. This element of character being an important one, it is well to go into a special course of training to develop and strengthen it.

1. Take any sentence; select the emphatic words, having but one word to an elementary thought; commit these words to memory in their order, then endeavor to complete the entire sentence mentally or aloud.

2. In going from your home to any other house or place of business, try to recall all the persons by name whom you met, and in the order in which you met them.

3. On retiring for the night, recall the events of the day in the order in which they have occurred.

4. During meditation carry on a train of thought directed by the active will, and recall all the topics in reverse order, then in the order in which they came to the mind.

5. A most excellent practice, and probably the very best for developing a quick and ready memory, is to listen closely to a sermon, and, on the first trial, seek to recall the text and the most important points made during the discourse. On the second trial recall the two most important points established by the sermon, and so on, increasing by one each time. Do not seek at first to recall more than one point, for, although you will undoubtedly be able to remember very many, it will prevent the scale of increase if you do not follow the plan here given.

All these means of developing the magnetism of the brain help each other. The power to send a thought to another mind is helpful to the memory, for both require the utmost clearness and intensity, although mere imitative memorizing is of the opposite character and lacks strength. This is seen in the case of one who has committed a recitation and forgets a line somewhere in the middle of it, and must go back to the beginning to straighten it out. That implies no mind; it is merely a succession of sounds. The Chinaman memorizes by a succession of sights, copying or imitating merely, but holding the ideas with tenacity. This is a mental gift, but it is not true memorizing, and cannot therefore become magnetic.

The clergyman is charged with the most solemn duties of the orator. We do not believe that the parish work should be imposed upon him. By divine command he is called upon to preach, not to enter into the financial problems of the church, nor the social intrigues of the choir. He is ground down under the pressure of labors not properly in his province. With such a handicap, he is useless in many cases, and worse than useless in most. We believe in the minister and in the church. They alone are particularly endowed with the power and the business of maintaining the moral standing of the world. But we do not believe in the cart-horse.

To preach to the souls of men the minister must possess magnetism in the highest degree, as well as mental clearness and the other qualities of his profession. Out of mind alone come thoughts only. Out of subconscious power comes inspiration, and magnetism takes no step and makes no advance that does not lead constantly upward toward that faculty. A magnetic preacher can impress, convince and win; but the drudge who visits his parishioners and grinds out a week of toil far more distracting than the method of getting a living by the wits, is not possibly capable of developing or even maintaining his magnetism. To say that the humble church cannot afford it is not true. In a community where there is but one church, there are not members enough to require labor from the pastor outside of his pulpit duties. Where there are two churches in the same community, let the minister of one do the drudgery and the other do the preaching. They will agree to this if they are honest. If the congregations object to amalgamation, let them think how ashamed they would be if God were to appear in their midst and ask what objection there could be to one church working as a harmonious whole, instead of two at war with each other in creed.

Power in the ministry is greatly increased by magnetism. This should not be conformed with zeal and excitement that take the mind off its legs; they are too often run away energies that are not fruitful in worthy results. Magnetism never strains, never pulls, never tugs, never shouts for mere noise, although the thunderburst comes when the period is ripe for it; but, on the other hand, it draws the people away from themselves up to the plane whither the speaker would carry them. What is said on this subject in the earlier pages of this realm, applies to the ministry and to all branches of oratorical use. For very many years we have watched the progress of our students in this art, who are ministers, and in every case they have bettered themselves. Of those who have been engaged in the study of magnetism for more than two years, we do not know of a single one who has not reported extraordinary success.

Power over juries has also been secured in a remarkable degree by our students. Lawyers who were accustomed to fail in their trials, have become the most successful in their counties. How this has been done can be learned from one who sends us his report while the present book is being brought to its completion (October, 1924). We embody the greater part of the account, as it is in itself a lesson in magnetism. "Like the lawyers whom you spoke of a number of years ago, I was poor and unsuccessful. I could not get a case to try for over two years. When I did go into court I was defeated, and lost a good cause. My client was ashamed of me. The public quietly ridiculed me, so much so that I was anxious to quit the law or move away where I was unknown. This would not save me, for I was unfit for the court part of my profession. Yet I was well read in the law. I could floor much older lawyers on legal questions, and I could talk; but I was tiresome. When in this predicament I saw your book on Personal Magnetism; it was what I had been wanting for years; I got that, and then went one better by buying the expensive book of Advanced Lessons, although I borrowed the money. This was three or more years ago, perhaps four. I depended on those two books and nothing more. I am going to tell you what I accomplished, and make it brief. I accumulated mechanical magnetism. Being a leaker I had room for much and it came. That was step number one. Everybody knows how that is done; it is easy. The second step was to control all my energies, by bringing them under one harmonious law; the third was the greatest, the will. I cultivated that. Now, I was ready for the world, for the battle of life. One thing I needed, and I am going to teach you, my teacher. It is this. I have an enormous fund of power, but it needed the diversified uses to give it escape without waste. I organized a debating society; I spoke at public meetings; I was invited to speak oftener; I attracted attention by my so called wonderful improvement in so short a time, and here I am today credited as the most eloquent and most successful jury lawyer of my county." He told the whole story in a succinct manner, and his report goes with the many other victories won by the power of magnetism. It is, as we hope your report some day, will be, one of the stars in this galaxy of glory.

Power in the medical profession is rapidly gained through the practice of advanced magnetism. In no other calling is there so much opportunity for the exercise of this art. In the first place let the physician accumulate all the magnetism possible by the aid of the first volume, and let him compress all his energies into one chain of power, for confusion in him distracts the sensitive patient. The latter looks to the face of the doctor for hope, or for the story of the case; the very entrance of the physician is one of assurance, inspiring confidence, or it is one of confused energies, disturbing the confidence already secured. To make the sick one nervous or depressed is sure to throw back the patient and retard the progress toward recovery. Perfect calmness of mind, perfect peace of all the energies held under absolute sway, and a clearness of vision into the nature of the malady accompanied by a determination to affect a cure, are preliminaries that every physician should regard.

A distinction should be recognized between the so called magnetic healers and the regular physician. The former cannot be other than charlatans. There is no escape from this conclusion. Disease cannot be driven out of a patient by the magnetism of another. Self-magnetism may effect a cure, but only by supplying vitality with which to govern the appetite and the assimilation of food; two processes that often fail because of a lack of functional life. This is afforded by magnetism, as is the increased vitality of the heart which is rapidly failing and bringing its owner to the grave. Even in such cases the proper nutrition must be supplied to the system. There is no cure of any disease, no matter what its kind, except by rebuilding the body. Medicines may shift the abnormal conditions, but never did and never can effect a cure. How absurd is it for a magnetic healer to attempt to "throw off" such a malady as rheumatism by rubbing or other processes, when the uric acid is being momentarily formed by perverse habits which the patient makes no effort to correct? As well open the faucet and flood the house, then call the healer to rub the house instead of turning off the faucet. The cure of diseases is effected by turning off the fountain of their supply, and rebuilding the injured body. The fact that neuralgic headaches are overcome by the outer influence of magnetism, is not of itself sufficient to prove extensive powers. One swallow does not make the springtime.

Power in business is founded upon the same laws that have been repeatedly stated in this volume. To restate them would be to rewrite the book. The first essential is a stock of magnetism of enduring force, such as is derived from the practice of the exercises of the first volume. The confusion that inevitably attends the career of an active business man, and which may sooner or later unfit him for any other duties, should be conquered. Calmness, peace, will, determination, and every social charm that can be acquired, should be used. Never fretted, never made angry by the angularities of his customers, always conciliatory and pleasant, always bound to please, even when patience ceases to be a virtue, always honest in his dealings, and bright enough to see that the wholesalers do not impose dishonest goods upon him, he cannot help succeeding if he is magnetic. He should be prompt in his correspondence, never allowing a minute to pass unnecessarily when an answer is needed; for it takes no more time to be prompt than to lag behind, and he should make the wishes of his customers paramount to his own, when he can properly do so. Honesty pays a larger dividend in this age of trickery than any other quality.

Power in social relations is purely magnetic, and always derived from this art. Wealth and rank may force the leadership over others, but it is a following of sycophants that will permit it. There are requisites of admission into every set, into every clique, into every circle; sometimes these are titles and wealth; sometimes ancestry or birth; sometimes merit, office, fame or style; but the queen of women is always the possessor of charms of personality, whether she belong to the upper or the humbler caste. So with true men who win recognition in society. We have shown the possibility of merit alone rising out of the lowest scale and taking the possessor to the highest plane, even amid wealth and rank, while neither came to lend aid. The best society is governed by the most sensible rules, and it is to the credit of some circles in every part of the civilized globe that they place no barrier against the entrance of worth, unattended by any other quality.

Power over the opposite sex has been referred to so often in this volume that we need devote no large space to it here, except to take a glance at its opposite side. We believe in the law of affinity by which one ideal, schooled in magnetism, will eventually find one of the opposite sex that nature and destiny have intended for each other; although fate steps in too often and ties the knot otherwise. Too many men have married too soon, or have not succeeded in welding that chain that should have bound them to another. Too many women have also been mis-mated. There is now no remedy. Maintain the marriage relation at all hazards, and make of your counterparts all that you would have found in your ideals. Much has been said in previous pages of this volume on the same subject.

What we now wish to say upon the matter of power over the opposite sex is on its reverse side, the attempt of a person of superior magnetism to rob a lesser individual of chastity. It is supposed that the man or male is always the aggressor; but this is far from being true, as it is also untrue that no female is in danger if she does not give some kind of invitation to the opposite sex. Leaving out of the question the class that plies the profession of unchastity, we need only refer to the others who are innocent in toto, and to those who are bad sub rosa. When one of the last-named class meets another of the same class, and there is doubt as to the fact of virtue, either may avoid the needed suggestion and so pass by untrammeled; or either may take the initiative. One is as likely to do so as the other. The man, fearing to make a mistake, looks for some sign or signal. The woman, hating to be despised if she should reveal her nature to one who would not wish her company, will likewise be wary. Thinking herself correct in the opinion she forms of the man, she throws out a hint that is capable of being construed either way, in case a turn is necessary. This is the moment of her fall, though not of the first she has experienced. The man accepts the hint as a challenge, with some bit of conduct that he can explain on either side of the fence on which both are poised; and, these preliminaries over, the toboggan is easy. The pivotal point may be assumed by either; the man gets some cue from the woman in most cases; while the woman acts on the theory that every man is vulnerable.

If honor is a tawdry jewel there is nothing on which to base the use of magnetism. No person will exert an influence to do some thing that is not desired in his own heart. There is no glory in conquering the virtue of one who has it for sale or loan. There is only shame in throwing a magnetic influence over an innocent human being, with the purpose of despoiling the one chief charm of life. But there is both glory and honor in winning the heart and mind of one who is worth the battle and who resists the victor, if won for marriage. We are proud of those of our students who have taken Cupid by the ear, thrust him aside, and leveled their own shafts of love at the hearts of unwilling mortals. A wife or a husband who has been lassoed by magnetism has never been lost. It is the only cord that never breaks in marriage. Many notable cases have been cited in previous realms of this book.

Power in temptation is the needed friend of the honest girl who is unable to withstand the magnetism of some man who seeks her virtue. We believe that our students are incapable of such defilement; but there are men everywhere who have some small degree of native magnetism, just enough to overpower the girl. It is useless to claim that the percentage is small of young women who are misled. The fact is quite the contrary. Every physician of extensive practice knows that a rather large, though relatively small, percentage of females have been wronged prior to the age of twelve; as many are likewise dealt with between that age and fifteen; then comes the horrible era which ranges from fifteen to twenty, in which more than ninety per cent, of all who are left to their own control, fall prey to man. Mothers, fathers, sisters, brothers and husbands go to their graves ignorant of the evil which has been visited upon their loved ones. Those who see only the surface evidence will indignantly and vehemently deny this assertion. Those who know the facts will recognize its truth.

There is but one remedy. There is but one aid for the weak who is tempted, and that is magnetism. It is well worth the cost, for what it saves is above all price. Let the girl learn to control herself, not by the empty boast that she can always take care of herself, for this vaunting is a bubble that some certain man can prick at the first glance of the eye. Let her study the full course of magnetism, and fortify herself especially under the realm of the will as presented in this volume, and she need not fall. Not even the promise of marriage, affirmed in hot tears and indented with burning kisses, can unbalance that power which she thus acquires. So in all temptations the rule of safety is the same. It is, and has been, the tower of strength to those young men, and older men too, who have fallen into lines of evil and are likely to yield.

MYSTIC UTOPIAN SUPERMEN

Power in self-cures should be studied very thoroughly, as it is by far the most certain of all means of removing disease, if there is a basis, in the shape of nutrition, to work upon. Nearly all disease is due to foreign matter in the system, coming in through adulterations in the food or a wrong selection of drinking fluid. This is explained in our "Life Building" book. The body must have fourteen elements daily, and in seventeen compounds. Give it more or give it less, and something will go wrong. The kidneys are the source of some of the most disagreeable as well as the most quickly fatal of maladies; yet these organs would never become diseased were it not for the introduction of foreign matter in the system. On the other hand, it is the lack of sufficient quantities of the right kind of food that causes heart failure and neuralgia; while many improper methods of cooking, combined with foreign matter in the diet, lead to dyspepsia, and so on through the whole list.

The facts concerning the curative powers of magnetism are so apt to be distorted, that we prefer to first sum them up, and then explain them. Concisely stated, they are as follows:

1. One person cannot cure another person by magnetism; the most that can be accomplished is to render a minimum assistance, which must be based upon hygienic laws.

2. One person may supply a slight amount of vitality to another through the power of magnetism; and this has but a small temporary, and no permanent, virtue, unless obedience is yielded to hygienic laws.

3. The erratic action of the nervous fluids that sometimes causes headaches or other pains, may be corrected by the magnetism of another.

4. Self-magnetism is the most certain of all methods of cure, and its efficiency must depend on the proper supply of the exact nutrition demanded by the body.

5. All disease represents one of three conditions; either a deficiency of nutrition in whole or in some particular part; or in the introduction of foreign matter in the body through food, drink or drugs; or the lack of due vitality. The last-named often results from the first or second. In some cases, perhaps in a majority, all these causes are at work together.

6. There is no way known to science, or to man, nor has there ever been, nor will there be any way of overcoming disease and curing its effects, except by rebuilding the body.

7. As in childhood and youth, when the body grew because the vitality was excessive, so in maturity a fullness of vitality is needed to maintain the daily waste and rebuild the system with new and perfect material; and this process of rebuilding must occur faster than the ordinary waste of the body.

8. Artificial magnetism cannot supply vitality. Life springs from its own impulses, not from those that are thrust upon it. The more dependence is placed upon outward influences, the less the life of the body will generate its own vitality.

9. Self-magnetism is the source of the greatest and most buoyant life.

These are facts that have been proved times without number in the cure of disease; and on the other hand, is the perverted doctrine of magnetic healers, who claim that they are able to produce sleep, cure pain, and accomplish other results by this power, when the fact is that much of their work is hypnotic. The best opinions are decidedly against the use of this degrading power to cure disease, and we have found many potent reasons why it should not be employed, which have been stated in the earlier realms of this book. Do not let us be misunderstood as to the value of magnetism itself in curing ordinary pains, headaches and any disorder that is due to an erratic action of the nerves; but there is a vast difference between a disorder and a disease. Self-magnetism is the proper agency for curing the latter, and this must have for its basis the same regime that rebuilds a diseased body. In fact, the latter process is often impossible or very slow when unaided by self-magnetism.

The practice of curing headaches in others is valuable as a means of testing your growing magnetism, and we shall review some of this power, at the same time asking you not to confound so slight a disorder as headache with any disease. You may control another person by the voice, the eye or the touch in this experiment, which is a very simple affair. If discrimination were to be made, the relative value of each would be stated as follows: The eye's power is generally the strongest, and is rated at 100 per cent, in value, the voice at 80 per cent., the touch at 60 per cent., the eye and voice at 180 per cent., the eye and touch at 160 per cent., the eye, voice and touch at 240 per cent.

Some persons have a more magnetic touch than others; and some have on hand a crude supply of touch magnetism furnished by nature, while the eye and voice may not possess any appreciable quantity. In grasping a person's hand it is better to hold the body, arm and hand dead still, while the nerves are exceedingly tense. The mind may say what it will, either silently or openly. The touch is capable of accomplishing many physical effects, and the exhibition is most satisfactory. It is a pleasant evidence of the power of generating animal electricity. The fingers can arouse and give escape to more magnetism than any other part of the body in the way of touch. The balls, or the very tips, of the fingers are the best points of escape, but only slightly better than the palms. It is well to remember this in attempting to remove pain from others.

The capture of the belief of a sick person is a valuable aid to his being cured. Confidence in yourself, free from a consciousness of it, is the surest way of obtaining his confidence. No being should be forced into any belief against his will. These combinations in you and your patient open the way to the exercise of curative powers. Then comes the necessity of using the mental assertion, of which so much has been said in previous realms of this volume. Direct your whole mind upon the patient, and make use of the following inward observation: "I am sure you believe I can remove this pain," or some similar expression. There are many cases where an attempt to cure in this way would be entirely useless. While it is possible, it is grossly improbable, that such a method as that of personal magnetism could effect a cure of a dangerous illness, and it would be criminal to neglect to call in a physician at such a time.

The only illness that a person ever ought to attempt to cure by magnetism is such as would be considered too trivial to require the immediate aid of a physician. We make these remarks because persons often acquire considerable power, and this leads them into the belief that they are infallible. There come times to all of us when the nervous system is unmanageable, and its magnetism unreliable. These times are few, however; but even at our best we are fallible. The method of checking the violent escape of electricity may be effected by either medicine or magnetism. If by the former, the flow is counteracted by exciting a lesser degree of it somewhere else, thereby establishing an equilibrium until nature restores the normal condition. We all know that the tendency in nature is toward a cure of every malady.

The same methods may use magnetism only, and it is here that the best results are obtained. The person suffering with a pain in the head is still waiting for that soothing touch which, if directed aright, will counteract the escaping electricity of the patient. Imagine yourself a battery (with plenty of power in store, capable of directing it at will), seated before a suffering friend, who is no battery worth mentioning, having no power to direct, but losing it all, and that loss caused by some pressure on the nerves, or some irritation of them that excites a violent escape of the vital fluid. You have to overcome this violent loss. You will have done well if you restore the loss to its everyday or ordinary escape— that which attends all nervous people. The nerves of such people are often very sore, without experiencing any real pain, showing that any escape of vitality may be slightly painful.

It will generally suffice to cure headache to have the patient sit near you, your hands resting on opposite sides of his or her head, the balls of the fingers coursing gently over the forehead and scalp, from the front of the head to the back, following the general direction of the pain. It requires three things to make unequivocal cures.

1. That you possess accumulated magnetism.

2. That you firmly believe you can cure.

3. That you so express yourself mentally during the process of the attempt.

An active mind will be able to direct the course of the magnetic current down the arms and out of the balls of the fingers into the very nerves of the patient. In many cases the escape of vitality is overcome at once by the counter current. The cure is instantaneous. In others the escaping vitality is checked gradually. The reports of cures are so numerous that it is useless to attempt to select any for publication. The students of advanced magnetism, unless grossly careless, have been uniformly successful.

The voice may always aid the magnetic touch, by speaking in soft, gentle, low and sympathetic tones. Holding the palm over the part affected by the pain is sometimes quick in its results. The whole palm should touch, and very lightly. In touching other parts than the head, and in coursing the balls of the fingers gently over these parts, but one direction should be taken. Rubbing back and forth will only warm the body, not magnetize it. Rub always in the same direction. Do not reverse, but bring the hand back through the air, and so continue. All movements along the arm or hand should be toward the shoulders, following the line of pain; all on the legs should be toward the hips, and generally toward the spinal column.

The power of the imagination may deplete the magnetism, or invite hypnotic belief.

This is the One Hundred and Fourteenth Principle. It is not the effect of magnetism on the body, but the effect of the imagination over all else, and thus the law is different from any yet presented. You may know of many instances of the use of this force. We can do nothing better than to cite the case of a celebrated French physician of Paris, author of many excellent works on the force of imagination, being desirous to add experimental to his theoretical knowledge, who made application to the minister of justice, to be allowed an opportunity of proving what he asserted by an experiment on a criminal condemned to death. The minister, by order of the Emperor, delivered over to him an assassin who had been born of distinguished parents. The surgeon visited the prison and told the unfortunate man that several distinguished persons had taken an interest in his family, and had obtained permission of the minister that he should suffer death in some less disgraceful way than on the public scaffold, thereby saving the feelings of his family, and that the easiest death would be by bloodletting.

The criminal gladly agreed to the proposal. At the time appointed the physician repaired to the prison, and the criminal being extended on the table, his eyes were then securely bound, and he was slightly pricked near the principal veins of the legs and arms with the point of a pin. At the corners of the table were placed little fountains or basins filled with warm water, from which poured several streams falling into tubs placed on the floor to receive the water. The poor criminal thinking it was his blood that trickled down his arms and legs, into the tubs, became weaker and fainter by degrees. The remarks of the medical gentlemen present in reference to the pretended quality and appearance of the blood increased the delusion, and he spoke more and more faintly, until his voice was at length scarcely heard. The profound silence in the apartment, and the constant dripping of the water, had so extraordinary an affect on the brain of the patient, that all his vital energies were soon gone, although a very strong man, weighing one hundred and ninety-five pounds, and he was dead in one hour and forty minutes, without having lost a single drop of blood.

A gentleman having led a company of young children beyond their usual journey, they began to weary and cried to him to carry them; which, from their number, he could not do, but he told them he would provide them with horses to ride on. Then cutting little sticks, he gave one to each, and provided a larger one for himself, he bestrode it; whereupon they straddled each their stick and rode home without the least complaint. Such is the "power of mind over matter."

The religious fanatic and the martyr to political excitement have exhibited resistance to physical agents to a degree of inflexibility most incredible. The Shakers believe that, in their trances and visions, their souls visit the heavenly world. In this state the lancet has been applied to them, and their flesh scarified without producing a particle of blood. This will plainly show the power the mind exercises over the physical system, or in other words, over the body, and its great influence in producing a cure in many diseases.

Dr. A. T. Thompson, of London, an eminent man in his profession, related many highly interesting cases of this nature. "I give you a case," said the doctor, "as an illustration of the control of the mind over the operations of medicine, where the whole effects must have been induced through the nervous agency, modifying the functions of the organs concerned. A lady was laboring under an affection of the bowels, attended with severe pain and the most obstinate costiveness. She was physicked, the warm bath used, and administered with injections and anodynes, but without the least effect upon the bowels, and without affording any relief from pain. At length the physician was informed that she had expressed her conviction, that if her usual medical attendant, who was then in the country, and alone understood her constitution, could be called, she would be relieved. This physician was accordingly sent for, and on his arrival, although no change either of measures or medicines was resorted to, her bowels were quickly moved, sleep and entire relief of pain followed, and in a few days she was perfectly well."

Dr. James has related a case communicated to him by the late Professor Coleridge, which strikingly illustrates the power of the imagination in relieving diseases. As soon as the powers of nitrous oxide were discovered, Dr. Beddoes of the London Hospital, at once concluded that it must necessarily be a specific for paralysis or palsy. A patient was selected for the trial, and the management was intrusted to Sir Humphrey Davy. Previous to the administration of the gas, he inserted or placed a small pocket thermometer under the tongue of the patient, as he was accustomed to do on such occasions, to ascertain the degree of animal temperature with a view to future comparison.

The paralytic man, wholly ignorant of the nature of the process to which he was about to be submitted, but deeply impressed with the representation of Dr. Beddoes as to the certainty of success, no sooner felt the thermometer under his tongue than he concluded that the gas was in full operation, and in a burst of enthusiasm, declared that he already experienced the effect of its benign influence throughout his whole body. The opportunity was too tempting to be lost. Davy cast an intelligent look at Coleridge, and desired the patient to call again on the following day. The man again called at the appointed time, when the same ceremony was performed, and repeated each succeeding day for a fortnight; the patient gradually improving during that period, when he was dismissed as cured, no other application having been used.

Professor Woodhouse, in a letter to Dr. Mitchell, of New York, has given a recital which also tends to show what singular effects can be caused if the imagination be previously and duly prepared for the production of wonders. At the time that the nitrous oxide excited almost universal attention, several persons were exceeding anxious to breathe gas, and the professor administered to them ten gallons of atmospheric air, in doses of from four to six quarts. Impressed with the belief that they were inhaling the nitrous oxide, quickness of the pulse, dizziness, vertigo, difficulty of breathing, great anxiety about the breast, a sensation similar to that of swinging, faintness, restlessness of the knees and nausea, or sickness of the stomach, which lasted from six to eight hours were produced—symptoms entirely caused by the breathing of nothing but common air under the influence of an excited imagination.

A magnetic brain may separate the senses from the body.

This is the One Hundred and Fifteenth Principle. The body of flesh and bone is the product directly and indirectly of the vegetable kingdom, and its functions are inherited from that realm. Trees breathe by their leaves; the body by its lungs; plants grow by the circulation of their life-fluid, the sap; the body grows by the circulation of its life-fluid, the blood; plants, trees and all get nutrition by the digestive action of their root fibres; the body gets nutrition by the digestive action of the nerve fibres of the stomach, exactly reproducing the work of the root fibres, which is selection and absorption into the life-fluid. Thus we possess a vegetable body, called flesh as an easier means of expression. But we have five senses, emanating from the head, while the tree has no head and no senses. Its existence is fundamental; so is ours, except for the addition of the senses.

To be able to separate the senses from the vegetable body is an attribute which, it seems, only the great men and women of the world have possessed. It should be acquired by all. The exercise of the willpower in that direction, aided by the experienced use of proper magnetic lines, will accomplish the desired result. History merely repeats itself over and over again in the lives of the great men and women, as far as this power is concerned. Nearly all the biographies of the truly great mention this as a gift. Napoleon could charge his mind with any subject he pleased, and instantly discharge all thought of it. He never worried. In the midst of the most terrible wear and tear of anxious, nervous thought he could select any period of the day or night for sleep, and slumber for an exact time. This has been stated as true of scores of others. General Butler, when tired by a too long continued mental strain, could step into a private room and sleep at will. "Excuse me for twenty minutes," he would say; then disappear. In ten seconds he was snoring. In nineteen minutes more he was awake. In twenty he appeared bright and new, as though refreshed by a full night's rest.

The most singular instance of the power of the will over the functions of the body, and taken altogether, perhaps, the most remarkable case on record, being supported by the most unquestionable testimony, is related by Dr. Cheyne, in his English Malady, pages 208-310. The case is that of Hon. Cornel Townshend, who for many years had suffered from an organic disease of the kidneys, from which he was greatly emaciated. He was attended by Dr. Cheyne, Dr. Baynard, and the distinguished surgeon, Dr. Skine, three of the most eminent men in England. These gentlemen were sent for, in great haste, early one morning, to witness a singular phenomenon, or strange case.

He told them he had for some time observed an odd sensation by which, if he composed himself, he could die or expire when he pleased, and by an effort come to life again. The medical gentlemen were opposed, in his weak state, to witness the experiment, but he insisted upon it, and the following is Dr. Cheyne's account: We all three felt his pulse first; it was distinct though small and thready, and his heart had its usual beating. He composed himself on his back and lay in a still posture for some time; while I held his right hand, Dr. Baynard laid his hand upon his heart, and Dr. Skine held a clean looking glass to his mouth. I found his pulse sink gradually until, at last, I could not feel any by the most exact and nice touch. Dr. Baynard could not feel the least emotion in his heart, nor Dr. Skine see the least soil of breath on the looking-glass. We then each of us held to his lips the glass several times, examined his pulse, heart and breath, and could not by the closest scrutiny discover the least symptom of life in him. We reasoned a long time on his strange, odd appearance, as well as we could, and all of us confessed it unaccountable, and beyond our power to explain so strange and inexplicable a case. He still continued in that condition, and we concluded that he had indeed carried the experiment too far, and at last being quite satisfied he was dead, we were about to leave him. He had continued in this situation about half an hour, it being then nine o'clock in the morning, in autumn, when, just as we were leaving, we observed some motion about the body; and, upon further examination, found his pulse and the motion of his heart gradually returning; he then began to breathe gently and speak softly. We were all astonished, to the last degree, as this unexpected change in a man we confidently believed to be dead, and after some further conversation with him among ourselves, went away fully satisfied as to all the particulars of this astonishing case, but confounded and puzzled, and unable to form any rational scheme, by which to account for it.

He afterward, several months subsequent to this event, tired and worn out by his mental and bodily sufferings, sent for his attorney, made his will, settled legacies on various servants, received the sacrament, and calmly and composedly expired in one of those extraordinary and powerful influences of the mind over the physical system. His body was examined and all the viscera, with the exception of the right kidney which was greatly diseased, were found perfectly healthy and natural. This power of will, manifested at pleasure, is perhaps one of the most remarkable phenomena connected with the natural history of the human body. The distinguished Dr. Benton in his work alludes to cases of the same kind, and reports that the celebrated Carden Hagged could separate himself from his senses when he pleased.

The health of the plant and flower, its changing shape and diversified form, are all dependent upon purpose,— but that purpose is the will of the creator. In the animal and man the vegetable functions are the result of the will of a Creator. The three brains, the cerebrum, the cerebellum, and the medulla oblongata, are separate purposes at work to enact the will of the being—a gift from the will of a Creator. In this separate will-life rests the independent control of the body.

The question now confronts us: "May a human being step in between the will of the Creator and his own life and body?" The answer is "Yes." The Creator so intended, and has waited patiently these many centuries for man to grasp the great meaning of his own existence. In moments of unreckoned mental dominion, the mind is seen in its sway over the body. History is full of this evidence. The whispered secret is heard but not heeded.

That the mind has a powerful influence on health is well known to medical men, and in fact to all persons of observation; and this is the reason why physicians encourage their patients. Not infrequently, mental emotions such as fear, grief, or any great anxiety of mind, have turned the hair gray in a single night. Man is more or less the creature of passion, prejudice, habit and education. The heart, alas! despite the stern philosophy which justice bids us exercise, invariably warps the understanding. Even when most disposed to place reliance on the impartiality of our discriminating faculties, the sympathies and prejudices of our nature still triumph; the leadings of a mode of thought and reasoning, that has been instilled into us through training and education. This shows the importance of proper moral instruction, and the necessity of correct early habits. We are also often misled by the force of imagination.

Some persons suffer more from pain than others; it is well known that all do not bear surgical operations equally well. That is, doubtless, greatly dependent upon their organization, although it may be modified by habits of endurance, or on the contrary, in particular diseases, depending on the condition of the nervous system at the time, which should be particularly and strictly attended to, for it is remarkably susceptible of impressions. The slightest motion of the muscles, the slightest breath of air, will often induce the most excruciating torment where it is morbidly impressed; the operation of medicine is interfered with, and regular physiological action must be importantly modified. The influence of hope is also necessary to procure relief, and the alleviation or removal of disease is, in a great measure, dependent upon the condition of the mind.

The agreement between mind and body is constant.

The administration of new medicines without possessing anything particularly novel or powerful, will frequently induce an amendment of the disease, and this is often the reason why medicine prescribed by physicians of celebrity, or professors, has been known to succeed better in their hands than in those of other persons. It is greatly the confidence and hope of the patient that works the cure. Disease is known to depress the powers of the understanding as well as the vigor of the muscular system, and will also deprave the judgment as well as the digestion. A sick person in particular, is extremely credulous about the object of his hopes and fears. Whosoever promises him health, generally obtains his confidence; and this is the reason why so many become the dupes of quacks and patent medicines.

The force of imagination, the power of fear, exercised on the animal economy, are admitted by every medical observer, and indeed by every one of common sense; and the limits to which their operations are to be assigned, no one can designate. This subject is of great importance to the medical man, if he wishes to practice successfully; and how very much is it to be regretted that so little attention is paid to this important subject, the influence of the mind upon the vital functions. Research in such a field of inquiry would display many phenomena, which in ancient times were attributed to supernatural causes, and latterly to magnetic and other causes, which might be satisfactorily referred to the operations of the nervous system alone, without the supervention of other agencies. The modus operandi is not understood and the opinions entertained by distinguished physiologists are various. The operations of the moral feelings and emotions in the production of corporeal diseases are far from being yet understood, and hundreds have died from fear during the prevalence of the cholera who would have been living at this time had they possessed moral courage.

Poor human nature! How fearfully does it deceive itself when it flies to drugs to relieve every disease! Look into our large and commercial cities, where more work is done with the head than with the hands; where every kind of food for the passions is not only superabundant in quantity, but of the most stimulating quality, and thousands who never labor at all, are found who, through the unnatural degree of excitement kept up in the brain and nervous system, and the full play of the passions, bring very great injury to their health. An attentive examination of every class of society will convince us, that in proportion as the intellect is highly cultivated, improved, and strongly excited, the body suffers, till a period at length arrives when the corporeal deterioration begins to act on the mental powers, and the proud man finds that the elasticity even of the immortal mind may be impaired by pressure too long continued, and that, like springs of baser metal, the body requires occasional relaxation and rest, instead of dosing and drugging. See that pale cheek, that eye that has lost its luster, that careworn countenance, that languid step, that flaccid muscle, with great weakness, and the indisposition to exertion, and you will behold the results of a mind worn down by the cares and disappointments of life, and a body exhibiting a faithful picture of its influence upon it.

RINGS of influence far overspreading the sky, span the mighty realm wherein man has sought to peer since first he knew his relation to the universe that canopies him. Shut in on this earth with all its dangers, he hopes for some destiny that shall separate him from the rolling hall on whose crust he clings. He sees life made up of the material that lies on the ground beneath his feet, and operated by the forces that come from the sun. So ignorant is he of the laws that govern the universe that he does not know where the parent orb of the solar system had its origin, or whence it receives its vital supply. He believes that, if he were given wings with which to fly a billion miles in each billionth part of a second, he could scour the heavens from one extreme to the other, going through all the heights, the depth and breadths, and find nothing but suns and solar systems.

If it is true that we see all there is of the universe in kind though not in extent, then the powers that make, keep and control it are diffused and scattered, and suns are gods, and gods are beings of fire. But if it is not true, then heaven and the abode of God are designedly hidden from our little dot in the sky, and only His presence pervades matter. There is no such thing as an existence suspended in empty space, apart from the architectural structure of the universe. The home of the Ruler is somewhere or everywhere. All forces operate on the material; they are powerless to find leverage except in matter. The day is not far distant when science will declare that the ether which fills space and is omnipresent within all gases, liquids and solids, is all there is of spiritual existence; being capable of containing and transmitting every influence hitherto known.

Magnetism lives in ether; and leaps its bounds under pressure to seek release through more solid lines of matter. The water-sea that encompasses our continents is more free than the earth and its minerals; the aerial-sea that bathes the planet is lighter yet; but the ether-sea, itself expanded matter, is freedom idealized. Strike the water into waves, and their highest speed is childishly slow compared with the undulations of air that rive the wind; yet both give way before the flight of ethereal fire that counts its millions of miles in each minute of time. The sun is close enough to the earth to almost scorch it, yet sound would require fourteen years to pass from this earth to that orb. We regard the railway train that moves at an average speed of forty miles an hour as the embodiment of high speed; but if it were to maintain this swiftness night and day without ceasing, it would require 263 years in which to reach the sun. It travels at the rate of forty miles an hour; light goes nearly two hundred thousand miles a second, and would reach the sun in about eight minutes.

This speed is all too slow for thought, and much too slow for feeling. Yet within the mind's mind there is another kind of thought, another kind of feeling, far more subtle and intense than the conscious faculties are able to detect, that sends its messages many millions of miles in every millionth part of a second, and catches answers ere the vibrations cease; which must require a more sensitive ether-sea for its transmissions. As mental messages and impressions seem to require no time whatever, it is possible that they are received at any distance the instant they are created. It is not reasonable to suppose that God must wait for knowledge, even though it comes from the farthest limit of space. The discussion of what the universe is, of its height as compared with its other relative dimensions of length and breadth, and the nature of the abodes within its central spaces, together with questions that are necessarily involved in that connection, may be found amply set forth in the highest degree book of this series, namely, Future Seeing. We are now to consider man's relation to the general forces beyond those of commonplace life.

MYSTIC UTOPIAN SUPERMEN

There are superhuman realms of power.

This is the One Hundred and Sixteenth Principle. By superhuman we mean but one thing; that is, beyond the uses of the ordinary senses. We do not mean to refer to the claims of spiritualism. The proofs are abundant that such a realm does not exist, for the reason that every manifestation can be traced to some activity of the ether-sea. The superhuman need not necessarily exclude the grander nature that coexists with the human. Man is composed of his body and its forces; the former being the tools of the latter. The forces are vital when they relate to mere physical expression; they are mental in thought only; yet the blending of the two are needed in so simple a range of faculties as may be seen in the use of the senses. By these channels all things are known, felt and experienced; and from them all reasoning proceeds. The deepest thought is but a divergence or expansion of an idea founded upon somebody's sense impression.

Despite the deep veiling that obscures the faculties that exist apart from the ordinary senses, they are well recognized as actual agents of life, which, for some reason, have never been openly visible to the common gaze. As they have come to manifest themselves from time to time, their strangeness and infrequency of occurrence have produced alarm. Being superhuman, they have been at once associated with the only thing which man had ever regarded as superhuman; so the theories and supposed complete proofs of spiritualism, occultism and what else, were immediately founded, only to be foundered when the breath had returned and sense could be summoned to the investigation.

As we proceed we shall see the proofs of powers, long associated with the ordinary faculties, but which have always been partners at least with the superhuman, and these grow into others without limit. Man may be a creature of dust, but magnetism is not of earth. The sun that holds these mighty orbs to its heart by a chain of influence great beyond comparison, sends to all life such share of that influence as each individual is able to use, and the power behind the sun lives in and through the endowments that have been transmitted to earth by the varied vitalities of that orb, giving us the clew to possibilities yet unrealized. As we proceed to unfold the plot of destiny, light is always growing more intense, and new domains loom up in the distance. Over the horizon of hope the skies hang brightening into rosy gleams of promise.

The ether-sea reaches every realm of power and washes the shore of Heaven.

This is the One Hundred and Seventeenth Principle. This law is fully recognized by science, and has no doubters except so far as the latter portion of the principle is concerned. It is true that science does not recognize either the existence or nonexistence of heaven, as understood in religious theories. It is not material, either as to whether such admission is made or not, or as to the kind of heaven that may exist in the sky. If it is not in some special section of the universe, it is everywhere; for no person of sense believes that the great system that is perfected in space is without government, and whatever governs it is located somewhere or everywhere, and that is what we mean by heaven, for the purposes of this principle. We have fixed scientific reasons for believing that heaven is specially located, and is not a scattered or diffused presence, which reasons will be amply stated in the forthcoming volume, Future Seeing. It has no place or part in this book.

MYSTIC UTOPIAN SUPERMEN

Having proved that heaven exists in fact, the principle which says that the ether-sea reaches every realm of power and washes the shore of heaven, is a self-evident truth. No well read person, whose attention has been called to this subject, denies the omnipresence of the ether-sea. The long exploded Newtonian theory of the materiality of flight made that force a molecular activity, not realizing the extreme thinness of the ether. The attempts to concentrate the atoms of which ether is composed and reduce them to matter, was just as senseless as would be the effort to condense the atmosphere by focusing the sound. No matter how much loudness may be compressed into a small space, nor how many voices, horns and whistles may be directed and reflected upon a given spot, the air is not increased in bulk by this excess of sound, and the same is true of the ether. While the Newtonian theory of the material nature of light is denied today because of the inability of experiments to collect light and turn it into matter, the fact of the existence of the ether-sea is universally admitted.

As such a sea exists, and as it fills all the universe, even to the outermost limits of occupied space, there can be no doubt that it is omnipresent within those limits. Being so, it must connect the kind of heaven we have mentioned with all the suns and planets. This proposition is of immense importance. It tells us that there is a means of direct communication between our earth and all the orbs of the sky; with heaven itself, with God, the angels and the souls of those who still live, although not in form visible to the eye of flesh. The importance of the fact goes much further than our first thought would carry it, and here we come to the serious part of the present realm. There is within the human breast a reverberating chord of sympathetic union with the powers beyond. There is in every life some evidence of superhuman faculties ever at work seeking to make the story plain. Time brings new steps in the progress of mind and matter, and there is nothing in the universe that is capable of standing still. Today amazing revelations follow one after another as never before in this history of mankind.

As evil and good are everywhere present, so the subconscious faculty has two opposite extremes.

This is the One Hundred and Eighteenth Principle. It is not possible to find good unless evil exists as its opposite pole. There is this exact negative of every quality of the mind, of the body, of the heart. Man steers clear of one by taking his course toward the other. The sanity of the mind has its opposite nature in mental unsoundness; the health of the flesh is threatened by disease; love counterbalances hate; hope, despair; pride, shame; resolution, fear; excitement, depression; day has its night; winter, its summer; spring, its autumn; the flowers, its weed; food, its poison; the bird, the reptile; the church, the saloon; the Bible, the press; heaven, hell; God, the devil; and it need not surprise us to find in so powerful an influence as magnetism its opposite pole in hypnotism; and that the subconscious faculty is likewise built of two extremes.

There can be no communication from one point to another, from one mind to another, or from one being to another that is not carried on by means of an agency. Influence cannot leap the clear gulf of nothing. When hypnotism puts the conscious mind to sleep and arouses the subconscious faculty in its basest form, it places those who are with the subject in communication with scenes, thoughts and impressions that are not approachable through the ordinary channels of life. Surprise follows ; for it is most natu-

298

ral to wonder at unusual occurrences. We call such hypnotic subject a medium because the consciousness of others is brought into connection with the doings of the realm of apparent mystery, and we call the process clairvoyance, because the subconscious faculty is endowed with a sight that peers through matter as though it did not exist. But all this extraordinary power must act upon something; it requires an agency, and what water is to the billows, and air to sound, so the ether-sea is to thought and feeling. A vision of the eye travels the immense vault of heaven, seeing the remote stars in a second of time, because their waves of light wait already upon the gaze. So a glance of the eye within the mind of subconsciousness travels all distance immediately, making use of the ether-sea in some one of its many functions.

We have said that this ether washes the shore of heaven. It is needless to discuss in this volume where else its waves proceed, or what influence, worlds or peoples they connect us with, for these interesting questions are fully considered in our advanced books; they have no place in this volume. What does concern us now is the fact that there is such a thing as the subconscious faculty; also the further fact that it is called clairvoyance when developed by self half-hypnotism or by the hypnotic influence of others. All science admits these things. Neither of these propositions is in dispute. Then comes the long search into the meaning of such a power, and a thorough examination of its product to see what the fruitage of the remarkable faculty.

For a long time science let it alone; then came the spasmodic efforts to test the genuineness of the clairvoyants, and the discovery that most of them were pretenders; after which the matter lapsed, and the experiments were conducted in a manner calculated only to arouse further doubts. In late years the claim that spirits were talking through these clairvoyants led to a fixed belief in the existence of a world of disembodied souls that were waiting somewhere for something to turn up. Without a single item of proof, with the absence of all logical reasoning, these claimants have leaped the gulf between facts, and have come to the totally unwarranted conclusion that whatever cannot be explained until one knows how to explain it must be proof absolute of a spirit world. That, with the supposed abundance of evidence at hand, the vast majority of mankind and all the scientists refuse to be convinced of the existence of such a world, is sufficient to show what little progress the claim has made, and the fact that the following of that erratic creed was greatest soon after the close of the civil war, and has been on the wane since science is now learning how to explain the phenomena, is indicative of the fate of spiritualism among the intelligent classes. All crazy doctrines will find followers among the weak-minded, and brainy charlatans will lead them on for greed.

Today all science is changed in its views of the clairvoyant power. That it really exists is admitted. The universities of the world, including all the greatest as well as the more humble, not only admit the fact, but have established departments of education which include the treatment of this subject under the head of psychology; and eminent investigators in every civilized country are banded together in societies of research endeavoring to gather more facts and get more light on the meaning of the phenomena. One of the most careful of scientists recently said: "I have been associated with others for twenty years, seeking to find an explanation of the existence of the subconscious faculty, and all the gain that has been made is in the accumulating of proof. Nothing new has been added. By accumulating the proof, I mean that we have more evidence today of the existence of the faculty, simply because we have acquainted ourselves with more instances of its activity. We have confirmed into positive knowledge a former belief that this power was clairvoyant; but the remarkable keenness of it as evinced twenty or more years ago has never been surpassed by any subsequent evidence. It is a record of more cases, with no one of them rising above a certain watermark." This statement has been confirmed everywhere.

Looking at the most startling instances of this power as developed by hypnotism, or in any form of the trance condition, which is the same thing, it is impossible to find one lofty act, or one noble tendency in the whole business. Search may be made in every direction, and it will be made in vain. "What does spiritualism teach?" we asked of a score of accredited leading representatives of that creed, as we met them from time to time. "It teaches immortality." "Let us see the evidence." And they have made but two points in all their mass of testimony; the rest is unwarranted conclusion. The points are, first, that mediums (of a low order of intelligence in nineteen cases out of twenty) have revealed things that nobody else in the immediate companies had known; and, second, that the same mediums had been made to talk in the voices of the departed and tell where the departed were at the time, though in a fearfully broken, disjointed and unwilling manner. By the admission of the "priests and apostles" of spiritualism, these voices were known to somebody living to be the voices once used by the departed, or else they could not have been so identified; and the statements as to where they were as shades were contradictory and false on their face, showing that they might have been reflections and echoes of the living. Yet it is claimed that such evidence proves the fact of spirit existence, and the spirit-existence proves immortality. No grosser piece of false reasoning was ever perpetrated.

From the statements of professional manipulators of clairvoyants, and from the many times confirmed assertions of those who seek the truth honestly and for truth's sake, even those who believe in the conclusions which every free mind may freely make, no matter how erroneous, it is clear that the highest level of this use of the subconscious faculty is a very debased plane. One person, speaking frankly, says, "I am puzzled to know what the influences are that sometimes give such accurate information. I thought they indicated a spirit-life, for they utter that claim so often; but I see now that they are really reflecting the supposition of those who are about the mediums. We all think they are spirits, and the mediums catch that idea. Then we expect spirits to come and talk to us; and the mediums are looking-glasses, giving back to us the contents of the room in which we sit. Then these spirits we believe to be those of the departed, and this the mediums reflect. Much of the talk we hear from them is lost memory stored away in our own minds and forgotten. What I most wish to say is that the use of the word hell and devil predominates in the tongue of the spirits? This statement has been many times corroborated by others. There is nothing inspiring, nothing ennobling, in the uses of subconsciousness as developed through hypnotism. " This is the universal verdict.

On the other hand, or at the other extreme, there is abundant and overwhelming evidence of the potency, the loftiness, the grandeur and exaltation of the powers that are associated with the higher uses of this faculty. One is debased because its plane, atmosphere and temperament are low, and it comes not out of the uplifting of the human mind, but by deadening it. We never hear of clairvoyance as the offsprings of magnetic wakefulness; but always as the dark fruitage of hypnotic sleep. The subject ever remains in ignorance of facts that pass through his brain, except as they are told to him after he awakes. To him it is a gloomy, joyless, unsatisfactory proceeding. But magnetism brings the better personality into a full appreciation and consciousness of all that transpires, and there is reward at every turn.

Each life has some knowledge of the tendencies within itself toward these higher goals. Certainly all is not bound down to earth and the machinery of human activities. Self-experience has much to report on this subject. Apart from inward evidences, is the long summary of history in the lives of exceptionable men and women. The world calls it genius, and that name may as well remain as any other. The fact that most interests us is the leap out of the limited conditions of human life into the fellowship of some other and always better realm. The magnet is in the skies, and man's yearning for the superhuman is the response to its drawing call.

Exalted subconsciousness is established by self-magnetism.

This is the One Hundred and Nineteenth Principle. That there is such a condition as that described is well known. It is not only public history, but private and individual experience also. The only doubt to be cleared away is that which relates to its subconscious association. This we shall proceed to discuss. There is one difficulty at the outset, and that is the blending of various grades of subconsciousness in the lines of genius. What seems a contradictory condition is often met with, and, although this faculty is undoubtedly present in all cases of extraordinary ability, its uses are varied. It may be set down as an established fact that the union of magnetism with the subconscious power, is always productive of genius, not all of which is exalted. Then comes the necessity of defining that word.

It has not been credited to any great warrior that victory in battle is a goal to be admired, because its attainment costs suffering and death. So Wellington is not regarded as an exalted genius outside of English domains; nor Napoleon outside of France. Poe is regarded as a hypnotized poet, since his writings were weird and gloomy. Byron dealt with the sensual, even though he gave birth to the noblest of thoughts. It is not what the work shows, nor how much of the human is blended into the exalted that furnishes the measurement of genius; nor is morality necessarily involved at all in such consideration. Nature has no moral code. "Thou shalt not steal" is an absurdity to the creatures that are taught to get their food by theft and murder. The supposed immorality of Shakespeare is never apparent outside of its reference to the sexes; an innocent wrong in a state of dawning civilization, and never immoral until mankind agreed to call it so. Byron's enemies find no other fault with him. It is all a question of standards.

The gifts of exalted subconsciousness are pure when in the condition in which they are imparted, they become gross and untrue only when mingling with the mind of human existence. What the wicked Napoleon might have been had he used his powers of genius solely for the uplifting of mankind, we cannot tell. When at war he was a glorious victor until he fell into the cataleptic condition that caused him to ride into Waterloo asleep in his saddle. It is a scale of ascent and descent. The subconscious faculty, aroused and sustained by magnetism, makes the genius a man of wakefulness and a conqueror, and the same faculty, in the same genius, possessed by the same individual, may slide headlong down the scale into the hypnotic condition of catalepsy when the brilliance of the career has outshone itself. So Napoleon the Great was a cataleptic in the later years of his life; so the conquering Caesar and the battle-garlanded Alexander were cataleptics. Can it be true that the mighty men and women of earth sometimes fall from their pinnacles, and that the fall carries them into the extreme opposite of that in which their power was wielded? If so, it is but natural, for there are two poles to the subconscious world. If it is not true, then it seems strange that genius has so often fallen into catalepsy.

A person who has acquired mechanical magnetism may turn it about and apply it to self, after a complete absorption of the principles of advanced magnetism. The realm of the will is directly concerned in the development of this power. The goal should be to subject self to this acquired power, instead of turning it always upon others; yet it may be used freely both ways at the same period of one's life, though not at the same moment of time. The condition and inconveniences of the lapse are always present, and must be mastered by carefully allotting the duties of the day. Thus a person should set apart a particular hour and location when he will be alone, or he will carry his lapsed state into the business of life, and suffer from the imposition of others, as we have said of Webber and many men who do not come into full possession of their commonplace faculties when swayed by others of grander scope. Exaltation leads away from earth. On this very principle, every minister should live apart from the drudgery of daily existence, for each step upward carries him nearer to God, and gives him a more minute knowledge of humanity by the law of intention.

Self-magnetism is the product of magnetic temperament and mental vision.

This is the One Hundred and Twentieth Principle. We must learn the way into the realm of exaltation, and the process needs to be explained. The habits of geniuses, especially in those periods when their power was developing, are valuable aids to our present understanding of the subject. They were magnetic by reason of an excess of vitality in the nervous centers, which their habits of life turned into a positive fund from which they drew at will. All true geniuses of real power have led their fellow-beings because of a superior instinct which drew followers and commanded recognition. Mere eccentricity, that gives birth to erratic conduct, is not genius, even if some of its products may strike the popular fancy.

The habits of the great personages have been such as would favor the development of magnetism. The shortcomings so often noted are due to lack of system. Where the power has been uniformly maintained, the life has been one grand highway of success. It so happens that every great career has been centered upon some leading theme and purpose. This of itself attracts the magnetism into narrow and consequently powerful channels, unless the character is deep and broad enough to admit of wider scope. Then again all great personages have intuitively cultivated mental flights into lofty realms, and this, added to the high development of magnetism, has resulted in making themselves the subjects of their own peculiar charms.

What comes carelessly or accidentally out of habits, may be more effactually acquired by a system of development founded upon the same laws. Some persons, by chance, have secured so-called gifts, and believing them to be inherited, have lost them by abuse or failure to nurture them. Others, seeing the supreme value of such powers, have carefully studied them, and thereby given increase to their effectiveness. But, of all gratifying experiments, the most satisfactory is that class which depends upon the regularity and certainty of system. It is necessary to know the laws that are involved, and the methods of building upon them, after which the results rest solely upon the character of the use to which the faculties are put.

The plan of this realm's development may be outlined as follows: As a basis it is necessary to master the first volume, which relates to the acquisition of mechanical magnetism. On this must be built the whole system of advanced magnetism of the present volume as far as it relates to the affirmative side of the art, and the negative must be studiously avoided. All this may be accomplished as a matter of certainty. It is not a question of gift, but of work. No person need fail, unless failure is due to lack of interest. Any individual who will make the effort, and continue in it, may surely acquire mechanical magnetism. This, coming into this advanced volume, the third realm should be read and reread until it is mastered. Gradually its laws will be assimilated into one's life as regime. The same is then true of the fourth realm, and so on to the end. The particular principle which relates to the magnetic temperament is the key to this progress. Habits of daily life may be swung around, little by little, until they have influenced the whole current of magnetism, without requiring much specific exercise.

Mental vision stimulates the fancy.

This is the One Hundred and Twenty-first Principle. Here we refer to the ordinary plane of mental vision. It is not, for such reason, a commonplace acquisition, nor is it a flight of unwarranted imagination. It does take the mind away from the ordinary uses of the day, away from the mere functions and faculties of life, away from the hard abstract as well as concrete thoughts of study, up into an unaccustomed realm. In its first ascent it touches upon the well-known attribute of genius, which is popularly termed fancy. This is not its correct name, but is the only word that conveys to the mind of the general reader what is meant by the idea within its compass.

This quality is of so great a value that it should be fully understood. Remember that we are now dealing with the lowest plane of mental vision, that of the ordinary genius. It is occupied by large numbers of men and women in every generation who do not succeed in climbing higher; yet who are far happier than the vast hordes below them. Their habits of mental vision have come to them by native temperament, or else through the ambition to acquire fame in some specialty, as in art, poetry, oratory, invention or leadership. The study of the future years of earthly existence, with the possibilities of triumphant achievement, necessarily excites the mind and leads to the building of ideals out of which success is to be molded. So, by the hope of making a name, the faculties involved in the attempt are aroused from oblivious sleep, are stimulated into operation and impelled onward to the conflict.

The simplest use of mental vision is seen in the effective conversation, as in business matters where the talker hopes to make his statements clear as well as convincing. Here is the law, condensed from the principles of a previous division of this book: A person, possessing accumulated magnetism, who sees in his own mind a clearly defined picture of the thought he is uttering, will in every case irresistibly impress it upon his hearers. But, you ask, will that convince? It will make your hearers see what you see and feel what you feel. Of this there can be no doubt. And this is as far as the magnetic speakers ever seek to go. The lawyer needs no more; the minister's usefulness will increase 1000 per cent.; the actor, adding to his dramatic education, can never be second rate; and all classes of persons will find it a means of wielding great personal power wherever the voice is employed.

The earlier practice in mental vision should be confined to quotations of other authors. We will take a line at random; one from the lore of our youth. "The boy stood on the burning deck." Did you ever see a ship, or a picture of one, or read a description of a vessel, so that you can bring its shape before your mind? If not, there can be no mental vision. Never attempt to talk about anything you are not familiar with. But if your answer was in the affirmative, close your eyes, and do not open them until you can see before the mind's eyes, in the very brain, a ship. Bring to your view mentally, the width, the length, the decks, the bow, the stern, the masts, the ropes, sails, men and all. If you are subject to the disease called mind-wandering, this will cure it. Who is entirely free from mind-wandering ? Who at church listens to every word, and keeps the attention fixed upon the thoughts that are being uttered? Lack of interest, you say. That is no excuse, and it is a dangerous practice to hear a part and not the whole of anything. Mind wandering is developed in that way, and once incurred is a pathway of intellectual ruin, often ending in softening of the brain.

Mental wandering destroys mental vision.

This is the One Hundred and Twenty-second Principle. The result of this malady, for such it must be regarded, is to cut off all of the higher powers of the mind, as well as to weaken that organ for everyday use. The author has often been called upon to treat this evil for professional gentlemen, and in over two thousand cases coming under his care, he found but two persons entirely free from mind-wandering. They were exceptionally brilliant and capable men and full of the freshness of life.

Of the others (who were all unfortunate enough to have the disease) he succeeded in every instance in curing it. The result proved most satisfactory. The change in the intellectual calibre was quite marked. The cure was established solely by the exercises in mental vision. One gentleman could not, on shutting his eyes, perceive anything at all. Instead of keeping him on one exercise too long, he was carried from exercise to exercise repeatedly and for many weeks. At last, he began to see mentally the dim outlines of a ship.

"I have it!" he exclaimed. The outlines deepened and finally stood out in bold relief. Moral, never give up the ship. Unsuccessful people try a thing a few times, do not succeed and throw it up in disgust. Unsuccessful people are full of disgust for everything, and for everybody. The fault is due to their impatience and their incredulity; unless, perhaps, their laziness is also in the case.

Continue the exercise by closing the eyes, and again calling up the ship before you. What kind of a ship do you see? What color? Where is the boy? Do you see his face? What expression do you see upon the face? What part of the ship is on fire ? Do you see the curling smoke, the red and yellow flames? Are they near the boy? Is it night or day?

MYSTIC UTOPIAN SUPERMEN

Open the eyes and see in the air before you, mentally, every detail as above called for, as you repeat the line orally: "The boy stood on the burning deck."

Mental vision must bring the mind to a focus.

This is the One Hundred and Twenty-third Principle. It may be called the positive side of the preceding law, but it means much more, as may be seen by examining its process. To prevent a wandering of the mind, its whole attention should be devoted to one subject at a time, even with all its branches and variations, and the thought should revert at every step to the main thread by which it is held to its purpose. This is all in the estate of commonplace life.

On the other hand the exercise of the faculty under this principle implies, first, that it has magnetism, which is not involved in the prior law; second, that the mental flight is away from the range of ordinary thought; third, that it does not wander or indulge in imaginings; and, fourth, that it concentrates its full power upon the pith and very essence of the idea which it affects. The ability to bring the subconscious mind to a focus should not be confounded with the pernicious habit of thinking upon one thing to the exclusion of other matters. This distinction is an important one and must be clearly understood. There is quite a difference between looking at one spot until all else is obscured, and the one line of gaze has wearied the eye. In a similar way it is not by any means the same thing to cast the mind upon one idea and hold it there as it is to concentrate many other ideas together toward a given focus. In one case the mind is injured by its useless exertion; in the other its vision is immensely improved by the great variety of lines which are knitted together in one central rope of influence.

Many theories and exercises have been invented by teachers of this subject, and some have founded whole systems of training on the one principle which is now under discussion. We had seen the law worked out in many ways long before we made use of it. One of the most common of methods is to throw the mind on any given subject to the exclusion of all ideas else, and wait for further development; but magnetism is not invoked and the result is commonplace. Thus, an artist is taught to create imagination by this process; to think of any theme that he wishes to develop, and keep his mind upon that one theme an hour at a time in the deepest concentration. If he is to produce an ocean, he will see the water, the green, the blue, the waves, the crests, the billows, and all else, until his mind at last holds still to one selected view. This is not the art of making a focus.

In order to turn the theme just mentioned into a powerful flight of fancy under the skill of mental vision, it would first be necessary to possess a large fund of magnetism, so that the temperament of the genius would be established; then the direction of the mind upon a single subject, even with the commendable variations mentioned, should not be favored, for there is much more to be attained by making a focus. The ocean scene is very properly the central idea of this theme, but much else should be gathered around it and thrown upon it, like influences standing near ready to be called into service. The waves of the ocean do not originate in its own nature, but obey the power of the wind that plays on its surface. This wind is gentle, soft, insinuating, steady, rough, wild, powerful, or mighty, as the elements may determine, and the waves change their character to suit the atmospheric condition. Then the clouds are always in harmony with wind and wave.

305

MYSTIC UTOPIAN SUPERMEN

The black ruinous mass accompanies the rolling vapor of the thunderstorm, before whose wide path a dead calm lies on air and wave, but under whose angry mountain the tearing wind upheaves the piling billows which are again assuaged by the torrential flood. Here are ideas that stand about to wait upon the ocean scene.

But there are more to be considered, before all may be brought together upon the central theme. The colors of the ocean are due in part to the water, but very largely to the air, the clouds and the sky. There are reflections from rocks, shores, islands, ships and everything around as well as above the surface of the deep. The blue sky, clear and open, imparts that rich and fresh coloring that is most entrancing to the eye. The fleecy argosies, like sail-spread boats, are mirrored in calmer surfaces below. The snowy cliffs of heaven, the long veils of leaden gray, the lace-like haze, the hurrying islands, these and more are influences that effect the ocean's hue, its character and its waves. Then the birds that wing their flight across the sky or skim the crests below, the craft that may here and there dot the horizon edge, the floating weeds or wreckage, and the limits that hem in the scene on every hand must be given their affecting rank in the interest of the picture. But the stars at night must not be forgotten, nor the influence of the sun at high noon. The rising orb at morn overspreads the horizon with colors peculiar to its period, and these involve the water and the clouds in far reaching floods of light. The sunsets of art are as numerous as the Oriental alphabet. The moon in all its phases commands the central position in many an ocean scene, and cannot be accidentally placed.

Thus we may see the radii of the picture, and all the influences that bear upon its full garniture. Let each part be held in sway and made to strengthen the central theme; let these outer parts be multiplied and intensified as they are drawn toward the focus, and you have an idea of the importance of our principle. On the contrary, if the mind be wandering or indulging in its imaginations, there is no possibility of attaining the power of self-magnetism, which is the product of the temperament of which we have spoken and mental vision; and, until self-magnetism be acquired, there can be no hope of reaching the realm of exalted subconsciousness. These are distinct propositions. They are laws of exact value, and must be strictly observed. Looking over the steps that lead to this result, we see that each one is possible in every earnest life, and the summary should not contain a single element of failure.

Mental vision is a creative function.

This is the One Hundred and Twenty-fourth Principle. The plan stated herein was reported to us from a well-known poet, through the kindness of an intermediate. What is true of poetry in this regard is true of oratory, art, invention and all other uses of the higher faculties of the mind. Before making the experiment, recall the music of some river you have heard flowing; the rhythm, the murmur, the ripple, the dash, will all live again. Then repeat aloud the following lines:

"Oh, a wonderful stream is the river time, As it runs through the realm of tears, With a faultless rhythm and musical rhyme, And a boundless sweep and a surge sublime, As it blends with the Ocean of Years."

Close the eyes, and repeat the first line silently. Call up before your mind the stream, a river, a long river, just like some river you have seen or heard about. Have you ever been upon the banks of a river, or on its bosom? Recall the same stream. Was it in the summer? At twilight, or in the morning? Who was with you? Was the occasion pleasant? Where did this river have it source? Where do all rivers originate? Can you see the mountains or hills, the upland scenery where a small stream babbles among the rocks, and can you follow it down through the country it must pass through ere it reaches you? It skirts little towns and villages, divides farms, runs mills, and bears the one sad story of life at every turn it makes.

Time is compared to a river. The mental vision carries us far back beyond the record, even of geological data, and we see the on-flowing stream, until it has reached us.

The second line of the verse is capable of great enlargement. The pupil must now begin to create. Earthly life is a vale of tears. The river time did not originate in this life. It was flowing on long before, and on its course passes through the vale of tears. Thought flashes in an instant over a thousand scenes of life. A dying man may recall in a few seconds the wickedness of a life time. So we can now think of every great sorrow we have witnessed. One scene will, perhaps, stand out above all others. The habit of mental vision, once formed, will always enable us to see everything in the boldest relief; and the strongest pictures occupy but the fractional part of a second.

Let the pupil fill out the mind pictures for the rest of the verse. All the five senses come in for a share of the creative ability of the brain; as, for instance, the perception of sound may be made very acute in recalling beautiful songs, or the voices of loved ones, long since counted among the memories of the past; we can taste the delicacy; we can feel the blow, the pain, the wound, the touch, the kiss, once more; we can inhale the fragrance of the rose; or the balmy air of some spring day just freshening into blossoming May or the evening odors wafted to us by some gentle summer zephyrs, as we walked in hope when love breathed its first sign into confessing words; all these and thousands more of experiences of the past can be summoned into the active present, by the aid of mental vision.

The acquirement of the art is rather slow, but when the wedge is once entered the hardest part of the battle is over. You will soon find your mind making creations of its own. Whether these are used for poetry, for composition, for oratory, for the dramatic profession, for painting, for drawing, for sculpture, for invention, or for any of the sublimer ambitions of life, is not material. The process interests us because it is a step toward the great exaltation which the highest mind alone can reach; highest, not in the sense of hook lore, but in that better quality of forceful energy.

Mental vision, by practice, may be made a natural attribute of the brain.

This is the One Hundred and Twenty-fifth Principle. The extent of the power acquired seems to be without limit, and many very emphatic cases have come to our notice from the reports of our pupils, or those who have carefully studied and pursued these lessons. So important is the success in many an instance that it has been the cause of completely revolutionizing the life of the student. The examples herewith given are the same that we have used for fifteen years or longer, and they will be recognized by those who have formerly employed them.

The emphatic ideas generally should receive the mental vision. " Winter/' Close the eyes and recall all the past winters of your life. Which one was the pleasantest? Which the saddest? What occurred in each? Where were you at the time? Do you now see the people who were with you then? the house? the town or country site? Do they come back as vividly as they were once real? "Snow." Enlarge this. See before you some great drifts; see the long expanse of fields, all white. "Summers." Can you with the mind's eyes recall the verdure everywhere, the blossoms opening into flowers, the outdoor

life, the old times, and one, perhaps, happier or sadder than any other. In a flash all these should be present. "Sheaf." The harvest; the fall of fruit, flower and grain. Enlarge this, and put the results on paper, then call them up as mental pictures. "Glides. " You can see very easily the gliding movement of a river; the overhanging banks and cliffs, and trees' that mirror their shapes on the glassy surface; here you glide into the shadow, and out again into the sunlight. Do you see this or any part of it? Do not practice one exercise too long.

"Friends, Romans, countrymen." Close the eyes. What do you see? Where are you? Marc Anthony is addressing the Roman populace, upon the conclusion of Brutus' speech. The impression made by his predecessor is unfavorable to Anthony, and the latter must overcome it. There are the faces of enemies hedged about the scene, their distrust of the speaker and their hatred of the dead Caesar being everywhere disclosed. What are these faces? Of what caste, age, and order of intelligence are the people? What are their costumes as to material, style, shape, richness or poverty, cleanliness or dirt, and how are they worn, handled and managed by the populace? "I thrice presented him with a kingly crown, which he did thrice refuse."

Imagine yourself standing before the Roman populace. Have the mob well pictured in your mind, their various heights, sizes, facial expressions, and attitudes; see all these details in the air before you and around you; then shut the eyes, keeping the mob still imprinted upon the mind and call up a scene within a scene,—a vision within a vision,— the event of a previous day when the crown was offered to Caesar and he refused it. Picture the occasion as well as you can, allowing the imagination to take such flights, as it will in supplying the details. Do not have the "presentation scene" too empty. See the building, or place, its surroundings, its furniture, its people; behold Caesar's face; call before you the crown, what it looked like, and so continue through the entire process of mental vision.

Having given examples for this practice, and having partially supplied the visionary scenes for the pupil, we now ask the pupil to create his own scenes, supplying all the details himself. The examples below are divided into four classes:—

1. Things.
2. Qualities.
3. Nature.
4. Supernatural.

Each pupil should write out, after each attempt at mental vision, what he saw; and keep adding any new details with each attempt until he has filled the scene. Do not sit down and compose, but shut the eyes and imagine, then write the sights seen. It may require months to even "start" the process of mental vision; but when once started, it grows very rapidly. Each one of the following examples should be practiced upon for a long time, and when you think you have a perfect scene, send it to us for examination. Persons with genius will possess this gift at the start. Practice slowly, deliberately, wait for the vision to come, and focus all surrounding details upon the main theme. Great men and women always think in the form of pictures.

Intense mental vision develops great clearness of perception.

This is the One Hundred and Twenty-sixth Principle. While the law stated may seem to depend upon a higher degree of the same power already set forth, it really opens up a new phase of the whole matter. The statements we are about to make are founded upon reports made to us by our students, and are so strong as to possess the flavor of exaggeration. One of our advisers, a gentleman who looks only to the business side of this great study, counselled us as follows: "What you have written is true; you knew it to be true; I do, also, in cases sufficient in number and authenticity to convince any reasonable person; and there are proofs in abundance to sustain the claims made in these reports; but what of the general public? In order to convince them you must produce your proofs, and these would involve you in a breach of trust toward the men and women who have sent you the reports in good faith under the promise that their names should never be divulged. On the whole, it is the part of wisdom to lay down the principle and expunge the facts which are embodied in the accounts of the students who have used that principle. My only reason for giving this advice is to save your page from being doubted by those of the public who are ignorant of the workings of the principle." We have presented one side of the case; the summary of which is to the effect that the time is not yet ripe for the world to accept the truth in this matter.

The other side of the case is very brief and simple.

The statements made are true. If they are to be doubted by the public, it must be a very limited portion of the public, for no person who does not possess this hook in his own name has a right to know what it contains, and every person who does so possess the hook may easily verify the assertions by proving them in his own life. The great number who have proved the principle in the past have furnished us with reports sufficient in bulk to make a large book. The import of one and all is this: intense mental vision develops great clearness of perception. This is clairvoyance, it may be claimed; if so, it is easily disposed of, but it is certainly a higher grade of the power than is derivable from hypnotic conditions, and is free from the baneful influences of that practice.

Some of the more important accounts may be drawn from in this connection. The abundance of minor experiences cannot be ignored; but it is gratifying to know that substantial rewards have come to those who have worked to secure great results. In one case, now an old one to us, a former student of this system, who has risen high in his profession of artists, has, through the aid of mental vision been able to conceive the true costumes and faces of the ancients; he discovered this fact after painting several important pictures solely from imagination, and then receiving proofs of their correctness, which he had not at hand at the time the work was done. His friends, not being satisfied with his claims, tested him by giving partial descriptions of scenes which he reproduced with such perfection as to excite charges of collusion.

Another pupil, a lady of twenty, whose ancestors came from another country, and whose paternal grandmother was buried in a graveyard near a German farm, had occasion for the first time in her life to visit the place. She had never even been in the country. Arriving at the graveyard she found her grandmother's grave at once, and exclaimed: "The white fence is down." This fence had been there at the time of the funeral thirty years before, and had lasted but eleven years. To some of the old residents this lady described her grandmother's home, with the garden, farm, orchard and vineyard as they used to be, although great changes had been made since her death, of which the granddaughter could have had no knowledge. More of these incidents will be presented in other forms in these pages. New principles are associated with the present law. Its importance is so great as to demand the best attention. The conditions of clairvoyance are absent, while the results are better obtained.

Sincerity of belief is necessarily the basis of all self magnetism.

This is the One Hundred and Twenty-seventh Principle. While this law seems somewhat like another, it is founded upon an opposite purpose and runs on under opposite conditions. When one seeks to control an hypnotic subject, it is necessary to convince the latter of the ability to do so. He looks into the eyes of the operator and there reads the fact. While a thorough belief is a help to the operator in acquiring the force of will needed in the effort, the real value of it is in its effect upon the subject.

The contrary is true in the case of self-magnetism. In the first place the sincerity of belief serves to marshal all the energies and vitalities into one column of strength and determined purpose. This increases the magnetism; and, being founded on magnetism, doubles on itself and grows continually, making the combination the most powerful thing in all human life. But there is another reason why it is important; it selects a goal and goes toward it with irresistible purpose; thus not only serving to increase the magnetism but to make its action the greater. It is like a storage battery of electricity in which an already large fund has been greatly increased, and to which machinery has been connected capable of executing more effective work. Some exceedingly important victories in this art have been achieved by this use of the personal powers.

Here magnetism almost reaches its height. There would seem to be no loftier planes, but one yet remains to be considered at the end of this series of principles; the last and the grandest. Next to that is the power that comes from the union of the energy, after its acquisition, with the thorough sincerity of belief in one's ability to use it at will. Such sincerity may be cultivated, and falls back upon all the principles started since the second estate of this book, as a basis for its development. It makes no difference how it is acquired; but it must be associated of necessity with the practice, the regime and the temperament of magnetism. The most helpful of the specific aids to its growth, are the laws that relate to the will and those that relate to mental vision. The former will invariably build magnetism; the latter gives it clearness of brain and accuracy of judgment. These, then, are of leading value.

The ganglia are separate cells of energy capable of union at will.

This is the One Hundred and Twenty-eighth Principle. We have, in the first volume of this study, referred to the fact that there are ganglia everywhere connected with the nervous system, as a part of it; their purpose being to collect and to hold the electricity or life-principle ready for use. Each ganglion is a nerve cell of gray matter, the most powerful substance of the entire body. At each side or end there is a fibril, which is composed of protoplasm and terminates in finer branches.

These ganglia hold the nerve life of the being, and are found throughout the system, but principally in the brain, when mass is considered. They seem to be numberless. The great fact connected with them is their separate existence, each being disconnected from the other. According to the histological scheme of Gerlach, the mass of the substance of the brain is a meshwork of cells and fibrils; and science asked the question: How is it then possible that various sets of cells are shut off from one another, then connected in part with others, and so arranged in countless millions of probable combinations? Attempts of every kind were made to meet this problem, and it was not till 1889 that the solution was found. A short time before this the Italian histologist, Dr. Camille Golgi, had discovered a method of impregnating hardened brain tissues with a solution of nitrate of silver, with the result of staining the nerve cells and their processes better than was possible by the method of Gerlach, or by any of the methods that others had introduced. Now for the first time it became possible to trace the cellular prolongations definitely, for the finer fibrils had not been rendered visible by any previous method of treatment. Golgi himself proved that the set of fibrils known as protoplasmic prolongations terminate by free extremities, and have no direct connection with any cell save the one from which they spring. He showed also that the axis cylinders give off multitudes of lateral branches not hitherto suspected.

The discovery did not go far enough, however. It remained for another scientist, Dr. S. Ramon y Cajal, to follow up the investigation by means of an improved application of Golgi's method of staining, and to demonstrate that the axis cylinders, together with all their collateral branches, though sometimes extending to a great distance, yet finally terminate, like the other cell prolongations, in fibrils having free extremities. In a word, it was shown that each central nerve cell, with its fibrillar offshoots, is separate. Instead of being in physical connection with a multitude of other nerve cells, it has no direct physical connection with any other nerve cell whatever.

This was of more than ordinary importance, and when Dr. Cajal announced his discovery, in 1889, his revolutionary claims amazed the mass of histologists. There were some few of them, however, who were not quite prepared for the revelation; in particular His, who had half suspected the independence of the cells, because they seemed to develop from dissociated centers; and Forel, who based a similar suspicion on the fact that he had never been able actually to trace a fibre from one cell to another. These observers then came readily to repeat Cajal's experiments. So also did the veteran histologist Kolliker, and soon afterward all the leaders everywhere. The result was a practically unanimous confirmation of the claims, and within a few months after his announcements the old theory of union of nerve cells into an endless meshwork was completely discarded, and the theory of isolated nerve elements—the theory of neurons, as it came to be called—was fully established in its place.

The discovery served to make clear what was previously unexplainable. In modified view, the nerve cell retains its old position as the storehouse of nervous energy. Each of the lines extending from the cell is held, as before, to be a transmitter of impulses, but a transmitter that acts when controlled. The fibril operates by contact and not by continuity. Under proper stimulation the ends of the fibrils reach out, come in contact with other end fibrils of other cells, and conduct their destined impulse. Again they retract, and communication ceases for the time between those particular cells. Meantime, by a different arrangement of the various conductors, different associations of nervous impulses induced, different sets of cells are placed in communication, different trains of thought engendered. Each fibril when retracted becomes a nonconductor, but when extended and in contact with another fibril, or with the body of another cell, it conducts its message as readily as a continuous filament could do—precisely as in the case of an electric wire.

The method of operation is fully sustained by every kind of experiment; and answers the question as to how ideas are isolated, and also, as Dr. Cajol points out, throws new light on many other mental processes. One can imagine, for example, by keeping in mind the flexible nerve prolongations, how new trains of thought may be engendered through novel associations of cells; how facility of thought or of action in certain directions is acquired through the habitual making of certain nerve-cell connections; how certain bits of knowledge may escape our memory, and refuse to be found for a time, because of a temporary incapacity of the nerve cells to make the proper connections; and so on indefinitely.

There is another importance attached to the discovery. If these ganglia are scattered throughout the body, as they in fact are, it is at once seen how the nerve-force or magnetic-vitality may be collected and preserved, to be used at will, or to be wasted when the impulses are not controlled. The whole secret seems to be locked up in this power of the cells to separate or to unite as they may be controlled. All the power, the life, the energy of the body can be traced to these ganglia. The mysteries of thought, and even the inner clearness of the subconscious faculty are held in these little disconnected cells. An ordinary idea makes use of but few, while the vast numbers lie idle. A change of thought causes a few others to unite, while the hordes are yet unemployed. Magnetism calls more than a few into union; it needs more to propel its thought. Self-magnetism uses still more, for the power now is mighty; and the greater the nervous energy or magnetism becomes, the more of these cells are called into service. This is necessarily true. It is an axiom almost. What if the entire mass, or a majority at least should at one impulse be made to serve the will? The greater includes the less. Nothing would be lost and much gained.

Facts are inspired by the use of the subconscious faculty.

This is the One Hundred and Twenty-ninth Principle. It must not be misunderstood. The facts that come to a gifted speaker are generally those of a stored memory; things supposed to have been long ago forgotten, but now called forth in their exactness of truth. This rule has been tested in many ways. The cause of the exercise of such power may probably be found in the principle previously stated. The little ganglia or nerve-cells that abound in countless numbers through the brain as well as elsewhere, produce thought by their methods of uniting and combining with each other. It would naturally follow that the more of them that are employed in every thought impulse the more powerful the impulse must become.

This is not all. There are facts surrounding all minds. The world is full of facts. They abound in the universe. Their influences are as numerous as the sands of the sea. Few persons are able to appreciate the force of this law, until they come to the startling keenness of mind that the genuine clairvoyant exhibits. Professors of the leading universities of England and America join voices in the exclamatory questions. What does this mean? How did this person obtain the information? Traveling over land and sea, in and out of buildings, in and out of closets, of minds, of books, papers, letters, this power of true clairvoyance goes and comes, extracting facts and revealing them to the amazement of all, without committing a single error.

Before the volume closes we shall show that what is possible to the hypnotized or cataleptic subject, is equally and even better possible to the self-magnetized individual. We see no way of attacking the law. It is everywhere acknowledged that clairvoyance can touch facts, no matter where they are, no matter how remote in time or place, no matter how intricate or how difficult of abstraction; this must be accepted as the impregnable truth, for it is always maintained by tests and always believed. Then it is equally certain that there are as many facts in the world surrounding the normal life, as there are surrounding the clairvoyant.

Better than all is the fact that self-magnetism, employing the exalted power of subconsciousness, is able to touch more information, to see it more clearly and to draw it forth into the world of uses in greater strength, than all the combined powers of clairvoyance. Given a due amount of magnetism, as well as a magnetic temperament with strong mental vision, and facts can be unfolded in surprising clearness. This should be so, and is so. We remember some years ago supplying a piece of missing information that was not discoverable by any method of research or study. The question was then raised as to the correctness of the information, as there was no way at the time of ascertaining. After a lapse of time, the accuracy was confirmed so that all doubt was removed; then came the inquiry as to how we got possession of the facts when they were not obtainable at the time.

This kind of proof has been often secured not only by us but by our pupils. It is a very common occurrence with some. Says a teacher in one of the leading schools of the North, "I come to possess facts, the truth of which I cannot prove for a long time after securing them. I hesitate to make open use of them, as I am in doubt as to their honesty. Sooner or later I learn of their truth. This is the strangest of strange things." Poets are necessarily gifted with mental vision, and they often see existing facts in the universe that no man has yet called forth. Tennyson was peculiarly gifted with this power. Shakespeare went everywhere with his subconscious mind; and there is no other way of accounting for his remarkable genius. He died several years before the circulation of the blood was discovered, yet described it in his writings. Swedenborg wrote scientific matter, deep, broad and voluminous; scientists of his day were compelled reluctantly to admit the accuracy of all his statements while knowing that he had no means of access to the information he divulged.

Were it not for the truth of the principle, that facts are inspired by the use of the subconscious faculty, there would never be a discovery in science, never an invention, never a step in the progress of civilization. Feeling for facts, reaching out after them, studying hard to unearth them, will not bring them to light. They come, when they come at all, with startling suddenness, like a bolt out of a clear sky, like a shaft of light into the shadows of the groping brain. The Wizard Edison has a completely endowed subconscious mind, whose theme is electricity, and the facts which his mind has drawn out of the vast deep into his possession are revolutionizing the nations of the nineteenth and twentieth centuries.

Intuition is a subconscious knowledge of facts.

This is the One Hundred and Thirtieth Principle. This is a peculiar commonplace power that is possessed by nearly all persons at times, though not clearly enough to give them any remarkable prestige. It shows that the mind occasionally touches all its realms, even though it does not make a prolonged stay in the better of them, unless invited by culture. Popularly described, intuition is the feeling that a thing is true, without any evidence of the fact obtained from the usual sources. Once let a person understand the nature of this power, and ignorance will construe every impression into such knowledge.

Most presentiments and impressions are not intuition. If they are founded upon the least fact as an instigation, they are then merely deductions, conclusions or estimates, and are right or wrong as the mind may be of good or bad quality in its judgment, or the guess may hit or miss. When the habit of inference has grown on a person it becomes morbid in proportion as the brain is shallow. This is seen in such moods as those of jealousy, envy and revenge; in which all reason is dethroned and nothing of value is substituted. This depletes the mind by soon exhausting its vitality at any given place. It is well known that to weary any one point of the brain is equal to destroying its whole action for the time being. Size has very little to do with the quantity of vitality involved. In the center of the medulla oblongata is a little dot, too small to seem of any use; yet if it be touched with the point of a needle the heart will stop beating and death ensue in the instant. So the exhaustion of a single line of thought in the brain, will lead to the temporary collapse of the whole organ. This is supposed to be a step in the art of hypnotizing a person. The evil moods of which we have spoken are capable of holding the thought a long time, with the consequences mentioned.

Intuition is quite the opposite of this process. It comes without preparatory thinking, and generally when the mind is most receptive by being most inactive. It is one of the most valuable aids to a human being, and, in lesser life is really necessary to save the too vulnerable animals from being overwhelmed and exterminated. Many a man has owed his life's preservation to the callings and warnings of this little power. Sometimes it speaks with the distinctness of certainty, and always brightly; never on the dark side; never terrorizing by alarms and appalling apparitions. That the habit may be cultivated is well known, and by the same process that is used in stimulating the visions of dreams. It seems to keep pace with the development of exalted magnetism.

Subconscious visions in dreams are stimulated by intensifying them.

This is the One Hundred and Thirty-first Principle. A dream is a waking process. It occurs under excitement due to external causes that appeal to the senses, or to internal causes that are aroused by a current of magnetism passing along a series of ganglionic cells and stimulating them to action. Reference has been made to the histology of these cells, and their methods of disconnecting for rest, and uniting to produce given ideas; which may be found a few pages back. The inward flow of an inciting current is sufficient to produce the dream; first always leading up to wakefulness, although many persons relapse again into profound slumber. It is in the moment of getting awake that the dream occurs.

When the nervous system is in the realm of confusion, the dream is always hypnotic, and may or may not be startling or terrifying. When the nervous system is in the realm of peace, the dream never fails to be refreshing, happy, inspiring and exalted. Few and rare are the cases where such dreams occur unless the faculties of life have been brought into their full magnetic power. Some of the hypnotic dreams are true because they possess the clairvoyant faculty found in the lower stratum of subconsciousness. On the other hand many of the exalted dreams are incapable of being verified, as they reach realms that are superhuman; but not one has ever been found untrue, and some have shown the pathway of success with unerring accuracy.

The process is simple and the explanation is easily understood. There are facts all about us and beyond us. This proposition cannot be disputed. Of these facts some are close at hand and probable; others are greater than human life. This earth with its opportunities, is not all there is of the universe. Man is not master of creation. There is something to be known that he has not yet found out. Facts are things. They are everywhere. A faculty that is clear in its perception is able to see what cannot be viewed by the use of the ordinary human senses. Mankind is something of earth, more of the human, and something of the superhuman. Occultism, or any other ism, is not needed to construe the process whereby the mind within is able to catch facts not obtainable by the ordinary faculties.

The visions of dreams are intensified by repeating their details in the mind, creating more surroundings, producing the focus through the aid of mental vision and throwing all the energy of magnetism upon them. The brain-cells are given a double use; each takes its share in the production of conscious and subconscious ideas; or else the same cells in one combination make the ordinary mind, and in other combinations, the extraordinary. Which ever may be true is not material. The fact we seek to impress is that the same idea is given a greater impulse and vitality by being supported on a larger number of brain cells. This is what may be accomplished by the process just stated. It is wrong to allow the incidents of an exalted dream to become lost. Lazy habits drive away this blessed influence. Activity, quick and alert to every detail, secures the valuable theme and preserves it for future reference. The more frequently it is repeated, the more intense becomes the power of that faculty which first produced it. Here is the secret of the growth of subconscious visions in dreams.

Inspirations are intensified by recording them.

This is the One Hundred and Thirty-second Principle. The record must be made at the time of the inspiration. We do not use this word intending to take it into that higher realm of influence where divinity has exclusive sovereignty. There is every grade and kind of inspiration. The word by common consent, is made to apply to whatever action of the mind the user chooses to describe. The scale of power runs a gamut from the least energy to the greatest; and there is every opportunity for taking advantage of any part of it one chooses. Inspirations, whether in dreams or in waking hours, are evidences of power of the highest order.

MYSTIC UTOPIAN SUPERMEN

One individual progresses, another falls back into the rear of the masses; because one takes advantage of the opportunities of advancement, while the other gives them no heed. For instance, it is known that many an inspiration has knocked at the door of life and been shut out. A man falls asleep and dreams; he awakes, remembers the dream and goes to sleep again. In the morning he does not seek to recall the details; at noon they are vague; at night again he has no idea of what his dream consisted of,—it is lost. Another man dreams, he awakes, remembers it, falls asleep and in the morning on arising he writes down the details as he dreamed them. At night again he looks at the details; he lies down to sleep, thinking of the dream of the night before. That dream came to him in sleep; thinking of its details excites the sleeping functions of the brain, and brings on sleep. This is a parallel base only. The brain standing as the soul's interpreter, has a variety of functions. Away, in some remote corner of its life, is the crevice that lets in the light from another world. A gleam trembles on the edge, and we shut it out; it appears less distinctly, and is gone. Yet, after years of absence, it is time to shine again. If we had not shut it out, or if, when it comes again, we encourage it the presence grows.

Every life has its awakening, its thrill, its yearning, its song of hope, its dawn of genius. They come when we are least prepared to receive them, always unexpectedly; and they linger with us but a brief time. Like the brilliant flights of poesy they are inspired. Genius long ago learned how to save the fruit of these great moments— for they are the greatest moments of life—by instantly recording the thought which the creative function of the brain had inspired. Few persons care to put themselves to the trouble of finding paper and pencil and writing down an idea, at inconvenient times. They think it will last until some more opportune moment; but that department of the brain which opened to give vent to the effusion, closes tightly, and few persons can recall, even an hour later, any line of the beautiful jewel. It goes away offended, and when it so departs it leaves forever.

Many a grand idea has come to a person in a dream. Genius would arise at the first waking moment and record the facts. Mediocrity would wait until after breakfast in the morning and often hunt in vain around the alcoves of the brain for the idea. Many an orator, or a candidate for the title, while walking along the street alone or in company, finds an idea of great value running in his mind. In ten minutes it will be gone. It can never be recalled in just the shape in which it came to him. The great poets and many of the greatest orators have seized this opportunity to save this gem of thought. The principle involved is this: The brain was exercising its creative function at the time; and this function may be stimulated by preserving the thought, and afterward referring to it.

The reason why a subsequent reference to the thought will stimulate this valuable condition of the brain, is because the thinking powers are concentrated upon that part of the brain which produces or creates these thoughts. On the same principle, if any word, feeling or impulse of an inspired nature, should occur, it must be fixed at once; and any after reference to it is called recurrence, and excites it very much in the same way as the functions of the brain are excited. Added to this habit must be a magnetic temperament and the full development of mental vision. Experiments have been made in these uses for many years. The principle is everywhere proved not only true but easily possible to one who sets the goal as it is demanded under the laws in the estate of the will. Aim high and reach the mark. No training in which self is master and pupil can exceed this in rich fruitage.

Inspirations will carry the ready mind to unlimited heights.

This is the One Hundred and Thirty-third Principle. These visitations are the natural outgrowth of the mental powers heretofore described. All persons have at times hoped to catch a glimpse of the borderland of the hereafter. What this glimpse is cannot be told to one who has never known its character. To a deaf man you cannot explain the exquisite deliciousness of sweet music; to the blind there is no avenue of joy in flowers. Yet sometimes in soul-dreams the waking heart pulsates to the harmony of life, and the inner sense is startled, though not awakened; and in its filmy foresight catches the spirit of the better man.

Inspiration is an attribute of subconsciousness; it is to soul-life what color is to light, or contour to grace, or weight to gold; its relationship is present, but hard to appreciate, if not experienced. Yet, although the relationship is difficult to define, the real nature of inspiration in and of itself is easily understood. It knocks at the heart of every human being some time during life. Great occasions fire the heart, and lo! the world is made richer by newborn patriotism, love of country, true eloquence, grandeur of thought, of word and of deed. In the quiet thrill of still moments, when the man that lives within the man seeks recognition, there comes the poet's lofty genius, the artist's dream of beauty, the author's inspired utterance.

These are the soul's better life, and they lift the curtain that veils eternity; not high enough to show the realm beyond, but sufficiently to reveal the trailing light that burns along the horizon's edge. In these supreme moments of life there are degrees of intensity; and inspiration is likewise graded, depending upon the person, and the circumstances. All greatness is inspired; all genius is inspired; yet they consist originally of tendencies. These tendencies may be neglected or encouraged; and, from an unremitting observation of over forty years, we are convinced that they may be created in every human being. In other words the opportunity of being great is open to all. It all hinges upon what a man does with his fundamental endowments.

Inspiration comes like a bird, and is wary. It must be coaxed and encouraged. Inactivity repels it. The habit of constant application is the first essential. Idle moments, idle conversation destroy it. The successful men and women all are full of busy activities; have on hand as much, and almost more than can be attended to.

Inspired thoughts and deeds occur every day, among the lowly as well as among the powerful. In every age they have had their office, their usefulness and their fate. Inspiration makes a man better than his fellow beings. Born for a destiny, cleaving to one main purpose through life, he becomes great. Opening the listening ear of the soul till it drinks in the purpose of divine life, man becomes a saint. Writing from the tablets of revealed knowledge, he becomes an agent of the Deity. Rising higher yet, and above the plane of the human, he is Christ. Every being in every age, and of every race and condition, who speaks one word for the good of his fellow man, who utters one sublime truth, who acts one noble deed, is to that extent inspired; and, it matters not how a doctrine, or a religion came about, whether by accident or design, whether by the invention of man or the will of the Creator, by the artifice of priests or the command of God; it stands for what it is, and in so far as it draws humanity Heavenward it is glorious and inspired.

Epigrams, felicitations, and all rare thoughts are gifts of exaltation.

This is the One Hundred and Thirty-fourth Principle. The meaning of the law stated is well understood by every person who has had occasion to tit himself for the highest usefulness in this life. Here is a man engaged in conversation; he suddenly stops, takes out a paper and writes. If one dares to ask him what it is that he has written, he may learn the fact that an idea of value, an apt phrase, a peculiarly impressive thought, or some happy fancy has come to his mind, and he wishes to secure it at the earliest possible moment.

Why is he not willing to wait till some more opportune time? For two reasons; first, he knows that even the most retentive memory will fail to recall it a few moments later; second, the catching of the inspiration, for such it is, and the future reference to it, will stimulate the very faculty that produced it, and lead to greater growth hereafter. This is why Tennyson would arise from a party, excuse himself, and reappear a few minutes later; this is why Longfellow, Tennyson, Bryant and nearly all great poets have got up out of bed at night, written down certain lines, and gone back to bed. Pope saved his ideas by the use of his cuffs, a collar, or a scrap of paper; anything he could get at to write upon, if there was no sheet of paper at hand. The habit is one of common occurrence among geniuses in every department of life. The most successful of American playwrights confesses to have "saved" his sudden ideas for years in advance of each play, by instantly noting down the exact phraseology of each thought. "It was not the idea in the words, but the precise arrangement of the words that I found valuable." This is the secret. Looking at the writings of Shakespeare, you will find that all his ideas may be reproduced in different phraseology, but that their charm and power are lost. Nowhere in all his works is it possible to substitute one word for another and yet preserve the effect. Each word seems to fit in its place like the stones in Solomon's temple. The speed with which he must have written precludes the use of deliberation. His inspiration walked with him.

Epigrams are the best products of the mind. They are not met with every day. Speakers, knowing their value, attempt to create them out of the reasoning faculties, but they do not come in that way. Their advent is spontaneous. The machine-made epigram is artificial, it seeks to shock the mind by an absurd contradiction of ideas, like the phrase, "His youth increases with his age," or "I believe it because it is impossible." In one case the statement is not true, even if it intends to say that exuberance grows as the years advance. In the other case, the phrase is silly, yet has been passed around as an effective remark. Some of the contradictory epigrams are good, although they are never inspirations. We state a few by way of illustration, so that the mind may not be led into considering their culture as valuable. "He was so dishonest that he could deceive nobody," is true or may be true, if the person referred to is well known. "Failure is a stepping stone to success," is a very good homily, for it tells us that the right kind of man will take lesson by failure and, avoiding its mistake, approach success. "The more a man has the more he wants," and "The more we know the more there is to know," serve their purpose as compressed statements of philosophy. They pass for the machine-made epigrams of the world.

MYSTIC UTOPIAN SUPERMEN

The true epigram is always inspired. It comes quite freely if the habit has been secured under the plan we have stated; that is, by writing them down at once, and afterward giving them many reviews in the mind. The function that creates them is thus stimulated and nourished. The word epigram comes from the Greek, and refers to a short, pithy, powerful, compressed statement. It was in use originally on tombs, and its purpose was to praise the dead by stating as much as possible in the fewest words. Such is the true meaning of the epigram of inspiration. The phrase, "True art is to conceal art/' serves as an illustration of an apparent contradiction, while coming very close to inspiration. "Thirty centuries look down upon you," has often been cited as an effective epigram. It served to inspire the soldiers of Napoleon who, amid the repose in Egypt, saw the works of three thousand years before gazing upon their conflict. "Shakespeare's worst rises above Bacon's best like a palace above a but," is an inspired epigram of tremendous force. "Fit the same intellect to a man and it is a bowstring; to a woman and it is a harp-string," is another richly laden thought.

Felicitations come out of the same faculty but in possibly lower degree; though all influences that count for joy and happiness are blessed. The habit of creating felicitous phraseology is one to be encouraged but never forced. A very low stratum of this art appears in the cheap talk of every day, and has no real connection with the exalted faculty. Such writers as Thackeray, Dickens, Irving, Holmes, Lowell and others of their peculiar brilliancy, have depended largely upon felicitations in order to hold their perpetual charm over their readers. "Fate tried to conceal him by naming him Smith," is a good illustration of this power. It sets the mind to thinking for a long while and always with increasing pleasure. Depew is the most effective of orators today, because of his mastery of felicitation. His ideas, as far as their pro rata value is concerned, sink deeper and live longer in the memory.

Written thoughts may be magnetic.

This is the One Hundred and Thirty-fifth Principle. A writer is in one of two moods, if his work has any merit at all. He is the tool of mere intellect, which is commendable ; or he is more or less within the realm of an exalted estate. If his intellect alone commands his work, it has the merit of accuracy to a greater or less extent, and becomes a means of reference; but the writers who have proved themselves the most trustworthy have failed to do genuine service as teachers of mankind. This duty they cannot well neglect, for their food should be made as attractive and presentable as possible. Dry thoughts, even if without error, are always dry, except to minds dryer yet. A sponge without moisture might perceive some dampness in hay and seek to draw it out.

Magnetic thoughts in writing are charged with the vitality of their authors. This, if at all in the realm of subconsciousness, is first seen in the art of clearness. Flowery style is of no help in describing commonplace facts, but clearness, and picture effects are decidedly valuable. These are magnetic. Then there is an undercurrent of energy, not apparent in the surface gleam of thought, that quietly takes hold of the reader and holds his interest in spite of himself, and, when his brain is weary from excess of use in hard problems, he comes back to the study or the reading with renewed brightness. The power of the simplest phraseology is seen in the following question from Shakespeare in which the king seeks sleep in vain: "Wilt thou upon the high and giddy mast seal up the ship-boy's eyes, Canst thou, 0, partial sleep! give thy repose to the wet ship-boy in an hour so rude, and, in the calmest night, deny it to a king?

Then, happy, low, lie down; uneasy lies the head that wears a crown." In the same easy flow, the following description of rain is given by Byron in his poem of the Alpine Storm: "Far along, from peak to peak, the rattling crags among, leaps the live thunder! Not from one lone cloud, but every mountain now hath found a tongue, and Jura answers through her misty shroud back to the joyous Alps, who call to her aloud! * * And the big rain comes dancing to the earth." This is a clear picture, even to one who has never witnessed a thunderstorm in the mountains. Examples without number may be readily collected from each and every grade of description. The testimony of writers confirms the fact that when the subconscious mind is awake or partly so, the production is better and the task of composition easier. Goldsmith's greatest work was written in an incredibly short time; and the same is true of Sheridan's masterpiece, and many another gem of literature. It is also true of Daniel Webster's greatest oration; it fell from him without time for preparation.

The arrangement of words may be magnetic.

This is the One Hundred and Thirty-sixth Principle. It differs widely from the one preceding. That referred to written thoughts, intending to show that there could be magnetism without the use of the voice, and without the personal influence that is generally present in a speech that wins. In writing, in conversation, in argument, and in elaborate address, it is possible to inspire the arrangement with magnetic construction. This is a gift, and one of no small consequence. It may be illustrated in every kind of way. The best practical use that may be made of the charm, is perhaps seen in the law professor who many years ago impressed himself upon his hearers by clothing the dryest of subjects in attractive phrases. It was then said of him that the future would place him high among men of his profession, and he since rose to the very top rank, having achieved an international reputation. The same subjects, the same details expressed by the ablest lecturers of his time, even charged with personal magnetism to the highest degree, were made more fascinating by him because of the arrangement of words.

Many persons acquire magnetism and yet are unfortunate in their arrangement of the words they employ, especially in conversation. Take the case of the young man who really was magnetic, but had no speech outlet for it; he proposed a number of times to the girl he loved most dearly, but his use of the words was bad; the words themselves were well selected, but he put them together in a very unfortunate manner, and she rejected him. In his utter helplessness he resorted to the last resource, that of pouring out his love in writing. In personality he was magnetic; in the arrangement of words in speech he was otherwise; but, in writing, his magnetism came again to him. She could not resist the strong appeal of the letter, and accepted him. Left to himself he could master the slower process of the pen. In her presence he spoke as fluently, but not as effectively.

There are many ways of saying the same thing. The phraseology of the Bible must ever stand as the masterwork of inspired arrangement, both in the original tongues and in the translations. It fails only in the Septuagint. One can collect tens of thousands of beautiful and wonderfully effective phrases that are full of this charm, and the close student of that sublime work receives some of the inspiration that belongs to its creation. Shakespeare, Milton and Homer complete the quartet of grand magnetic forces in the noblest literature.

One should fairly revel in these works, if charm of style, plentitude of epigrams, and exalted flights of mind are sought.

A person may be self-magnetized and greatly benefited by the operation of hope.

This is the One Hundred and Thirty-seventh Principle. It brings us on new ground, although still in the realm of exaltation. The law here taught has its opposite in that earlier estate where the faculties were darkened by baneful influences, and there we learned that a person may be self-magnetized and greatly injured by the operation of fear. Without hope life is not at any time worth living. A low instinct, prevailing among animal creation, teaches the individual to struggle for its life; but there is nothing to hope for beyond food and shelter.

The true man or woman of today looks upon the necessaries of life as incidents only of existence, useful in maintaining the faculties at their best; and beyond these aids as of no value, certainly not goals for which the race has been created. He who has nothing beyond the care of the body in this life to look forward to, is poor in the most abject sense of the word. It is well to be able to earn a living, to be affluent enough to provide a home, and to ward off the enemy of life's last years, a helpless and dependent old age. There is more than enough ten times over in this world to shelter, clothe and feed every human being on earth, and to provide the main luxuries of the day; and the time may come when men and women, endowed with personal power, may win a full share from the unequally distributed fund of supply. But the human race is on earth for other reasons as well as this. There is no power worth having that is not held by magnetism. The blessings of wealth are lacking even with abundant accumulations, if there is not the ability to command its influence. Misery is personified in the homes of those weaklings who are puppets of hoarded riches. They know nothing of the affirmative pleasures of existence. Ask them what hope they have, and it is in the next ball or the next card-party. There is no far horizon, no streaming rays of light bursting from the golden bed of a rising sun. All is fenced in by narrow walls and false landscapes. Progress ceases with hope. There is no magnet ahead to draw the mind and soul on to their better estates. In proportion as hope is strong, character is sturdy, effort is increased, power enlarged and magnetism intensified. It is better to create this magnet, if none exists; for without it the rudderless, aimless, drifting ship has neither course nor port, and the mariner no object in living or dying.

Hope, in its highest exaltation, spiritualizes life.

This is the One Hundred and Thirty-eighth Principle. It may be argued that the process of salvation, whereby the new birth takes place, is induced by self-magnetism. Indeed several of our students have advanced the claim and attempted to sustain it by arguments and proofs. We at one time came very near entertaining the same opinion, but found that the real facts broke down the theory. Conversion, so-called, is a creative act, if it is genuine, and a temporary delusion otherwise. The subject is properly a phase of immortality. Our present principle has a far different meaning.

MYSTIC UTOPIAN SUPERMEN

In the last principle we saw the operation of hope in this life; the care of the body as an incident, and some real reason for living and progressing, as a magnet. Here we meet another kind of magnet; we see hope in its highest exaltation shedding its influence over this existence. Between the common or even the lofty hope of a life limited by the confines of earth, and the expectation that is based upon a hope that reaches beyond all human experience, there is a breadth of territory as wide as time. The poor lover who sees the moon shining in the zenith of the sky, and knows that its light is kissing the cheek of a maiden beyond the palace walls that shut him out, would fain catch the reflection of her beauty in the same light that bathes his own face. So the eye of imagination, conjuring up the splendors of a princely kingdom in the far Orient, sees the same sun that daily beholds the distant glories, and envies him his knowledge. Earthly ambition is the moon of our lesser life; exalted hope is the dazzling sun that shines over realms we cannot reach. Of that sun we are far away beholders, and we can see it even when its rays fall alike on us and on the kingdom beyond the separating mists. If it could reflect its vision we would possess its secrets.

That which is superhuman in man is aroused and called into life by the magnetic impulse of any lofty aspiration large and high enough to draw it forth. It is everywhere agreed that man as he is, without the aid of the inducements that are thrown around him by systems of ethical training or by the excitement of exhortation, contains the ground-soil in which the spiritual plant may grow. By this is not meant the ghost-theory of spiritualists. If there were such a condition as spirit-life, in the sense in which such a theory thrusts it upon us, the fate of humanity would be deplorable. All the lore of spiritualism, of which but little is honest, presents not one ray of hope,' not one gleam of happiness, nothing but fear, fright, lunacy and misfortune, wherever it is intensified.

The operation of an exalted hope is quite the opposite. The higher the ambition, the greater the goal. The more we intensify its power, the more delightful is the sensation of its magnetism. It leads to light, always opening out a brighter realm, always revealing the whiteness of our inner life, and telling us that the more we cast away of the dross of existence, the nearer we shall come to an understanding of what heaven is like, and the better we shall qualify ourselves for the hereafter. On earth certain moral, mental, and spiritual qualities give a man the citizenship of the world; leaving the mental behind him after death as suited only to these environments, his moral and spiritual qualities must give him the citizenship of the universe. He who has a pure heart, who loves justice and lives by principle would be at home anywhere in God's domains.

Magnetism perfects itself in the charms of absolute happiness.

This is the One Hundred and Thirty-ninth Principle. There are many systems of development offered to humanity; some great, some exalted, some small and some very low. Left to natural selection each individual draws to himself whatever his temperament most easily affiliates with. The scale of choice is of interminable length. Like attracts like. A coarse country bumpkin, fed on delicate quail, would not assimilate it; hog and cabbage best suit his temperament. A refined stomach will not assimilate rough food. A Georgia cracker will digest clay. Villains hate flowers. Beautiful music scrapes on the soul of a murderer as a nail scratching window glass. Poetry impresses the modern journalist as art impresses a clam. A stretch of lovely landscape affects the horse-racing gambler as a woodpile affects a tramp—he does not care to see it.

A noble temperament rises out of this bumpkin condition of body, mind and soul, and assimilates something from the inner atmosphere that enters the body; while a low order of being, so far from drawing in love, refinement, beauty, fragrance and divine aspirations, can assimilate better the fumes of beer and tobacco, two allurements that tempt only the lowest temperaments, despite the fashion of smoking. As an illustration of the rule that like attracts like, we find then an overwhelming majority of people who possess the beer or tobacco temperaments are passionately fond of rotten cabbage in the form of sauerkraut; rotten milk in the form of old cheese, and rotten kidneys in the form of sausage meat, a diet that is the religious pinnacle of some people, and rises in importance above the affairs of state. The governmental party in England was overthrown and routed by a proposed tax on beer. The majority of the sovereign voters of America sell their birthright,—the holy privilege of voting,—for a few drinks of whiskey and beer. To change the fortunes of existence it is necessary to change the temperament.

A physical temperament draws nothing but earth to itself; it is made of clay, feeds on the products of the soil, no matter what may he its diet and drink, and gets its happiness in this debased realm. The world is full of such people. You promise a man a position worth more money in the year than the one he now holds, and he will be pleased; but ask him to take something into his stomach in the way of food of extra choice quality, and his pleasure is excessive; ask him to take a drink' and the superlative state of happiness is at once reached! He is magnetized by a merely physical influence. Ask him, instead of the beer or whiskey, to follow in the footsteps of greatness, to enter upon a kingly manhood, and he will entertain for you and your proposition the most profound disgust of which the human mind is capable.

These beast-temperaments are not happy. The rich tell the world they are not happy; but most of them are of the beast-temperament; there are some magnificent men and women ill the homes of wealth. No person is happy who is held under by any influence, and this is true in all ranks. The genius of mastery, first over self and then over others, is the source and soul of true happiness. Poverty or even ordinary success, financially as well as in all other respects, is inexcusable. We not only believe, but we know that every human being who is capable of appreciating the power of this training in magnetism, is able to win wealth, position, success and happiness in life; to realize full contentment and pleasure here without lessening the heritage of the hereafter; in fact to ascend to the heights of earth in order to be closer to the plains of heaven.

There is no study of magnetism that does not teach the acquisition of control by one person over another. This is considered the climax of success. There the power ends. There are facts, however, that dislodge the security of such position. As hypnotism is the negative as well as the debased side of magnetism, so its realm of vision is likewise mean in nature and limited in scope.

On the heights above, the power is of an opposite character, and has so many points of difference that a whole book might be devoted to the consideration of its greatness without exhausting the subject. Here are some comparative propositions:

NEGATIVE. Hypnotism opens the subconscious faculty by degrading and temporarily destroying the consciousness of the mind.

MYSTIC UTOPIAN SUPERMEN

POSITIVE. Magnetism opens the crystal mind by uplifting and strengthening the consciousness of the mind. NEGATIVE. Hypnotism uses one individual for the enlightenment of another in subconscious operations.

POSITIVE. Magnetism may give the powers of mental clearness to its own possessor.

NEGATIVE. Hypnotism allows to its victim no knowledge of the wonders of subconsciousness, and reveals to others a broken and limited interpretation only.

POSITIVE. Magnetism allows to its possessor a complete knowledge of the wonders of the universe through the most exalted uses of the faculties.

We might go on for pages showing the difference between these two powers, as there are other points almost without number. The faculty of the crystal mind is the youngest yet of human discoveries. Science has given due attention to the forces of the mechanical world, and is now turning its eye to man's own wondrous composition. In the inevitable uplifting of the race a new form of humanity must ere long come upon earth and its mind will unfold, adding to material consciousness the keener limitless vision of a mental force whose nature and value we are fast learning.

Everywhere in science it is admitted, as far as thought has been given to this particular line of investigation, that the subconscious faculty is destined to be the next great subject of interest. You would be surprised to know the number and the names of the great men who are busily at work in this direction, investigating and experimenting, and all the leading universities and schools of the civilized world are working with them. The one objectionable feature in the whole study is the fact that subjects must be found and used. Science is dependent upon the mere clairvoyant or cataleptic; generally a person of dwarfed mind in one case, or of a diseased nervous system in the other. The broken nature of the revelations and the many contradictions of statement, despite a marvelous accuracy in a few instances, have lent a flavor of uncertainty to the whole matter. It seems as if the power were there, but buried under a weight of incumbrance from which no one is able to extricate it. And, were it procurable for use in such way, no person would wish to carry about a subject who must be manipulated, put to sleep or otherwise used, and then dealt with at certain times only, for the class of information to be afforded.

The secret has been discovered by accident, and in the lowest uses, as has been the case with many of the greatest blessings of invention and research. What has been shown to man thus far, in the form of glimpses, was intended to excite his curiosity and lead to a full investigation into the whole realm of discovery. This is nature's plan, for she can do nothing grand except through the agency of civilized man. Take him away and all progress would come to a standstill. Whatever is to be known of the further endowments and powers of nature, man, religion and God, must await the zeal of human advance. Something has been ascertained in the past hundred years; much more is at hand and fast being given to the public by the thinkers at work upon the subject.

The chief end to be attained is the union of the wonderful mind of man with its fullness of conscious power, and the faculty of the crystal mind of which nature has so often and so astoundingly given us hints. It is the case of a mind within a mind; the inner brain having omnipotent knowledge, seeing all things as clearly as if there were no obstructions, and yet cut off from the normal mind by the mere lack of a communicating agent.

MYSTIC UTOPIAN SUPERMEN

There are but two propositions to be considered: First, is there such a faculty? Second, is it possible to connect the mind with it in the same person, so that the knowledge may be known and acted upon? That there is such a faculty is acknowledged by all persons who have examined the question. Science admits it, all important institutions of learning admit it, and nature proves it.

Some of those who are certain of the existence of an inner mind having omnipotent knowledge, seem inclined to believe that it is intended for another world than this; but as its knowledge is useful in this world, it certainly has a place here. Others are disposed to regard it as a form of inspiration, simply because it is possessed by geniuses in secular matters, and by the loftiest morality in religious cases. The mental vision of St. John was of this kind. There is no doubt that he saw into his inner mind, which had been exalted by his intense force of religious fervor, and it does not detract from the theory of inspiration to say that his purity of life and vigor of feeling had united the two faculties. Inspiration is a plane that all may reach who are able to climb so high.

In all ages there have been two classes of people; one has been too ready to believe anything strange, and the other has been too ready to pronounce as a fraud anything that smacks of the supernatural. In the case of Mahomet, the latter class never stopped to think that the so-called prophet was a cataleptic, and that subconsciousness was attached to that disease. By some process the vision that came to him in his cataleptic conditions were transferred to his normal mind, and this indicated a most superior power. His life was that of a man of extraordinary gifts in many directions. It is assumed that he invented the subject-matter of his visions. Still he delved in the realm of subconsciousness, probably entering at the lower stratum and coming out near the top. His conquests of friends and enemies were marvelous; and the fact that his wife was his first convert and her relations were his most ardent followers, shows that there was less of fraud than is commonly supposed. His closest friends believed most thoroughly in him. History, in our religion, calls him an impostor; yet countless millions have died in his faith, and his work filled in a void that only another Mahomet could occupy.

Gaming nearer to our own times we see the case of one who was discredited by the leading scientists of his day, yet who has out-written and outlived them all. Take the history of Swedenborg from the testimony of impartial biographers and honest though opposing critics, and you will find much that cannot be accounted for except under our principle. During his entire life he was honored by the potentates of his country and retained their fullest confidence to the day of his death. He changed his name to Swedenborg because of being ennobled by his sovereign in earlier life. Scientists knew that his many works on subjects of the deepest value, especially his philosophical books and his great system of cosmogony, could not have been written from any information at hand; yet, after his death, the severest critics and the most learned of scientists could not find many serious flaws in his treatises, except where he expressly theorized, and they found an enormous number of scientific truths, far in advance of the age in which he lived; so many, indeed, that it required nearly a hundred years after his last book was written to verify all he had said.

Whence came the power if not under our present principle? Theophilus Parsons, himself a great American, says of Swedenborg: "He exhibited in many instances a knowledge of facts which, as it seemed, implied an opening of his spiritual senses." His chief opposing critic was Kant, the famous German philosopher; yet he said of him: "I declare we must either suppose greater intelligence and truth at the basis of Swedenborg's writings than first impressions would give, or that it is a mere accident. Such a wonderful agreement exists between his doctrines and the deepest results of reason, that there is no other alternative whereby the correspondence can be explained." Then Theophilus Parsons goes on to give many instances of Swedenborg's exhibition of the crystal mind in secular matters, so clearly proved that his contemporaries admitted that the " evidence is unanswerable." His revelations were often public, and in some cases to the king or queen; as when he stated the details of the fire in Stockholm (three hundred miles away) on July 19,1759, describing the hour it commenced, what was burned, how it spread, when it was extinguished, and the various incidents, all to a large party in Gothenburg. The Governor, hearing of the statements, sent for Swedenborg, who repeated the full details; yet it was two days later when a courier arrived with news of the conflagration, exactly confirming all that had been told. This is but one of many instances. The enemies of Swedenborg base their opposition to him on the following statement which he made public: "The Lord Himself manifested Himself to me in person." He also stated that his eyes had been opened to visions beyond earth. How shall we account for his powers, and for the following that he now has in this age among the intelligent classes? His errors were due to his theories and not to his vision-power; they were the product of his brain, not of his crystal mind. The dross of earth attends everything. Gold comes out of mud. Radium, that metal of marvelously concentrated energy, comes from dirty pitchblende.

We might go on citing cases without limit; but we have taken those of persons whose powers cannot be explained except by the union of the two faculties, the conscious brain and the crystal mind. They are more readily verified. We have an abundance of personal evidence, the chief value of which is to prove to us the genuineness of our principle, as a law in science. As the law involved is fully discussed in the next and final principle we will consider the matter under that.

Magnetism may be made the agent of distant control.

This is the One Hundred and Fortieth Principle. It is peculiarly worded. Where powers exist, there must be agencies, and agents through which they operate. Every thing has something controlling it. Human life is the direct object of the contact of many influences; but not one of them passes through empty space. As sound and light must have some medium each, through which to pass, so thought and feeling require means of connecting the influence with the object controlled.

Our principle works both ways. Magnetism is the power by which a person may control or be controlled; and its cultivation may lead to either result. That is to say, it is in the power of a person to so develop magnetism as to place himself under the influence of other realms above him, or in touch with forces of which his natural mind knows nothing, as well as to throw out a control toward those who are weaker than he is. Thus magnetism is the law of the universe; and it makes the possessor a receiver and a giver; always being influenced by the greater power, and influencing the lesser; provided always there has been established a means of communication. One person may be given this power from another, and yield back a greater force in payment of the gift.

The operation of distant magnetic control is best started by the cultivation of mental vision; and it is needless to say that this must be based on the acquirement of magnetism in the way so often stated in this volume. A review of the various principles will give full light on that part of the subject. The practice of mental vision must be conducted in privacy until it is strong enough to bear interruptions and diverting influences. No person is aware, who has not tried it, of what may be accomplished by a determined will turned in on one 's self in periods of long seclusion. Experiments of every land have been made, and are being made, under these principles ; and the unvarying testimony of the lives of geniuses and gifted men, proves the same law. Seclusion, a turning in of the magnetic will on one's self, and a giving up to the power of an exalted purpose, have ripened the faculty and opened the inner mind without loss of natural consciousness.

The experiment that tells the most and is the most severe, is that which enables a person to so intensify his magnetism as to force his presence upon other persons at a distance. "I will appear to you at such a place and at such an hour," he says. He may or may not succeed. The fact that he can do so, has been amply proved. If he tries nineteen times and fails every time, but succeeds the twentieth, he has done something wonderful. The failure is nothing unusual; the success is, and it carries with it the proof of a great power somewhere. Such experiments have been carried on by design, and often with results in every respect satisfactory, showing that the phenomenon of appearance is not accidental.

We will not continue the consideration of this side of this question. Our purpose here is to deal with the receiving side of magnetic control, or the question, What can a man draw to himself from out the mists of the unknown? There are thousands of ways in which the power may be used, and we will name but few of them, as the whole subject belongs to another work. If you wish to know what is going on in the mind of another, the crystal mind will reveal that person's brain. Suppose you wish to take advantage of that thought, knowing it, by displacing it with another idea more in accord with your purposes toward that person; that is magnetism founded upon the crystal mind. It is magnetism because it is power over another. Its foundation rests upon power by which the knowledge of what exists is made clear.

Many a person is gifted with the ability to look into transactions at a distance; but few are magnetic enough to control them. The former power is very common in embryo; for there is scarcely a man or woman who does not exercise this faculty daily, or, at least, who is not played upon by it. Yet its presence is rarely ever recognized; its messages not often interpreted. You are the recipient, no doubt, of a hundred impressions in every twenty-four hours, not one of which are you able to understand; first, for the reason that you are ignorant of their coming; second, because you have only a vague idea at best of what they mean even when they are strong enough to arouse your attention. Let us examine a very simple law; one not great enough to grow into a principle at this place. To start with, the premises must be proved.

These premises are embraced in the well known fact that all persons, or nearly all, are recipients of messages. We have talked with or heard from a vast number of men and women, and never yet have we learned of the existence of an individual who has not received such messages. The question has been put to countless thousands, "Have you ever read the thoughts of another, caught an idea before it was expressed, or received impressions of transactions?" and the answer is always "Yes." We will not take the time now to extend further the discussion of this part of the subject, as the premises are admitted to be true by all persons. The simple law to which we referred was that which is naturally based upon such premises.

Nature has been hammering away for centuries, trying to give man the hint of the power that lies within his control, yet is seemingly out of it. In some cases, she has made the evidence of this power so strong that he ought to have followed it to its end; but he remained frightened and passive. The cry of ghosts, witches, demons, and what not, has alarmed the masses and ridiculed the investigator, merely because everything that cannot be explained by the ordinary senses has been ascribed to the realm of spirits.

The brain with its powers of magnifying is able to connect forms of microscopic images into demons of more than life size, as in fever and delirium; and this terrifies; but no one is alarmed when the microscope itself reveals as much and more. Yet this same brain, stimulated by the force of impressions, is able to take a peep into transactions that are beyond the reach of the ordinary faculties, and the cry of spiritualism is raised. So every hint of nature that is intended to arouse an interest in this undeveloped power is at once charged to the same realm of spirits.

The powers of the crystal mind have always existed; they have been waiting for man's invention so that they might be opened out in all their wonders, as electricity and all natural forces have waited. What we know of the magnificent uses of the electric fluid has been discovered in the most recent years; yet something has always been known of it, and hints enough have been thrown out to attract man's attention, even for two thousand years and more. Mental clearness is a greater power, and, when developed, will make the world a heaven and man a god. It has in it the elements of omniscience, all-knowledge, and this is the basis of omnipotence, all-power. There is but one agent capable of developing it, and this agent is magnetism. Hints enough of this agency have also been given to man, to no use.

We have said that magnetism is the only agent capable of developing the higher powers of the crystal mind, and this is true. The process is not difficult, once the magnetic temperament is established; and there are very few men and women who cannot establish that. Due attention to the exercises and regime of the first volume, and the influences that arise from the mere reading of this volume, if earnestly done, will come very near establishing the magnetic temperament. The more your life is saturated with this book's principles, even from thought alone, and from that shifting of one's daily habits that attends a thoughtful mind, the more speedily will your magnetic temperament be founded; and it will grow. We advise always the use of these pages, the reading of all the principles, a continual reference to the laws and facts stated, and a natural influence will naturally follow.

Then comes into play the simple law that tells us if any faculty is encouraged, it will grow. This is seen in the culture of epigrams, of felicitations, of rhythm, of rhyme, of poetical fancy, of flights of the imagination, of invention, of discovery, of mental impressions, and of the crystal mind. Let any person of magnetic temperament take advantage of any impression that comes to him, study it out and develop it by the use of mental vision, and although it may take a long time at the first trial to obtain a clear sight of the incident the effort will be well spent, for every subsequent trial will be easier and shorter. This is tested without difficulty by any one who has developed the magnetic temperament. This discerning of an impression is not easy at first. It may take one of three moods, happiness, gloom or dullness. We will look at instances of each.

A man who proposed to follow out the origin of a certain impression found himself one evening under a weight of despondency due to nothing that he had any knowledge of through the ordinary senses. Had something gone wrong in his business or otherwise, the mood would have been natural. So he concluded that it was due to some form of telepathy. He had studied and had acquired a magnetic temperament; he also knew what the power of mental vision could accomplish, and he set to work to probe this impression. It is necessary to be alone—at least until the habit is formed of penetrating such influences. He retired to a room where no sound or act of another could distract his thoughts; and he had nothing left on which to work except the despondency that had come over him. It was not a strong mood. He sat and thought of it, but refused to allow his mind to take flight at will; for, had it done so, he would have gone out of the depressed condition into a score of other thoughts. The process is not difficult to any person; and his method is the guide to all others.

He merely asked himself why he was despondent; and he thought of it to the exclusion of everything else. Then he tried to trace the events back to the moment when he first recognized the mood. He was walking home, having alighted from the car; and, in passing a house at the corner, he felt a heavy weight within. It was to this moment that he turned his mind, going over the brief distance he had walked, and trying to put himself in the same mood. It was a very easy thing to do, sitting now alone and calling up the bit of unimportant experience. He kept his mind upon the trifling incidents until the mental vision suddenly enlarged. This was right. It is always the result of concentrated thought; and all persons are able to do as much, although those who have cultivated the power, as under the lessons of this book, make more speedy progress and go further. He saw in his mind a brick building; it faded away like a dream; he rebuilt it again and again, and soon he saw it more distinctly. It was one with which he was familiar; but he could not locate it. The signs were on it, but not distinct enough for him to read. He was not yet an adept in the use of the mental faculty. Satisfied that the sight of the building meant something, he resolved to keep his mind upon it until a more distinct view was obtained. The despondency was deepening, and he had some doubt as to his wakefulness; but he refused to be disturbed; having given orders that no one should interrupt him as he had important work to do. So he had.

Store doors now appeared; they were somewhat familiar ; but he could not satisfy himself as to what building or to whose store they belonged. He saw within, piles of goods stood on either side; a counting room was lighted up, and the inner shades were drawn, but he saw beyond them as easily as if they were transparent. Two men were at work on books, and his name was written on a page of paper, as though heading the list. Yet, with all this help, he could not discern their faces nor read any words except his own name. The gloom increased. He was very despondent. Under his name and to the right of it a large sum of money was distinctly written. Then he thought of a firm that owed him more than any other three debtors, and at once he knew the men. He now saw their own signs on the building and by the doorway. He recognized the faces of these men; and realized that both partners were at work in their office concocting some scheme whereby he would lose more than his own business could stand. This firm was as good as gold, so the phrase went; nor did he even have a suspicion of their weakness. He believed what he now saw through his mental faculty. He possessed magnetism and must use it.

Arousing from his lethargy, and keeping his mind on the two men, he sent into their counting room a bolt of intense thought that came from all the concentrated energies of his nature, now thoroughly in earnest. This he followed by bolt after bolt. The influence took effect; he saw the two men look at each other, then go to the door and look around. They thought they had heard something. They came back in alarm. He saw them open their ledger to a page bearing his name; they were both talking of their indebtedness to him. He must act at once, and he did. A few words reached them ere their night work was done; and they came like another bolt. "Everything known. Account must be settled at once, or attachment will be made." It was settled. The men asked him how he had obtained the information, but he kept the matter to himself. He pounced upon them a few days too soon for their convenience; but they told him that it was their intention to pay his claim prior to suspension. This they had decided upon in that night-conference. He then knew that his magnetism had reached and influenced them.

In happy moods for which there is no visible or connected cause, it is possible to trace their origin in just the way we have described. But many telepathic messages come when the mood is neither bright nor dark, but just dull. The brain seems stupid without cause. The method of procedure is to trace it back to your condition when you were first aware of the immediate dullness, and this is always possible, if you are seeking to give it attention. Then do as the man did whose experience we have just stated. Above all things, prevent the wandering tendencies of the mind; keep the thought concentrated. Mental vision is the most rapid developing power associated with man's faculties. The moment you secure the least clue, then throw all your powers of thought upon it. Watch it, and it will grow. Intensify your will power, and the details will become sharper, while the scene will assume greater depth and breadth. As soon as you have divined the vision and found it a fact, though far away, then you hold the reins of control; a line of communication is now established, and your influence, like a voice, a thought or a transfiguration, will come into some other person's mind or presence and dictate your will.

These things are going on all the time but in embryo conditions. No life is altogether free from them, except that a person who is self-mastered through the culture of magnetism, may invite or reject them at will. It has been proved possible to step into the room where friends or relatives may he, and become one of their party though thousands of miles away; and even to become the controlling member of such party, while unseen and unknown. If you do not believe this, try it. You need as the basis, a large stock of magnetism and the magnetic temperament, to which must be added the thoroughly developed powers of mental vision. Then the results are easy. Do not make the mistake of supposing that you can locate a person at will by general thinking; and do not make the blunder of believing that what you see is spiritualism. You will see facts, not spirits. A woman whose son was in Europe, thousands of miles away, wished to locate him and influence him; but, try as hard as she might, she could not succeed in either; as she possessed neither mental vision nor magnetism. Another woman under similar circumstances accomplished the full purpose of her wishes; as she had both powers under control, and acquired them solely by leisurely study. In trying to locate her son, she did not merely think of him and hope for him; that was too general; she devoted her thoughts to some specific act of his that was associated with herself, as his last promise to her. This she pondered upon and set it again in motion at a time and place where no counter influence could disturb her. Soon she saw a room, a table, cards, chips of different colors, and villainous eyes all about the form of her son. She knew he was in a gambling den, and her magnetism was aroused to an intensity of white heat. Suddenly the young man dropped his cards, arose, and looked at her, then went out. He wrote her a letter stating the circumstances, and adding, "Mother, I saw your form distinctly appear before me; and I never will, never in all my life will I gamble again." She saved him by her magnetism. He thinks he saw a ghost. She knows it was merely the action of the crystal mind. That you may accomplish the same results and acquire even greater power is as certain as that you breathe.

The true crystal mind tends upward toward perfection. A complete machine is a work of the highest skill; it is an example of integrity; for, were some part missing or defective, the integrity of its construction would be marred or broken. There is but one item in the moral code of the universe, and that is honesty. The ten commandments are different ways of saying, "Be honest." The criminal codes of the world with their thousands of restrictions are all variations of the one command, "Be honest." The man or woman who is perfectly honest, needs no creed, no decalogue, no code, no religion. Grand and ennobling as all true theology must ever be, it crumbles into dust before the standard of integrity; it pales and is lost in the light of perfect honesty. When a human being has reached that moral stage where nothing can deviate him from this one quality, he has outstripped all others in the race to heaven. Some day before the twentieth century has far advanced, when men and women are using their crystal minds, and they can see into the motives of their fellow beings, then there will be a burning light shedding its piercing rays into all brains and hearts; then the criminal codes of the world will have but one interpretation, "Be honest;" then religions, Protestant, Catholic, Jewish, pagan and all, will cluster about the rock-built temple of God, whose every stone bears the whole story of salvation, "Be honest." That we can see minds and motives now, is true; that the faculty is coming rapidly to the front, is true; that its development will be full and wide, is true; and then it must also be true that humanity, with its guise thrown off, must be honest.

Thus the proof is abundant and clear that magnetism, employing the exalted state of the clear crystal mind, must rebuild the human race, giving it the powers of omniscience and omnipotence, relatively speaking. This is no idle statement; no hasty remark made in a moment of enthusiasm ; it is a conclusion founded upon long years of investigation, long years of growing powers, long years of common, sensible, practical observation among students of a faculty which, like electricity, has always been suspected, but only recently developed. The world is destined to advance from one plane to another, ever higher and better; but it plunges before it leaps. So history has always recorded its past.

MYSTIC UTOPIAN SUPERMEN

We are in the abyss at the close of the dying century. Confusion everywhere reigns. The church is sick at heart; the honest man is in a fog; sensuality, drunkenness, cupidity, greed and infidelity are the five stars that lure the race on to its plunge. Then the great leap will be taken; the air will clear; the sun will shine; and a new plane will be reached. This is the past. It is the future.

The tendency of all nature, in and out of life, is toward honesty, because honesty is integrity, and integrity is perfection. This tendency accompanies progress, and is the channel through which omniscience is reached. We are not preaching, any more than the engine-builder preaches when he makes a flawless machine. Integrity is a mechanical idea. We say that the race and the world are on an upward incline, and that perfection is the goal. Humanity is, thus far, the best product of this part of the universe, but it is quite short of perfection. In its imperfectness it is unsatisfactory and unsatisfied. It lacks knowledge and it lacks power, because it is imperfect. Honesty is almost an unknown quality as a flawless guide. To do one thing and intend another, to speak and think in opposite directions, to deceive any human being, to make a wrong, to mar the heart, these are conflicts with self; they weaken the powers of life; they scatter magnetism, for they are dishonest. Imagine a machine striking its parts against each other, or scraping with friction, and you see the weakness of the being who lacks honesty. This quality is sincerity of purpose in all things, with no contradictions, no conflicts. Suppose God were dishonest, how easily the planets might crash into each other. See the sincerity of His handiwork in the celestial realms.

In the present estate it is necessary that the whole personality and all the faculties should be exalted into this one commanding quality of absolute sincerity, perfect honesty. It is not impossible. If you use your will power, as directed in a previous realm of this book, you may step at once into this condition. It is worth the strongest effort, the utmost self-denial. What a wonderful power is at once secured! The active, energetic, magnetic, honest man or woman is a tremendous engine of influence; for all jarring parts of the machinery of life are harmonized, and all the myriad energies are working together. Then may a man call upon himself without fear or trembling for the best uses of all his faculties. Now comes the true exaltation. There is hardly any limit to the power that may be acquired through the simple process we have described. The uses of the crystal mind may be extended as far as one wishes to give the time to this development. You will be richly rewarded for every hour devoted to the study.

It is said that solitude is society if one is good company to himself. Among the pleasantest periods of life are those which have been spent in communion with the angels of thought. An empty nature is lonesome and restless when the hours are not crowded with events of outward interest; the finer minds grow weary with too much of such clatter. The power of magnetism is used on others amid the stirring scenes of life; but its richest fruits are found in the development of the exalted crystal mind under the principles set forth in this book. The plan of procedure has been stated over and over again, and need not be repeated. Ordinary mental vision accomplishes much when persistently pursued; but, with a high degree of magnetism behind it, the results are more than you would be induced to believe. Add to these the power of an exalted soul, and the theme rises to the sacred domain of the superhuman, without touching the morbid realm of spiritualism. At the base of humanity the moods are dishonest, criminal and chaotic; at the summit of life they are honest, pure and full of peace. In one extreme we find serfdom and abject slavery; in the other, power and control; in one, hypnotism; in the other, magnetism.

We might draw this work to a close at this place, were it not for the fact that all has not been said. Yet how can we say it? The rest is life history; not of one person but of many. It is not easy to pour out the experiences of heart and mind where they are too sacred to be viewed with the eyes of commonplace observation. When we say that there is no limit to the powers that may be attained through the use of these principles, we speak more than the reader will grasp at the first, or even the second perusal of these words. The exalted crystal mind knows all, or may know all if it seeks such knowledge. It is a telescope that can see into other minds, into the dead air of blackest night, into the sealed houses, into the earth or sky, even far away into space. This telescope rests in obscurity because of the barrier that separates the consciousness of the ordinary senses from its own clear light. Magnetism has been employed to search out its secrets. Turning now to the height above, it becomes exalted and omnipotent. The trinity of power is the crystal mind, magnetism and mental vision. It is a trinity that every true person may possess.

We could recite at this place the personal history of our students who studied these subjects privately with the author, and have since unfolded some of the powers indicated; but to repeat them would necessitate the publishing of statements that the reader would refuse to believe. It is better to learn for yourself what may be accomplished by the alliance of the three powers which constitute the trinity we have mentioned. We receive no more private pupils, for the information is fully presented in the pages of this volume, and private lectures would prove an unnecessary expense. Among those who have reflected the highest purposes of this course of training was a clergyman of the best university training, a doctor of divinity of the keenest judgment as well as the most profound learning. He applied in the following language: "I have a friend whom hitherto I considered qualified to advise me on subjects of extraordinary interest; but he has surprised me by a tenacious belief in the powers of the crystal mind. I could not obtain peace with him until I had promised to investigate the matter for myself. I will come to you as an unbeliever, even as one who professes to challenge your claims." He spent two years in acquiring a magnetic temperament in the manner stated in a previous part of this volume; and then leisurely devoted himself to the development of mental vision. Slowly and by almost imperceptible degrees he acquired the crystal mind and became aware of its knowledge. At length he felt constrained to admit the sublime truth. "It is too sacred to be told," he said, and continued, "We all possess an omniscient faculty; and God gives us the power to get at it if we will. Perhaps the time is not yet ripe for such development; but when it comes, as come it must, there will be consummated the climax of human history." With perfect calmness of judgment we should one and all accept the story of the coming change. The facts are impregnable. They cannot be ignored. They have convinced the best minds of civilized Europe and America; they are today carrying conviction everywhere before them. Not one of these facts can be assailed. What are they?

1. The human mind may be made crystal clear.

MYSTIC UTOPIAN SUPERMEN

2. This is clear-seeing.

3. Under the influence of perfect honesty, it becomes exalted.

4. With the guidance of mental vision it becomes intensified in its clearness and strengthened in its powers.

5. Aided by magnetism its powers become limitless.

The first step in the impending change will be the acquisition of the knowledge of the crystal mind. The second step will be the transparent condition of all that is now hidden; and when men and women are able to read the minds, thoughts, purposes and motives of all other men and women, evil must necessarily vanish from the earth. No wrong can long endure in the fullness of light.

The wonder of scientific investigators has always been excited by the fact that God was not known to the great majority of mankind when the civilization of Greece and Rome was at its resplendent height, some two thousand years ago. The arts flourished, and literature as well as philosophy reached a degree of grandeur that has hardly been known since; the Indo-Europeans, hailing from the south of Central Asia, or the north of India, had streamed again and again into the countries where their descendants now rule the civilized world; yet a little band of Hebrews wandering into Egypt and out again through the wilderness, was the only people that knew anything about the Creator; and today less than one per cent, of all mankind pretend to have any fixed belief in His existence, and that only through faith, because knowledge renders faith unnecessary. The proof of God's existence is within the reach of all intelligent men and women; but they cannot discern the infinite with the finite senses.

All ages have had their geniuses, and they have been men and women of crystal minds; for there all genius takes its root. Those who have risen to the plane of supreme greatness have added magnetism to the faculty mentioned; and the most magnificent personages of history have claimed an intimate knowledge of God. The life of a genius has already been referred to; it was but one of ten thousand, all greater than he; and the most searching criticism cannot find dishonesty or self-deception in the life of any of them. The one great conclusion is this: The knowledge of God's existence, of the universe, of destiny, of life and death, and of all things now hidden, is not intended for the uses of the ordinary mind, nor is it attainable through that channel. A higher faculty is indwelling in man. Omniscience, like wisdom, is useless without the power of execution; and omnipotence is summed up in the most kingly of all powers, Universal Magnetism.

THE END.